OXFORD CLASSICAL

*Published under the supervision of a Committee of the
Faculty of Literae Humaniores in the University of Oxford*

The aim of the Oxford Classical Monographs series (which replaces the Oxford Classical and Philosophical Monographs) is to publish books based on the best theses on Greek and Latin literature, ancient history, and ancient philosophy examined by the Faculty Board of Literae Humaniores.

The Roman Army at War
100 BC–AD 200

Adrian Keith Goldsworthy

CLARENDON PRESS · OXFORD

Oxford University Press, Great Clarendon Street, Oxford OX2 6DP
Oxford New York
Athens Auckland Bangkok Bogota Bombay Buenos Aires
Calcutta Cape Town Dar es Salaam Delhi Florence Hong Kong Istanbul
Karachi Kuala Lumpur Madras Madrid Melbourne Mexico City
Nairobi Paris Singapore Taipei Tokyo Toronto Warsaw
and associated companies in
Berlin Ibadan

Oxford is a registered trade mark of Oxford University Press

Published in the United States
by Oxford University Press Inc., New York

British Library Cataloguing in Publication Data
Data available
Library of Congress Cataloging in Publication Data
The Roman army at war: 100 BC–AD 200
Adrian Keith Goldsworthy.
(Oxford classical monographs)
Based on the author's thesis (doctoral—Oxford).
Includes bibliographical references.
1. Rome—History, Military. 2. Rome—Army.
3. Rome—History—Republic, 265–30 B.C.
4. Rome—History—Empire, 30 B.C.–284 A.D. I. Title. II. Series.
DG89.G65 1996 937–dc20 96–7430
ISBN 0–19–815090–3 (Pbk)

1 3 5 7 9 10 8 6 4 2

Printed in Great Britain on acid-free paper by
Bookcraft (Bath) Ltd., Midsomer Norton

In Memory of my Father,
Alan Keith Goldsworthy

PREFACE

to the paperback edition

In writing the preface for this paperback issue, I would like to thank all those who have passed on their comments to me. I must also mention a few works of direct relevance to the theme of this book, which appeared too late for inclusion in the hardback. N. J. E. Austin and N. B. Rankov's *Exploratio: Military and Political Intelligence in the Roman World from the Second Punic War to the Battle of Adrianople* (London, 1995) has at last provided a thorough treatment of this subject, aspects of which are touched upon in Chapter 4. P. Sabin's article, 'The Mechanics of Battle in the Second Punic War', in T. Cornell, B. Rankov, and P. Sabin (edd.), *The Second Punic War, a Reappraisal*, BICS Supplement 67 (London, 1996), 59–79 deals with some of the issues raised in Chapters 4 and 5. It is especially gratifying that so many of our conclusions, for instance on the nature of heavy infantry combat, are so similar, deriving as they do from the study of different sources. I suspect that some of the differences reflect genuine changes in the warfare between the two periods. There are encouraging signs that the study of Roman military history may be starting to rival the imaginative work done in recent years on Greek warfare.

ACKNOWLEDGEMENTS

I HAVE been fascinated by military history for almost as long as I can remember. My interest in the Roman army is about as old. As a boy I sought out every book that I could find on the subject and, before I was skilled enough to understand the original texts, read translations of the works of ancient authors, such as Tacitus, Caesar, and Josephus. The picture of the Roman army presented by the latter was markedly different from the army depicted in modern works. At first I assumed that it was the ancient writers who were in error: Tacitus was not a military man, whilst both Caesar and Josephus were propagandists. This was certainly the reasoning of the modern scholars who had studied the Roman army. Slowly I began to wonder about the wisdom of this line of reasoning. It is logical to assume that the ancient writers are more likely to be accurate than commentators writing nearly two thousand years later. The classical writers are far more concerned with the behaviour and morale of soldiers than the technical aspects of warfare which have been the main interest of modern scholars. This strengthened my faith in their accuracy. It is my belief that I have learnt far more about war from talking to former soldiers, and reading the diaries and memoirs of men who have fought in battle, than I have through reading a great number of technical manuals and conventional histories.

This book is the work of a civilian. I have never been a professional soldier, nor am I ever likely to participate in a real battle. It is common for historians to study subjects of which they have no practical experience, but I hope that none of my comments concerning the behaviour of men in battle cause offence to those who have actually seen combat. My sole military experience has come from a couple of years in the university OTC. This taught me much about the practical difficulties of moving large numbers of people around, and of trying to ensure that they arrived as a unit in the right place at the right time. I also feel that it taught me about unit pride. I remain convinced that the two sub-units I served in, Cambrai Platoon and the Royal Artillery Troop, were without doubt the finest parts of the whole corps. I learnt much from this practical experience, but do not think that it altered my status as a civilian. I hope that this may be an asset, making me explain things that a more military man might take for granted.

This book is based on my Oxford D.Phil. thesis. Many of the staff and other students at Oxford helped in its development, if only by creating so favourable an environment for research. I must acknowledge my great debt to my supervisor, Dr Alan Bowman. His patient guidance have made both the thesis and the book far more coherent. I would also like to thank my thesis examiners Dr Roger Tomlin and Mr Mark Hassall, both for the interest they showed in my ideas and their very helpful comments and criticism.

I must also thank Ian Haynes for his support, interest and friendship. It was a very fortunate chance that brought two of us to Oxford at exactly the same time to study different aspects of the Roman army. In addition I would like to thank all those of my family and friends who helped, especially with such time-consuming tasks as proof reading.

CONTENTS

FIGURES

MAPS

TABLES

ABBREVIATIONS

ad Att.	Cicero, *Letters to Atticus*
ad Fam.	Cicero, *Letters to his Friends*
AE	L'Année Epigraphique
Ann.	Tacitus, *Annals*
Appian	*Roman History*
Appian, *BC*	*Civil War*
ANRW	H. Temporini, W. Haase (eds.), *Aufstieg und Niedergang der römischen Welt* (Berlin, 1972–)
BC	Caesar, *The Civil War*
BG	Caesar, *The Gallic War*
BJ	Josephus, *The Jewish War*
CIL	*Corpus Inscriptionum Latinarum* (Berlin, 1862–)
Class. Phil.	*Classical Philology*
CQ	*Classical Quarterly*
Dio	Cassius Dio, *Roman History*
Diodorus	Diodorus Siculus, *History*
Ectaxis	Arrian, *Expeditio contra Alanos*
Gell.	Aulus Gellius, *Noctes Atticae*
Germ.	Tacitus, *Germania*
Hist.	Tacitus, *Histories*
IGLS	L. Jalabert and R. Mouterde, *Inscriptions grecques et latines de la Syrie* (Paris, 1929–82)
ILS	H. Dessau, *Inscriptiones Latinae Selectae* (Berlin, 1892–1916)
JRS	*Journal of Roman Studies*
Jug.	Sallust, *Bellum Jugurthinum*
NH	Pliny the Elder, *Naturalis Historiae*
RIB	R. G. Collingwood, R. P. Wright (eds.), *The Roman Inscriptions of Britain* (Oxford, 1965)
RMP	R. O. Fink, *Roman Military Records on Papyrus* (Cleveland, 1971)
Strabo, *Geog.*	*Geographica*

TAPA	*Transactions of the American Philological Association*
Vegetius	Epitoma Rei Militaris
Velleius	Velleius Paterculus *Roman History*
Xenophon, *Hell.*	*Hellenica*
Xenophon, *Mem.*	*Memorabilia*

Quotations from ancient works are normally given in translation. The translations used are the most readily available, usually the Penguin Classics series in the case of Latin works, and the Loeb editions in the case of Greek texts. The works used are listed below.

TRANSLATIONS OF ANCIENT SOURCES

Appian, *Roman History*, trans. H. White (Loeb Classical Library; London and New York, 1912–68).

Caesar, *The Gallic War*, trans. S. A. Handford and J. Gardner (Pengiun Classics; London, 1982).

Caesar, *The Civil War*, trans. J. F. Gardner (Penguin Classics; London, 1967).

Cassius Dio, *Roman History*, trans. E. Cary (Loeb Classical Library; London and New York, 1914–25).

Cicero, *Letters to his Friends II*, trans. W. Glynn Williams (Loeb Classical Library; London and New York, 1952).

Josephus, *The Jewish War*, trans. H. St J. Thackeray (Loeb Classical Library; London and New York, 1989).

Strabo, *The Geography of Strabo*, trans. H. L. Jones (Loeb Classical Library; London and New York, 1917–49).

Tacitus, *The Agricola and Germania*, trans. H. Mattingly and S. A. Handford (Penguin Classics; London, 1970).

Tacitus, *The Annals of Imperial Rome*, trans. M. Grant (Penguin Classics; London, 1971).

Tacitus, *The Histories*, trans. K. Wellesley (Penguin Classics; London, 1972).

Introduction

THIS book is about the Roman army's methods of waging war. In it I examine the army's structure and organization and the effects of these on its military performance, placed in the context of the military institutions of some of its chief opponents. Building on this assessment, I then discuss the way the Roman army fought a campaign, the strategy it adopted, and the factors which decided the outcome of a conflict. In greatest detail of all I discuss the behaviour of the army during a battle, assessing how its members at every level of the command structure performed or failed to perform. In short this is a study of the Roman army as a military force.

There is some need to justify the appearance of yet another book on the Roman army. The literature on this subject is already vast and growing all the time. Scarcely a year goes by without several volumes appearing devoted to some aspect of the Roman military, ranging from the strictly academic to the more popular. In part this is a reflection of our evidence for the Roman world. We know more about the army than almost any other section of Roman society.[1] The army played a vital role in Rome's history. The Roman Empire was conquered and held by it. The Republic fell, and the Principate was created, in a series of civil wars made possible by the willingness of professional Roman soldiers to fight each other. Almost all successful Roman statesmen were also soldiers. The interest shown in the Roman army is understandable in this context. There is also a widespread popular interest in all periods of military history which has grown up out of all proportion in the Western World since the Second World War. Yet there is a peculiar fascination with the Roman army which goes beyond this interest in warfare. This fixation is based on the institution itself. The Roman army, with its clearly organized structure and uniformity of dress, equipment, and tactics, was something apart. No comparable force had ever been seen in Europe, and perhaps the world, before,

---

[1] See the review of Speidel *Roman Army Studies*, vol. 2 (1992) by N. Purcell in *Classical Review* 44 (1994), 138–9.

and nothing like it was seen again for nearly a thousand years after Rome's fall. Throughout Europe, the Middle East, and North Africa the army left tangible signs of its presence in the roads it had built and marched on, the forts and camps it had lived in, and the monumental frontier barriers it had defended, notably Hadrian's Wall. Our image of the Roman army is one of massive organization, rigidly disciplined might, and, most of all, incredible modernity. The Roman soldier served in a unit much like the regiments of modern armies. He might hold a series of ranks or posts, much like those of modern soldiers. Like them he took part in regular parades and ceremonies, and might receive medals for gallantry. His day was regulated by duty rosters which would be familiar to soldiers serving in European armies in the twentieth century. The idea of the Roman army is still a powerful one even today.[2]

The general fascination with the Roman army and the wealth of literature devoted to it makes it all the more surprising that no comprehensive study of its military performance has been attempted this century. Many books have devoted sections to the army's tactics, organization, and weaponry, but have failed to discuss how the army actually fought.[3] There has been a tendency to shy away from the waging of war. This is the ultimate function of all armies, including the Roman, a statement that is true even for a force only rarely engaged in actual fighting. The failure to analyse properly how an army fought its wars is not unique to Roman historians. To understand it, we must look more generally at the writing of military history.

The style and conventions of military history have been little influenced by scholars working in the academic community. Few professional historians have looked at armies.[4] When they have, it has

---

[2] E. N. Luttwak, a modern strategic analyst, saw the strategic situation of the Roman Empire as very similar to that faced by the Western powers in the Cold War era. The long-term success of the Roman army in defending the Empire's frontiers offered an ideal for NATO to emulate. Luttwak's study of Roman grand strategy was written with this aim clearly in mind, encouraging an idealization of the army's behaviour, and also some anachronistic thinking concerning its role. See E. N. Luttwak, *The Grand Strategy of the Roman Empire* (Baltimore 1976), pp. xi–xii, 'The paradoxical effect of the revolutionary change in the nature of modern war has been to bring the strategic predicament of the Romans much closer to our own.'

[3] e.g. G. Webster *The Roman Imperial Army* (London, 1985), contained a section entitled 'The army in the field', 231–68. This included long quotations from Vegetius, Caesar, and Josephus without any real analysis of these, and also sections on medical services, diet, and pay scales, 257–68.

[4] G. R. Elton, *Political History: Principles and Practice* (London, 1970), 53.

almost always been from the perspective of the social historian, whose methods may best be employed in examining an army in peacetime. As Michael Howard commented, 'the trouble with this sort of book is that it loses sight of what armies are for.'[5] The reason for this avoidance of the subject of war and battle is a deeply emotional one. Firmly embedded in the Judaeo-Christian culture of the West is a deep abhorrence of war and the violence it brings. The detailed study of this violence might imply an acceptance of, and acquiescence in, the existence and importance of war, ideas unacceptable to any liberal-minded scholar working in a modern university. The same emotion can be seen at work in the conference of behavioural and social scientists who produced the Seville Statement of 1986. The Statement, since then adopted by the American Anthropological Association, rejected utterly any claim that man as a species was naturally predisposed towards violence and war.[6] Whether or not its conclusions were correct, the Statement owed little to academic reasoning and a great deal to the feelings of scholars as to how the world should be.

The tone of military history was set outside the universities, and due largely to the course of the great conflicts of the last 150 years, it was set in English. One of the most influential works was Edward Creasy's *Fifteen Decisive Battles of the World* (1851). Creasy provided an excuse for the writing of military history which did not force the historian to feel a morally unjustifiable interest in violence: battles are important because they decide things—the world today is a product of centuries of warfare. The concept was typically Victorian. At the same time constitutional historians were charting the growth of the institutions of the British State through the years of bloodshed, rebellion, and civil war into the grandeur of Victorian England. Soon afterwards Darwin produced his theory of evolution, with its doctrine of progress and development through struggle and competition. Creasy looked not only at the results of battles, but at the factors which made them decisive, in particular strategy and tactics. This approach became a popular one.

There was one distinct group of military historians who felt less need to justify their choice of topic. These were the serving or former soldiers (and here we are invariably dealing with officers, often of field

---

[5] Quoted by J. Keegan in *The Face of Battle* (London, 1976), 28.
[6] See J. Keegan, *A History of Warfare* (London, 1993), 80–1.

rank) who turned in great numbers to the writing of military history. To this they brought their professional knowledge of the practicalities of soldiering. It is often forgotten that many of these men were deeply involved in trying to influence the military thought of their own day. Captain Basil Liddell Hart and Major General J. F. C. Fuller, two of the most influential British military historians of this century, developed theories of armoured warfare during the inter-war years, which they hoped the British army would adopt. Both had been effectively forced out of the army itself, but continued to attempt to influence its tactics from outside, in part through the writing of history. Their own doctrines of modern war could as a result sometimes cloud their judgement of the past.[7] More importantly than this, their deep interest in modern war led them to concentrate overwhelmingly on those aspects that warfare has had, or has appeared to have, in common throughout the centuries. In the main they concentrated on strategy and tactics and the commanders who dictated these.

The essence of this style of writing was that there existed certain 'Principles of War', unchanging throughout the centuries. Victory in war went to whichever commander best employed these principles. The campaigns of Alexander the Great and Caesar, of Frederick the Great and Napoleon, of Rommel and Montgomery all obeyed these same basic rules. The theories of Clausewitz expressed essentially the same idea. Outside Germany these gained little favour until the Cold War. Many, including Liddell-Hart, blamed Clausewitz for the rise of German militarism that had led to the carnage of the Great War, and so rejected his specific doctrines.[8] Yet none disputed the idea that there could be a general theory of war applicable to all periods. Clausewitz's own studies of specific campaigns were neither as impressive nor as influential as *On War*. The doctrines of the latter were inseparably linked with the conditions of his time, with their assumption of the existence of nation states and professional standing armies, making them of little value for the analysis of other periods.[9]

These two ideas, of the unchanging principles of war and the

---

[7] Fuller believed lessons applicable to tank warfare could be learnt from the campaigns of Alexander the Great. This fundamentally influenced his comparison of the Macedonian and Roman armies. See Ch. 4.

[8] See M. Howard, 'The Influence of Clausewitz', in Carl von Clausewitz, *On War*, ed. and trans. M. Howard and P. Paret (Princeton, 1976), 43–4.

[9] For a discussion of this see Keegan, *History of Warfare*, 3–23. For a criticism of Keegan's approach see C. Bassford, 'John Keegan and the Grand Tradition of Trashing Clausewitz: A Polemic', *War in History* 1. 4 (1994), 319–36.

importance of the results of battles, dominated the genre of accounts of warfare and battles. The activities of generals and the strategy and tactics they employed received most attention. A battle was reduced to greatly simplified tactical moves and the actual fighting and killing glossed over, a neat order being imposed on chaos. The resulting accounts, of a type John Keegan has described as the 'battle piece', appeared to offer detailed descriptions of the fighting, without explaining in any way what actually happened.[10] The tactics themselves, represented in precise and inevitably over-simplified and artificial maps, mattered more than the experiences and behaviour of the participants. The principles of strategy and tactics are readily understandable to the most unmilitary reader, making this type of narrative very attractive. The chaos of battle was reduced to order, its violence and bloodshed made so impersonal as to remove any moral repugnance.

Many of the professional soldiers must have realized that their accounts of battles were in many respects artificial, but they failed to communicate this to their readers, leading less knowledgeable authors to believe that they had understood the truth of war. Some soldiers did argue that more could be learnt from military history if it focused less on the tactics and the principles of war and more on what actually happened. In the thirties Field-Marshal Lord Wavell, lecturing to Staff College candidates, stated that,

To learn that Napoleon in 1796 with 20,000 men beat combined forces of 30,000 by something called 'economy of force' or 'operating on interior lines' is a mere waste of time. If you can understand how a young, unknown man inspired a half-starved, ragged, rather Bolshie crowd; how he filled their bellies; how he out-marched, outwitted, out-bluffed and defeated men who had studied war all their lives and waged it according to the textbooks of the time, you will have learnt something worth knowing.[11]

Elsewhere Wavell suggested to Liddell-Hart that he should concentrate most on the 'actualities of war—the effects of tiredness, hunger, fear, lack of sleep, weather'.[12]

In the previous century a French soldier, Colonel Ardant Du Picq, had attempted to do just that. He had concentrated on the behaviour of the individual soldier under the stress of combat. As well as looking at

---

[10] See Keegan, *Face of Battle*, 28–9, 35–45, 61–7.

[11] Quoted in J. Connell, *Wavell, Scholar and Soldier* (London, 1964), 161–2.

[12] Quoted in J. Connell, 'Talking about Soldiers', *Journal of the Royal United Services Institute* (1965), 224.

his own day, Du Picq also examined the battles described by Polybius and Caesar, believing that the ancients were far more honest about the reasons why men ran away during a battle.[13] Du Picq's aim was not primarily historical, to understand the past, but directed towards producing tactical reform in the contemporary French army. A similar ambition motivated the American Army's Official Historians in the Second World War, chief amongst them General S. L. A. Marshall.[14] This group looked at the behaviour of the US soldier in combat, reaching many startling conclusions. Many of these were influential in the development of the US Army's tactical doctrine and organization after the war. Both Du Picq and Marshall suggested that battles were completely unlike their depiction by military historians, but their ideas had virtually no effect on the way that military history was written.

Accounts of battles continued to be centred around 'battle pieces' and criticism of the tactics of the 'Great Commanders'. Then in 1976 John Keegan produced his radically different master-piece, *The Face of Battle*. Keegan rejected the conventions of military history and tried instead to explain what actually happened in his three chosen battles, Agincourt, Waterloo, and the Somme. He concentrated on the behaviour of individual soldiers, how bodies of such men interacted with and fought each other, basing his analysis as far as possible on the personal accounts of participants. The result was far more satisfying than the traditional battle pieces. Armies ceased to be impersonal masses, the neat blocks on a tactical map, and became instead collections of individuals facing the stress of the chaos and violence of battle, their behaviour influenced by the ideas of their society. Amongst Keegan's later works came *The Mask of Command* (1987) and *A History of Warfare* (1993). The first book discussed the role of the general in history, examining how the expectations of each culture led army commanders to behave in different ways. In the second book he rejected the idea that all wars have been essentially the same throughout history and suggested that each society defined what a war was and how it fought one.

Others have followed Keegan's lead to produce far more satisfying studies of warfare and warriors. Richard Holmes in his *Firing Line* (1986) examined the motivation of the individual soldier in the last few centuries. Concentrating on much the same period Paddy Griffith, an

---

[13] Col. Ardant Du Picq, *Etudes sur le combat* (1914).
[14] S. L. A. Marshall, *Men against Fire* (New York, 1947).

example of the rarest of breeds—a tactical historian—has looked at armies' tactical doctrines, why these were adopted, and how and why they succeeded or failed.[15] Others have employed the techniques of *The Face of Battle* to look at specific conflicts in greater depth. Victor Davis Hanson's *The Western Way of War* (1987) revolutionized thinking on hoplite warfare between Greek city-states. Charles Carlton produced in his *Going to the Wars* (1992) a view of the English Civil Wars that is at once illuminating and far more humane than past studies of these conflicts. Not all attempts to apply Keegan's methods have been so successful. Robert Egerton's *Like Lions They Fought* (1988) attempted to combine this technique with anthropological analysis to study combat in the Anglo-Zulu War of 1879, but was marred by his limited knowledge of the British army and British society in this period.

Keegan's approach offers a pathway to a far greater understanding of warfare and battle. It has not however wholly altered the way in which military history is written. The genre of the 'battle piece' is still strong and works of this kind continue to be written every year.[16] Some authors pay lip-service to *The Face of Battle*, but show no indication in their text of any influence by Keegan's ideas. Although the study of battles has become more respectable, there are still very few professional historians working in this field, slowing any change in the perception of the purpose and scope of military history.

As stated at the beginning of this section, the literature on the Roman army is vast, but has included little discussion of how the army actually fought. Few significant changes in our understanding of the Roman army in battle have been made since Hans Delbrück examined this in his monumental *Geschichte der Kriegskunst im Rahmen der politischen Geschichte*.[17] Parker, Harmand, and others have attempted to modify the details of Delbrück's conclusions, but have not questioned the fundamental validity of his approach.[18] Delbrück's Roman soldiers

---

[15] See P. Griffith, *Forward into Battle*, rev. edn. (Swindon, 1990), *Military Thought in the French Army, 1815–1851* (Manchester, 1989), and *Rally Once Again: Battle Tactics in the American Civil War* (Marlborough, 1989).

[16] e.g. N. Bagnall, *The Punic Wars* (1990). The author, a former Chief of the General Staff, attempted to draw useful parallels between the situation in the 3rd cent. BC and that facing NATO today.

[17] H. Delbrück, *History of the Art of War within the Framework of Political History*, i, *Antiquity*, trans. W. J. Renfroe (Westport, 1975).

[18] H. M. D. Parker, *The Roman Legions* (Oxford, 1971), and J. Harmand *L'Armée et le soldat à Rome de 107 à 50 avant nôtre ère* (Paris, 1967).

are not individuals whose personal emotions played much part in their behaviour during a battle, but are something close to automata, small parts of some massive machine. The historian's task was to reconstruct this machine, building up piece by piece a picture of its organization, the formations adopted by its units, and the tactics which they employed. It was assumed that the army's success was rooted in a fixed tactical formula or 'battle drill', applied in all circumstances. Scholars are still attempting to discover this formula.[19] This view of the Roman legion as a military machine, its components the impeccably disciplined legionaries who never deviated from their perfect formations, is close to the popular idea of the Roman army.[20] The idea did not originate with Delbrück. Some have believed that it is a reflection of the ancient accounts of the Roman army. As Keegan noted 'no military institution of which we have detailed, objective knowledge has ever been given the monumental, marmoreal, almost monolithic uniformity of character which classical writers conventionally ascribe to the Legions.'[21] Keegan was incorrect in asserting that all, or at least most, classical authors represent the Roman soldier as an unemotional and unreacting fighting machine. This view is derived from a small body of authors writing in a specific genre, the military manual. The most influential of them all was Vegetius.

Vegetius' *Epitoma rei Militaris*, written in the late fourth or early fifth century AD, had as its theme the need to restore to the contemporary Roman army the military virtues and institutions of the past.[22] Thus it seemed to offer a precise description of the Roman army at its best. Vegetius also offered practical advice on how to fight a war and it was for this reason that copies of his work, either in full, as an epitome attributed to Modestus, or an extract based on his 'General Rules of War' (Vegetius 3. 26) were so frequently produced throughout the Middle Ages and the early modern period.[23] How far his ideas actually influenced the conduct of medieval warfare is unclear. A conscious

---

[19] M. P. Speidel, *The Framework of an Imperial Legion*, the Fifth Annual Caerleon Lecture (Cardiff, 1992).

[20] A recent book expressed this idea in its title, almost certainly unconsciously, J. Peddie, *The Roman War Machine* (Gloucester, 1994).

[21] Keegan *Face of Battle*, 68.

[22] For Vegetius in general see N. P. Milner, 'Vegetius and the Anonymus De Rebus Bellicis', D.Phil. thesis (Oxford, 1991).

[23] See N. P. Milner *Vegetius: Epitome of Military Science* (1993), p. xiii.

attempt to adapt the military theories of classical authors to modern warfare was made in the sixteenth and seventeenth centuries, in particular by the Dutch under Maurice of Nassau and the Swedes under Gustavus Adolphus. One example of the military thinking of this time is the 1616 edition in English of *The Tacticks of Aelian* produced by John Bingham. The text was accompanied by diagrams depicting Aelian's drills and formations being performed by seventeenth-century pikemen. An appendix was provided detailing the Dutch adaptation of these drills for practical use. The philosophy behind the work is best summed up by the frontispiece illustration showing Alexander the Great handing over his sword, and presumably also his military ability, to Maurice of Nassau. In attempting to create modern 'Roman' legions, drill books like Aelian's and manuals like Vegetius' were far more useful in providing hard facts than the narrative accounts of battles given by Caesar and Tacitus, which were rediscovered around the same time. Nevertheless the latter, and particularly Caesar, seemed to confirm the general impression of military perfection and were scanned for any stray details of drill and tactics. They were not analysed with the purely historical aim of reconstructing the past, but the practical object of physically recreating it. When the seventeenth-century 'legions' failed to operate as perfect machines it was the modern soldier who was blamed and not the tactics and ideas themselves.[24] Modern men were simply not the equals of the iron legionaries.

Although the specific drills derived from classical sources soon developed out of all recognition, the idea of the Roman legion, of its clear organization, uniform equipment and behaviour, has remained powerful to this day. It remained a strong influence on scholars studying the Roman army. Military manuals, chief amongst them Vegetius, and also the idealized descriptions of the army provided by Polybius (Polybius 6. 19–42) and Josephus (*BJ* 3. 70–109), seemed to offer the best evidence for the type of reconstruction attempted by Delbrück and others. Increasingly the study of the Roman army focused less on its military role and more on its daily routine, a reflection of the common tendency to study most armies in peacetime rather than wartime. Recently, in an article entitled 'Work to be Done on the Roman Army', M. P. Speidel, one of the most influential

---

[24] Keegan, *Face of Battle*, 67–8.

workers in the field of Roman army studies in recent years, singled out Vegetius as the most useful literary source.[25]

What is often forgotten is that military manuals are more concerned with theory than practice. They describe an ideal, the army as it should have been, rather than as it actually was. To assume, as has so often been done, that in the singular case of the Roman army such perfection was the normal state of affairs is both naïve and unsupported by our other evidence.[26] Furthermore a military manual by its nature sought to impose a scheme of order and simplicity upon the complicated chaos and disorder of battle. A discussion of drill and formation tells us nothing of what actually happened when two bodies of men armed with swords or spears came into contact. Examination of the latter reveals far more about the course of a battle than the former.

The evidence exists for a detailed examination of how the Roman army actually fought its wars and battles after the style of Keegan's investigations. Descriptions of warfare and especially battles are a major feature of the narratives of most ancient historians. In these they are far more concerned with the psychology of soldiers, both as individuals and collectively, than with the topography of the battlefield or the technical details of drill and tactics. Their accounts provide a picture of a Roman army that was certainly highly efficient, but far from perfect, of Roman soldiers who were often well disciplined and highly motivated, but not mindless machines. Added to the literary evidence we have the epigraphic record of individual soldiers and units, and the monumental representations of the army's triumphs. Archaeological work has provided many examples of the army's equipment and weaponry and occasionally, as in the graves at Maiden Castle near Dorchester, a direct illustration of their effects on the enemy. However, by its very nature much archaeological evidence concerning the army is concerned with long-term trends, for instance in the development of the buildings within a fort. Such information is too clumsy to reveal what the soldiers in the fort were doing on a day-to-day basis.

This book, then, is an attempt to understand how the army actually

---

[25] M. P. Speidel, 'Work to be Done on the Roman Army', *Roman Army Studies*, 2 (1992), 13–16, p. 15.

[26] e.g. many of the very fine articles written by R. Davies, collected in R. Davies, *Service in the Roman Army* (Edinburgh, 1989), show a tendency to regard the Roman army as perfect, to a great degree because of extensive use of Vegetius, 3, 28–30, 68, 205–6, 230–1.

worked on campaign. That in itself is of interest, but it will also seek to put other aspects of the army's behaviour into their proper perspective. The amount of academic attention devoted to the army, to its recruitment and career pattern, its religious beliefs and ceremony, its role in and effect on society, the artistic and technical developments of its equipment, and the specifications of its buildings, needs to be put in its proper perspective. The army existed to wage war. All other aspects of its behaviour and the relics it has left behind, however interesting and informative the study of these may be, should not obscure this truth. To understand them properly, we must appreciate more clearly the army's military role.

I

The Organization of the Roman Army 60 BC–AD 200

THE theme of this book is the behaviour and methods of operation of the Roman army. Later chapters will deal with the way the army moved on campaign, the strategy it adopted and how it fought the enemy in battle. If all these aspects are to be properly understood, it is first vital to examine the army's organization, since this affected all of its activities. This chapter describes the development of the army's unit structure during this period.

A great body of information on the unit size and organization of the Roman army has been amassed by the patient work of several generations of scholars. The literary sources are often obscure or contradictory on the details of unit structure, but much information has been derived from the epigraphic and papyrological record. As a result a fairly coherent picture of the army's structure has emerged. The first part of this chapter will be a summary of much of this information. The forces of the period under discussion are by far the best documented of any Roman army, yet there are still gaps in the record, details that must remain in doubt. It would be impossible to discuss these properly in the present study, without digressing too far from our theme. Here I shall present the generally accepted view of unit structure, but it is important to remember that there is room for doubt in some cases. New discoveries might well alter our view entirely.

This chapter summarizes the work of many scholars on the army's organization. On only two major issues does it go beyond this. The first is a warning against rigid thinking concerning unit strength and internal structure. No army in history has managed to maintain all its units at their exact theoretical strength at all times. This is especially true on campaign, when units' strengths are continually eroded by disease, combat, accident, and the need to provide detachments for innumerable tasks. There is ample evidence to show that the Roman army was no different in this respect. Military organization exists to enable the army to perform its role. Local circumstances might require unit size and structure to be altered. The Roman military system was highly flexible and able to accommodate such changes.

The second issue is linked to this. The banding together of men into units and the creation of a command structure are not ends in themselves, but means to facilitate the army's operation. All aspects of army organization have some purpose, even if it is not related directly to the army's military role. The size of a unit and the number of internal divisions and officers it possesses directly affect how it will manœuvre and fight on a battlefield, and how quickly it will march between battlefields. The size of an army's most important sub-units reveal the scale and type of conflict it anticipated fighting. Any changes in this suggest changes in the current military situation. No real attempt has been made to understand the military significance of unit structure.[1] The last section of this chapter will begin to assess the influence of unit organization on the army's methods of fighting a war. This is a theme we shall return to in later chapters.

UNIT ORGANIZATION: THE THEORY AND PRACTICE

Throughout our period the legions were the largest units of the Roman army.[2] Each legion was composed of ten cohorts. Each cohort had an overall strength of 480 men, sub-divided into six 80-man *centuriae*, each commanded by a centurion.[3] The centurions were titled in order of seniority:

---

[1] F. W. Smith, 'The Fighting Unit: An Essay in Structural Military History', *L'Antiquité Classique*, 59 (1990), 149–65, discussed Greek and Roman army units without any real discussion of the military factors involved. M. P. Speidel *The Framework of an Imperial Legion*, the Fifth Annual Caerleon Lecture (Cardiff, 1992), did make an attempt to establish the order of battle of the legion of the Principate and infer his tactics from this. His conclusions were marred by a failure to examine fully the conditions of the battlefield and by too inflexible an interpretation of the evidence; see Ch. 5.

[2] The most recent discussion of their organization is Speidel, *Framework*. For the legions in general see H. M. D. Parker, *The Roman Legions* (Oxford, 1971).

[3] For centurions and *principales* in general see A. von Domaszewski, *Die Rangordnung des römischen Heeres*, 2nd edn. ed. B. Dobson (Cologne, 1967), 1–121; E. Birley, 'The Origins of Legionary Centurions', and 'Promotion and Transfer in the Roman Army II: The Centurionate', in E. Birley, *The Roman Army, Papers 1929–1986* (Amsterdam, 1988), 189–220; D. J. Breeze, 'The Career Structure below the Centurionate during the Principate', *ANRW* II. 1. 438–51; D. J. Breeze and B. Dobson, 'The Roman Cohorts and the Legionary Centurionate', *Epigraphische Studien 8, Sammelband* (Dusseldorf,

> *pilus prior*[4]
> *pilus posterior*
> *princeps prior*
> *princeps posterior*
> *hastatus prior*
> *hastatus posterior*

The centuries themselves were usually identified by the centurion's name, but sometimes his title was used.[5] Below the centurion were the three *principales*, the *optio*, *signifer*, and *tesserarius*. The men were divided into ten *contubernia*, each of eight rankers, who lived and messed together. Amongst these there were men ranked as *immunes*, that is exempt from fatigues, and others such as *beneficiarii*, who held junior staff posts. It is uncertain whether someone, perhaps an *immunis*, had command of a *contubernium*, but this group of eight was clearly of vital importance in the morale of the army.[6]

For at least some of our period the first cohort of the legion had a strength of 800 men instead of the usual 480.[7] These 800 were divided into five *centuriae*, each of 160 men. The five centurions, the *primus pilus*, *princeps*, *princeps posterior*, *hastatus*, and *hastatus posterior* were the *primi ordines*, the senior centurions of the legion, and enjoyed immense prestige. In a permanent fortress these men lived not in a suite of rooms at the end of a barrack block, as did most centurions,

---

1968), 100–24; B. Dobson, 'The Significance of the Centurion and *Primipilaris* in the Roman Army and Administration', *ANRW* II. 1. 392–434, and 'Legionary Centurion or Equestrian Officer? A Comparison of Pay and Prospects', *Ancient Society*, 3 (1972), 193–207, and 'The Centurion and Social Mobility during the Principate', in C. Nicolet (ed,), *Recherches sur les structures sociales dans l'antiquité classique* (Paris, 1970), 99–116.

[4] G. Webster, *The Roman Imperial Army* (1985), 114.

[5] e.g. *RIB* 341, 2001, 2023, 2032; see M. P. Speidel, 'The Names of Legionary Centuriae', *Arctos*, 24 (1990), 135–7.

[6] On *principales* and *immunes* see G. R. Watson *The Roman Soldier*, (London, 1969), 75–88; on *beneficiarii* see Ch. 4, n. 21; on morale see Ch. 6.

[7] Hyginus, *De Munitionibus Castrorum* 3, 4, claims that this unit was roughly double the strength of the other cohorts, cf. Vegetius 2. 8. The fortresses at Caerleon and Inchtuthil seem to bear this out. For Caerleon see G. Boon, *Isca* (1972), 88; for Inchtuthil see L. F. Pitts and J. K. St Joseph, *Inchtuthil: The Roman Legionary Fortress Excavations 1952-1965* (1985), 164–9. For opposing views on the first cohort see S. S. Frere, 'Hyginus and the First Cohort', *Britannia*, 11 (1980), 51–60; E. Birley 'The Dating and Character of the Tract *De Munitionibus Castrorum*', in Birley, *Roman Army Papers*, 53–7; and D. J. Breeze, 'The Organization of the Legion: The First Cohort and the Equites Legionis', *JRS* 59 (1969), 50–5. On one occasion Caesar refers to a *centuria* of 120 men, which might be taken to mean that the first cohort was larger at this period, *BC* 3. 91.

but in their own spacious houses. The date when the first cohort was enlarged is unknown, but the best evidence for this comes from the Flavian period. It is unclear why the first cohort was larger than the rest. There is no evidence to suggest that it included many of the specialists or administrative personnel contained in the legion. The first cohort was commanded by the picked officers of the legion and guarded the unit's precious standard, the eagle. Therefore it might be that this unit was considered a special élite. Vegetius claimed that men in the first cohort ought to have been chosen from taller recruits than the rest of the legion, which would reinforce its special status as an élite within the legion.[8] The information for the organization of the legion's cohorts is summarized in Table 1.

The cohort was primarily a tactical, not an administrative unit. It has been suggested that because of this the cohort possessed no permanent commanding officer.[9] Certainly there was no officer equivalent to the prefects and tribunes of the similarly sized auxiliary units. Yet if a body of men is to function as a unit on the battlefield, then it must have somebody in charge to tell it what to do. If it has not, then it will be little more than a mob, incapable of manœuvre. It is undisputed that centurions differed in seniority, if not in rank. Therefore it would seem eminently reasonable to find the commander of the cohort from its senior centurion, the *pilus prior*. It seems also likely that these nine men were included amongst the *primi ordines* when a general summoned his *consilium*.[10] Tacitus refers to *Legio VII* in AD 69 losing six centurions *primorum ordinum* (*Hist.* 3. 22). If the *primi ordines* included only the centurions of the first cohort then there should have been only five or six of these in total (depending on

Table 1. *The organization of the legion's cohorts*

Unit	Centuries	Strength of each	Total
First Cohort	5	160	800
Second to Tenth Cohorts	6	80	480

[8] Vegetius 1. 5. A parallel might be the grenadier companies of 18- and 19th-cent. infantry battalions, composed of the tallest and strongest men to act as shock troops.

[9] e.g. D. J. Breeze, *JRS* 59 (1969), 55, 'the legionary cohort . . . was a tactical unit . . . and yet it had no officers or organization.'

[10] See Ch. 4, 131–3.

whether the cohort was milliary or not.)[11] If the cohort was milliary then we have one extra centurion. If quingenary why did Tacitus not say *omnes* instead of *sex*? The answer could simply be that Tacitus was not overly interested in military detail, and was simply being vague. Nowhere are we specifically told that the *pilus prior* commanded the cohort, but it does seem highly likely.

The only other distinct units within the legion were the cavalry and the veterans. The cavalry contingent of 120 men was included within its order of battle from at least the early Empire.[12] The number of veterans varied according to how many men were eligible. The legionary horse provided a useful source of scouts and messengers. Many cavalrymen seem to have received quick promotion and perhaps had a better than average level of education and initiative.[13] If these men were to function as dispatch riders, then a good appreciation of the tactical situation would have been an advantage.[14] The veterans may not have been forced to remain with the colours until Augustus established fixed terms of service for legionaries of 20 years plus 5 as a veteran. They seem to have formed a separate unit and might be used as garrisons.[15] There is one reference to a *centurio veteranorum* and another to a *praefectus veteranorum*,[16] but their organization is unclear. It is possible that the expansion of the first cohort was due to their inclusion, and if so the addition of a body of experienced men might have enhanced the suggested élite status of this body.[17]

Although there appear to have been no other definite sub-units within the legion, many men with specialized skills were included within its ranks. These included engineers, architects, and technicians of all kinds. Most legionaries seem to have possessed some building skills, especially in siegecraft.[18] Other specialists with a military function within the legion were the men who manned its artillery. Of most use during sieges, lighter engines might also be employed on the

---

[11] *CIL* VIII. 18065 dated to M. Aurelius' principate records cohorts of *III Augusta* which had seven or eight centurions, so that it is possible that some cohorts at some periods had more centurions than *centuriae* (assuming that the units in question did not have seven and eight *centuriae* respectively.)

[12] K. R. Dixon and P. Southern, *The Roman Cavalry* (London, 1992), 27 suggest this may only have been true for the legions in Judaea in AD 67.

[13] See M. P. Speidel, 'The Captor of Decebalus. A New Inscription from Philippi', in M. P. Speidel, *Roman Army Studies*, i. (Amsterdam, 1984), 353–68.

[14] See Ch. 4, 'The Giving of Battle'.   [15] *Ann.* 1. 44, 3. 21, Suet. *Tib.*32.

[16] *ILS* III. 2817 and *AE* 1941, 165.   [17] See Ch. 1 n. 7.

[18] E. Luttwak, *The Grand Strategy of the Roman Empire* (Baltimore, 1976), 40.

battlefield.[19] Vegetius suggested an allocation of one light bolt-shooter to each century and a larger stone-thrower to each cohort, but it is difficult to know if he was speaking of an hypothetical ideal, never attained in reality, or of an actual practice at some period (Vegetius 2. 25). Overall it is likely that a legion had numerous engines at its disposal and took a number considered appropriate to the operations in hand. It is asserted generally that only the legions were allowed, or had the skills, necessary to operate artillery. This may have been true in some cases. During the revolt of Civilis the Batavian auxiliaries showed little aptitude for siegecraft (*Hist.* 4. 28). Yet according to Josephus the Jewish rebels operated engines captured from the Jerusalem garrison and in the defeat of Cestius Gallus, having been instructed in their use by prisoners taken then (*BJ* 5. 267). If the implication that these men came from the garrison is correct, then they ought to have been men from an auxiliary cohort. It is possible that seconded legionaries were attached to the garrison of Antonia before the revolt, but it may simply be that there was no official ruling which restricted artillery to the legions and that it was allocated as required.[20]

Otherwise, throughout our period, most legionaries were armoured, heavy infantry.[21] Defensive equipment consisted of a bronze or iron helmet; a scale, mail, or segmented cuirass; and a large semi-cylindrical body-shield (initially oval but in most cases cut down to a lighter rectangular form.) Offensive weaponry included a heavy javelin, (the *pilum*), the short, thrusting sword (the *gladius*), and perhaps a dagger. Some of the hastily formed units raised during the civil wars may have lacked the full panoply. There were also other exceptions to this uniformity: Arrian's Cappadocian legions were divided into *contophori* and *lonchophori*, troops armed probably with the *pilum* and *lancea* respectively. He does not say whether individual cohorts had standard weaponry or whether each had half its men armed in each manner. Lucian writing a little later referred to this same division in the Cappadocian armies (Lucian, *Alexander* 55). This may well have been a local phenomenon, suiting the legions more to the warfare of the area. There is no evidence that it was adopted on an Empire-wide

---

[19] *BG* 2. 8, *Ann.* 1. 56, *Ectaxis* 19; see Ch. 5, 190.
[20] See D. B. Campbell, 'Auxiliary Artillery Revisited', *Bonner Jahrbücher*, 186 (1986), 117–32, and D. Baatz, 'Recent Finds of Ancient Artillery', *Britannia*, 9 (1978), 1–7.
[21] H. Russell Robinson, *The Armour of Imperial Rome* (London, 1975), 11–81, 147–89, for a discussion of legionary defensive equipment, and see M. C. Bishop, and J. C. Coulston, *Roman Military Equipment* (London, 1993), for equipment in general.

basis at this time. It cannot have required any significant retraining for a man to throw a lighter *lancea* rather than a heavier *pilum* on certain occasions, and it seems likely that all units possessed this flexibility (*Ectaxis* 16–17).

In the legionary fortress of *III Augusta* at Lambaesis, the store-rooms for weapons included inscriptions referring to *arma antesignana* and *arma postsignana*.[22] Two tombstones of *antesignani* have been found, one from Strasbourg dated to AD 70, another from Syria in 172.[23] Caesar made four references to *antesignani*.[24] In two of these the men had for the occasion, or perhaps always, less equipment to carry and fought in support of the cavalry in the same manner as the Germans. In another passage the *antesignani* were part of a picked force of volunteers including many centurions, chosen to fight in a fleet action. On the other occasion they were sent ahead to occupy a piece of high ground in advance of the army (*BC* 1. 43–6). In this case they were worsted by the Pompeian legionaries' use of Spanish light infantry-style tactics. This suggests that the men were not themselves light troops. Each of the four passages suggests an élite status for these men, but whether this was because of higher morale, or *ésprit de corps* or was actually linked to a distinctive role, must remain in doubt.[25]

The Roman army had traditionally relied upon allies or auxiliary troops since early in the Republic. It is difficult to be precise, but for much of our period the *auxilia* probably equalled in number the citizen troops.[26] By the end of the second century they may have significantly outnumbered them.[27] The number of *auxilia* with field armies varied considerably. Varus had only six cohorts and three *alae* with his three legions in AD 9 (Velleius 2. 117), whilst in AD 14 Germanicus with the army of the same province had a far higher proportion (*Ann.* 1. 49). Agricola may well have fought Mons Graupius with considerably more

---

[22] Y. Le Bohec, *La Troisième légion Auguste* (Paris, 1989), 188.

[23] *AE* 1978, 471; *IGLS* 2132 respectively.

[24] *BC* 1. 43–6; 1. 57; 3. 75; 3. 84.

[25] Parker, *The Roman Legions* 36–41 and Speidel, *Framework* 14, both suggested that these men were skirmishers, but this cannot be supported. All we can definitely say is that these troops operated in advance of the main body of the legion.

[26] On the *auxilia* in general see D. B. Saddington, *The Development of the Roman Auxiliary Forces from Caesar to Vespasian* (Harare, 1982); P. A. Holder, *Studies in the Auxilia of the Roman army from Caesar to Trajan*, *BAR* 70 (Oxford, 1980); and G. C. Cheesman, *The Auxilia of the Roman Imperial Army* (Oxford, 1914).

[27] Cheesman, *Auxilia*, 53–6.

auxiliaries than legionaries.[28] Overall, numbers seem to have been dependent on availability and the local situation. This is also true of the type of unit involved. Arrian's Cappadocian army contained a high proportion of horse and foot archers. In a different tactical situation, for instance in Britain at the same period, there were far fewer bow-armed units [29]

The *auxilia* had several roles. The cavalry provided an arm in which the legions were almost totally deficient in effective numbers.[30] Most seem to have been able both to skirmish and perform shock action, with only a few units specializing in one or the other. Cavalry of the regular *auxilia* was better organized, disciplined and trained, than anything prior to this. Much about their internal organization is now obscure. For instance, were some decurions senior to others? It would have been inordinately difficult for one prefect to control sixteen 30-strong *turmae* in anything but the simplest of battlefield formations. Arrian's cavalry seems to have been able to act in at least two sections, but the prefect can only have been with one, and someone must have been in charge of the other (*Ectaxis* 1–2, 27–8). Probably as with centurions some decurions had greater responsibilities and controlled more than their own *turma*.[31] In at least some units, the *turmae* themselves were as much as twice as large as the normal size.[32] Cavalry were useful in reconnaissance and communication duties, as well as in battle. Perhaps their most crucial role came in the latter, with the ability not only to influence its progress, but to make it decisive by turning a defeat into a rout through a concerted pursuit.

Archers provided a valuable missile capability, as would slingers, who perhaps were included within some units, although no specific cohorts are known.[33] Yet the role of the ordinary infantry is less clear.

---

[28] See Frere, *Britannia*, (1987), 95.

[29] *Ectaxis* 1, 12, 14, 18, 21, 25; see Saddington, *Development of Roman Auxiliary Forces* 179–86, on the role of the *auxilia* within the army.

[30] On cavalry and its role in general see Dixon and Southern, *The Roman Cavalry*, and A. Hyland, *Equus: The Horse in the Roman World* (London, 1990), 63–197; for cavalry in battle see Ch. 5, 'Cavalry against Infantry' and 'Cavalry against Cavalry'.

[31] At least some units included a *decurio princeps*, e.g. *AE* 1892, 137.

[32] Fink, *RMP* 1, 6, 8, 17. There are problems with these documents as they give far higher totals for the strength of the *turmae* than the sum of the names listed. Even so the totals of names are on average just over 60 per *turma*, the listed strengths more than twice this. Whatever the actual strength of these units, it was significantly larger than the assumed normal strength of a *turma*.

[33] e.g. *CIL* VIII. 18042, where Hadrian complimented the cavalry of a *cohors equitata* on its skill with slings.

Traditionally, these have been viewed as some form of light infantry, perhaps following Tacitus who contrasts on more than one occasion the weaponry and formations of the legions and *auxilia* (*Ann.* 12. 35, *Hist.* 2. 22). Elsewhere auxiliary troops seem to operate in close order, using the traditional sword-fighting techniques of the Roman army at Mons Graupius, and standing up to and beating legionaries in AD 70 (*Agricola* 36, *Hist.* 4. 20). Josephus refers to *psiloi* (light infantry) but these may be allied units from the armies of client kingdoms rather than regular *auxilia* (e.g. *BJ* 2. 116). The equipment associated with most units of auxiliary infantry on monuments such as Trajan's Column and on tombstones appears remarkably regular.[34] Most seem to have had a helmet (usually of bronze), a cuirass of scale or mail, a long oval, flat body-shield, a sword (either a *gladius* or *spatha*), and several javelins and/or a short spear. The javelins might have given them a short-range missile capability greater than a legionary, although not on the occasions when these, as has been suggested above, also carried lighter missiles. The mail cuirass cannot have been very much lighter than the armour of citizen troops. This equipment is not that of a skirmisher. Both legionaries and auxiliaries could have operated for short periods of time in a looser order or perhaps contained an element within the unit trained to do so. For most purposes, the auxiliary infantry operated in close order like the legions and like them had an advantage over most of the non-Roman infantry opponents they met. The *auxilia* were a cheaper and, given their primary organization at a lower level, more flexible way of providing the army with the manpower required to fulfil its role. It was in this sense, rather than by providing novel fighting techniques, that they supported the legions.

The essentially similar fighting techniques of the legions and many auxiliary infantry, emphasized the degree to which the *auxilia* became an essential and very efficient part of the Roman army. Many of Caesar's *auxilia* were not trained in Roman discipline and often got out of control.[35] The same seems to have been the case in the armies of the early Principate.[36] Yet by the 60s AD, Josephus often made little distinction between the soldiers of different types of units.[37] Tacitus

---

[34] For a discussion of distinctions between legionary and auxiliary equipment see Bishop and Coulston, *Roman Military Equipment*, 206–9.

[35] *BG* 2. 24, 3. 12, 5. 16.

[36] e.g. *Ann.* 2. 10 where the Batavians attacked without orders.

[37] Both can be referred to as hoplites, see Saddington, *Development of Roman Auxiliary Forces* 100.

can refer to the Batavian rebels, who perhaps uniquely, even at this time, were led by officers from their own tribe, as *veterani*, soldiers as effective as any in the Roman army (*Hist.* 4. 20). Then and indeed later, the Batavian and other auxiliary units enjoyed a high reputation. The increased regularity of auxiliary units was not a sign that they were losing the specialist abilities which had led to their recruitment, but rather that they had become a truly effective branch of the Roman army. Therefore, the creation of the *numeri* and ethnic units in the second century AD probably represented a new approach to frontier policing rather than a drop in ferocity amongst the *auxilia*.[38] Similarly the suggestion that the legions were always positioned to prevent any possible revolt on the part of the *auxilia*, and always equipped to outclass them, is an invention of modern scholarship. No hint of such a role appears in our ancient sources.[39]

The actual size and organization of auxiliary units has been a subject of much debate, revolving largely around the corrupted text of Hyginus, the few surviving documents recording unit strength, and the excavations of auxiliary forts.[40] The latter is an especially difficult method, since the identity of a fort's garrison is often uncertain, as is the proportion of the unit present at any one time. The unit strengths recorded on *pridiana* are unlikely to represent the proper strength of the units in question, so cannot finally solve the problem. The strengths given in Table 2 are those generally accepted, and the ones which I believe most likely, but I freely acknowledge that there is room for doubt. Quingenary units were normally commanded by a prefect, milliary and citizen units by a tribune.[41]

No army in history has been able to maintain its units at their theoretical strength all of the time. Peculiarities of local situation often make an army's units alter their organization immensely. Unit organization is intended to allow an army to carry out its assigned role.

[38] P. Southern, 'The *Numeri* of the Roman Imperial Army', *Britannia*, 20 (1989), 81–140, who deals with the vagueness of the term. See also M. P. Speidel, 'The Rise of the Ethnic Units in the Roman Army', *ANRW* II. 3, 202–31.

[39] e.g. Luttwak, *Grand Strategy*, 42.

[40] e.g. Cheesman, *Auxilia*, 21–56, Holder, *Studies in the Auxilia*, 5–13, E. Birley, '*Alae* and *Cohortes Milliariae*', in Birley, *Roman Army Papers*, 349–64; M. Hassall, 'The Internal Planning of Roman Auxiliary Forts', in B. Hartley and J. Wacher (eds.), *Rome's Northern Provinces* (Gloucester, 1983), 96–131; D. P. Davison, *The Barracks of the Roman Army from the 1st to the 3rd Centuries. BAR* 472 (1989); and J. Bennett, 'Fort Sizes as a Guide to Garrison Types', in C. Unz (ed.), *Studien zu den Militärgrenzen Roms*, iii (Stuttgart thesis, 1986), 707–16.

[41] See Holder, *Studies in the Auxilia*, 77–80.

Table 2. *Size and organization of auxiliary units*

Unit	Foot	Horse	Centuries	Turmae
Cohors Quingenaria Peditata	480		6	
Cohors Quingenaria Equitata	480	120	6	4
Cohors Milliaria Peditata	800		10	
Cohors Milliaria Equitata	800	240	10	8
Ala Quingenaria		512		16
Ala Milliaria		768		24

It does not exist for its own sake. Therefore to adapt it to suit local requirements or conform to available manpower is a sensible reaction and not a sign that the organization has failed. All the indications suggest that the reality of the Roman army's deployment was just as messy and irregular as any other comparable force.

The legions in Caesar's day normally seem to have been understrength. By the Alexandrian campaign *Legio VI* had as few as 1,000 men.[42] This was an extreme case, in a formation that had been engaged in nearly constant campaigning for about a decade. The legions of the Principate increasingly had a permanent base or depot, which might perhaps have continued training recruits whilst the legion was on campaign, preventing its numbers from dropping so low. Even so, the *Legio X* at Masada may have had fewer than 3,500 men.[43] To judge from the arrangement of the tents, there were somewhere between 200–300 men per cohort. A duty roster of a century in *III Cyrenaica* in the 90s AD shows a century at about 50 per cent strength.[44] Records of the discharges made by various legions in the second century vary from *c*.100–*c*.330 in one year, at an average of *c*.213.[45]

---

[42] *Alexandrian War* 69, cf. *BC* 3. 6 where legions average 2,150, or 3. 89 where they average 2,750 and Pompey's *c*.4,000.

[43] C. Hawkes, 'The Roman Siege of Masada', *Antiquity*, 3 (1929), 195–213, and I. A. Richmond, 'The Roman Siege-Works at Masada', *JRS* 52 (1962), 142–55.

[44] Fink *RMP* 9 and 58. *RMP* 9 has 31 men initially and 5 added later, whilst 58 probably accounts for 9 immunes actually with the unit (line 17 and n. 16), but due to its fragmentary nature this is less certain. The totals for the century would be initially 40 men and later 45.

[45] J. F. Gilliam, 'The Plague under M. Aurelius', in *Roman Army Papers* (Amsterdam, 1986), 227–51. See also R. Alston, *Soldier and Society in Roman Egypt: A Social History* (London, 1995), 39–52).

This is just over half of what might be expected if the unit contained 5,000 men. Therefore, unless there was a very high mortality rate in the army,[46] most units were understrength. Certainly, the very low numbers of veterans recorded in some years suggests that the latter was at least sometimes the case.

The records of auxiliary units suggest the same pattern. Those of three *cohortes quingenariae equitatae* are given in Table 3. All three units are below their theoretical strength of around 600. *I Apanenorum* by over 25 per cent. Interestingly, in all these units, the better-paid cavalry were far closer to their theoretical strength. It is known that infantrymen were often promoted to the cavalry troops and it seems to have been easier as a result to keep these higher-paid soldiers nearer their full complement.[48] *Cohors XX Palmyrenorum milliaria equitata* from Dura-Europus to some extent reverses this trend.[49] Since this unit does not seem to have followed the model normally thought appropriate for milliary units (an indication that these and probably other units varied their organizations according to the local situation), it is hard to estimate its theoretical strength, but in AD 219 it had 1,210 men and in AD 222 1,040. This suggests that it fluctuated between being at, near, or perhaps over full strength in these years. Finally, the strength return of *Cohors I Tungrorum* from Vindolanda around AD 90, records a total of 752 men under six centurions.[50] If, as seems likely, this unit was milliary, then it was only under-strength by about 6 per

Table 3. *Composition of the* cohortes quingenarine equitatae

Source	Unit	Date	Total	Foot	Horse
RMP 63	*I Hispanorum veterana*	*c.*100	546	417	119
RMP 64	*I Augusta Lusitanorum*	156	477	363	114
P. Brooklin 24[47]	*I Apanenorum*	213–16	434	334	100

[46] A. R. Burn, '*Hic Breve Vivitur*—Life Expectancy in the Roman Empire', *Past and Present*, 4 (1953), 2–31.

[47] See J. D. Thomas and R. W. Davies, 'A New Military Strength Report on Papyrus', *JRS* 67 (1977), 50–61.

[48] *Hist.* 4. 19, where the Batavian cohorts demanded an increase in the proportion of cavalry in each unit. [49] *RMP* 1, 6, 8.

[50] A. K. Bowman and J. D. Thomas, 'A Military Strength Report from Vindolanda', *JRS* 81 (1991), 62–73.

cent. It would be rash then, to estimate an average strength for any Roman unit, and must be acknowledged that these varied immensely.

A unit might fall significantly below strength as a result of battle casualities, sickness or from failure to recruit sufficient men. As great a drain on the unit's manpower was the number of men on the unit's strength, but posted on detached service. It is vital to remember that there were many non-military roles that the army was called upon to perform, in part because there was no one else to do it. In Egypt and the East, in particular, there is evidence that the army performed a policing or even counter-insurgency role.[51] This role necessitated a widespread dispersal of forces. Legionary vexillations seem to have been quite common in the cities of the East.[52] In the letters dealing with Pliny's governorship of Bithynia there are many references to soldiers detached from their units, performing roles as varied as the escort of procurators and the regulation of traffic. Pliny refers to Trajan's desire to reduce the number of men away from their units to the barest minimum of those employed on essential tasks.[53] The *pridiana* refer to many men absent from their unit for various reasons. *Cohors I Hispanorum Veterana Quingenaria Equitata* had men in Gaul to fetch clothing and horses and perhaps grain, in other garrisons, and at the mines in Dardania—all of whom were considered to be outside the province. Within it, other detachments served on the staff of the legate and procurator, attached to an expedition across the Danube, on a scouting mission, at headquarters, and as guards to cattle and draft animals, amongst other tasks. The total number of men absent as a result of these detachments is not preserved, but the high proportion of one centurion and three decurions on detachment is mentioned.[54] At Vindolanda only 295 men (including 31 unfit for duty) and one centurion were in garrison, the rest being at places as far apart as Corbridge and London.

The continual absence of many men, and most especially officers, can only have reduced the military readiness and efficiency of the remainder. A unit scattered in small detachments over a wide area can have had few opportunities to exercise as a single body. Such a

---

[51] B. Isaac, *The Limits of Empire: The Roman Army in the Eoot*, 2nd edn. (Oxford, 1992), 101–60, and Davies, *Service in The Roman Army*, 175–85. For the army in Egypt see Alston, *Soldier and Society*, 69–101.

[52] e.g. Isaac, *Limits of Empire*, 36–8, 125.

[53] Pliny, *Epistulae* 10. 19, 20, 21, 22, 27, 28, 77, 78.

[54] *RMP* 63, lines 17–40.

dispersal of personnel deprived a unit of internal cohesion and weakened its *ésprit de corps*. The most efficient units in the Roman army were those which had campaigned together successfully for a long period of time, like the eight Batavian cohorts by AD 70 (*Hist.* 4. 20). The sporadic nature of the fighting in many conflicts meant that many years of operations were required for a unit to reach the peak of its efficiency. Hirtius' description of Caesar's army in 51 BC is instructive:

He had three veteran legions of exceptional valour—the VII, VIII, and IX— and also the XI, a legion composed of picked men in the prime of life, who had now seen seven years service and of whom he had high hopes, although they had not yet the same experience or reputation for courage as the others. (*BG* 8. 8)

In the civil wars of the last decades of the Republic, veteran legions had an effect on the course of battles out of all proportion to their numbers (e.g. *Alexandrian War* 76, *Spanish War* 31).

This evidence suggests that the Roman army's units were far from static even in what may be termed peacetime. By the end of the first century AD many units occupied permanent sites, which they would continue to hold for decades or even centuries.[55] It has become conventional to describe these sites as forts if their garrison consisted of an auxiliary unit and fortresses if they housed a legion.[56] Neither term is really appropriate, since both suggest that a site's function was primarily defensive. Compared to medieval castles, the fortifications guarding Roman sites appear very weak. The Roman sites were seldom built on strong natural positions. Their defences invariably consist of a low curtain wall, with towers at the corners and vulnerable gateways, and one or more ditches. Only to an enemy unskilled in siege technique (and admittedly many of Rome's opponents fell into this category) were such defences formidable. There was no technological limitation preventing the Romans from producing far stronger fortifications, as they were to do increasingly from the third century onwards. Rather the modest defences of most military sites indicate that they were not defensive strongholds, but bases housing troops.

---

[55] e.g. *Legio II Augusta* went into garrison at Caerleon in the 70s, remaining there until the second half of the 3rd cent.; *Ala Petriana* occupied the fort at Stanwix under Hadrian and was still there in the *Notitia Dignitatum* (*Not. Dig. Occ.* 40. 18.) See P. A. Holder, *The Roman Army in Britain* (London, 1982), 104–5, 108–9.

[56] See Webster, *The Roman Imperial Army*, 167.

Under normal conditions these units moved out to fight any enemy in the open and did not wait behind their walls to receive an attack.[57] In peacetime detachments from a garrison were sent wherever they were needed for a specific task. In the strength return from Vindolanda mentioned earlier, more of the cohort was at Corbridge than at its home base, where the headquarters and its records were located. The attested presence of a unit at a site for a century or more may mean no more than its records were kept there. In the Vindolanda material several units have been recorded as being in the garrison in a relatively short space of time. This was not previously apparent from the epigraphic record. There are also a few references to legionary personnel. Therefore to assume, in default of other evidence, that other forts were occupied soley by a single unit for centuries is highly dangerous.[58]

Much debate has recently centred around the question of identifying the garrisons of forts on the basis of equipment finds,[59] including the suggestion that, since legionary equipment has been found in forts of auxiliary size, these pieces of equipment were not restricted to the citizen troops. This is possible, but there is no positive evidence in its favour, and a little against it.[60] It seems far more probable that this is an indication that legionary detachments often operated far from the *castra* of the parent unit, forming all or part of a smaller garrison. The evidence for mixed garrisons of infantry and cavalry of both legions and auxiliary troops is fairly strong. Such garrisons were common in Britain of the conquest period, varying in scale from Hod Hill (*c.*1 cohort and 7 *turmae*) to Longthorpe (*c.*2,500–2,800 men), but some are evident in such positions as Newstead, on more permanent defensive lines.[61] The term Vexillation Fortress was originally created to describe those camps, which were not considered to fit any perceived unit size. It now seems increasingly likely that these sites of irregular dimensions are in fact so common as to be almost the norm.[62]

[57] See Ch. 3.

[58] Bowman and Thomas, *Britannia*, 18 (1987) 128–9, 134.

[59] V. A. Maxfield, 'Pre-Flavian Forts and their Garrisons', *Britannia*, 17 (1986), 59–72; M. C. Bishop, 'The Distribution of Military Equipment within Roman Forts of the First Century AD', in Unz (ed.), *Studien*, 717–23, and '*O Fortuna*: A Sideways Look at the Archaeological Record and Roman Military Equipment', in C. Van Driel-Murray *Roman Military Equipment Conference 5*. *BAR* 476 (Oxford, 1989).

[60] *Hist.* 1. 43. See Bishop and Coulston (1993), 206–9.

[61] S. S. Frere and J. K. St Joseph, 'The Roman Fortress at Longthorpe', *Britannia*, 5 (1974), 1–129, and D. P. Davison (1989), 164–208.

[62] Maxfield, *Britannia*, (1986), 59.

The Roman army's use of vexillations emphasizes its essential flexibility more than any other aspect of its organization. When the allocation of entire units to a specific task was unsuitable or impossible a vexillation was formed. Vexillations varied in size from the 16 men Pliny gave to the procurator Maximus in Paphlagonia (Pliny 10. 27, 28.) to forces of several thousand, such as the 1,000 horse and 6,000 foot under a tribune sent by Vespasian to garrison Sepphoris in AD 67.(*BJ* 3. 59.) Many detachments had essentially civilian tasks, such as mining or construction work, but those with more strictly military functions fell into two types. Firstly, we have the detachments sent to reinforce the army in a particular area. These bodies might operate as a brigade within the army of the area, but were not intended to act independently, so were not usually mixed forces of horse and foot. The 2,000 men from the Egyptian legions who served under Titus at Jerusalem in AD 70 were an example of this type.(*BJ* 5. 43 and 287–8.) They reinforced an army weakened by drafts sent to support Vespasian's imperial ambitions in Europe. Auxiliary vexillations drawn from several *alae* and cohorts are known, but legionary detachments are most common.[63] In these, the men do not seem to have been all drawn from the same cohorts or centuries.[64] This may well be another indication of units being under strength, making it necessary to draft men from other parts of the legion into the chosen cohorts to make them into viable units. Since these were then organized after the manner of ordinary units, and in most cases took time travelling to the area of operations, then the morale links within the unit and familiarity of officers and men had time to grow up. If units were up to strength, it would seem undesirable to break them up before sending them into action. The basis of selection for such a detachment may have varied. If the vexillation was to represent the legion amongst the army of another province before returning to the parent unit, then the best men might be picked. If, however, it was to be a permanent draft into another legion, then the temptation must have been for a unit to get rid of all the worst soldiers and trouble-makers in the ranks. Such a reinforcement may have been a mixed blessing to the legion concerned. On specific occasions, vexillations of volunteers or the

---

[63] e.g. *BJ* 5. 43, *ILS* 2723 (a cavalry vexillation commanded by a legionary Tribune), *ILS* 9200 (A vexillation from several legions).

[64] M. P. Speidel, 'The Role of Legionary Cohorts in the Structure of Expeditionary Forces', *Roman Army Studies*, i. 65–75.

picked élite of units were formed for some particularly difficult operation, for instance the storming of the Temple in Jerusalem in AD 70.[65]

The second type of vexillation was the mixed, temporary battle group, containing both infantry and cavalry, detached for a certain operation. Sometimes, as with the 'divisions' within Arrian's army, they operated as large sub-units within an army, easing the general's control over his forces.[66] Elsewhere their operations were independent. Their commander was often the senior officer from the units involved, often an auxiliary prefect, such as the Antonius who commanded the garrison of Ascalon (*BJ* 3. 12). Larger forces may have had a more senior officer such as a legionary legate in charge, who may or may not have had troops from his own unit within the command.[67] These arrangements, although events might dictate otherwise, were never planned to be anything other than temporary. Obviously, the longer a collection of units operated together, the better their co-ordination would become, but permanent mixtures of troop types could not have covered the variety of possible tactical situations so well.[68]

Before we move on to examine the effects of unit organization, it is worth pausing to consider what type of men composed the army. The majority of men in the legions under the Principate were volunteers. A mass conscription or *dilectus* was sometimes held just before or during a major war to bring existing Legions up to strength or to raise new ones.[69] Nero's *Legio I Minervia*, composed entirely of men over 6 feet tall, was almost certainly composed of conscripts (Suetonius, *Nero* 19. 2). The *dilectus* may have been a formally organized process or little more than a press-gang.[70] Pliny refers to a class of recruits known as *vicarii* (substitutes) as opposed to *voluntarii* (volunteers) and *lecti* (conscripts) (Pliny, *Epistulae* 10. 29). Conscription may have been

---

[65] *BJ* 6. 131–2, cf. *BC* 1. 57, 1. 64.   [66] *Ectaxis* 1, 3, and 9.

[67] e.g. During Civilis' revolt, Herennius Gallus, the legate of *I Germanica*, seems to have commanded the main body of XVI Primigenia, *Hist.* 4. 19, 26.

[68] See Ch. 4 n. 11.

[69] *Ann.* 13. 35. See P. A. Brunt, 'Conscription and Volunteering in the Roman Imperial Army', *Scripta Classica Israelica*, 1 (1974), and J. C. Mann, *Legionary Recruitment and Veteran Settlement during the Principate* (London, 1983), 49–63, for contrasting views of the frequency of conscription.

[70] Polybius' description of the *dilectus* of the 2nd cent. BC is firmly based in the institutions and magistracies of the city of Rome. It is difficult to see how this process could have been transferred to the provinces (*Polybius* 6. 19–21).

more common in auxiliary units, with a tribe or state being obliged by treaty to provide a certain quota of troops for the Roman army. This was certainly true of the Batavians (*Germ.* 29). The brutal behaviour of the officers conducting the *dilectus* amongst the Batavians in AD 70 was the final provocation for the tribe's revolt (*Hist.* 4. 14).

Vegetius gives a detailed description of the best type of recruit, including the region he should come from, his previous occupation, age, physical size and fitness, and education (Vegetius 1. 2–7). Most scholars discussing recruitment have assumed that these high standards were met by the average recruit, rather than representing an ideal seldom realized in practice.[71] A rigorous selection process for recruits is held responsible for the high quality of Roman soldiers.[72] There is much evidence to suggest that the legions could not afford to be so particular in their selection of manpower. Tiberius complained of a shortage of suitable recruits for the army. In Italy, only the poorest vagrants were volunteering (*Ann.* 4. 4). Dio attributes a speech to Maecenas, in which he advised Augustus to maintain a strong regular army, since this absorbed many men who would otherwise have become bandits (Dio 52. 28). The laws contained in the *Digest* dealing with recruitment are informative. Men who had been condemned to the wild beasts, deported to an island, exiled for a fixed term not yet expired, were, if discovered in the ranks, to be discharged and punished. Men who had joined to avoid being prosecuted were also to be discharged.[73] The existence of this legislation suggests that such men had been discovered in the army. It is noticeable that only men guilty of such major crimes were barred. The army may have contained many petty criminals.

Our ancient sources may praise the deeds of the army, but they are hostile to the soldiers as individuals, representing them as brutal and unruly.[74] Soldiers seem to have often taken money or property from civilians by force.[75] In the New Testament, John the Baptist instructed the soldiers, who may have been Roman auxiliaries or from Herod's

---

[71] See R. W. Davies, 'Joining the Roman Army', in *Service in the Roman Army* (Edinburgh, 1989), 3–30, and G. R. Watson, *The Roman Soldier* (1985), 37–53.

[72] Davies, *Service in the Roman Army* 28–30.

[73] *Digest* 49. 16. 2. 1, 49. 16. 4. 1–9, 49. 16. 6.

[74] e.g. Juvenal *Satire* 16. See J. B. Campbell, *The Emperor and the Roman Army* (Oxford, 1984), 9–13. For the provincial's view of soldiers see Isaac, *Limits of Empire*, 269–310.

[75] See R. W. Davies, 'The Supply of Animals to the Roman Army and the Remount System', in *Serivce in the Roman Army*, 156 n. 26.

army to 'Do violence to no man, neither accuse any falsely; and be content with your wages' (*Luke*: 3. 14). In the previous century one governor of Cilicia had extorted money from the cities of the province by threatening to billet troops on them (Cicero, *Ad Att.* 6). In part this threat may have been based on the cost of feeding the troops, but their behaviour may have been as great a fear.

The army seems to have been most attractive as a career to the poorest citizens. For such men, the army offered a roof over their heads, a steady diet and income in coin, perhaps a sense of purpose, and legal and extra-legal advantages over civilians. Overall a soldier's life was more secure than that of an itinerant labourer. In theory the soldier was worse off than the civilian in one major respect, his inability to contract a legal marriage. In practice this legal restriction seems to have been ignored by most units. A significant proportion of soldiers formed alliances with women and raised children, many of their sons entering the army.[76] In contrast to the advantages of a soldier's career, we must remember its harsher side. A soldier ran the risk of being killed or crippled by battle or disease, but also on an everyday basis was subject to the army's brutal discipline. This as much as anything else, probably contributed to the frequency of desertion throughout our period.[77]

Certain ranks of the army's officers came from distinct levels of society. The most senior—army commanders, legionary legates, and *tribuni laticlavii*, or senior tribunes—were drawn from the ranks of the senate.[78] The five *tribuni angusticlavii*, or junior tribunes, in each legion, and the tribunes and prefects in charge of auxiliary units were equestrians.[79] Recruitment into the centurionate was not confined to any one group. There are examples of men joining the legions as ordinary *milites* and being promoted to the highest grades of the centurionate after around 15–20 years service. At the other end of the scale we have men, some of them equestrians, being directly commissioned. It is normally asserted that the latter were heavily

---

[76] J. B. Campbell, 'The Marriage of Soldiers under the Empire', *JRS* 68 (1978), 153–66, and J. C. Mann, *Legionary Recruitment*, 62–3, 65. *Canabae*, or civilian settlements occur outside many forts and camps, see C. Sebastian Sommer, *The Inner and Outer Relation of the Military Vicus to its Fort*, *BAR* 129 (Oxford, 1984).

[77] *Ann.* 13. 35, Sallust *Jug.* 103, *Ann.* 2. 52, Dio 65. 5. 4, 68. 9. 5, *Digest* 49. 16. 4. 1–9.

[78] On these officers, see Ch. 4.

[79] For equestrian officers in general see H. Devijver, *The Equestrian Officers of the Roman Imperial Army*, i–ii (1989 and 1992).

outnumbered by the former, but the evidence is not really good enough to be too dogmatic.[80] A high proportion of auxiliary centurions were drawn from provincial aristocracies.[81]

The rank of centurion was very prestigious. This is emphasized by the willingness of equestrians to serve as centurions. Promotion to centurion was a great step for an ordinary soldier. Both his pay and living expenses increased dramatically. When the Younger Pliny secured the rank of centurion for one of his clients, Metilius Crispus, he presented him with 40,000 sesterces to equip himself (Pliny 6. 25. 2). This sum was the equivalent of many years pay for an ordinary *miles*. Many centurions owned slaves and had large households.[82]

It is normally assumed that promotion in the Roman army, especially in the centurionate, was dictated by merit. This is at best a half truth. Patronage seems to have been far more important, as it was for securing favours and advancement throughout the Roman world.[83] We have already seen that Pliny secured an appointment to the centurionate for Metilius Crispus, a man with no prior military experience. Later, whilst he was governor of Bythinia, he wrote to Trajan requesting promotion for one Nymphidius Lupus, the prefect

---

[80] For centurions in general, and for views of their promotion, see the works cited in n. 3. There are twelve definite cases of men promoted from the ranks in the 1st and 2nd cent. AD *CIL* 111. 7556, *AE* 1902, 41, *CIL* XII. 2234, III. 2035, XI. 390, V. 522, III. 12411, V. 7004, VIII. 2354, VIII. 217 = *ILS* 11301, *AE* 1939, 101, *CIL* XIIIL. 6646. G. Forni, *Il Reclumento delle legioni da Augusto a Diocleziano* (1953), 152–6, lists more, but either the dating or reconstructions are dubious. There are also twelve inscriptions of men directly commisioned as legionary centurions, *CIL* XIV. 2989, II. 2424, VI. 3584, X. 1202, X. 5829, *AE* 1957, 249, *CIL* VIII. 15872, VIII. 14698, *AE* 1913, 215, *CIL* III. 1480, V. 7865, *MEM.Junta Sup.* 133, 1929, 66+. Five of these men are equestrians. Three more men were directly commissioned as legionary centurions before transferring to the Praetorian Guard. Two others who were transferred may also have been, *CIL* XIV. 2523, II. 4461, XI. 6057, X. 1127, *AE* 1935, 12. The majority of centurions' career inscriptions either do not mention service before the centurionate or refer only to *principalis* rank. The same trend is discernible with *primi pilares*. Of the 100 *primi pilares* listed by A. von Domaszewski, Die Rangordnung des römischen Heares, 2nd edn. (Cologue, 1967), 64 record no service prior to *primus pilus*. Examples of centurions recording no prior rank include *CIL* VIII. 2877 = *ILS* 2653, *CIL* VIII. 2891, VIII. 2786 = *ILS* 2659, *CIL* VIII. 3001.

[81] See J. F. Gilliam, 'The Appointment of Auxiliary Centurions' *TAPA* 88 (1958), 191–205. Cornelius, the centurion of the *Cohors Italica* mentioned in *Acts* 10, probably came from a prosperous family in Caesarea. See M. P. Speidel, 'The Roman army in Judaea under the Procurators', in *Roman Army Studies*. ii. 224.

[82] One is recorded as owning 9 slaves *CIL* III. 8143, c.f. *Matthew* 8: 5–13 and *CIL* XIII. 8648 = *ILS* 2244.

[83] For patronage in general see R. P. Saller, *Personal patronage under the Early Empire* (Cambridge, 1982).

of a cohort (Pliny 10. 87). In the letter he describes his long acquaintance with Lupus and the man's virtues. Juvenal jokingly mentions the importance of letters of recommendation for a recruit (Juvenal, *Satire* 16. 4–6). Papyri from Egypt confirm this, recording men who were appointed to administrative posts, the status of *immunis* (exempt from fatigues) and even *principalis* rank on enlistment through letters of recommendation from influential men.[84] The importance of patronage and influence within the army's career structure explains some of the more exceptional individuals recorded. One is Publius Aelius Tiro, appointed prefect of a cohort at the age of 14 (*ILS* 2749). The youngest recorded directly commissioned centurion was 18 (*CIL* III 1480 = *ILS* 2654). At the other end of the scale are men who served in the same rank for many years without being promoted. There are cases of men in their sixties and seventies still serving as centurions with their legions.[85] Of the eighteen centurions known to have served over 40 years, only four became *primus pilus*. There are cases of men in junior posts remaining there for a long time. One man was a *beneficiarius tribuni sexmestris* for 24 years (*CIL* III 7758), another a *cornicularius tribuni* for 16 (*CIL* III 895), another an *aquilifer* for 13 years (*CIL* III 11027), and yet another an *optio* for 10 (*CIL* XII 2234). In the section on unit organization we noted how many officers served away from their units.[86] The choicer postings, offering the best chance of enrichment and further advancement, were doubtless filled by those with the most influence. The importance of patronage in the career structure of the Roman army does not mean that merit had nothing to do with a man's success. There was little to be gained by a patron in recommending large numbers of incompetents for vacant posts. The final words on patronage come from a letter written by Pliny to a provincial governor.

> For two reasons I have singled you out to approach with a request which I am most anxious to be granted. Your command of a large army gives you a plentiful source of benefits to confer, and secondly, your tenure has been long enough for you to have provided for your own friends. Turn to mine—they are not many. (Pliny 2. 13. 1–3)

---

[84] e.g. *P. Mich.* 465, 466. See Davies, *Service in the Roman Army*, 21–5.
[85] e.g. Petronius Fortunatus *CIL* VIII. 217 = *ILS* 2658 and T. Flavius Virilis *CIL* VIII. 2877 = *ILS* 2653.   [86] See above, pp. 24–5.

THE SIGNIFICANCE OF UNIT ORGANIZATION

It is now time to see how the Roman army's organization effected its wartime behaviour. Throughout our period the legions were the largest and most significant units in the army. By the beginning of the first century the long process whereby the citizen militia of the Republic became a professional army was virtually complete.[87] The earlier Republican legion had retained many of the aspects of the simple infantry phalanx from which it developed. The five sections of the legion—namely the heavy infantry *hastati, principes,* and *triarii,* the light infantry *velites,* and the cavalry *equites*—were equipped differently and had specific places in the unit's formation.[88] Its principal strength was the thirty maniples of its heavy infantry, the *equites* and *velites* acting in support of these. These units of about 120–160 men were deployed in three lines of ten maniples each. It was a force for large-scale battles, for standing in the open, moving straight forward and smashing its way through any opposition. The essential philosophy behind it was that of winning a straightforward, mass engagement with the enemy. Only in the method of doing this did it differ from the Greek hoplite phalanx or Macedonian combination of this with shock cavalry. The same, quick decisive clash with the enemy was desired. In this role the manipular legion performed very well. Hannibal's skill as a general inflicted several massive defeats on this army, yet the same type of army, when better led and with higher morale, beat him in turn. The inclusion of allied troops within the armies of this period did not change the essential tactical doctrines behind them, since many allied units were organized as legions and acted in a similar fashion, whilst any additional light troops or cavalry were deployed to help achieve the same aim of breaking the enemy's line.[89]

The legion of the late Republic and early Empire replaced the maniple (of 120–160 men) with the cohort (of 480 men) as the most important subdivision of the unit. It also did away with the *velites* and probably the *equites.* Each cohort consisted of three maniples, one from each of the lines of the old legion. The actual equipment of the individual legionary was standardized, but did not alter significantly. This has sometimes obscured the massive difference between a legion of 5,000 men divided into thirty maniples and one divided into ten

---

[87] See R. E. Smith, *Service in the Post-Marian Roman Army* (Manchester, 1958), 1–26 for this period.
[88] L. Keppie, *The Making of the Roman Army* (London, 1984), 33–40 on the manipular legion. [89] Ibid. 22–3.

larger cohorts. A legion of ten cohorts was a more complex structure than one of thirty maniples. An additional, intermediate level had been added to the command hierarchy. The commander of a manipular legion had to relay any orders directly to his thirty immediate subordinates, the centurions in charge of each maniple. He had then to co-ordinate personally their operations. This process would inevitably have been slow and prevented the legion from adopting a subtle or complicated plan with any chance of success. This, as much as anything else, explains why the tactics of Roman armies in this period were invariably simple. A legate in charge of a legion of ten cohorts could control his force far more easily. Instead of having to deal with thirty immediate subordinates, he had only to direct his ten cohort commanders. These men could themselves be left to control the 480 men under their command. A cohort was far more than the sum of the three maniples composing it. It possessed a clear command hierarchy and was accustomed to operating together as a unit. The result was a far more flexible legion, capable of successfully undertaking complex plans. Throughout his campaigns Caesar displayed a mastery of exploiting this flexibility. More than anything else, it is this that distinguishes his operations from those of earlier Roman commanders. The flexible cohort structure seems to have been made possible by the professionalism of the army. It seems unlikely that earlier Roman forces could have adopted this organization successfully.

Three lines of cohorts provided a similar concentration of force to three lines of maniples in order to break through an enemy army. Therefore, a legion of ten cohorts was at least as well suited as one of thirty maniples to winning a decisive large-scale battle. In both, the deployment in depth provided readily available reserves to exploit any success and turn a mild defeat of the enemy into a rout.[90] The greater flexibility of the cohort gave it advantages over the maniple in this type of warfare. Yet, whilst the legion of ten cohorts could win large-scale battles, it could equally be divided to operate effectively in smaller-scale warfare. A detachment of one or several cohorts would have been far less unwieldy than a numerically similar collection of maniples. The cohort was adaptable to more types of warfare, not just that waged on the largest scale. It seems likely that the cohort developed amongst the Roman legions in Spain, where the broken country and dispersed

[90] See Ch. 4.

opposition often required the use of forces smaller than a legion, yet larger than a maniple.[91]

The army of the last century of the Republic was firmly based around the legion. It was capable of adapting to smaller-scale warfare, but a body of 5,000 men was considered the most useful size for the principle sub-unit of the army. This suggests that large-scale warfare was anticipated as its main role. The general enfranchisement of Italians following the Social War, although increasing the citizen body, did not significantly affect the balance of the army. Legions were recruited from a larger citizen body, but performed essentially the same role of winning large-scale battles. Many armies included foreign allied contingents of cavalry or light troops, since the new legions lacked any significant number of these. Caesar's cavalry in Gaul was recruited from Gallic allies, German hostages and mercenaries and included some Spaniards. Numidian light infantry, Cretan archers, and Gallic infantry were also present in the army, at least in the early years.[92] Pompey accumulated a vast selection of allies for the Pharsalus campaign (*BC* 3. 4). In most cases these allied troops were recruited locally, and as a result fought in a manner which the terrain of the region favoured. Without the large numbers of allied cavalry, Caesar's army would have had great difficulty in coping with the numerous horse of Gallic armies in the open country in which most of the war was fought. Caesar raised a legion from non-citizens in Transalpine Gaul, a unit which later became the *Legio V Alaudae* (Suetonius *Caesar* 24). Both sides in the civil war raised legions from non-citizens, often, it seems, without bothering with the formality of granting citizenship to the men on enlistment (e.g. *African War* 19). Other foreign legions appeared at this time, such as the two Galatian formations raised by King Deiotarus, which served under Cicero in Cilicia in 51 BC and later in the civil wars.[93] All of these were recruited from the type of men who, under the Empire, would have been drafted into the auxiliary cohorts or *alae*. This is a clear indication of the scale of warfare in the last decades of the Republic. The wars against the Eastern kingdoms of Pontus or Parthia, or Caesar's operations against

---

[91] See Keppie, *Making of the Roman Army*, 63, and M. J. V. Bell, 'Tactical Reform in the Roman Republican Army', *Historia*, 14 (1965), 404–22 who argues convincingly for the cohort first becoming common in Spain.
[92] Gallic cavalry *BG* 2. 24, infantry 7. 50; Germans 7. 13; Spanish 5. 26; Numidians and Cretans 2. 7.   [93] Cic. *ad Att.* 6. 1, *Alexandrian War* 39, 40, 77.

the often large Gallic tribal units were decided by battles fought on a large scale. Similarly, in the Civil War, several actions involved over 50,000 men. It therefore made sense for the Roman armies involved in these conflicts to have the majority of their troops organized into comparatively large sub-units. A legion would have been more effective in a large action than ten individual cohorts, even if these had been 'brigaded' together by some _ad hoc_ arrangement. The legion had a clearly defined command structure and was trained to operate as a unit. As a result, the commander-in-chief of an army had to direct, not each unit of 500 or so men, but groups of ten of these. When an army might be made up of twenty, thirty or more cohort-sized formations, this was a clear advantage.[94] The Romans never developed any formation of greater than legion size. Battles were seldom large enough to require this. It is also unlikely that a general's staff would have been able to control such large forces.[95]

After the Pannonian revolt of AD 6–9 and the German rebellion of AD 9 (and even in these the enemy was often disunited) wars with well-organized kingdoms fielding massive armies became comparatively uncommon. Parthian wars occurred every few decades, the Dacians required large forces to defeat them under Domitian and Trajan, as did the Marcomanni and Quadi under Marcus Aurelius, but on the whole warfare was on a smaller scale. It is no coincidence that the imperial _auxilia_, as they began to emerge under Augustus, were not organized as legion-sized units, but as independent cohorts of infantry and similarly sized _alae_ of cavalry, more suited to warfare on a smaller scale. At the same time legionary troops began to operate more often in vexillations than as full legions. A 'corps', such as the eight Batavian cohorts, might serve together and be attached to a legion either acting as a small army in its own right or forming a sizeable sub-unit within a larger field force (_Hist._ 2. 27). A single cohort of _auxilia_, lacking firm attachment to any larger body, could operate as effectively on its own. The _cohortes equitatae_ which became increasingly common as the first century progressed, encapsulated this flexibility perhaps more than anything else.[96] As a combination of infantry and cavalry, they were ideal for garrison or outpost work, could fight on their own as a small,

---

[94] See Ch. 4 for a discussion of command.
[95] According to Velleius 2. 113, Tiberius found an army of 10 legions too difficult to control in Pannonia.
[96] See R. W. Davies, 'Cohortes Equitatae', in _Service in the Roman Army_, 141–51

balanced army, or could combine with other units as part of a larger force. The army of the early Empire was, as a result of the combination of legions and *auxilia*, capable of both large and small scale warfare with a considerable degree of flexibility.

CONCLUSION

There has been a tendency in the past to fail to relate studies of the Roman army's organization to either its prime purpose or the society that produced it. The army's ultimate function was to win wars by defeating the enemy in battle. This was not altered by the fact that many soldiers may never have been involved in a conflict. The permanence of the Roman army, as a full-time force of professional soldiers, gave it a significant advantage over most of its enemies. Roman campaigns could become seasonal because of problems of supply, but were not forced to become so by the need for soldiers to follow another occupation. In subsequent chapters we shall see that this allowed the Romans to attack and defeat enemies at a time of year when the latter were incapable of fighting.[97]

The organization of units, particularly the changes in legionary structure, tell us much about the changing scale of warfare. A legion of 30 maniples was suited to only one style of fighting, at which it excelled. This was the straightforward, large-scale battle, involving little or no prior manœuvre. In this period most campaigns were decided by one or more of these major confrontations, with little small scale fighting before or after these. The legion of 10 cohorts was as good at winning a large scale battle as one of 30 maniples, but it could also adapt itself to smaller-scale, less intensive fighting. A cohort possessed a clearly defined command structure. As a result it was far more efficient acting independently than 480 men divided into maniples. The adoption of the cohort produced a far more flexible legion. This change was made possible by altered recruitment patterns, which allowed legions to become more permanent, and made necessary by the type of warfare waged by some of Rome's enemies. The warfare of the first century BC was predominantly fought on a large scale, in which set-piece battles were decisive. Therefore in this period the legion was the principal unit of Roman armies and legions were commonly raised from non-citizens.

[97] See Chs. 2 and 3.

Under the Principate provincials recruited into the army were organized into much smaller basic units, the *alae* and *cohortes* (of 500–1,000 men). Similarly legions served on campaign in detachments, or *vexillationes*, far more often than as whole units. Clearly the warfare of this period was usually fought on a smaller scale than that of the previous century. When major wars of conquest were planned, complete new legions were often raised, and the subsequent conflicts fought by large armies, in which a body of 5,000–6,000 men was a useful sub-unit. No permanent unit larger than a legion was ever created, because armies were seldom large enough to require it, nor was there ever an enemy capable of organizing an army large enough to produce such large-scale warfare.

The evidence for the realities of unit organization shows that units were seldom kept at anywhere near their theoretical strength. There were two reasons for this. The first was that recruitment could not hope to anticipate the number of losses suffered due to illness, accident, enemy action, and desertion. On campaign the level of attrition from all these causes would have significantly increased. In 47 BC the Sixth Legion was reduced to less than 20 per cent of its 'paper strength' (*Alexandrian War* 69). The second factor reducing the number of effectives available to a unit for active service was the number of men, and particularly officers, detached on some of the many duties required of the Roman army. The result was that there was far less standardization and uniformity of size between units than has been assumed in the past. Adaptation to local requirements, for instance the unusual weaponry and organization issued to Arrian's Cappadocian legions, produced even more variety. The Roman army was an inherently flexible organization, able to cope with this variation.

This clearly defined and highly flexible organization was there to allow the army to perform the roles required of it. To study army organization as an end within itself is to misunderstand its significance. The great degree of variation within the strengths and internal organizations of Roman units was a sign of the system's great advantage, namely its ability to adapt to the local situation. Had it not possessed this, and instead slavishly adhered to its theoretical organization, then it would have had great difficulty coping with a changing military situation.

2
The Opposition

THE organization of the Roman army played a great part in determining its conduct on campaign. In the next chapter I shall discuss Roman strategy and methods of operation. It is important to remember the obvious fact that there must be at least two sides in any conflict. The organization and methods of operation of the armies of Rome's enemies must have influenced the course of a campaign fought against them. We must study the military institutions of Rome's opponents before we can hope to understand fully Roman strategy.[1] During our period the Roman army fought against a great range of opponents, however, virtually no information has survived for many of these armies. I intend to discuss the armies of the three best-documented opponents that faced Rome in this period. These are the Germans, Gauls, and Parthians. The differences between the warfare of these peoples may suggest something of the overall variety of opponents faced by Rome.

There have been very few works dealing with the organization, strategy, and tactics of German, Gallic, and Parthian armies in this period. In the case of the Germans and Gauls, this is almost certainly because they produced no commanders responsible for tactical innovations, and were therefore attributed little importance in the development of the art of war.[2] The Parthians have often been credited with a high level of military efficiency, largely because of Rome's failure to conquer them.[3] However, the evidence for the Parthian army is actually very poor, which has deterred any attempt at a

---

[1] See Ch. 3 for Roman strategy and the ways in which this was altered according to the nature of the enemy.

[2] Even studies of specific campaigns tend to concentrate on the Roman viewpoint, e.g. J. Harmand, *Une Campagne Césarienne: Alesia* (Paris, 1967). When attempts have been made to assess the strategy and tactics of Rome's opponents these have normally been judged by anachronistic standards, see Ch. 3.

[3] e.g. E. N. Luttwak, *The Grand Strategy of the Roman Empire* (Baltimore, 1976), 43–4.

real analysis of the army's capability. Set against the scant attention paid to the military organization of Rome's enemies is the vast literature dealing with the equipment of the individual warrior of each army. The evidence for this is primarily iconographic and archaeological, and, particularly in the case of the latter, constantly expanding. Many of these studies concentrate on the artistic form of particular items and do not discuss their use in warfare. Yet there is clearly a belief that the study of weaponry can fully explain the warfare of a people and that the equipment of the individual reveals how an army of many such individuals fought. Todd attempted to understand Germanic warfare by studying the weapons of the individual warrior.[4] Brunaux and Lambot did pay a little more attention to army organization and tactics in their study of Gallic warfare, but still devoted most space to weaponry.[5] The fighting technique and equipment of the individual warrior may tell us much about the way in which he fought during a battle, although I shall argue later that this was not the most important factor even in this.[6] However, the equipment of an individual will tell us nothing about how an army fought a war. To appreciate this we must understand the organization of the army.

The organization of an army limited its actions on campaign. The arrangements for command and control dictated the degree to which commanders could influence the actions of their troops and so the tactics that these might employ. The army's logistical arrangements placed limits upon the length of time that it could operate in the field and also the speed at which it manœuvred. The organization of an army can tell us much about the assumptions of a society concerning warfare. An army that was incapable of speedy or subtle manœuvre and only capable of supplying itself in the field for a short period was forced to seek a quick decision to any conflict by fighting a massed confrontation with the enemy. Such a society would have expected a war to consist of a single decisive battle with the enemy.

Every culture has its own concept of the nature of war.[7] A people's cultural assumptions about warfare are as important as its military organization in dictating the behaviour of its army during a conflict. The two aspects are closely interrelated, so that it is often difficult to

---

[4] M. Todd, *The Northern Barbarians* (Oxford, 1987), 140–62.
[5] J. Brunaux and B. Lambot, *Armement et guerre chez les gaulois* (Paris, 1987).
[6] See Ch. 5.   [7] See J. Keegan, *A History of War* (London, 1993), 3–60.

discern whether a people's military institutions dictated its expectations of the form a war would take, or had themselves been moulded by these. Both aspects probably developed together. Military institutions placed ultimate limits on what an army might achieve. Cultural assumptions might limit its actual activities even more. Later in this chapter I shall argue that the organization of Gallic and Germanic armies made it impossible for them to fight a guerrilla war. At the same time their cultural assumptions about warfare assumed that everything would be decided in the massed clash of open battle. Massed battle played an important role in maintaining the distinctions between different sections of society. As a result these peoples were incapable either of waging a guerrilla war or even of considering fighting in this way. Realization of the importance of these limitations is vital to any understanding of the military practices of a people.

An army's organization must reflect the socio-political organization of the people that produced it. Political centralization could produce more effective armies, which were capable of fighting protracted campaigns. Therefore it is vital to study an army in the context of the society that produced it, and not to judge it by the standards of more recent military history. However a full discussion of the economy and society of each of our three examples would require a lengthy digression and draw us away from our main object. I therefore intend to deal only with those aspects that had an immediate affect on warfare. More detailed discussions can be found in the works listed in the footnotes.

In any study of the armies of Rome's opponents it immediately becomes clear that these were markedly inferior in discipline, organization, and tactics to the Roman army. As a result any direct confrontation in open battle with the Roman army was most likely to end in a Roman victory. Scholars have suggested that the Roman army was less likely to be successful in the more sporadic fighting of a guerrilla war.[8] Many scholars have gone on to assume that this was the style of fighting that was used, or should have been used, by many of Rome's enemies. As mentioned above, I shall attempt to show in this chapter that many armies, for instance those of Germanic and Gallic peoples, were not capable of fighting in this manner. In this and the next chapter I shall argue that it was in this type of fighting, and not in guerrilla warfare, that Rome was more likely to suffer a serious defeat.

[8] Luttwak, *Grand Strategy*, 40–6.

The final section of this chapter will deal with the absorption of former enemies into the Roman army. I shall attempt to identify those aspects of the military traditions of Rome's enemies that allowed many to transfer their loyalty to their conqueror, and form highly effective units of the *auxilia*.

THE GERMANS

Our sources maintain a clear distinction between the Germanic and Gallic tribes, but the degree to which this reflected reality is now hotly debated.[9] In the main, the debate has revolved around linguistic and cultural distinctions, and not military differences, and so it need not concern us here. This section will include evidence regarding any people that our sources considered to be German.

There must have been many differences in the political and social organization of individual tribes, and developments in these during our period, which are now obscure.[10] The tribe, or *civitas*, was normally divided into several clans, or *pagi*. Each *pagus* was led by a combination of a monarch, a group of powerful nobles, perhaps organized into a council, and an assembly of all free, adult males. The more unified tribes might also have a similar set of institutions at the level of the *civitas*. In most tribes the general assembly, composed of all warriors other than those who had disgraced themselves in battle, had the greatest authority (*Germ.* 6). It was there that the *duces* or military leaders were elected. In AD 70 it was at such an assembly that the Canninefates elected Brinno as their leader, symbolically raising him on a shield (*Hist.* 4. 15). Leaders were normally selected from the nobles of the tribe, in particular the royal house or *stirps regia*. The nobility controlled many members of the tribe through client relationships, made possible by wealth. A noble's power depended on his wealth and reputation, but individual ability was required to exploit these. This period saw a significant growth in the power of individual nobles. A clear indication of this was the growing importance and size

---

[9] See M. Todd, *Northern Barbarians*, 11–13 and *The Early Germans* (Oxford, 1992), 8–13, and C. M. Wells, *The German Policy of Augustus* (Oxford, 1972), 14–31.

[10] On Germanic society in general see Todd, *Northern Barbarians*, 77–114, and *Early Germans*, 29–46, E. A. Thompson, *The Early Germans* (Oxford, 1965), 1–71, cf. N. Roymans *Tribal Societies in Northern Gaul* (Amsterdam, 1990), 17–45 for much of relevance to Germanic society.

of the noble's retinue or *comitatus*.[11] According to Tacitus, a man's prestige was measured by the number and fame of the warriors permanently supported by him (*Germ.* 13). These *comites* were loyal to their leader above anything else (*Germ.* 7 and 14), but required considerable wealth to support them. The increasing tendency for land and cattle to come into private hands allowed these followings to be maintained. This development gave a noble a basis within the tribe for real power, which, combined with exceptional ability and charisma, led to attempts at, and the establishment of, tyranny or kingship. Arminius and Maroboduus are examples of this process. Arminius based his position on the prestige gained from fighting Rome and, in particular, the defeat of Varus in AD 9. This allowed him to dominate his own people, the Cherusci, and also lead a collection of allied tribes.[12] Maroboduus linked many subject and allied peoples to the Marcomanni, acquiring sufficient force through wealth to impose his will on unwilling subjects (Velleius 2. 108–9). Maroboduus was forced into exile after his defeat by Arminius in AD 17 and soon afterwards Arminius was himself murdered by rival nobles from his own tribe (*Ann.* 2. 63). The position of such strong, charismatic leaders was always vulnerable, dependent on maintaining their reputation for military success. No leaders of power comparable to Arminius and Maroboduus were to emerge in either the Cherusci or Marcomanni for a long period after their fall.

Although not by any means completely absent, *oppida* were comparatively rare amongst the Germanic peoples in our period, and those that there were never developed into the political and economic centres of central and southern Gaul.[13] Caesar left a picture of a constantly wandering society without fixed settlements (*BG* 6. 22). It is unclear if this was really the case even at the beginning of our period, but in Caesar's day Germanic society was becoming more static. The archaeological record shows a steady growth and considerable stability in a large number of German villages.[14] Caesar seems to have been right in viewing cattle as the most important type of wealth (*BG* 6. 22), especially since these herds were easily concentrated in the hands of

---

[11] See L. Hedeager, 'The evolution of German society 1–400 AD', in R. Jones, J. Bloemers, S. Dyson, and M. Biddle (eds.), *First Millenium Papers: Western Europe in the 1ˢᵗ Millenium AD. BAR* 401 (1988), 129–401.

[12] *Ann.* 2. 88 on the career of Arminius.

[13] See Ch. 2, 'The Gauls'.

[14] Todd, *Early Germans*, 17–19, 62–78.

individuals (*Germ.* 5). Yet his claim[15] that little attention was paid to cereal crops, is undermined by his own testimony, where the Usipetes and Tencteri were forced to migrate when attacks from the Suebi prevented them from tilling the land (*BG* 6. 1). In fighting the Germans, Roman armies frequently made their villages, cattle, and crops the object of attack with considerable effect.[16]

The chief source of wealth allowing a noble to keep a large retinue, was warfare, which provided booty, especially cattle. Added to the physical rewards in raiding, military success gave a leader prestige in a society in which all free men were warriors. Caesar mentions the pride taken by tribes in the depopulated areas around their land, which symbolized their own martial strength as well as reducing the immediate threat of being raided themselves (*BG* 6. 23). The leader of a famous or strong retinue might receive gifts from outside the tribe from those wishing to avoid his attention (*Germ.* 13). Warfare and the raid especially, which could be mounted by a leader's *comitatus* alone, played a vital role in Germanic society and made these tribes uncomfortable neighbours for the Roman provinces. The extent of Germanic raiding across the *limes* is unclear, since our sources tend only to record forays of the largest scale.[17]

This discussion of Germanic political and social organization has of necessity been brief, but was required to place an investigation of the organization of a tribal army in context. The only permanent forces in any German tribe were the *comites* of the nobles. These were formed of warriors dependent for their means of living on their leader, and as a result, loyal to him. They often included men from outside the tribe, eager to serve a famous leader (*Germ.* 14). Numerically, these retinues were comparatively small, their exact size dependent on the wealth and prestige of the noble. By themselves they were suited only to raiding and very small-scale warfare, but they formed a highly motivated and well-equipped nucleus for the main body of any army (*Germ.* 13). A leader such as Arminius not only had a large number of famous *comites*, but was also able to attract a proportion of the ordinary warriors to form a more permanent field army.[18] Maroboduus was reputed to have

---

[15] *BG* 6. 29 perhaps also the lack of large central stores of food made this real.

[16] e.g. *BG* 4. 19, *Ann.* 1. 49, 1. 54; see Ch. 3.

[17] *BG* 6. 35; Velleius 2. 97; Suet. *Galba* 4; Dio 54. 11, 20; 55. 10; 71. 15–16, 19. 2; 72. 1. 1a, 3. 2; *Ann.* 4. 72; 11. 18; 12. 27; 13. 54.

[18] Tacitus' claim that by AD 17 his army had become more disciplined seems simply due to prolonged service. *Ann.* 2. 45.

included a body of guards trained and drilled almost to Roman standards in his army of 70,000 foot and 4,000 horse.[19]

It is unclear just how broad a section of society was comprised of those adult males considered capable of bearing arms. It seems at least possible that the right to bear arms was granted to all those able to equip themselves. The assembly of warriors decided when to take offensive action and elected a leader. The tribes' reaction to an enemy attack depended on the amount of warning it received. When Caesar crossed the Rhine in 55 BC the Suebi decided to remove or hide their property and non-combatants, whilst the men gathered in the centre of their territory and planned to meet the Romans there (*BG* 4. 19). The tribe behaved in a similar way on his second crossing of the river two years later (*BG* 6. 29). On many other occasions, Roman armies attacked a tribe and ravaged its territory without being opposed.[20] In most circumstances a German army only appeared to attack the Roman force as it withdrew.[21] This does not appear to be a type of guerrilla tactic, since the tribesmen were quite willing to fight the Roman army as it retired. Rather it seems that the process of massing the tribal army was a slow one, so that by the time it had been formed, the Romans were already moving away. Tacitus noted that the tribal assembly, composed of all warriors and thus identical to the tribal army, took days to gather together, because the Germans were not punctual (*Germ.* 11). This suggests that the mustering of an army was a long drawn-out process. When faced with an invasion by the army of another tribe, the slow speed of its advance might well have allowed time for a force to be gathered to confront it. When attacked by a small raid or a swift-moving Roman column, this was normally impossible.[22]

Once assembled, the army was divided into bodies based on the *pagus*, which were in turn split into units based upon family and regional relationships.[23] If such units had an appointed or natural leader, it would have been difficult for him to have manœuvred them on the battlefield, let alone off it, given the absence of training or

---

[19] Velleius 2. 109: note also the deserters fighting with Gannascus *Ann.* 11. 18, cf. Decebalus, Dio 68. 9. 6, who would also have provided permanent forces.

[20] *Ann.* 1. 50, 1. 55; 2. 8.

[21] *Ann.* 1. 55 where it is noted as exceptional that the Chatti did not do so.

[22] The role of the depopulated strip around a tribal territory is clearly vital in this aspect of warfare, *BG* 6. 23.

[23] Tacitus noted (*Germ.* 6. 10) that *scuta tantum lectissimis coloribus distinguunt.* It is unclear whether units or individuals were distinguished in this way.

discipline. For the overall *dux* or duces of the army the direction of a
large collection of such units must have been immensely difficult.[24] All
leaders could have hoped to do was deploy their army on the terrain on
which they intended to give battle. Normally, the Germans occupied
their position before the Romans approached, giving them time to
arrange their forces.[25] It is no coincidence that on the occasions of
German attacks upon withdrawing Roman armies, the tribesmen
massed on the likely line of retreat and there awaited the Roman
column.[26] The Suebian plan to gather and then wait for Caesar's army
to approach was similar (*BG* 4. 19, 6. 29). It is likely that in warfare
between two tribes a degree of mutual consent, to meet at a certain
place for a decisive battle, was common. Both armies could only move
slowly and desired a quick result, making a swift confrontation
desirable. According to Plutarch, 'Boeorix, the King of the Cimbri,
rode out with a small body of cavalry to the Roman camp and
challenged Marius to fix a day and a place and then come out and fight
for the ownership of the country' (Plutarch, *Marius* 25). Even if his
account is accurate, such formal challenges may not have been
common, but the way armies moved into contact on a convenient patch
of ground would have had the same result in practice. The primitive
organization of these armies prevented anything more complicated
from being attempted. It would be missing this point to describe such
warfare as ritualized. Tribal armies were not supple, manœuvrable
forces, but clumsy masses capable only of open battle or an ambush on
a grand scale.

According to Tacitus, *alios ad proelium ire videas, Chattos ad bellum*
('Other tribes may be seen going forth to battle, the Chatti come out
for a campaign').[27] One of the practices he claims to be unique to this
tribe was the carrying of food by the individual warrior. How the
individual warrior fed himself in other tribes is unclear. It is likely that
it was the responsibility of each man to provide for himself, since none,

[24] Note the poor march discipline of Arminius' troops, *Ann.* 2. 12.
[25] Arminius and Segimerus had gathered their army before leading Varus towards it
in AD 9, Dio 56. 19. 5.
[26] e.g. *Ann.* 1. 50, 63, cf. *BG* 5. 32, where the Eburones deployed two ambushes, one
on each of the routes available to the Roman column. It would clearly not have been
possible to wait until the Roman choice of path was visible before deploying a single
ambush.
[27] *Germ.* 30 where he notes the Chatti carried food. Elsewhere he states that the
wives of warriors carried provisions, suggesting that the Chattan practice was unusual
(*Germ.* 7).

save, just possibly, the most organized states, can have possessed a commissariat service. Most probably this function was carried out by those in the train of women (*Germ.* 7, 8), and slaves (*Ann.* 12. 27), which followed the army. However, few German armies had the capacity to maintain themselves for a long time in the field unless living off enemy lands, so that armies swiftly dispersed after a battle, whether a victory or defeat.[28] The armies of exceptional leaders such as Arminius were more able to undertake a campaign. Long service under a strong leader made them more amenable to command (*Ann.* 2. 45). The host of Ariovistus was able to maintain itself for a long period in the face of Caesar's army without offering battle. Arminius could attempt a night advance and attack on Germanicus (*Ann.* 2. 12), or a feigned flight drawing the enemy into a trap (*Ann.* 2. 63). The element of regular auxiliary troops in the Batavian revolt of Civilis allowed greater tactical subtlety in the latter part of the rebellion than in the earlier actions. In the first battle of the campaign the tactics were simple. Civilis lined up his forces in the open for a direct frontal attack on Munius Lupercus, and had the women of the tribe standing behind the line and providing moral support (*Hist.* 4. 18). Later in the campaign, a complex attack, made by four columns simultaneously, was mounted by the rebels (*Hist.* 5. 20). It is unfortunate that we have no detailed description of the Chatti on campaign and so cannot tell if their greater organization allowed them to adopt more complicated plans. Nor do we know what type of political organization made this possible. Tacitus' description of a large number of warriors who had no other occupation than war seems to suggest a concentration of, presumably noble, wealth to support these (*Germ.* 31). The army of this tribe and those of other tribes under an exceptionally strong leader were clearly dangerous and required large Roman armies to defeat them, as well as increasing the chance of the Romans being defeated. With the possible exception of the Chatti, whose use of tools Tacitus mentions, no German army, even the partially Roman-trained Batavians, showed much capacity for siege warfare, perhaps because few strongholds were of importance in tribal warfare (*Germ.* 30; *Hist.* 4. 28). The better-organized armies might have been able to maintain themselves in the field for long enough to blockade a garrison into

---

[28] The Chatti were unique in organizing supply, *Germ.* 30. 3 Caesar notes the importance of gathering food into places of security to cause raiders to starve, see *BG* 2. 10, 6. 10.

submission, but stood little chance of success if direct assault unaided by siegecraft was of no avail.

Apart from the Tencteri (*Germ.* 32), cavalry seems to have made up only a comparatively small proportion of German armies.[29] It has been suggested that the *comites* of nobles were normally mounted,[30] and Tacitus mentions that at least some were given horses by their leader (*Germ.* 13). Even if these did have horses, they may have ridden to battle and fought on foot (*BG* 4. 12). It seems equally possible that the cavalry was drawn from the wealthier of the ordinary warriors, that is, those who were able to afford a horse. Caesar's re-equipping of his German cavalry with better horses suggests that their own mounts were often of poor quality (*BG* 7. 65). Certainly Tacitus mentions their ugliness and lack of speed (*Germ.* 6.), and modern studies suggest that they were small.[31] The large size and weight of the rider reduced speed significantly. In the same passage Tacitus notes their lack of manœuvrability in formation. The only tactic that German cavalry seem to have employed was the headlong charge. These charges were often successful, despite the lack of saddles noted by Caesar.[32] In the 50s BC the high reputation enjoyed by German warriors in Gaul in part explains the advantage in morale they enjoyed over Gallic horse. Lack of missile weapons and training, probably as well as their military philosophy, ensured that German cavalry made poor skirmishers or scouts (*Germ.* 6). The vital function played by the infantry of the *centeni* or 'the hundred' in cavalry tactics is noted several times.[33]

Infantry was the main strength of most German armies. Our sources tend to concentrate on the formidable appearance of individual warriors, with their large frame and red hair.[34] Tacitus gives the best description of their equipment:

Only a few of them use swords or large lances: they carry spears—called *frameae* in their language—with short and narrow blades, but so sharp and easy to handle that they can be used, as required, either at close quarters or in long-range fighting. Their horsemen are content with a shield and a spear: but the foot-soldiers also rain javelins on their foes; each of them carries several, and they hurl them to immense distances, being naked or lightly clad in short

---

[29] Although the figures themselves are unreliable, the proportion of 6,000 cavalry out of the army of 120,000 led by Ariovistus in 58 BC may be instructive. In other armies, cavalry remained a small minority.   [30] e.g. Todd, *Early Germans*, 32.

[31] See A. Bantelmann *Tofting: Eine vorgeschichtliche Warft an der Eidermündung* (Newmunster, 1955).   [32] *BG* 4. 12; 7. 67, 70, 80.

[33] *Germ.* 6, *BG* 1. 48.

[34] Note the use of hairstyles to make the warriors more frightening, *Germ.* 31 and 38.

cloaks. There is nothing ostentatious about their equipment: only their shields
are picked out in the colours of their choice. Few have breastplates; and only
one here and there a helmet of metal or hide. (*Germ.* 6)

Elsewhere he implies that at least one tribe tended to use longer
spears than the *framea* (*Ann.* 2. 14). In a speech attributed to
Germanicus it is claimed that many in the rear ranks made do with
clubs.[35]

The archaeological record seems to confirm Tacitus' claim that
armour was scarce.[36] Shields provided the main means of defence for
the majority of warriors. Roman monuments depicted these as
sexagonal, rectangular and round, which the cavalry seem to have
favoured.[37] Until recently, swords were comparatively uncommon in
the archaeological record, leading Todd to estimate that on average
about one in ten warriors were swordsmen rather than spearmen.[38]
The swords discovered include La Tène long, two-edged types,
Roman swords or copies of them,[39] as well as the increasingly
uncommon single-edged knife or short sword of the pre-Roman
period. The Ilerup Ädal votive offerings, dated to the very end of our
period at around 200 AD, may greatly alter our view of German
weaponry in the period, once the findings have been published. This
find which seems to be composed of the spoils of an army from
Southern Norway or Sweden included along with 1,500 spear and
lance heads, several hundred Roman-type swords, many with makers'
names in Latin or clearly Roman inlays.[40] Whether these were taken in
a Roman defeat or sold by traders is unclear, but if an army so far from
the *limes* possessed such a large amount of high-quality equipment,
surely we might expect those nearer to possess comparable or even
greater amounts of such gear.[41] It is reasonable to expect the better
equipment to have been concentrated amongst the nobles, their *comites*
and the wealthier warriors. If there were humbler warriors armed only
with clubs, their complete absence from the archaeological record
would not be surprising.

---

[35] *Ann.* 2. 14, cf. the 'German' *symacharii* on Trajan's column scenes 95, 96, 177.
[36] The Hjortspring lake find included 20 suits of mail from the pre-Roman period,
but this represents the highest stratum of society.
[37] Todd, *Northern Barbarians*, 151–52.   [38] Ibid. 149.
[39] E. Nylam, 'Early *Gladius* Swords in Scandinavia', *Acta Arch.* 34 (1963), 185.
[40] J. Ilkjær, 'The Weapons' Sacrifice from Ilerup Ådal, Denmark', in K. Randsbourg,
The Birth of Europe (Rome, 1989), 54–61, and Todd, *Early Germans* 111.
[41] e.g. *Ann.* 2. 45, where Tacitus noted the use of captured weapons by the Cherusci.

No widespread finds of arrows appear until the fourth century, but since the bow seems to have been the weapon of the poor, and so, unlikely to be represented in the burial record, this may not reflect the complete absence of bows from German armies.[42] Men are recorded skirmishing with javelins, but it is unclear whether they specialized in this function, or were merely warriors from the main line, running forward to harass the Romans as individual enthusiasm dictated (*Ann.* 1. 64). Overall, it seems that the greatest prestige was attached to prowess in hand-to-hand combat.

The main tactic of German infantry was the charge in dense formation at great speed. Tacitus referred to their battle line as a row of wedges or *cunei*, but did not give details about this formation.(*Germ.* 6). Vegetius tells us that the *cuneus* was a formation wider at the rear than the front (Vegetius 3. 17). However Caesar describes the battle line of Ariovistus as a phalanx and it is possible that Tacitus used *cuneus* to mean a dense formation of no particular shape (*BG* 1. 52). It seems clear that in German armies the better-equipped, nobler warriors and those especially keen stood in the front rank (*Ann.* 2. 14). It may be that there were fewer of these individuals, so that a mass of less enthusiastic warriors tended to bunch behind each group of the boldest, thus producing a wedge-shaped formation. Equally, the formation may have been deliberate, and the result would in any case be a manœuvrable, relatively fast and intimidating body of men.[43]

It is easy to emphasize the stereotype of the wild barbarian. Clearly some aspects of the Germans' appearance were intended to intimidate an enemy, and did so. The war-cry called the *barritus* served a similar purpose. According to Tacitus:

By the rendering of this they not only kindle their courage, but, merely by listening to the sound, they can forecast the issue of an approaching engagement. For they either terrify their foes or themselves become frightened, according to the character of the noise they make upon the battlefield; and they regard it not merely as so many voices chanting together but as a unison of valour. What they particularly aim at is a harsh, intermittent roar; and they hold their shields in front of their mouths, so that the sound is amplified into a deeper crescendo by the reverberation. (*Germ.* 3)

German units were not simple mobs of individuals and it is

---

[42] See Todd, *Northern Barbarians*, 155–6.
[43] See Ch. 5, 'Close-Order Infantry against Close-Order Infantry', for a discussion of the *cuneus* and of the Germans in battle.

noticeable that Tacitus mentions as the greatest crime the discarding of one's shield in battle, a sign of the worst cowardice to the Greeks of the hoplite era, who possessed often as little formal training or discipline as the Germans.[44] German bands were perhaps not disciplined into rank and file, but did keep together and offer a coherent front to the enemy. Although German armies often employed cover to conceal their initial positions from the Romans, they always attempted to fight on open ground. In tribal warfare perhaps any convenient open plain was employed.

German armies were clumsy forces, incapable of subtle manœuvre. Their logistical organization was rudimentary, which ensured that they were unable to stay together and operate for any length of time. As a result they were best suited to fighting individual massed battles and not protracted campaigns. The massed battle seems to have been the most important, and perhaps the only part, of full-scale tribal war. The centrality of battle was confirmed by its vital role in maintaining distinctions in society. During the fighting a noble lost status if he was surpassed in courage by his *comites*, whilst these in turn were obliged to equal his bravery (*Germ.* 14. 1). The individuals within the *comitatus* competed with each other in prowess and courage, for status within the group and rewards from the leader (*Germ.* 14. 3–4). Non-combatant members of the tribe, in particular the wives of the warriors, watched the battle from behind the main line and assisted the wounded (*Germ.* 7–8, *Hist.* 4. 18). Their presence encouraged the warriors to conform to the standard of courage expected of them, for if they failed to do this then the whole community witnessed their failure. Tacitus noted that the Germans considered it a matter of pride to carry away their own dead and wounded, even before the fighting had been decided (*Germ.* 6). After a victory the Germans were more inclined to loot than to mount a concerted pursuit aimed at destroying the enemy army's capacity to fight another battle.[45] This is of course a sign of poor discipline, but may also indicate that once an advantage had been gained by one side in a battle, the other was expected to give up. It suggests that the warriors expected some visible, and perhaps profitable, symbols of victory to accompany the glory gained. It seems

---

[44] *Germ.* 6, see V.D. Hanson, *The Western Way of War: Infantry Battle in Classical Greece* (New York, 1989), 64–5 for Greek parallels where the shield was considered to protect not just the hoplite himself, but his comrades on either side.

[45] *Ann.* 1. 68, *Hist.* 4. 60, Dio 56. 22. 2–3.

likely that in tribal warfare the whole conflict was normally decided by a single battle. There was no need to pursue and destroy the enemy, since he would concede defeat in the war because of the loss of this battle. Victory in battle was connected to physical possession of the battlefield, which allowed the victors to preserve their own casualties and plunder the enemy dead.

Battles, and therefore wars, between two German tribes contained a strong element of ritual, limiting and defining the actual fighting. Some of the rituals they shared with hoplite warfare between Greek city-states and with the warfare of many primitive societies.[46] It is vital that this element of ritual should not blind us to genuine violence and the dramatic consequences of Germanic warfare. When the Hermunduri and Chatti fought a battle over the possession of a salt-producing river, with economic and religious significance to them both, each side took a vow to Mars and Mercury promising to sacrifice their foes to the gods if they were granted victory. The Chatti were beaten and all their captured warriors and their horses were ritually executed, their arms and equipment destroyed (*Ann.* 13. 57). Even when the defeat of a tribe in battle did not involve such heavy losses to the warriors involved, it often forced a tribe to vacate its land and move elsewhere. The Usipetes and Tencteri were forced to migrate when defeated by the Suebi (*BG* 6. 1). During the reign of Nero the Ampsivarii attempted to occupy an area of land reserved for the Roman army, having been driven out of their own territory by the Chauci (*Ann.* 13. 55). In the *Germania* Tacitus describes how the Bructeri were destroyed by the Chamavi and Angrivarii, who then occupied their land (*Germ.* 33.). Clearly the limits imposed on the actual fighting did not limit the decisiveness of Germanic warfare. The appropriation of the best land by the victors is a frequent, if sometimes gradual result, of the most ritualized and primitive warfare.[47]

German armies were not capable of fighting a guerrilla war because they were unable to remain in the field for a long campaign. Small bands however, often of the noble and his *comitatus*, could and did mount raids effectively. These raids served a vital role in society by providing the nobility with the wealth, chiefly in the form of cattle,

---

[46] On hoplite warfare see Hanson, *Western Way of War, passim.* On primitive warfare in general see Keegan, *History of Warfare*, 94–115, especially on the Maring of New Guinea.
[47] Keegan, *History of Warfare* 55–8 on 'territorial displacement'.

required for systems of clientship to operate. Yet these raids would not decide a war. Only the tribal army could do this and the army was only capable of fighting individual battles. Whenever the Romans attacked them, a German tribe attempted to gather an army and meet the invaders in battle. They did this even though, with the benefit of hindsight, we can see that they were almost certainly going to be beaten. In most cases the process of massing the army took so long that the Germans were only able to meet the Romans when the latter were already retiring from their territory. The instinctive reaction of a Germanic tribe to an attack was to meet the enemy in battle. Therefore, not only were they incapable of fighting a guerrilla war, but it seems unlikely that they would even have thought of fighting in this way. It was not a question of the Roman army having to provoke unwilling Germans into a massed encounter which these were likely to lose. Normally the Germans were only too willing to confront an attacking Roman army. This being so, the most dangerous opponents were the tribal leaders who could unite their own and other tribes. It was the men like Arminius and Maroboduus, who posed the greatest threat. These men led confederations of tribes and massed armies that were not only exceptionally large, but also capable of staying in the field for a long time. Very large Roman armies were needed to defeat such leaders, but there remained the danger that the Romans themselves would suffer a reverse, as happened in AD 9. The conquest of Germany failed, not because the Roman army was incapable of attacking the important assets of the German tribes, but because it failed to defeat Arminius decisively in battle. Eventually Tiberius decided to abandon further attempts at conquest, a decision not altered by Arminius' murder (*Ann.* 2. 26).

THE GAULS

In contrast with the last section, I intend now to deal with a much shorter period of time, examining Gallic armies during Caesar's campaigns of 59–51 BC. In central and southern Gaul, Gallic society displayed a far higher level of stratification than that of contemporary Germanic peoples. It possessed many of the institutions of the early state, including annually elected magistracies and popular assemblies,[48]

---

[48] B. Cunliffe, *Greeks, Romans and Barbarians: Spheres of Interaction* (London, 1988), 106–24, and Roymans, Tribal Societies, 17–45.

as well as *oppida* which were economic and political centres rather than mere places of refuge. Within these the archaeological record emphasizes the clear social divisions between classes. Despite the formal institutions of government, the influence of individual nobles tended to dominate the politics of the tribe. These might possess personally both cattle and, most of all, land. As among the Germans, prestige was measured in the size of retinues (*BG* 6. 15). Again recruitment seems to have included men from outside the tribe. Caesar frequently refers to wandering warriors seeking employment, who may not in Gallic society have been seen as the robbers and vagabonds that he described (e.g. *BG* 7. 4, 8. 30). At least in some instances the followers may have been bound to the noble by an oath of loyalty which demanded that they should not outlive him, as with king Adiatuanus of the Aquitani and his 600 *soldurii*. Little is known of the nature of this relationship, for instance whether it was common throughout Gaul or merely a local phenomenon. According to Caesar:

The Sotiates call such persons *soldurii*. The friend to whom they attach themselves undertakes to share all the good things of life, on the understanding that, if he meets a violent end, they shall either share his fate or make away with themselves; and within the memory of man none has yet been known to refuse to die when the friend to whom he had sworn allegiance was killed. (*BG* 3. 22)

Added to these were the nobles' dependants or clients, the freemen attached to him in a somewhat obscure relationship. With these forces at his back, Vercingetorix was able to defy the chiefs and magistrates who had expelled him from Gergovia, and seize supreme power in the *civitas* (*BG* 7. 4). Caesar continually emphasized the ambition of individual nobles for tyranny or kingship within their tribe[49] and although he perhaps exaggerated this to justify his own intervention, it seems unlikely that it was not essentially true. An interesting proof of the personal loyalty of retinues and retainers is the ease with which these served the Romans as *auxilia*. The only Gallic troops drawn from the mass of the citizen body mentioned by Caesar, the 10,000 Aeduan infantry in 52 BC, performed badly and seem largely to have been used to guard the lines of communication (*BG* 7. 34). Not only did Gallic cavalry effectively fight for their leader on behalf of the Romans, but

---

[49] e.g. Orgetorix *BG* 1. 2 and Vercingetorix *BG* 7. 4.

equally, if the leader chose to transfer his allegiance, as Commius and later Roucillus and Egus did, they automatically followed him.[50]

Any of these organized *civitates* was capable of putting a large army into the field but, as importantly, they could also mobilize many allied tribes in their support. The various alliances between tribes, seen most notably in the groupings around the Aedui and the Sequani, appear frequently in Caesar's narrative in explanation of his actions.[51] Tribes to the east might well have hired mercenaries from, or have been allied to, German tribes, the obvious case being the invitation made by the Sequani to Ariovistus (*BG* 1. 31). Individual nobles within a tribe used marriage alliances to gain extra-tribal links in a parallel way, increasing their own power.[52] Such states had armies willing to be confronted in battle, but these were large formidable opponents.

The tribes of the north-west were described in less detail by Caesar. Their *oppida* seem to have been less important than those in the south, and their armies smaller, but in many respects they were similar. In the north-east, a more egalitarian society seems to have existed, which had much in common with the peoples of Germany.[53] Most were willing to fight open warfare, forming comparatively large field armies, but their *oppida* were small refuges of little political importance. Leaders seem to have been temporary, elected for wars and less able to strive for supreme power.

The *oppida* of central and southern Gaul provided a clear target for Roman offensives. If the enemy was unwilling to meet the Roman army in the field, then these strongholds could be stormed and the tribe forced to capitulate.[54] The presence of large stores of food and equipment often made these especially attractive targets.[55] To set against this, sieges of these strongholds were often long drawn-out and arduous, and, even if usually successful, presented considerable problems of supply. Direct assault without preparation risked a bloody repulse (*BG* 3. 20, 7. 52). The *oppida* of the Veneti could all be evacuated by sea. These were of less central political importance and

---

[50] Commius *BG* 7. 76, Roucillus and Egus *BC* 3. 59–60.

[51] e.g. his support of the Remi in 57 BC, *BG* 2. 3–5, of the Boii in 52, *BG* 7. 9–10, on the importance of alliances in general see *BG* 1. 31, 6. 11.

[52] Dumnorix' own wife was from the Helvetii, his mother was married to a noble of the Bituriges, and his half-sister and other female relations to men of other tribes, *BG* 1. 18; Ariovistus had two wives, one Suebian, the other a sister of King Voccio of Noricum, *BG* 1. 53.

[53] See Roymans, *Tribal Societies*, for a full study of these.

[54] *BG* 2. 12–13, 7. 13.   [55] *BG* 1. 38, 7. 32, 7. 55, 8. 3.

offered little advantage when taken. In this case the tribe's main
fighting force, its navy, had to be defeated before it surrendered (*BG* 3.
16). In the village-based economy of the north-east, the Romans were
able to attack these communities, as well as livestock and crops, and
through their devastation force a surrender (*BG* 6. 43). Both were
alternatives to confronting the enemy field army, which may not have
been possible or desirable depending on circumstances.

'Before Caesar's arrival in the country, the Gallic states used to fight
offensive or defensive wars almost every year' (*BG* 6. 15). The scale of
these conflicts is hard to judge, but it is probable that the aim was the
reduction of the enemy to a subject tribe through a moral defeat rather
than his destruction. For the nobles, warfare offered the opportunity of
wealth, prestige, and reputation to further political aspirations at home.
As in Germany, a retinue could only be maintained by actual fighting.
The reason given for the migration of the Helvetii, that the geography
of their homeland did not allow them full scope for raiding (*BG* 1. 1),
and the subsequent raids on Rome's allies (*BG* 1. 2), reinforces the
importance of warfare in Gallic society. Again, both factors are similar
to those discussed as encouraging endemic warfare in Germanic
culture.

This is the customary method of opening hostilities in Gaul. A law common to
all the tribes alike requires all adult males to arm and attend the muster, and
the last to arrive is cruelly tortured and put to death in the presence of the
assembled host. (*BG* 5. 56)

It is clear that forming and organizing a Gallic army was a difficult,
long drawn-out task despite such draconian measures. On several
occasions, Roman armies mounted surprise attacks on tribes and
devastated their territory before these were able to organize an
effective response.[56] The retinues of nobles seem to have been at least
semi-permanent and, added to their clients, formed a strong nucleus
for the tribal army. This seems to have been made up of units based on
clan, familial, and town groupings (*BG* 7. 19). These troops were
poorly disciplined, and lacked training above the level of the individual,
but were able to form reasonably tight formations on an open
battlefield (*BG* 1. 25). Movement to and from the battlefield was a
clumsy, ill-organized process, the column being encumbered with

---

[56] e.g. *BG* 6. 3, 4, 5, 30, 7. 8, 8. 3; see Ch. 3.

many wagons containing women and other non-combatants.[57] Therefore manœuvre in close proximity to the enemy, especially disengaging, courted disaster, and fighting a battle from the march was equally liable to confusion.[58]

Normally the Gallic army needed to occupy the ground to be fought over for a long time, in order to form up.[59] On some occasions contingents arrived during or after the action (e.g. *BG* 1. 25, 2. 29). Ambushes, which normally involved use of cover for concealment, but an actual attack into open ground, needed to be placed well in advance (e.g. *BG* 2. 18, 5. 32). Strabo seems largely correct when he claims that the Gauls 'come together openly and without circumspection, so that for those who wish to defeat them by stratagem, they become easy to deal with'. As a result, unlike the Spanish, they could be defeated all at once rather than piecemeal (Strabo, *Geog.* 4. 4. 2).

Leadership amongst the northern tribes seems to have been less permanent than amongst the southern, their armies able to feed themselves for a shorter time and as a result desirous of a quick decision. The Belgic tribes could still refuse to attack a strong position occupied by Caesar in 58 BC (*BG* 2. 8–9), but after waiting a few days had to disperse when grain ran short. A decisive battle, though one fought in favourable circumstances, was clearly the aim of warfare. Attacks on towns (*BG* 2. 6), and threats to supply lines (*BG* 2. 9) were attempts to force such a decisive encounter. Central and southern tribes with more developed economies, which provided surpluses of grain, were able to maintain an army far longer in the field.

This was seen most clearly in the campaign of 52 BC, a year when Vercingetorix enjoyed power and authority over a confederation of tribes that was clearly exceptional. He was able to seek to wear the enemy down by skirmishing, destroying supplies in their path, threatening their communications, and weakening the allegiance of their allies. Throughout the year, Vercingetorix himself maintained an army waiting to strike and destroy the enemy if an opportunity offered, but avoided joining battle if it did not. Both the leader and the times were exceptional, but earlier the tribes of the south-west joined by allies from Spain had adopted a long-term plan to defeat the Romans

---

[57] *BG* 8. 14, *BC* 1. 51, cf. Brunaux and Lambot, *Armament et guerre* 51–2.

[58] *BG* 2. 11, 7. 68, 8. 27.

[59] Gallic armies often occupied a position to await the Romans, e.g. *BG* 2. 7, 2. 19; 3. 20; 5. 49; 7. 12, 7. 19.

whilst maintaining a strong army in the field (*BG* 3. 23–5). Like Vercingetorix, a mark of their organization and mood had been the construction of a camp, something unheard of in Gaul (*BG* 3. 23, 7. 30). In neither case was the Gaulish army equal in terms of manœuvre, discipline, or control to the Romans, but they were a stage more advanced in that direction than ordinary tribal armies. Advances in siege warfare during these years were similar. The role of *oppida* in tribal warfare ensured that, unlike the Germans, the Gauls had some basic methods of attack. The Nervii were found to have copied Roman methods of attack, but were clearly still considerably less able (*BG* 5. 52). Although it may have been a close thing on several occasions, no Gallic tribe actually managed to storm any of Caesar's *hiberna*.

Apart from amongst the more egalitarian Nervii, cavalry provided the highest quality troops in a Gallic army. They were drawn chiefly from the nobles and their retinues and clients. Because of this recruitment from the wealthier and more prestigious warriors, equipment was of good quality and consisted of a shield, lance, sword, and javelin, and often a helmet and mail armour. Added to this was the secure seat provided by the four-horned saddle, later adopted by the Romans themselves. The morale of these bands was usually very high so that, allegedly, thirty once routed 2,000 Moorish horse (*African War* 6). Even when outclassed by the heavier Parthian cataphracts, the younger Crassus' Gallic horse fought fiercely (Plutarch, *Crassus* 25). However, German cavalry enjoyed an advantage in morale over their Gallic counterparts throughout Caesar's campaigns (*BG* 4. 12). The tactics of the Gallic cavalry were those of the headlong charge. Discipline was normally poor, so that they were difficult to rally from pursuit (*BG* 5. 16), or rout (*BG* 2. 24). As scouts they were inefficient. Caesar's cavalry failed to locate the Gallic army at the Sambre (*BG* 2. 19). It may have been rare for Gallic armies to send out scouts to locate the enemy. The Helvetii failed to notice the night-time approach of two Roman columns to their camp in 58, and marched on the next morning, oblivious to the Roman presence.[60]

The close-order infantry were always the most numerous element of a tribal army. Diodorus gave a detailed description of Gallic equipment:

---

[60] *BG* I. 21–2, see Ch. 4.

For armour they use long shields, as high as a man, which are wrought in a manner peculiar to them, some of them even having the figures of animals embossed on them in bronze, and these are skilfully worked with an eye not only to beauty, but also to protection. On their heads they put bronze helmets which have large embossed figures standing out from them and give the appearance of great size to those who wear them; for in some cases horns are attached to the helmet so as to form a single piece, in other cases images of the fore-parts of birds or four-footed animals. Their trumpets are of peculiar nature and such as barbarians use, for when they are blown they give forth a harsh sound, appropriate to the tumult of war. Some of them have iron cuirasses, chain-wrought, but others are satisfied with the armour which Nature has given them and go into battle stark naked. In place of the short sword they carry long broad-swords which are hung on chains of iron or bronze and are worn along the right flank. Some of them gather up their shirts with belts plated with gold or silver. The spears they brandish, which they call *lanciae*, have iron heads a cubit in length and even more, and a little under two palms in breadth . . . some of these javelins come from the forge straight, others twist in and out in spiral shapes for their entire length, the purpose being that the thrust may not only cut the flesh, but mangle it as well, and that the withdrawal of the spear may lacerate the wound. (Diodorus 5. 30. 2–4)

Infantry formations could be quite dense and were based on a familial or kinship link, making a man's relatives the witnesses of his behaviour. It is likely that the boldest and best-equipped naturally gravitated to the front rank. Armour seems to have been very rare and the combination of shield, long slashing sword, and javelins formed the equipment of most warriors. The appearance of the individual, his size, expression and shouts, added to the noise of clashing weapons and the *carnyx*, or war trumpet, were clearly intended to intimidate the enemy before actually reaching them. If the enemy was persuaded that he was going to lose before an actual mêlée began, then a Gallic charge would succeed, if not then the Romans' superior equipment and discipline was normally decisive.[61] Attacks from the flank were far more dangerous.

Light infantry armed with missile weapons appear relatively infrequently in Caesar's account and seem to have had a subsidiary role, weakening the enemy before a mass charge went in and most of all supporting the cavalry (*BG* 7. 80). In sieges their importance increased. Javelins seem to have been common and at least some

---

[61] For a full discussion of battlefield performance see Ch. 5.

peoples used the sling, whilst Vercingetorix was noted as having appealed for archers from all over Gaul (*BG* 7. 30). Overall it is probable that more honour was associated with killing at close quarters, so that the skirmishers were provided by the poorer or younger warriors.

Gallic armies varied in size and efficiency, but even the most organized was still a clumsy body to manœuvre compared to a Roman army. The vast majority of tribes produced armies geared towards massed combat and not guerrilla warfare. For many peoples, especially in the north-east, wars were expected to be decided by a single decisive battle, as was the case in Germanic warfare. The reason for this was that their armies could supply themselves only for a brief period and thus a quick decision was desirable. The *civitates* of central and southern Gaul produced larger armies, capable of operating for a longer campaign. This gave them the option of avoiding battle until it was advantageous to fight, as Vercingetorix attempted to do in 52 BC. These armies were still geared towards massed confrontations and expected a war to ultimately be decided in this way. These states also possessed important political and economic centres in their *oppida*, the loss of which was a severe blow. A war between one of these tribes and Rome was likely to be decisive, either through a massed battle between the respective armies, or when the Romans employed their skill at siegecraft to take the enemy *oppida*. Although the Romans were more likely to win such a conflict, we should not forget that there was still a chance of defeat, and that such a defeat would be on a large scale. Gallic armies required large Roman forces to defeat them. Caesar came very close to defeat on several occasions in Gaul, most notably against the Helvetii, at the Sambre, and in 52. If the Romans had been beaten by Vercingetorix, then the results might have been as serious as they were in Germany in AD 9.

THE PARTHIANS

They are really formidable in warfare, but nevertheless they have a reputation greater than their achievements, because, in spite of their not having gained anything from the Romans, and having, besides, given up certain portions of their own domain, they have not yet been enslaved, but even to this day hold their own in wars they wage against us, whenever they become involved in them. (Dio 40. 14. 4)

In this section we are again dealing with several centuries of history. As before, our literary evidence comes entirely from the Roman perspective. What is noticeable, given the importance modern scholars have attached to the threat of Parthia,[62] is how little evidence our sources actually provide for campaigns against Parthia. Only those of Crassus, Antony, and Corbulo are described in any detail at all. As a result there will inevitably be many generalizations in this section.

The Arsacid dynasty established itself by 100 BC in authority over a wide part of the former Seleucid territories from the Euphrates to the eastern borders of Iran.[63] At the time of the first conflict with Rome the supreme power within the realm rested, at least in theory, with the king. Exploitation of the well-managed agricultural systems of the many Hellenistic cities and of the important trade routes gave the monarch the wealth to support a large army. In practice, the situation was rather different. The stronger noble families had come to gather many of the king's prerogatives into their own hands, controlling large expanses of land personally. Although the king controlled the army, it was recruited on a feudal basis from the noble families and their retainers. The greatest of these provided the cataphracts and some horse-archers, the remainder the mass of the latter. Contingents served together under their own leaders and in most instances seem to have been loyal to them, following them into exile.[64] The greater nobles often possessed both the ability and the will to challenge the king for the throne or support one of his relatives in doing so. Many of the periods of long peace between Parthia and Rome, and most especially the diplomatic success under Augustus, coincided with times of internal strife and civil war in the kingdom.[65] Parthia, it must be emphasized, also had borders other than that with Rome and may often have been involved there. Given these factors it is perhaps not surprising that only once, when in AD 161 Vologeses III took Armenia

[62] See B. Isaac, *The Limits of Empire*, rev. edn. (Oxford, 1992), 20–3.

[63] For Parthian political and social organization in general see A. Bivar, 'The Political History of Iran under the Arsacids', in E. Yarshater, *The Cambridge History of Iran*, iii. 1 (Cambridge, 1983), 21–97, N. C. Debevoise, *The Political History of Parthia* (Chicago, 1938), M. Colledge, *The Parthians* (London, 1967), 57–97, and R. N. Frye, *The History of Ancient Iran* (Munich, 1983), 216–33 and *The Heritage of Persia* (London, 1963), 178–97.

[64] See D. C. Kennedy, 'Parthian Regiments in The Roman Army', in J. Fitz (ed.), *Limes, Akten des XI. Internationalen Limeskongresses* (Budapest, 1977), 521–31.

[65] On relations between the Parthians and Rome contrast Isaac, *Limits of Empire*, 19–53, with J. B. Campbell, 'War and Diplomacy: Rome and Parthia, 31 BC–AD 235', in J. Rich and G. Shipley, *War and Society in the Roman World* (London, 1993), 213–40.

and then invaded Syria, did the Parthians initiate an offensive war. Their invasion of Syria and Asia was a direct result of the defeat of Crassus and part of the same conflict. When offensives did occur in other campaigns, and probably in terms of strategy in that one as well, these were essentially large-scale raids, designed to pillage and inflict damage, but not to hold ground, something the army was singularly ill-suited to doing, if it was seriously opposed.

The Parthians possessed an army which was normally willing to fight in favourable circumstances. Although its effectiveness has been greatly exaggerated, it was a force that was very difficult to defeat decisively and destroy in battle. As a largely cavalry army it was able to retreat very quickly. Antony was disappointed when a concerted pursuit resulted in only 30 prisoners and 80 dead (Plutarch, *Antony* 39). When fighting the Parthians, the Romans tended instead to make the country's cities, and most of all the royal city of Ctesiphon, the target of their offensives. During Crassus' initial foray across the Euphrates in 54 BC the Romans captured several cities, including Seleucia. They encountered little opposition from the cities' pre-dominantly Greek populations, who felt little loyalty to their Parthian overlords. Plutarch and Dio took the view that had Crassus moved immediately on Ctesiphon he would have met with a similarly warm welcome there.[66] The great eastern conquests of Lucullus and Pompey may well have encouraged Parthia's Greek population to expect a Roman occupation to be permanent. The failure of Crassus' and Antony's invasions shattered this illusion. Future Roman invasions did not find cities so willing to defect. Ctesiphon was sacked by the Romans in AD 116, 165, and 198. The loss of Ctesiphon deprived the Parthian monarch of at least some of his wealth and significantly reduced his prestige, perhaps to the extent of prompting his deposition. When Corbulo attacked the Armenian capital, Artaxata, the Parthian-imposed king, Tiridates, was forced to fight if he was not to lose face (*Ann.* 13. 39). The capture of other lesser cities contributed to this process in a small way. Yet, unless the majority of the numerous cities in the vast expanse of Parthia were taken, it is unlikely that sufficient political and economic dislocation would have occurred to force the king to surrender.

The exact nature of the organization of the Parthian army is not

[66] Plut. *Crassus* 17, Dio 40. 16. 3, 20. 3–4.

recorded in detail in any of our sources. The majority of men were provided by prominent noble landowners. According to Lucian, who, given that he is writing a humorous work, is unlikely to be the best witness, the basic Parthian unit was the dragon of 1,000 men (Lucian, *Quomodo Hist.* 29). Whether this was so or not, the dependants of one noble clearly served together, although they might be divided into cataphracts and horse-archers. The force raised and led by Surena at Carrhae in 53 BC gives us an example of the higher levels of military efficiency these retinues might reach. According to Plutarch his army consisted of 10,000 horse-archers and 1,000 cataphracts, who co-operated well with each other (Plutarch, *Crassus* 21). The organization of pack-camels to ensure continued supplies of arrows is mentioned, though it is unclear how common this was (*Crassus* 25). This force, when confronted, inflicted losses and broke the morale of a larger Roman army. Yet, if the high level of military effectiveness Surena had built up amongst his retainers shows how good a Parthian army might become, his fate—being disposed of as a dangerous rival by the king—is equally instructive. Given that the Crown could not trust the greater noble families, it was not in its interest to allow them to have highly effective regiments, with the result that the royal army, consisting of these contingents could not be of too high a standard. The high proportion of the troops provided by individual nobles meant that mustering a sizeable army was a lengthy process. The king did not have an army ready for immediate action. In 54 BC Crassus was able to cross the Euphrates, capture and garrison several cities and return to winter quarters in Syria, before any significant Parthian force was gathered to oppose him (Dio 40. 16. 1–20. 4).

Although we have the reference to ammunition supply in Surena's army, we know virtually nothing of the logistical arrangements of the Parthian army. Dio expressly states that the Parthians did not have an organized system to supply and pay their army (Dio 40. 15. 6). Their poor showing at sieges may have been due more to lack of technical skill and the low quality of the infantry, rather than supply problems when the army became static, but it may be that it was hard to keep the feudal elements of the army serving long enough to make these truly feasible (Dio 40. 29. 1).

The Parthian army was essentially a cavalry force. Cavalry could not hold ground, but by its nature advanced and retired quickly. Parthian armies exploited the essential mobility of cavalry by attempting to attack the enemy where he was weak and withdraw from contact where he was strong. The principle of exploiting every advantage is common to all forms of warfare, but the acceptance of flight as sensible when the enemy had the advantage was not.[67] For the Romans when the enemy turned to flee, it was a sign that he had been soundly beaten and now was the time to pursue him vigorously and to make his defeat decisive. Many of Rome's reverses against the Parthians occurred when a detachment of troops pursued an apparently beaten enemy, became detached from the main body, and were surrounded and defeated in detail.[68] Flight for the Parthians was a normal, sensible reaction to enemy strength, an impermanent state, altered when supports were reached and local strength had been regained, when aggression was again possible. This philosophy was as apparent in the broader events of the campaign as on the battlefield. When Roman armies, as under Antony and Corbulo, were competently led and offered little chance of successful actions in the field, the Parthian reaction was to strike at their lines of communication, successfully in the first case, but not in the second (Plutarch, *Antony* 38, *Ann.* 13. 39). In 53 BC the Parthians sent only a small force under Surena to shadow and delay Crassus' army. The main Parthian effort, under the king Hyrodes, was directed against Armenia. The aim was to deprive Crassus of this strong ally before trying to defeat him (Plutarch, *Crassus* 21, Dio 40. 16. 1–2). In the event Surena was able to defeat Crassus unaided.

There is a marked difference between the behaviour of both sides in the earlier confrontations between Rome and Parthia, compared to the later. In 53 both sides seem to have expected an easy victory. The Romans remembered the successes of Sulla, Lucullus, and Pompey, when small Roman armies had effortlessly crushed huge eastern armies from Pontus and Armenia (Plutarch, *Crassus* 18). The Parthians were equally scornful of their opponents. Surena was fully prepared to give battle to Crassus' numerically larger army. According to Plutarch, he hoped by the sudden and spectacular appearance of his army so to terrify the waiting Romans that they could be swept away by his cataphract's charge (*Crassus* 24). Instead the steadiness of the Roman infantry deterred Surena from mounting a charge until the Romans had been weakened. The logic behind this decision mirrors

---

[67] See Hanson *The Western Way of War*, 219–28 on Greek attitudes which emphasized direct confrontation of the enemy's strength.
[68] Plut. *Crassus* 25, *Antony* 42–3, *Ann.* 13. 36, 13. 40, 15. 9.

the strategy discussed above. When the enemy was strong, he must be worn down before a decisive attack was mounted to destroy him. In a campaign he was weakened by attacks on his communications or allies, until his main army was made vulnerable. In a battle he was harassed by the horse archers before the decisive cataphract charge was mounted. At Carrhae the Roman army was steadily weakened by the day-long bombardment of arrows, but remained unbroken. The collapse of the army's and its leader's morale after the battle was the chief factor in its destruction.

After Carrhae the Parthians must have been convinced that their contempt for the Romans was justified (Dio 48. 40. 2). In 51 BC a strong force invaded Syria, but was incapable of besieging Antioch (Dio 40. 29. 1). Crassus' *quaestor*, Cassius, then employed the Parthians' own tactics against them. A small force confronted them and then immediately pretended to flee, luring the pursuing Parthians into a trap (Dio 40. 29. 3). The Parthians were surrounded and destroyed, just as Publius Crassus had been at Carrhae. This small reverse, perhaps because it had been delivered by their own methods, did not reduce the Parthians' contempt for Roman infantry. In 39 BC after Publius Ventidius Bassus had driven the Parthians' ally, Labienus, out of Asia, the two armies confronted each other waiting for reinforcements. When the Parthians arrived to reinforce Labienus, Ventidius remained positioned on top of a steep rise. The Parthians believed his reluctance to come down was a sign of fear and, confident that the Romans would collapse, charged straight up the slope, presumably led by the cataphracts. The Roman heavy infantry counter-attacked and routed the Parthians with heavy loss (Dio 48. 39. 1–40. 5). In the next year the Parthians, led by Hyrodes' son Pacorus again invaded Syria. With similar confidence they attempted to storm Ventidius' camp placed on high ground guarding a river crossing. Once again a sally by legionaries supported by slingers defeated the cataphracts with heavy loss, including Pacorus himself (Dio 49. 20. 1–4). After these two defeats the Parthian belief in their own superiority established at Carrhae was shattered. In later campaigns their behaviour was far more cautious. Horse-archers became more prominent than cataphracts, and as a result the Parthians placed more emphasis on wearing the enemy down than decisively defeating him. We do not have detailed accounts for any campaigns against the Parthians after Corbulo's and so it is impossible to guess whether this balance in morale between the two sides was ever altered.

Turning to the composition of the Parthian army, there is little information on its infantry. Dio notes that the foot were provided by the poorest men and were all archers (Dio 40. 15. 2–3). The least numerous, but most impressive cavalry were the cataphracts. A fully equipped cataphract had a bronze or iron helmet, perhaps with neck guard, a lamella, mail, or scale cuirass with arm and thigh guards attached, leg defences of mail or laminated strips, and mail-reinforced gauntlets. The horse wore a caparison of iron or bronze scales with further armour on the neck or head. The wealthiest may have worn the full panoply, but many in the rear ranks must have made do with much less. Offensive weapons were the 4 m. (12-foot) *kontos*, backed up by swords, axes, and the like. The *kontos* was normally employed in a two-handed underarm thrust, the horse being directed by the rider's knees. Clearly all this gear weighed an enormous amount, so it is unlikely that these heavy horseman charged at anything quicker than a trot. Cataphracts were immune to most light missile weapons, apart from the sling, which did not need to penetrate to incapacitate the target, and probably at short range the heavy pilum. When fresh, in a frontal charge they could expect to beat most less-armoured horse.[69] Against steady heavy infantry, a frontal charge was unlikely to succeed, the horses being unwilling to hit a seemingly solid object. The Parthian cataphracts at Carrhae did not charge home on Crassus' legionaries (Plutarch, *Crassus* 25). It seems likely that even these heavy horsemen did not normally directly confront a strong enemy, but waited until he had been weakened by the fire of the horse-archers. When cataphracts twice did so against Ventidius' legionaries they were routed (Dio 40. 40. 1–5, 49. 20. 1–4). One of the reasons for the inability to repeat the success at Carrhae, was the lack of a commander capable of co-ordinating the two elements of the Parthian cavalry to maximum effect.

It is the horse-archer, rather than the cataphract, that our sources tend to think of typical Parthian soldier (e.g. *Ann.* 6. 35). The composite bow used by the Parthians was a technologically advanced and highly effective weapon. With it a right-handed bowman might expect to have an arc of fire, assuming the horse's head to be twelve on the clock face, from about six o'clock to one o'clock. The advantages of the horse-archer were mobility and speed, which made him a more

---

[69] Arrian implies that the similar Alan cataphracts were vulnerable to a flank charge, *Ectaxis* 30, cf. Plut. *Lucullus* 18. For cavalry on the battlefield see Ch. 5, 'Cavalry against Infantry'.

difficult target for return fire. As a result the normal tactic was to ride parallel to an enemy on the left, being ready to turn away if he attempted to close the distance. To use an anachronistic term, a horse, most of all a moving horse, is a highly unstable gun platform, making the firing of a moving archer highly inaccurate. His aim was not to hit specific targets but to pepper an area with missiles and hope that some struck home. Therefore, a high rate of fire rather than precision was required. Roman legionaries were well protected by shield and armour, so relatively few arrows in the target area would cause losses, and these would mostly have been non-fatal wounds to arms and legs.[70] Unless the infantry had no missile weapons and were demoralized, the horsemen could not afford to come into the range at which their arrows might pierce armour. Even at Carrhae, where they had such an advantage and the Parthians fired for most of the day, the Roman infantry was not weakened to the extent that it would be unable to withstand a charge of cataphracts. Charges by the horse-archers themselves required the enemy to be weakened even more.[71] When the Roman army included, as that of Antony and most later expeditions did, a significant number of infantry with missile weapons (and a foot-archer would significantly out-range a bowman on horseback) to support the heavier troops, then the horse-archers became less of a threat than a minor irritant.[72]

The effectiveness of the Parthian army has been greatly overrated, largely because of a misunderstanding of the battle of Carrhae. One of the reasons for the defeat at Carrhae was that Crassus controlled an unbalanced army. The army of the Principate included amongst the *auxilia*, high-quality cavalry and missile armed troops. If a balanced army kept together and made no mistakes, even moving in battle formation, then a Parthian force could not hope to beat it even in the open. Its horse-archers would have been unable to weaken the enemy significantly enough for the heavy cavalry to have charged successfully. As a result Parthian armies tended to shadow Roman forces watching for an error to exploit, such as the detaching of a small force. When they made the mistake of actually attacking, they lost. Hence, the tendency to strike at supply convoys, on which the Romans depended

---

[70] Note the use of the *testudo* by Antony, Plut. *Antony* 45.

[71] Plut. *Antony* 45, see Ch. 5, 232–4, for a full discussion of combat between horse-archers and Roman infantry.

[72] Note the high proportion of archers in Arrian's column in the *Ectaxis* 12, 14, 18, 21, 25–6, see Ch. 1, 19.

to maintain their armies in the harsh landscape of these campaigns.[73]
If these were properly defended then there was little the Parthian
commander could do to prevent the Romans from taking his
strongholds, as Corbulo showed by taking successive cities in Armenia.
A more serious problem for the Romans was the climate and the
disease it fostered, causing a high rate of loss through sickness.[74]
Added to this was the need for troops to protect the lines of
communication and the province of Syria from raiding, and to garrison
captured strongholds without reducing the numbers in the field army
to the extent that it could not operate. As a result, any campaign
against the Parthians required a very large army and massive logistical
support to keep these troops in the field. These troops inevitably
suffered a high rate of attrition from the harsh conditions. In terms of
battlefield performance a Parthian army was no match for a well-
balanced and competently handled Roman army. Only without the
right balance of troops and under a poor commander was a Roman
army likely to be defeated. The scale of the task, probably more than
anything else, prevented the actual conquest of Parthia.

NATIVE TRADITIONS AND AUXILIARY RECRUITMENT

The ease with which former enemies were assimilated into the Roman
army as part of the *auxilia* was a highly distinctive feature of this
period. Caesar used Gallic horse from allied tribes against those Gauls
opposing him. After campaigning across the Rhine against Germanic
peoples he obtained German units, which he used with great effect in
both the rebellion of 52 BC and later throughout the Civil War.[75]
Parthian units were present in the Roman army at least from the time
of Augustus and probably before.[76] Such auxiliary units normally seem
to have operated highly effectively against opposition with whom they
had more in common than their Roman leaders, so that there was
more than a little truth in Civilis' claim that 'it was at the cost of
provincial blood that the provinces were crushed ... and sober
reflection showed that Gaul had succumbed to Gaul' (*Hist.* 4. 17). A
full examination of the process by which the allies of the Republic

---

[73] *Ann.* 15. 11 where Tacitus noted the problem of feeding an army in this area.

[74] Even with the harassed retreat, the majority of Antony's losses came from disease,
Plut. *Antony* 50.

[75] See D. B. Saddington, *The Development of the Roman Auxiliary Forces from Caesar to
Vespasian* (Harare, 1982), 5–14.   [76] Kennedy, 'Parthian Regiments', 521–31.

became the more formally organized and regular *auxilia* of the imperial army would be a large study within itself, but it is worth considering here how far the military practices of the peoples under discussion eased their incorporation into the *auxilia*.

The intense and personal bond of loyalty between a noble and his retainers, clients, or *comites* has been remarked upon in all of the three peoples discussed. It appears to have been a common feature, although it is probable that the exact nature of the bond and its significance was defined differently in each society. As I have already shown, should the leader have chosen to fight for Rome, or for one side or the other in a civil war, then his retainers would have followed him, fighting as keenly and for as long as he chose. Most of the earlier auxiliary troops are more like the allies of the Republic, organized in their own units or groupings and led by their own leaders. In 52 BC Caesar had 10,000 Aeduan infantry in addition to his other allies. These seem to have been part of the tribal levy, raised using the normal institutions of the Gallic state (*BG* 7. 34). Their morale and effectiveness was lower than that of the units of cavalry composed of a noble and his followers. This was in part a reflection of the strengths of any Gallic army, but due more to the uncertain political situation. The Batavians included in the army of Germanicus in AD 16 seem to have formed a larger contingent than might have been provided purely by the nobles of the tribe and their *comites* (*Ann.* 2. 10). They were led not by a Roman, but by their *dux* Chariovalda and may well have been the ordinary army of the tribe raised in traditional manner. There is no suggestion of these troops possessing Roman organization or discipline. They launched an impetuous attack across a river and were lured into a trap. Their *dux* Chariovalda led from the front and eventually fell along with many of his chieftains and *comites*, in a manner more typically German than Roman. Later in the century the Batavians, still led by their own nobles, although without an overall *dux*, were organized into cohorts and an *ala* and fought with far greater discipline. The history of the Parthian units of the *auxilia* is somewhat obscure, so that, although Kennedy has shown that these existed from at least the Augustan period, if not before, we know little of their earlier organizations or the identity of their leaders.[77] Quite possibly, the earliest units were led by Parthian mercenaries or exiles and organized in their native manner,

---

[77] Ibid.

but we cannot be sure. There is a significant difference between fighting as allies of the Romans, but being led by native nobles or chieftains, and joining the Roman army in a unit led by a Roman officer and possibly trained and disciplined in the Roman manner.

In the section on the Germans it was noted that the *comitatus* of a noble not only included notable warriors from his own tribe, but often men from outside. Amongst the Germans, noble youths were prepared to fight for the leaders of other tribes if their own people were currently at peace (*Germ.* 14). Many of the most famous warriors of the Chatti had no homes or property, but wandered the land, fighting for any noble who fed them (*Germ.* 31). Military reputation, which was chiefly gained through personal prowess, could apparently be gained in any warfare, irrespective of whether this involved defence of your own tribe or attacks on its specific enemies. There seems to have been a similar class of warriors, professional in the sense of having no other job, which crossed tribal barriers in Gaul seeking employment with those prestigious nobles who could afford a large retinue (*BG* 7. 4, 8. 30). In both cases this tendency for retinues to be drawn from a wide area can only have increased the importance of the personal bond of loyalty between the retainer and noble. In neither instance, despite the fact that essentially, since they fought for food and reward, these men were mercenaries, does this seem to have been considered a dishonourable career. Many of these men came from a comparatively high social background before their service, whilst conspicuous prowess afterwards increased their reputation and prestige. Thus it can be seen that the concept of fighting for an alien tribe or people, or more specifically a famous man amongst them, was readily understandable in both Germany and Gaul. Not only that, but the following of this career or profession was perfectly acceptable to those of a high social standing. As a result, service in units of the *auxilia* might be expected to have been attractive to this group of warriors, and perhaps also to those of lower social station seeking advancement.

The details of the organization of the late Republican *auxilia* are somewhat obscure. Caesar referred to *praefecti equitum*,[78] as opposed to *praefecti equitatus*,[79] who were generals commanding larger bodies of cavalry, in charge of the cavalry units which seem to later develop into the *alae* of the Empire. Whilst the latter were invariably Roman, the

---

[78] *BG* 7. 67, 8. 12, 8. 28, 8. 48.   [79] *BG* 1. 18, 1. 52, 6. 6, 6. 29.

ranks of the former included some Gauls as well as Romans, mostly it seems from the equestrian order. It is likely that the Gauls involved were nobleman leading their own groups of retainers. Is it possible that the Roman officers led units of Gauls attached to them in the same sort of relationship that existed between the Gallic nobleman and his followers? The idea of a bond with an individual foreign leader was far more readily understandable to both Germans and Gauls, than loyalty to a distant Rome. Thus during the Civil Wars of the late Republic, German and Gallic units remained loyal to their leaders and willingly fought both Romans and other German and Gallic units on the other side. By 49 BC Caesar had a body of 900 cavalry recruited from natives during the Gallic campaigns as his personal bodyguard (*BC* 1. 41). A unit of Germans performed the same function for Cleopatra and, later, Herod the Great (*BJ* 1. 672). Augustus had his German bodyguard until this was disbanded in the aftermath of the disaster in AD 9 (Dio 56. 23). The high level of loyalty of retainer or *comes* to their noble leader, transferred to a Roman or other foreigner, made Gauls and Germans highly desirable as personal bodyguards. It was not really until Tiberius' principate that auxiliary units generally had permanent names, which in many cases then lasted for centuries. Before this, it was common for many units, especially Gallic *alae*, which formed a high proportion of the cavalry of the army, to be referred to as the *ala* of a particular commander. His name was given in the genitive, whereas later units named after a person carry the name in adjectival form. There may well be other reasons for this phenomenon, but it is at least possible that it reflected the soldiers' own view of themselves as the *comites* or retainers of the prefect in command. If the *ala Scaevae* was in fact named after Caesar's famous centurion, then he was the type of man possessed of all the warrior virtues which might have attracted a band of Gauls into his service. It is generally accepted, for instance by Birley, Holder, and Saddington, that those *alae* defined by their commander's name in the genitive were permanent units, their title changing when their officers did so.[80] This assumes that in the late Republic and Augustan period, units of the *auxilia* were as permanent as they later became. The *socii* of the Republican army seem to have been raised not on a permanent basis, but for the

---

[80] See E. Birley, '*Alae* Named after their commanders', *Ancient Society*, 9 (1978), 265–71 = *Roman Army Papers*, 368–84, P. Holder, *The Auxilia from Augustus to Trajan. BAR* 70 (1980), 21–3, Saddington, *Development of Roman Auxiliary Forces*, 147–50.

duration of specific campaigns. Service in the *auxilia* under Augustus may not have been regulated at 10 or 25 years as was later to be the case. It is at least possible that the early Gallic *alae* were raised by a specific commander, and disbanded if he left the army. There was no reason, if this were the case, why individual men from the unit might not then have shifted their allegiance to another commander, but they did not have to do so.

If the above arguments are right, then the relationship between officers and men in the *auxilia* may have been rather different from that existing in the legions, at least in the early Empire. In a sense it was a bargain. The troops were loyal to their commander, who fed, possibly equipped them, and provided opportunities for the winning of glory and booty. More than this, the commander would have been expected to display the warrior virtues of bravery and prowess, in the same way that the German noble was expected not to be outshone by his *comites*. It is interesting that Tacitus regarded the Thracian rebellion of AD 26 as having been prompted by a rumour that Thracian *auxilia* were to be mixed with other peoples and sent abroad (*Ann.* 4. 44). In a sense the Romans were suspected of breaking their side of what may have been a similar bargain. Although there were probably other reasons for this, the mutiny of the Batavian cohorts in AD 69, was under the pretext that Vitellius had not granted them the privileges which they had been promised (*Hist.* 4. 19). If the loyalty of many auxiliary units was focused not on Rome, but on the persons of their leaders, then a perceived breach of faith on the latter's part justified disobedience on their part.

A striking feature of many cavalry tombstones from the first two centuries AD is the depiction of the soldiers' servant or servants, standing by his horse and often holding a bundle of spears.[81] Speidel has argued convincingly that many, if not all, ordinary troopers might have expected to own a slave.[82] Caesar's Gallic cavalry seem to have been drawn from those classes who provided the cavalry in Gallic armies, that is, from those wealthy enough to own a horse and cavalry equipment. Diodorus described how the Gauls 'bring along to war also their free men to serve them, choosing them out from among the poor, and these attendants they use in battle as charioteers and as shield-bearers' (Diodorus 5. 29. 2). The only occupation of such a warrior

---

[81] M. Schleiemacher, *Römische Reitergrabsteine* (Bonn, 1984), in which at least twenty of the stones illustrated include servants.

[82] M. P. Speidel, 'The Soldiers' Servants', *Ancient Society*, 20 (1989), 239–47.

class may have been battle, so that servants were required to care for their horse and equipment, to prepare food for them and attend to their needs. It seems reasonable that these men accompanied their masters when fighting for the Romans, as they did in tribal warfare. If the more regular cavalry of the Principate continued to be recruited from this class, or from those who aspired to join it, might not the tradition of troopers having servants have been retained? The practice was not restricted to Gallic units, but it is possible that similar social factors were at play in cultures about which we know even less.

CONCLUSION

There have been many studies in the past of the weaponry and armour of the Germans, Gauls, and Parthians.[83] The assumption implicit in these studies was that equipment determined the manner in which these peoples fought. Yet studies based purely on equipment cannot properly explain how an army behaved in battle or on campaign. The course of a campaign was shaped by the organization and the military philosophy of the participating armies. If we are to understand the behaviour of the Roman army on campaign, then we must also understand its opponents.

Army organization was heavily influenced by society. Each society defined which groups within it should bear arms. For most Gallic and German tribes, the main army was drawn from all free, adult males. These men were not full-time soldiers and were organized only on the basis of kinship. The army produced in this way lacked a clear, well-organized command structure and as a result was difficult to control and move. Such an army was not capable of subtle tactics. Since its men were not permanent soldiers, this army could not stay in the field for long. These two factors, its undeveloped command structure, and its fundamental impermanence, encouraged such an army to seek a decisive result to a campaign as soon as possible. The only way to do this with such a clumsy, unmanœuvrable army was to fight an open, decisive battle with the enemy as soon as possible.[84] In a war between two tribes there was a desire on both sides for such a simple decisive clash, so that the limitations of the tribal army was not a great

---

[83] See Ch. 2.
[84] See Hanson, *Western Way of War* 27–39, for similar factors encouraging Hoplite armies to seek decisive clashes.

disadvantage. The Roman army was a permanent force, capable of supplying itself for a long campaign. This gave it a massive advantage over German and Gallic armies. Political centralization, as for instance in the *civitates* of southern and central Gaul, produced larger and more efficient armies. In 52 BC Vercingetorix attempted to wear the Roman army down by depriving it of supplies, secure in the knowledge that he could keep a sizeable army in the field for a long period of time. Conversely on both occasions in 57 BC when the Belgic tribes gathered an army, they were forced to seek battle quickly before supply problems forced them to disperse.

The strength of a Parthian monarch affected the efficiency of his army. The royal army was recruited primarily from the retinues of the principal noble families. In an ideal situation, but seldom in reality, these contingents were to be both loyal and efficient. As an essentially cavalry force, a Parthian army was best suited to fast-moving, raid-like campaigns. This encouraged an attitude to war in which the aim was to attack the enemy where he was weak and avoid him where he was strong. In many respects this was the exact opposite to German and Gallic attitudes to war. Wars fought by Rome against the latter were consequently very different to Parthian campaigns.

This study has examined only a few of Rome's opponents in this period. Perhaps the only others that might be examined in detail are the British tribes. Elsewhere, especially on the eastern frontiers, we have glimpses of how the opposition operated, but little more.[85] As stated in the introduction, the selection of armies treated in this chapter was not intended to deny the importance of others about whom less is known. Some clearly show evidence of the same processes discussed here. For instance the importance of Dacia as a perceived threat coincides with the reigns of Burebista and Decebalus, both strong kings possessing greater authority than their predecessors. In the interval between their reigns, little is heard of the Dacians. Both controlled powerful armies[86] and certainly in the case of Decebalus, could call upon many allied peoples such as the Roxolani and Bastarnae in the fight against Rome. Several reverses were suffered

---

[85] Josephus supplies a detailed picture of the Jewish war effort in AD 66–73, but the rebels failed to create an organized army during the course of this conflict. There are no other sources dealing with a conflict in the east during our period that provide enough detail to reconstruct the military organization of Rome's opponents.

[86] Strabo, *Geog.* 7. 3. 12 claims Burebista led 200,000 men—see I. H. Crisan, *Burebista and his Time* (Bucharest, 1978), 89–94 for a discussion of this.

before Trajan, with a very large army, was able to defeat Dacia. The growth of the powerful, charismatic nobleman in Germany presented a similar problem to Rome. Such a figure, if he was not destroyed by rivals at home as were Burebista and Arminius, required massive military resources to defeat. Whereas the Roman army might suffer reverses fighting a low-intensity guerrilla war on the frontiers, the results of these were of relatively minor importance. A defeat in a large-scale campaign was far more serious: therefore, campaigns against developed states, such as those in central and southern Gaul, or the Dacia of Decebalus, and tribes led by exceptionally powerful leaders such as Arminius, were less desirable and presented greater risks of catastrophic defeats.

In this chapter I could not hope to examine fully the development of the nature of warfare in each society and that of the other peoples with which Rome came into conflict during this period. A proper history of the art of war, in the sense of the nature and philosophy of warfare, in all cultures of the Greek and Roman world has yet to be written.

3
The Army on Campaign

IN this chapter I shall examine the methods of operation of the Roman army on campaign. I shall look most of all at the strategy which it employed. For this study we shall define strategy as the means of attaining the army's aims and objectives in any campaign. It is important to consider how much of the army's behaviour was dictated by the local situation, and how much reflected standard practice applied in all situations. If we are to understand the strategy of these campaigns, we must first establish what each side needed to do in order to achieve victory. Would the enemy be forced to capitulate by the defeat of his main army, the capture of an important city, or attacks on his economic assets, such as crops and cattle? As the last chapter has shown, the political and social organization of a people determined not only the way in which its army fought, but also the event that caused it to acknowledge defeat in a conflict.

There have been surprisingly few attempts to study the strategic doctrine of the Roman army in this period. The main reason for this seems to have been the almost universal assumption that the principles of strategy have been a constant factor throughout history. Implicit in this assumption was the belief that it was legitimate to judge Rome's wars by the standards of more recent conflicts. Major-General Fuller based his assessment of Caesar's campaigns not only on comparison with the wars of Alexander the Great, but also on his own theories regarding the importance of mobility in twentieth-century warfare. In his view, the Roman army's strategy was fundamentally defensive. It paid obsessive attention to entrenching its position and so denied itself mobility. Fuller associated this emphasis on defence with the stalemate of the Western Front in the Great War, which his own theories of armoured warfare had been created to counter, and so he condemned both it and the Roman army.[1] In this chapter I shall argue that Fuller's

[1] Maj. Gen. J. F. C. Fuller, *Julius Caesar: Man, Soldier and Tyrant*, (London, 1965), 74–87.

view of Roman strategy as fundamentally defensive was based upon anachronistic assumptions.

The belief that the Roman army obeyed the same principles of strategy as more recent armies has been implicit in the vast majority of studies of individual campaigns. This has been especially true of examinations of campaigns for which there is little literary, but much archaeological evidence, as is the case for most of the campaigns in Britain.[2] In these studies, the tendency has been to plot the sites of Roman marching camps and forts on a map, to attempt to infer troop movements from this, and then to invent a strategy to explain these. Webster's study of the war fought by Ostorius Scapula in Wales attempted to describe the rival strategies of Scapula on the one hand, and Caratacus and the Druids on the other. These strategies are closely related to geography and the Druids (whose involvement is not attested by any source at this period) are credited with 'an intelligence service to keep them fully informed of Roman army movements and intentions'.[3] In short, the campaign is judged by the author's unstated assumptions about warfare. What neither he nor any of the other authors of similar studies has done, has been to place the campaign under discussion in the context of other Roman wars of the same period. For many of these conflicts there is far more evidence. Cumulatively the many literary accounts of Roman campaigns provide a vast body of evidence concerning the army's practices. These need to be properly studied before we can hope to understand the archaeological evidence of camp-sites. One immediately obvious difference between the literary accounts of campaigns and the studies of these by modern scholars is the complete absence in the former of the geographical emphasis which so dominates the latter. There is no evidence in the ancient sources for the Romans ever having fought a war to control a piece of land for its own sake. Wars were always fought against political entities, such as a people, tribe, kingdom or state. When a frontier of a province was established along a geographical line the army was active militarily and diplomatically far in advance of this, dealing with the political entities outside the province.[4] The fixation

---

[2] e.g. G. Webster, *The Roman Invasion of Britain* (London, 1998), and *Rome against Caratacus* (London, 1981), or S. S. Frere, *Britannia* (London, 1993), 16–180.

[3] Webster, *Rome against Caratacus*, 28–9.

[4] e.g. the early adoption of the Trent–Severn line as the frontier of the province of Britain, *Ann.* 12. 31. It is unlikely that this ignored political boundaries, which anyway often follow natural features.

with physical, rather than political geography, which has so characterized modern scholarship, is thoroughly anachronistic.

Luttwak is one of the few scholars to have examined the attributes of
the Roman army on campaign.[5] He believed that the military structure
of the army of the late Republic and early Empire was fundamentally
imbalanced towards close order, shock troops. This gave it great
advantages in what Luttwak termed 'High Intensity Warfare'—the
winning of large-scale battles and the taking and holding of fortified
positions. The Roman army certainly does seem to have been more
efficient at this type of fighting than any of its opponents in this period.
However Luttwak went further and claimed that the Roman army was
at a disadvantage in more sporadic fighting or 'Low Intensity Warfare',
where there was not an enemy field army to be defeated in the open, or
a stronghold to take by siege. In this way he explained Rome's failure
to conquer the Germans and Parthians, since neither possessed fixed
assets that the Roman army could attack and destroy.[6] Most scholars
seem to have assumed that the army was ill-prepared to fight a
guerrilla war and have expressed surprise when its opponents did not
oppose it in this way.[7]

The supposed vulnerability of the Roman army to guerrilla warfare
is a myth derived from a misunderstanding of the evidence and of the
nature of warfare in this period. The last chapter examined the military
practices of several of Rome's enemies and concluded that these were
unsuited to fighting a guerrilla war—a type of warfare much less
common in this period than is normally supposed. More importantly,
the fundamental flexibility of the Roman army has not been fully
appreciated. Not only was it capable of fighting a guerrilla war, but it
was actually better at this than most of its opponents, such as the
Numidians or the tribes of Mount Amanus, who traditionally fought in
this manner.

This chapter examines a series of campaigns in some detail and
compares these with other operations fought with similar objectives. It
would not be either appropriate or possible to deal with the political
background of each conflict. The causes of each war will only be

---

[5] E. Luttwak, *The Grand Strategy of the Roman Empire* (Baltimore, 1976), 40–6.
[6] Ibid. 45–6.
[7] For instance, when the Caledonians chose to fight Mons Graupius instead of
avoiding open confrontation with the Romans; see W. S. Hanson, *Agricola and the
Conquest of the North* (London, 1987), 128, and G. Webster, *The Roman Imperial Army*
(London, 1985), 239.

discussed in so far as they influenced the objectives of either side. In a civil war, political factors played a far more prominent role in determining the course of the fighting, and so for this reason no examples of these are included in the discussion. All the examples will be taken from foreign wars.

There is no discussion of the relative importance of different types of conflict in the army's overall role. The section dealing with the suppression of rebellion is the largest in this chapter. This does not necessarily mean that this was either the most frequent, or the most important type of operation in which the army was involved, although this may have been the case in some provinces at some periods.[8]

THE CAMPAIGNS

Most of the wars fought by the Roman army during this period were against enemies significantly inferior in organization and discipline. They were, to use the terminology of the turn of the century, 'Small Wars', fought by a regular army against an irregular opponent. The classic discussion of this type of conflict was written by Col. C. E. Callwell.[9] Callwell discerned three types of Small War, and this chapter follows his categorization. These were:

1. Campaigns for the suppression of insurrection or lawlessness, and of the settlement of conquered or annexed territory.
2. Punitive campaigns.
3. Campaigns of conquest or annexation.

THE SUPPRESSION OF INSURRECTION

1. *The Rebellion of the Belgic Tribes, 54 BC: Narrative*

At the end of the campaigning season of 54 BC Caesar's legions were distributed in *hiberna*. These were more scattered than usual to ease the shortage of corn resulting from a bad harvest. One legion under L. Roscius was stationed amongst the Essuvii, but the bulk of the army,

---

[8] For the army as an occupying force or as a defence against external threats contrast Luttwak, *Grand Strategy*, with B. Isaac, *The Limits of Empire* (Oxford, 1992), and G. Woolf, 'Roman Peace', in J. Rich and G. Shipley (eds.), *War and Society in the Roman World* (London, 1993), 170–94.

[9] C. E. Callwell, *Small Wars* (HMSO, 1906), 21–5.

seven and a half legions, was concentrated in north-eastern Gaul in
camps no more than 160 km (100 miles) apart (See Map 1). This
emphasis reflected the sphere of recent operations and the questionable loyalty of this area. C. Fabius commanded one legion in the
territory of the Morini, Q. Tullius Cicero another amongst the Nervii,
and Labienus a third on the border between the Remi and the Treveri.
Initially there were three legions in the territory of the group of tribes
known as the Belgae, but L. Munatius Plancus was dispatched with
one of these to winter amongst the Carnutes, whose king had been
murdered by rival factions within the tribe. The remaining two were
stationed close together. G. Trebonius occupied the *oppidum* of
Samarobriva with one, whilst the quaestor M. Crassus was stationed
with the other 38 km. (24 miles) away in the territory of the Bellovaci.
The last legion with a vexillation of five cohorts was stationed at

1. The Belgic tribes at the time of Caesar's campaigns

Atuatuca amongst the Eburones. This force was commanded by Sabinus and Cotta (*BG* 5. 24). Once each unit had established itself in its winter quarters, a messenger was sent to Caesar, who had remained with Trebonius at Samarobriva (*BG* 5. 25). When his army was positioned securely Caesar intended to follow his usual practice and spend the winter in Cisalpine Gaul.

About a fortnight later, the Eburones rebelled and attacked the *Legio XIV* under Cotta and Sabinus. They were led by Ambiorix and Catuvolcus, who were induced to revolt by Indutiomarus the Treveran. An attack on a Roman wood-gathering party was followed by negotiations and the surrender of the Roman garrison. All fifteen cohorts and their attendant allies were destroyed in an ambush 3 km. (2 miles) from the camp. The few survivors eventually made their way to Labienus, somewhat over 80 km. (50 miles) away. Cicero's camp was closer than this and Ambiorix led his cavalry there. The infantry are not heard of again, and probably, having gained such a large amount of plunder and glory, dispersed to their homes in the manner of most irregular armies over the centuries. The attack on Cicero's camp, although inspired by the now successful war leader Ambiorix, was largely the work of the Nervii. A similar attack on foragers began the assault, but here Cicero, who had chosen the camp-site himself (Cicero, *ad Att.* 4. 19. 2), held out. A full-scale siege developed, with the Gauls copying the techniques they had seen used by Caesar's men (*BG* 5. 52).

Caesar was ignorant of the plight of Cicero's garrison until a slave of the Nervian deserter, Vertico, managed to pass through the Gallic lines. Caesar was with the legion under Trebonius. As soon as Vertico's slave reached him, he arranged for Cicero's relief. M. Crassus, 38 km. (24 miles) away, was sent orders to march to and occupy Caesar's camp at Samarobriva and to protect the army's baggage train housed there. Further messengers were sent to Fabius, ordering him to join Caesar on the march, and to Labienus, instructing him to move onto the frontier of the Nervii, if this was feasible. Labienus replied explaining that the latter was not practical. Caesar force-marched his small army of two legions and 400 Gallic horse, barely 7,000 men all told, without heavy baggage. A further exchange of messengers occurred with Cicero as Caesar neared the camp. The Gallic army abandoned the siege on news of Caesar's approach. Caesar tempted them into a poor position and in a swift action routed them, joining Cicero the same day without mounting a concerted pursuit. Caesar then returned to winter with Cicero's, Trebonius', and Fabius' legions around Samarobriva. Labienus had been unable to move to join Caesar because he was threatened by the Treveri. Later in the winter Labienus mounted a sudden attack against the forces around his camp, driving them off and killing their leader Indutiomarus. For the remainder of the winter, both sides were hampered by the problems of supply, and concerned themselves with diplomacy and preparations for war rather than actually fighting.

However, Caesar began his campaign earlier than was usual, and having concentrated four legions, mounted a surprise attack on the Nervii (*BG* 6. 3). Their territory was ravaged before they were able to muster an army and the tribe surrendered. Two legions were then sent to escort the army's baggage to the camp of Labienus, whilst Caesar with the remainder forced the Menapii to surrender by ravaging their lands as he had those of the Nervii (*BG* 6. 5). At about the same time Labienus fought a successful action against the Treveri (*BG* 6. 7–8). Caesar followed this by a brief punitive expedition across the Rhine. Having deprived the Eburones of their allies in this piecemeal manner, the Romans waited for the crops to ripen before marching against Ambiorix. This permitted an army to live off the land, greatly increasing its mobility. Leaving the baggage protected by Cicero and the re-formed *Legio XIV* at Atuatuca, the army split into three columns led by Caesar himself, Labienus and Trebonius respectively, and went with a week's rations to ravage a wide area. The army was to have returned within a week. Despite a raid by Germans on Atuatuca, the territory of the Eburones was systematically ravaged until the area was fully pacified.

1. *The Rebellion of the Belgic Tribes: Commentary*

Caesar's account of this rebellion spanned two books of the Gallic Wars, yet was clearly unbalanced to make the narrative more entertaining to readers. Thus we have detailed accounts of the dramatic sieges of Atuatuca and the camp of Cicero, and Caesar's relief of the latter. The campaigns fought in the next year to ravage the lands of the enemy tribes are covered far more briefly. The book dealing with this year is more concerned with the digressions on the customs of the Gauls and Germans,[10] and a detailed account of the attack on Cicero's command at Atuatuca (*BG* 6. 35–41). Furthermore,

---

[10] Gauls, *BG* 6. 11–20, Germans, *BG* 6. 21–8.

the two accounts of the initial attacks, one against Cotta and Sabinus, and the other on Cicero were obviously placed in contrast. In the first, the leaders were brave but uncertain, the men valued their baggage over their lives, and the centurions' valour was unavailing.[11] In the second, the commander was steadfast, his men stayed on the walls whilst their possessions burnt, and the centurions' bravery was invincible.[12] Having said this, there does not seem any reason to doubt for our purposes the information relating to the strategic decisions of the campaign.

In 54 BC the Belgic tribes had only recently been conquered and were still capable of putting large armies into the field. Initial success against Cotta and Sabinus won support for the rebels and they continued to attack instead of awaiting Roman retaliation. Yet these rebels lacked a 'Jerusalem', a single capital, the capture of which would have broken their will to fight. Caesar's army was not positioned to occupy a peaceful province, but merely to pass the winter between campaigns. Thus Caesar was able to move immediately on receiving Cicero's message and marched to confront the Nervii and break the siege. The available forces were small and were not supplied for a long campaign since they took no heavy baggage and, as it was winter, they were unable to live off the land. The force needed to confront the enemy quickly since it was incapable of maintaining itself in the field for long. Yet the enemy were numerically stronger and confident after their recent success, which made a battle risky. In the event the gamble paid off, and prevented another victory which might have further swollen the rebel ranks. The only other offensive action made by the rebels was taken by the Treveri against Labienus, who eventually, on reinforcement, defeated them. Otherwise the initiative was entirely with the Romans. Caesar's troops systematically devastated the territory of the Eburones and their allies, forcing them out of the conflict. Although these tribes had no centres of major political importance, the seizure of their crops and cattle and the destruction of their villages collectively represented a massive blow. The surprise gained by the Romans in these operations is noticeable and highlights the difficulty of forming irregular armies at short notice.[13] Caesar's own admission of the unsuitability of his troops for fighting the

---

[11] *BG* 5. 28–30, 5. 33, 5. 35. [12] *BG* 5. 40–1, 5. 43.
[13] *BG* 6. 3, 4, 5, 30.

dispersed Eburones would have been less true of the Imperial army which was far better supplied with regular cavalry and light troops (*BG* 6. 34).

The close dependence of all armies on supply was clearly seen in this campaign, as were the various means of coping with this. The problem of controlling widely dispersed forces is also apparent, although it is interesting that the only messengers who are noted as not having got through were those to and from the beleaguered garrison of Cicero's camp. This campaign saw the Romans attempting to defeat enemies piecemeal with a mixture of force and conciliation. The Nervii, Menapii and Senones were forced to surrender, but were then well treated, whilst the Eburones were destroyed as a political entity.

2. *Cestius Gallus' March on Jerusalem, AD 66: Narrative*

The Campaign of Cestius Gallus against the Jewish rebels in AD 66 provides a good example of the initial Roman reaction to insurrection within a province (see Map 2). The auxiliary cohorts of the *procurator* of Judaea and the forces of Agippa II had failed to quell the disturbances and a series of small-scale Roman disasters had resulted. Masada had been taken, and the Roman troops in Jerusalem massacred (*BJ* 2. 408, 449). Cestius Gallus, as legate of Syria, commanded the most conveniently placed, sizeable Roman army with which to oppose the insurgents. Earlier Syrian governors had been called upon to control disturbances, which the garrison of Judaea had been unable to suppress on its own.[14] Cestius Gallus formed his field army at Antioch. Its principal units were *Legio XII Fulminata*, vexillations of 2,000 men from each of the other Syrian Legions,[15] and four *alae* and six cohorts. The forces supplied by various allied kingdoms totalled 14,000 men according to Josephus. Additional, but inexperienced, manpower was provided by volunteers from many of the cities passed through by the army. How long the marshalling of this army took is unclear. The first fighting of the revolt occurred in May and the Roman garrison in Jerusalem was destroyed in September. Gallus reached Jerusalem in mid-November.

---

[14] Under Varus, *BJ* 2. 39–79, and Petronius, *BJ* 2. 184–203.

[15] It is a little unclear which legions were in Syria at this date, since it is uncertain when all the troops posted there for the Armenian campaign were withdrawn. The most recent commentary on this campaign is M. Gichon, 'Cestius Gallus' Campaign in Judaea', *PEQ* 113 (1981), 39–62. Although good on some aspects, many of his conclusions, in particular his detailed timescale, are based heavily on conjecture. A former soldier himself, some of his thinking is inclined to be too modern.

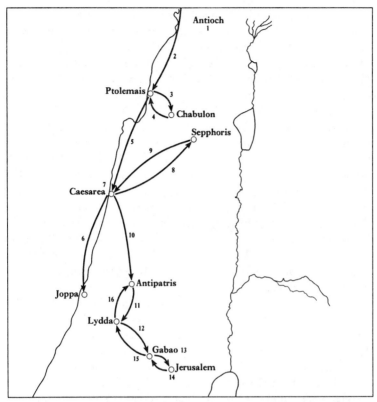

2. Cestius Gallus' march to Jerusalem in AD 66

1. Cestius Gallus musters his army at Antioch.
2. Gallus moves south to Ptolemais, raising levies in the towns en route.
3. Gallus takes a small detachment of the army to seize the town of Chabulon, on the frontier between Ptolemais and Galilee. He finds Chabulon deserted. The town is pillaged and burnt.
4. The Roman column returns to Ptolemais.
5. The main army marches to Caesarea.
6. A detachment is sent by sea to take Joppa.
7. A force of cavalry is dispatched from the main army to ravage the toparchy of Narbatene.
8. A large vexillation under Caesennius Paetus, legate of *Legio XII Fulminata*, moves to re-establish order in Galilee. The Romans are welcomed by the city of Sepphoris. A band of rebels occupying a strong position at Asamon are defeated.
9. Paetus' column rejoins the main army at Caesarea.
10. The entire army marches to Antipatris without meeting any opposition.
11. Gallus occupies the deserted town of Lydda and puts it to the torch.
12. The Romans begin the final approach to Jerusalem, climbing the Beth-horon pass.
13. They are attacked at Gabao at the head of the pass. After initial success, the Jewish attack is repelled. However a large part of the Roman baggage train is captured.
14. The Romans attempt to storm Jerusalem, but fail and begin to withdraw.
15. The rebels pursue eagerly, converting the Roman retreat into a rout.
16. The Roman army is harried back to Antipatris.

The Jews possessed no united army fit to oppose the Romans in open battle. Their forces consisted rather of small highly motivated groups, loyal to individual leaders, and supported with varying degrees of enthusiasm by the populace as a whole. It may have seemed to Gallus that no more than a display of force was needed to crush the rising. Moving south from Antioch he reached Ptolemais. He burned and looted the abandoned town of Sebulon, which was situated on the northern border of Galilee. After Gallus had moved on, many looters (2,000 according to Josephus) were massacred by the Jews (*BJ* 2. 50). Gallus proceeded to Caesarea and dispatched a force of cavalry to devastate the area around nearby Narbata. Another vexillation travelled by sea to seize Joppa. It is quite possible that the movement of the main army to Ptolemais and then Caesarea was also made by ship. These troops met with no effective opposition. A vexillation under Caesennius Gallus, legate of the *Legio XII*, was sent to Galilee to be welcomed by the city of Sepphoris. Most of the insurgents in the area fled but some attempted to hold a strong position at Asamon and were defeated (*BJ* 2. 511–12).

Having met no concerted opposition, Cestius Gallus was rejoined by the Galilean vexillation. He marched inland from Caesarea to Antipatris and then Lydda, joining the main road from Joppa to Jerusalem. Any signs of resistance were crushed brutally. Lydda and the nearby town of Aphek were both put to the torch. Continuing towards Jerusalem the Romans climbed the pass at Beth Horon and camped near the top at Gabao, about 8–9 km (5 miles) from the city. There they were attacked on the Sabbath and suffered a near disaster only retrieved by the arrival of reserves. At the same time, the army's baggage train was attacked, and many baggage animals captured (*BJ* 2. 511–12). It was clear that the insurgents had surrounded Gallus' army, although as yet they presented little threat to it. Gallus mounted assaults for six days, culminating in an attack on the Wall of the Temple. Josephus claimed that he came near to success (*BJ* 2. 540), but Gallus decided to withdraw from the city and suffered heavy losses whilst disengaging. The resultant retreat, harried by the heartened Jews, swiftly degenerated into a rout. The pursuit was halted more by the vast amounts of plunder acquired than any Roman action (*BJ* 2. 549–51).

The campaign had been an unmitigated disaster, the Romans losing 5,780 men and much material, including large numbers of siege engines. Even more importantly, the rebels had been given a major victory showing that Rome was not invincible, and perhaps suggesting that their cause had Divine support. The numbers of active insurgents and the area which they controlled increased significantly as a result. When the next, significantly larger, Roman army advanced into Judaea it was forced to recapture the province systematically, virtually city by city.

2. *Cestius Gallus' March on Jerusalem: Commentary*

The reason for Gallus' sudden withdrawal, despite Josephus' own claim that he was near to success, has often perplexed scholars.[16] It may be that the Romans did not realize that the Jewish leaders were wavering. However, two factors may have influenced Gallus. First, not all of his army had proved reliable. His largest regular unit, *XII Fulminata* was to lose its eagle during this campaign (Suetonius, *Vespasian* 5), either in the retreat or perhaps during the attack made outside Jerusalem on the Sabbath (*BJ* 2. 517). It is clear from Josephus that some Roman troops broke and fled during this engagement. *XII Fulminata* had been involved in the débâcle of Lucius Caesennius Paetus in Armenia in 62 AD, where it had been routed by the Parthians (*Ann.* 15. 10). It may be that the unit had not recovered from this defeat, or that the abuses or poor leadership that had led to this had not been dealt with fully by the time of the Jewish war. We should never assume that units of the Roman army were of uniformly high quality. Added to this were the bodies of irregular volunteers recruited in the many cities hostile to the Jews. These had little or no military training and were more inclined to loot than fight (*BJ* 2. 502–6). Their main value may have been to make Cestius' army appear larger. The use of such troops emphasizes the ill-preparedness of the Syrian garrison, and probably many provincial armies, for immediate, full-scale war.

Second, we come to the question of supply. Josephus provided very little information regarding the logistical arrangements of Cestius Gallus' army. It may well be, for instance, that he was supplied by sea whilst at Caesarea, but we have no indication of this. What is clear is that he can only have carried a limited supply of food and water with his baggage train on the march from there to Jerusalem. Once there,

---

[16] S. G. F. Brandon, 'The Defeat of Cestius Gallus in AD 66', *History Today*, 20 (1970), 38–46.

the surrounding bands of insurgents made foraging difficult. The capture of many baggage animals by the Jews may have represented a significant loss to available supplies.[17] When both these factors are considered, it seems questionable whether Gallus' army was in a fit state to pursue the siege of such a major city. A Caesar perhaps would have risked this and won, or suffered an even greater defeat. Gallus did not.

It is important to note that the Roman army contained only one full legion along with several vexillations. It seems quite possible that many units were significantly under-strength in peacetime and only capable of putting a proportion of their troops into the field at any one time.[18] The policing role of the army in the eastern provinces also involved many small detachments being dispersed around the country.[19] It may not have been possible or desirable to return these detachments to the parent units in a time of crisis. A further factor limiting the size of Gallus' army was the number of baggage and draught animals available to form its supply train. Both factors might have restricted the size of a force available for campaigning at short notice. The army that Gallus led against Jerusalem was not prepared for a full-scale, protracted war in the same way that the Titus' army, four years later, would be. Its units were understrength, inexperienced and of questionable morale. Its system of supply was incapable of maintaining it in the field for a long campaign.

The march to Jerusalem was not a full-scale military operation to besiege the city, but a display of Rome's strength. It was a bluff, intended to persuade rebels and potential rebels that Rome was invincible. At the beginning of a rebellion, inactivity on the part of the Romans might have been interpreted as weakness by the rebels. If the rebels appeared to be successful, then more of the population would have been encouraged to join them. In AD 66 and throughout the rebellion only a comparatively small proportion of the population was actively involved in resistance to Rome. The mass of the people was not committed to any cause, but might have been inclined to join whichever side seemed the strongest.[20] Therefore the longer the Romans waited before attempting to suppress the rebellion, the more

---

[17] See B. Bar-Kochva, 'Seron and Cestius Gallus at Beith Horon', *PEQ* 108 (1976), 13–21, esp. 18.

[18] See Ch. 1, 'Unit Organization: Theory and Practice'.

[19] See Isaac, *Limits of Empire*, 101–60.

[20] See Callwell, *Small Wars*, 71–83.

numerous the rebels would have become. The mobilization of a properly prepared and supplied Roman army, strong enough to fight a full-scale war if necessary, would have taken a long time, and allowed the rebellion to grow stronger. A quick reaction by the Romans, sending whatever troops were available at short notice, stood a chance of suppressing the rebellion before it had gained momentum, by daunting the rebels with a display of force, but little actual fighting.

This seems to have been what happened under similar circumstances in Judaea in 4 BC (*BJ* 2. 39–79). In the disturbances following the death of Herod the Great, the Roman prefect Sabinus had come under siege in Jerusalem. The legion under his command had attacked the rebels, but failed to break the siege. As soon as this was reported to Varus, the governor of Syria, he mobilized the two legions and four *alae* under his command and summoned allied troops. Then, following essentially the same route that Gallus would later use, he marched on Jerusalem. At the approach of his army, the rebels dispersed, although 2,000 were captured and executed. A report was received of a concentration of 10,000 rebels in Idumaea, so Varus marched quickly to confront this force, which immediately surrendered. Leaving the same legion as garrison of Jerusalem, Varus returned to Antioch. The campaign had been swift and involved little actual fighting. The speed with which Varus returned to Antioch suggests that his army was not prepared logistically for a long campaign. In this case a display of Roman strength was enough to break the will of the enemy to fight. Yet if Varus had met stronger resistance his army might not have been able to cope with it. A balance had to be struck by the Roman commander between striking swiftly before the rebellion grew and striking with sufficient force to crush it with one blow. Cestius Gallus, for a number of reasons, failed to achieve this balance and was defeated. In AD 9 Varus again reacted to a rebellion in Germany by immediately marching against the enemy with an army that was not properly prepared for war. The disaster resulting from this was even greater than that suffered by Cestius Gallus in AD 66.[21]

Judaea was not a recently conquered province in AD 66, and indeed Josephus frequently referred to the difficulty the rebels had in equipping themselves.[22] Thus the Jews were never able to establish a

---

[21] Dio 56. 18–22, on the unpreparedness of the army 56. 19.
[22] *BJ* 2. 576, 583 and cf. Florus and Sacrovir in Gaul, *Ann.* 4. 42.

field army capable of facing the Romans, their troops being especially vulnerable to the disciplined Roman cavalry in open ground.[23] Outside their many strongholds, their tactics were, as a result, generally those of the guerrilla. Therefore, since they were incapable of major offensive action, the initiative passed to the Romans after the first action inaugurating the revolt. The Roman reaction was to gather an army as swiftly as possible and march into Judaea seeking a major confrontation with the rebels in which the advantages of their organization, discipline, and equipment could be exploited. Although areas passed through en route were investigated briefly, the army marched straight at the head of the rebellion and country. If Jerusalem had fallen swiftly, there is some reason to believe that the revolt would have collapsed and all that remained would have been the mopping up of a few bands of fanatics. According to Josephus, this nearly happened.

The Suppression of Insurrection: Conclusions

Caesar's reaction to the rebellion in 52 BC again saw him adopting the offensive as soon as possible. After quickly strengthening the garrison in Transalpine Gaul, Caesar led a small force against the Arverni, achieving complete surprise by crossing the Cevennes when the passes were assumed to be closed for the winter. For two days his cavalry ravaged the tribal territory to intimidate the Arverni. Caesar then moved with all the troops that could be mustered to relieve Gorgobina, the stronghold of the Boii, which was besieged by Vercingetorix. Once again Caesar chose to take the field with a small army without heavy baggage, and so supplied for only a short time and unable to feed itself off the winter land. The reason given for this action was that he could not afford to lose prestige by failing to protect a tribe subject to a Roman ally. A loss of Roman prestige would have encouraged more Gallic peoples to join the rebellion against Rome. For the rest of the campaign, Caesar sought to maintain the offensive, advancing on Avaricum, Gergovia, and Alesia in turn. In practical terms this produced a decisive confrontation with the main enemy army under Vercingetorix. Yet as important at a time of crisis, when the loyalty of their allies was questionable, was the need for the Romans to demonstrate that they were dictating the course of the war and would eventually win. If the Romans had seemed vulnerable and at the mercy

---

[23] e.g. *BJ* 3. 12, 28.

of events, then the enemy would have been joined by many wavering tribes. By continually attacking, Caesar demonstrated that he was still strong.

In the campaigns discussed above, the Romans seized the initiative and took the offensive as soon as possible, attacking the enemy with whatever troops were available. In both 54 and 52 BC Caesar advanced against the enemy with small forces, unprepared for a long campaign. In Judaea in AD 66 the procurator Florus attempted to quell the disturbances with the auxiliary troops at his disposal, before aid was sought from Syria (*BJ* 2. 300–22). Cestius Gallus' army then, it seems, marched as soon as possible in a display of greater force.[24] In the rebellion of Boudicca in AD 60, the initial Roman reaction to the rebel threat, admittedly one that is scorned by Tacitus, was the dispatch by Decianus Catus of 200 ill-equipped soldiers from his staff (*Ann.* 14. 32). When this failed, Petilius Cerialis, with a vexillation of not more than 200 men of *Legio IX Hispana*, perhaps an *ala* and some auxiliary infantry, advanced quickly to attack the rebels and was in turn beaten (*Ann.* 14. 32). Finally, Suetonius Paulinus with the main field army confronted and defeated Boudicca (*Ann.* 14. 37, Dio 63. 8–12).

The practice of immediately confronting any rebellion with the forces available seems to have been standard throughout our period. In 51 BC Caesar immediately attacked any tribes showing signs of rebellion and, as in 54 and 52, did so even in winter with armies supplied for only a short operation (*BG* 8. 3–13). In Judaea in 4 BC and in Germany in AD 9, Varus moved without hesitation to attack any signs of insurrection. As soon as a rebellion in Thrace in AD 21 was reported to Publius Vellaeus, he sent detachments of auxiliary cavalry and infantry against enemy marauders and marched with the rest of his army against the main body, quickly defeating it (*Ann.* 3. 38–9). In the same year the risings in Gaul under Florus and Sacrovir were attacked by Roman forces as soon as possible and again quickly dispersed (*Ann.* 3. 45–6). When the Frisians rebelled against heavy taxation in AD 28, the local garrison was unable to suppress this and was besieged in the fort at Flevum. As soon as Lucius Apronius, the legate of Lower Germany, heard of this, he gathered available detachments of troops

---

[24] The time required to make an army ready to move from its bases should not be underestimated. In the recent Gulf Conflict, a fortnight was considered dangerously short time to prepare the British 4th Armoured Brigade to move from its bases in Germany.

and advanced to relieve the fort. Having done so, he advanced against the enemy. In his eagerness to confront the Frisians he launched a badly co-ordinated attack, was heavily defeated and forced to withdraw (*Ann.* 4. 73).

In Britain, in AD 48, Ostorius Scapula marched with the auxiliary forces available to crush the earlier revolt of the Iceni, even going as far as to use dismounted cavalry in an attack on fortifications (*Ann.* 12. 31). Later, Agricola was to gather troops from winter quarters and march with speed to punish the Ordovices for revolt, soon after arriving in the province (*Agricola* 18). When the Nasamones rebelled against Domitian, Cn. Suellius Flaccus, the legate of *Legio III Augusta*, immediately marched against them and after an initial defeat, destroyed their army (Dio 67. 4. 6). A similar pattern can be discerned in the revolt of Civilis, when various small Roman columns consisting of the only troops available, moved out to confront both the rebels and the mutinous Batavian cohorts (*Hist.* 4. 18, 20).

The natural reaction of even small and outnumbered Roman forces to the first signs of insurrection was to attack immediately. After the defeat of Cestius Gallus in AD 66, the Jewish rebels attempted to attack Ascalon. The city was garrisoned by one *ala* and one cohort under Antonius, a force numerically much smaller than the approaching Jews. Yet each time the Jews approached the city, Antonius led his garrison out to attack and defeat them in the open (*BJ* 3. 9–28). During the rebellion of Tacfarinas, a strong force of Numidians surrounded first the cohort stationed at Pagyda, and later a unit of 500 veterans holding the fort at Mala. On each occasion the Romans left the security of their walls to attack the numerically superior enemy in the open. At Pagyda the Romans were routed, but at Mala they drove off the enemy (*Ann.* 3. 20–1).

Roman forces always tried to seize the initiative and attack rebels. This did not mean that they always attempted to engage the enemy in open battle, to wage 'high intensity' warfare. After the initial reverses suffered in the Bar Kochba rebellion (AD 131–4), the Roman governor, Julius Severus, avoided open battle with the rebels. Instead he mounted a vigorous campaign of raid and ambush, employing his army in small detachments to wear down the enemy in many small defeats. Once the enemy had been weakened, the Romans were able to retake their strongholds one by one (Dio 69. 13. 2–3). A similar pattern can be seen in the revolt of the Boukoloi in Egypt in AD 172–3. At the beginning of the rebellion the Roman garrison of the province was defeated in a pitched battle. The new Roman commander, Avidius Cassius, avoided open battle with this confident and numerous enemy, but gradually wore them down by small scale aggressive action, until they were defeated piecemeal (Dio 72. 4. 2).

The rebellion of Tacfarinas is instructive since it shows not only the flexibility of the Roman army, which allowed it to adapt to the local situation, but also the fundamental importance of the offensive in Roman military doctrine. In the first phase of the conflict, Tacfarinas organized a field army based on the Roman model. A much smaller Roman army, consisting of *Legio III Augusta*, two alae, and some auxiliary cohorts, led by M. Furius Camillus, attempted to join battle as soon as possible. In the resultant engagement the Numidians were routed.(*Ann.* 2. 52) After this Tacfarinas resorted to raiding. As described above, Roman garrisons invariably attacked the raiders when they approached, rather than simply defending their positions. When the Numidians established a stationary base from which to mount raids, this was attacked and destroyed (*Ann.* 3. 20–1). Finally the Romans placed many small garrisons around the province and organized mobile columns to attack and ambush the raiders. These practices were continued for several years with many small-scale successes being achieved. Finally Tacfarinas himself was killed and his army destroyed by a surprise attack mounted by a Roman column on his camp at Auzea.[25]

Several aspects of this conflict deserve mention. The Romans had in a sense defeated the Numidian enemies by beating them in their own style of warfare. The Numidians used the tactics of raid, surprise attack, and ambush, and it was just these techniques that the Romans used against them. In part, the recruitment of Moorish auxiliaries enabled the Romans to fight in this manner. However not only auxiliary cavalry and infantry, but also heavily armed legionaries were included in the small mobile columns used to attack the enemy.[26] Although this was not the normal tactic for Roman units, these men were able to adapt to the local situation and perform effectively. The permanence of Roman units and the ability of the army to organize their supply actually gave these regular troops significant advantages over their opponents. Junius Blaesus was able to keep his army active

[25] *Ann.* 3. 73–4, 4. 23, in general see R. Syme, 'Tacfarinas, the Musulamii, and Thubursicu', in *Roman Papers*, i (Oxford, 1979), 218–30.
[26] Moorish auxiliaries *Ann.* 4. 23, legionaries 3. 21, 4. 24.

against the enemy even during the winter, when it was normally withdrawn to winter quarters. In the final surprise attack on the enemy, and on other occasions, the Numidians, who fought by ambush and raid themselves, were completely unaware of the presence of a heavily-armed Roman column until its advance began. A Roman force was not surprised as easily. In this conflict the Roman army showed itself quite capable of successfully fighting a guerrilla war.

In this final attack the Roman troops were ordered to seek out and kill Tacfarinas himself. The practice of removing the enemy leader occurred on other occasions in Roman warfare. The war against Jugurtha was finally ended when the king was captured by treachery (Sallust, *Jug.* 113. 5–6). When in 54 BC Labienus launched a surprise attack on the Treveri, he ordered his cavalry as their first priority to kill the enemy leader Indutiomarus (*BG* 5. 58). Caesar twice sought to arrange the capture or assassination of Commius (*BG* 8. 23, 48). Later Corbulo was to arrange the murder of Gannascus (*Ann.* 9. 19). A charismatic leader with the ability to organize and unite could do much to keep resistance going.[27] This tactic was not always considered appropriate. Tiberius rejected an offer to murder Arminius made by a Chattan chieftain, Adgandestrius, in 19 BC (*Ann.* 2. 88). Arminius was no longer actively fighting Rome, therefore his death was not needed to end a conflict.

Throughout the war with Tacfarinas the Romans sought to attack the enemy whenever possible. As in the other rebellions discussed, the normal Roman reaction to any insurrection was to confront it immediately with whatever troops were available. This often meant that outnumbered, poor quality, or inadequately supplied Roman forces took great risks in attacking apparently stronger enemies. When these weak Roman forces met solid opposition, they were often heavily defeated. There seem to have been two reasons for this emphasis on an immediate offensive in response to rebellion. The first was practical, in that a rebellion was always weakest in its early stages. A series of successes encouraged support for the rebel cause, whilst even inactivity on the part of the Romans was interpreted as weakness. Therefore an immediate attack, even by a weak force, might be enough to defeat the rebellion before it gathered momentum. The other reason for adopting the offensive and then maintaining it, was the effect that this had on enemy morale. If even small Roman forces were

---

[27] See Ch. 2.

willing to attack immediately much larger rebel armies, then it suggested that the Romans were confident of defeating the rebellion without difficulty. It suggested that Roman troops were so superior to any enemy that their success was inevitable. It did not matter if this impression was a façade, and that the Roman troops were inadequate for any heavy fighting. As on the battlefield, the appearance of force was often far more important than real fighting power.[28] A constant offensive was an attack on the enemy's collective will to fight as much as on his practical ability to do so.

Many rebellions fell into two stages. In the first, the Romans confronted and defeated the field forces formed by the rebels. In the second they ravaged the land to stamp out all the embers of revolt. The latter stage often became either a guerrilla conflict or a war of strongholds. In the case of the Jewish war, there was never a Jewish army in the field, so the war passed immediately into the second stage. The defeat of Sacrovir immediately ended the revolt before it developed into this latter stage. The rebellion against Caesar in 54 BC and that of Boudicca in AD 60 clearly passed through both stages. In the first, the concentration of Roman forces was necessary, in the second their dispersal. The conduct of a campaign in which the enemy was scattered and sought to avoid combat, but made small scale raids or ambushes, or fought from strongholds, seems invariably to have been arduous, time-consuming, and costly in manpower. Yet if the Romans had the will to keep a province, it was difficult for them to lose such a conflict, however long it took. Although rebels possessed of a field army were, in a sense, easier to confront and defeat, they were also far more dangerous, since the risk of a Roman reverse was greater and its results were potentially catastrophic. Thus Arminius' revolt in Germany was successful because his army defeated that of Varus and avoided being decisively defeated in any of the subsequent Roman campaigns.

PUNITIVE ACTION

1. *Cicero in Cilicia, 51 BC: Narrative*

Cicero's campaign against the bandits on Mount Amanus in 51 BC was on a far smaller scale than the campaigns of Germanicus, involving two understrength and inexperienced legions and lasting no longer than a

---

[28] See Ch. 5.

couple of months. It is probable that we only know of it at all because
of the identity of the Roman commander, but it seems likely that
operations on a similar or smaller scale were very common for the
Roman army of all periods.

Cicero had led his army to the area of Mount Amanus on the border
between Cilicia and Syria to counter the perceived Parthian threat.
When the latter faded, he decided that it was in the interest of both his
own province and Syria to punish the bandits of this area.[29] On 12th
October, he pretended to march away from the area to Epiphanea
(Cicero, *ad Fam.* 15. 8). Having left his baggage there, he force-
marched the army back at night, so that by dawn on the 13th he was
climbing the mountain. The army was divided into three columns, the
first led by Cicero and his brother Quintus, the second by C.
Pomptinus, the last by M. Anneus and L. Tullius. Surprise was
achieved and many tribesmen captured or killed. Pomptinus encountered the heaviest resistance at the capital Erana and nearby
Sepyra and Commoris, but these had all fallen by four o'clock in the
afternoon. The army reunited and camped by Issus for four days,
ravaging the surrounding country. Finally, Cicero considered it
important for Rome's prestige to take Pindenissus. He claimed that
this city had harboured fugitives and was said to welcome a Parthian
invasion. The capture of this stronghold made it easier to control other
tribes who showed hostility (*ad Fam.* 15. 10). After a 57-day siege, the
city capitulated and was burnt to the ground. The nearby city of
Lebara surrendered under the threat of similar treatment. Cicero then
returned the army to winter quarters. The campaign had been a one-
sided operation, yet the dangers inherent in such warfare were
illustrated by the reverse suffered soon afterwards in the same area by
the Syrian governor Bibulus, who lost his entire first cohort (*ad Att.* 5.
20).

1. *Cicero in Cilicia, 51 BC: Commentary*

Cicero's campaign did not provide a permanent solution to the threat,
sporadic though it may have been, posed by the tribes of this area.
Soon afterwards, the Syrian army was operating in the area, and it
seems likely that such operations had to be repeated at regular
intervals. Any success was only temporary. Yet the alternative, to have

---

[29] Cic. *ad Fam.* 15. 4. Most of the places referred to in Cicero's account are
impossible to identify. No useful map can be drawn to accompany this account.

garrisoned the area with sufficient troops to prevent lawlessness and banditry amongst the peoples of this area, was far more expensive.

Once again, peoples who tended to fight by ambush and raid were surprised by the sudden arrival of regular troops. Although these regular troops consisted largely of heavy infantry, they had adapted to the local situation and fought effectively in unsuitable terrain. It seems clear that the peoples of the area lacked political unity and were organized chiefly around the city or village. Although several *castella* other than the named towns were taken, and elsewhere crops devastated and herds confiscated, only those actually in the path of the army were directly affected. This operation demonstrated to the peoples of the area that Rome was not only capable of taking action against them, but willing to do so. A Roman army was capable of approaching and attacking a village, before the locals could gather together an army strong enough to stop them. Pindenissus was not a vital political or economic centre, but one stronghold amongst many. Its capture after a two-month siege showed that Rome was prepared to take the trouble to subdue even a minor enemy. In real terms, only a comparatively small proportion of the population of the region was directly affected by Roman action. However it showed the remainder that their mountain strongholds could not protect them from Roman action. As a result it weakened their desire to come into conflict with Rome. The effects might have been short-lived, but they were no less real for that. It is in this context that the defeat of Bibulus must be understood. After a demonstration of Roman strength, the locals had been treated to one of Roman vulnerability. In the relations between these peoples and Rome, the impression of power was more important than its reality.

2. *The German Campaign of AD 15: Narrative*

After the bloody suppression of the Rhine mutinies of AD 14, Germanicus mounted a punitive expedition against the Marsi, devastating the tribe's territory. The next year, AD 15 was to witness a series of similar operations largely intended to restore the prestige of Rome in the area after the mutinies and more importantly the Varian disaster in AD 9. The campaign began with a sudden raid on the Chatti in early spring (*Ann.* 1. 55). Germanicus led one section of the army, Caecina the other, both being based on the nucleus of four legions. Again, Germanicus achieved surprise, the Chatti were scattered, their tribal capital Mattium burnt and their land laid waste. Tacitus noted that the Chatti were unable to pursue as was normal with the Germans (*Ann.* 1. 56). Caecina had meanwhile with his forces deterred the Cherusci from intervening, although the Marsi attempted to do so and were defeated.

It is clear that the temporary union of tribes under Arminius was being weakened by these campaigns, since Germanicus received an appeal for aid at this point from Segestes, a Cherscan noble opposed to Arminius. The next operation was mounted against the Bructeri with Caecina marching overland to their territory whilst Germanicus moved by river. The Bructeri were swiftly defeated by a fast moving column in advance of the main force and their land ravaged. A major prize of this operation was the recapture of the eagle of *Legio XIX*. Whilst Caecina was sent forward to reconnoitre the forests and the bridges and causeways over the marshes, Germanicus performed an action directed, not by strategy, but by the morale of his own army and visited the Teutoburg forest to bury the dead of Varus' disaster.

An attempt was made to bring the main force of Arminius to battle. However, the former withdrew and even inflicted a check on the pursuit (*Ann.* 1. 63). Germanicus then withdrew his force by water, leaving Caecina to march his troops back to their *hiberna*. Arminius attempted to ambush and destroy this force and nearly achieved his aim. Although the Romans did break out they could hardly claim much of a victory (*Ann.* 1. 64). Even greater loss was inflicted on Germanicus' troops through storms at sea (*Ann.* 1. 70).

2. *The German Campaign of AD 15: Commentary*

In these campaigns, the Romans suffered heavy losses in both men and animals, largely as a result of attrition rather than enemy action (*Ann.* 2. 5). The next year saw campaigns with similar aims and methods, but also on two occasions Arminius risked a field action and was twice defeated. It may be that the Roman policy of attacking individual tribes in order to break up the fairly shaky alliance opposing them, presented a threat to Arminius sufficient to make him risk the chances of battle. The willingness to treat with Segestes, illustrated the Roman technique of dividing opposition by a mixture of force and conciliation.

The Germans had little political organization, and their capitals were not centres of rule, the capture of which would automatically have resulted in the defeat of the tribe.[30] It was not a practical

---

[30] See Ch. 2, 'The Germans'.

possibility to destroy a social and political entity such as a tribe by laying waste its land. The damage inflicted by ravaging tribal territory was moral rather than physical.[31] Cereal crops could have been burnt for a short time before harvest, and lasting damage done, but villages and houses could be quickly rebuilt.[32] Ravaging the land established fear in the hearts of the tribesmen opposing Rome. It may of course have also sown the seed of hatred which would be reaped in later years. Yet, if it was clear that the results of fighting Rome were dreadful, then a Roman army could hold sway over a far greater area than it might have physically controlled. Therefore to maintain with Wells[33] that the raid on the Marsi was 'a demonstration of little military value' would miss the point. In these operations, the Romans may have beaten no armies or captured no citadels, but they may well have broken the will of the people concerned to fight them.

The surprise the Roman army achieved against a people who normally fought from ambush is notable and reminiscent of Caesar's expedition against the Nervii and of the war against Tacfarinas (*BG* 4. 3). The tendency of the Germans to pursue any apparent Roman retreat, even if this was only a withdrawal after a successful operation, is also notable. Both factors were a noted feature of wars against certain irregulars in the nineteenth century.[34]

Punitive Actions: Conclusion

In several of the rebellions discussed in the previous section, the Romans mounted what were in effect punitive expeditions. The surprise attacks mounted by Caesar against the Nervii and the Menapii in the winter of 53 BC, were operations of this type. Potential allies of the Eburones from across the Rhine were treated to a similar display of force. Finally the territory of the Eburones themselves was ravaged. Often the second phase of a rebellion involved a series of punitive expeditions to stamp out the revolt after the main rebel army had been

---

[31] Although the physical damage inflicted by these expeditions only affected a comparatively small area, a series of campaigns could inflict massive political and social dislocation to a tribe. See N. Roymans, 'The North Belgic Tribes in the First Century BC: A Historical-Anthropological Perspective', in R. Brandt and J. Slofstra *Roman and Native in the Low Countries: Spheres of Interaction, BAR* 184 (Oxford, 1983), 43–69, esp. 57, on the consequences of Caesar's campaigns for the Belgic tribes, and the archaeological evidence for this.

[32] See V. D. Hanson, *The Western Way of War* (New York, 1989), 33–4.

[33] C. Wells, *The German Policy of Augustus* (Oxford, 1972), 241.

[34] Callwell, *Small Wars*, 71–84, 240–55.

destroyed. In these operations the aim was to break the enemy's will to
fight rather than his ability to do so. This meant that any enemy could
be defeated by such operations. Those physically affected by the
Roman action might have been few, but the remaining people had
been shown their own vulnerability. The very nature of the Roman
operation—a massive attack which often took the enemy by surprise—
contributed to the psychological defeat of the enemy. The conflict was
initiated by Rome and fought entirely on her own terms, so that the
enemy were little more than victims and certainly were not equals.
Even so the effect of this demonstration of overwhelming power might
be temporary, especially if a Roman reverse, however small, followed
it.

Luttwak argued that the Roman army was most effective in pitched
battles and sieges.[35] Yet in both these operations we have seen the
Roman army using the tactics of 'low intensity warfare', the raid and
ambush. Forces composed of a high proportion of legionary heavy
infantry were able to surprise completely the enemy in Cilicia in 51 BC
and Germany in AD 14–15.[36] In the former case the enemy's own style
of warfare emphasized surprise. Like the Numidians under Tacfarinas,
the enemy had essentially been beaten by their own tactics. Not only
had the Romans adopted the fighting methods of the local peoples, but
their superior organization and system of supply had given them major
advantages over their opponents.

WARS OF CONQUEST

It is hard to find descriptions of wars of conquest, outside the
Caesarean *corpus*, which are detailed enough to describe a single
campaign as an example. Therefore this chapter discusses only one of
these, but attempts to balance this by comparison with less-detailed
accounts of similar campaigns.

The Conquest of the Belgic Tribes: Narrative

Caesar claimed that his conquest of the Belgic tribes in 57 BC was
motivated by their attack on the Remi, a tribe allied to Rome (See Map
1). His initial actions were consequently directed towards relieving the
pressure on this tribe. Numidian, Cretan, and Balearic light troops
were sent ahead to reinforce the town of Bibrax which was threatened

---

[35] Luttwak, *Grand Strategy*, 40–6.   [36] See Ch. 2 and Ch. 3.

by the Belgae. The latter, after devastating the surrounding country, marched towards Caesar's camp with a view to fighting a decisive battle in the open field (*BG* 2. 7). Caesar proved unwilling to risk an action until it was favourable for him to do so. Neither side was prepared to abandon its strong position to attack the enemy at a disadvantage. The Belgae moved to take the bridge protected by a Roman fort and so threaten Caesar's supplies. This attempt failed, and the Belgae themselves began to exhaust their own store of grain. The tribes decided to disperse allowing each man to support himself at home, with the agreement to gather the army again in the area of the tribe which Caesar attacked first (*BG* 2. 10). Their withdrawal was not made in an orderly manner and the Romans inflicted some loss on the Belgae without risk to themselves (*BG* 2. 11). The problems encountered in mustering and supplying a tribal army were clearly shown by the next episode of the campaign. Caesar was able to attack, defeat, and force to surrender, the Suessiones and the Bellovaci individually. These were not aided by the other tribes (*BG* 2. 12, 15). It was only when Caesar began to give the same treatment to the Nervii that the Belgic tribes managed to bring together their united armies. The failure of Caesar's cavalry to scout efficiently resulted in a surprise attack on his army, which was building a camp near the Sambre (*BG* 2. 19–28). In the subsequent, hard-fought battle, the Belgae were decisively beaten. The contingent of at least one tribe, the Atuatuci, had not reached the Belgic army before the Sambre and this force returned to the tribal stronghold. Caesar proceeded to besiege the town, eventually forcing the surrender of the tribe and enslaving the survivors.

Wars of Conquest: Commentary

It is clear that in a war of conquest the invading army must adopt the offensive, abandonment of which will be a sign that things were not going well. It is more important to consider the target of the offensive. The ability of the Roman army in open battles and sieges has often been pointed out.[37] The Belgic tribes possessed an army confident of its ability to defeat an opponent in open battle. The total defeat of this ensured that the tribes involved capitulated. Yet initially, Caesar avoided battle with this force, and after its dispersal harried the territories of individual tribes. Although the Roman army could safely

[37] See Luttwak, *Grand Strategy*, 41–6.

have been assumed to be superior in the open field to any of its opponents, this does not mean that victory could always have been taken for granted. Whilst opponents with large field armies provided a tangible target for an offensive, there remained always the risk that the enemy would defeat and quite possibly, since they usually significantly out-numbered them, entirely destroy the Roman forces. The latter was a rare occurrence, but the large armies mustered by Trajan against the organized kingdom of Dacia, or by M. Aurelius against the numerous and powerful Marcomanni and Quadi showed that often exceptionally large Roman armies were required to minimize the risk of defeat.[38] These armies were not as numerous as the opposition, but they represented greater concentrations of troops than individual frontier provinces could usually muster. Nevertheless, campaigns against opponents with armies willing to take the field were generally more quickly decisive.

If the enemy possessed some centre of political importance, such as a capital, the capture of which would break their will to fight, this was a suitable target for an invading Roman army. In 54 BC Crassus made the cities of Parthia the targets of his attack. The predominantly Greek populations of many of these were more favourable to the Romans than their Parthian masters.[39] If the enemy possessed a field army, it seems likely that a threat to the capital might force them to risk a battle that they were most likely to lose. In the campaign in Armenia, Corbulo attacked Artaxata, thus giving Tiridates the option of fighting or appearing helpless (*Ann.* 13. 39). Jugurtha, who had been avoiding battle, was similarly forced to risk an action by a threat to Zama (Sallust, *Jug.* 56). A capital, either through the blow to prestige, or the political dislocation caused by its loss was thus a suitable target. Capitals of this sort were inevitably more common in the more politically centralized states, especially in the Hellenistic world.

A people or tribe who lacked a central political authority presented a different problem, especially if they lacked an army willing to fight and be defeated in open battle. In the Jewish revolt, which after the defeat of Cestius Gallus, resembled in many ways a war of conquest, the rebels were organized into diverse and often rival bands defending individual localities. The huge number of fortified towns and

---

[38] See L. Rossi *Trajan's Column and the Dacian War* (London, 1971), 92–6.
[39] Dio 40. 13. 1, 40. 16. 3, 40. 20. 3.

strongholds in the country made this a war of sieges, as the Romans, steadily recaptured one by one those areas and towns which failed to surrender. The conditions in the Bar-Kokhba revolt under Hadrian seem to have been similar. After the initial uprising, the Jewish rebels did not form a field army, but occupied a large number of strongholds and used these as bases for small-scale harassing raids. The Roman response was to capture systematically these strongholds. Dio claimed that the war involved the Romans taking 50 cities and 985 villages (Dio 69. 12. 3–13. 3). By its nature, such a war was arduous and imposed severe strain on the morale of the Roman troops, but as long as the Romans did not give up their will to reconquer the province (and this was never a realistic possibility in Judaea), then their eventual victory was only a question of time. Tribes of a less settled nature who lacked such strongholds, offered a different problem. Yet all peoples must have had some resources without which life would become difficult or unthinkable. Therefore attacks on villages, crops, and cattle, moved them either to surrender or risk open battle. Such operations were time-consuming, since only a small area could have been affected directly at any one time. In these circumstances, the war of conquest became in effect like the punitive expedition described earlier. In most cases, once the initial conquest was achieved, some garrisons were established in the area to guard against the threat of rebellion.

It is dangerous to rationalize the warfare of this period to the extent at which it becomes decided purely by economic factors. In a very real sense any war in this period was a conflict between the respective wills to fight on of the peoples involved. A war was decided when one of the participants admitted defeat and was no longer prepared to continue the fight. In some cases defeat in a single battle was enough to force a tribe or state to admit defeat, as most of the Belgic tribes did after the Sambre. The capture of a capital city could achieve the same result. The fall of Jerusalem in AD 70 effectively ended the Jewish War. When a people possessed neither a central political centre, nor a field army, but was organized at a lower level politically, then they might have to be defeated piecemeal. Operations on a much smaller scale would have been mounted to capture the local centres of authority (even if these were no more than villages) or to defeat the local forces (even if these were not numerous.) Therefore a war of conquest could involve the Roman army in operations on a very large or very small scale depending on the socio-political structure of the people under attack. Many of the forts and marching camps in Britain which can be dated to the early conquest period are small, housing vexillations of less than legion size. The invading army seems to have operated as a united body on very few occasions. More often it was divided into numerous miniature armies, almost certainly vexillations of both horse and foot, which operated independently. The political fragmentation of many of the British tribes made this necessary. Each group or clan within these had to be defeated, often individually, by the defeat of its forces or the capture of its strongholds. In the face of such disparate opposition there was little danger in dispersing the Roman army into a number of columns allowing several localities to be conquered simultaneously.[40]

If the enemy had to be persuaded that they had lost the war by some triggering event, or in the case of a politically fragmented opponent a series of events affecting each constituent part, then the Romans themselves had to be persuaded that they had lost the war by some defeat. The destruction of Varus' legions in AD 9 and the high cost of later operations convinced Tiberius to end the attempted conquest of Germany (*Ann.* 2. 25–6). If Caesar had been beaten at Alesia then perhaps the conquest of Gaul would also have been abandoned.

In all the campaigns discussed, the importance of maintaining a supply of food and material to the army is evident. Caesar frequently referred to the extent to which logistical factors influenced his strategic decisions and the course of operations.[41] However there is very little actual information in our sources on the details of the Roman commissariat. As a result, it is impossible to reconstruct this clearly. Information from other periods can tell us how much the various types of draught and baggage animals could have pulled or carried, but we do not know what each Roman soldier was normally issued with as rations for each day. Therefore we cannot assess how many animals were needed to transport the baggage of a Roman army on campaign. Since I do not feel that I can add anything to what has already been written on this subject, I do not propose to discuss supply itself, but

---

[40] V. A. Maxfield, 'Pre-Flavian Forts and their Garrisons', *Britannia*, 17 (1986), 59–72, esp. 60, 70–1, and 'Conquest and Aftermath', in M. Todd (ed.), *Research on Roman Britain 1960–1989* (1989), 19–29, esp. 24–5, notes the numerous small vexillation forts in Britain in the conquest period, but failed to link this properly to the political organization of the British tribes. She contrasts this pattern with Caesar's concentration of his legions in Gaul. Such concentration was only useful where the enemy, although tribal, was more united.

[41] e.g. *BG* 1. 16, 23, 27, 38, 49, 4.7, 5.24, 6.10, 29, 33.

merely to note its importance in shaping the course of campaigns.[42] For a more detailed examination of this question and some tentative calculations see Appendix 1.

THE ORDER OF MARCH

> Let me see two armies on the march, and I believe I could tell you the respective fighting value of each. No military quality is so frequently tested as that of marching.
>
> (Sir Garnet Wolseley, *The Soldier's Pocket Book for Field Service* (1882), 303)

The ordering of the column of march obviously depended on the local circumstances. The proximity or otherwise of the enemy was clearly a prime consideration. Caesar noted that his normal order of march placed each legion, with its own baggage, one behind the other. If there was a possibility of battle then transport of the whole army was massed and guarded, and the front of the army consisted of several unencumbered legions (*BG* 2. 17). In the campaigns in Germany where the wooded and broken terrain allowed the enemy to attack from any direction, it was important to ensure all-round defence. Here the standard practice seems to have been to send the *auxilia* and cavalry in the van, followed by the legions in virtually a hollow square formation, with the baggage of the army being in the centre, and to have more *auxilia* and cavalry bringing up the rear (*Ann.* 1. 54, 64). When threatened by an enemy strong in cavalry, Metellus and Marius in Numidia (Sallust, *Jug.* 46), and Crassus in Mesopotamia also used the hollow square (Plutarch, *Crassus* 23). Alternatively, Agricola in Scotland, threatened by an enemy who preferred to fight from ambush, divided his army into three columns, so that if one were ambushed, one or both of the others could march to its relief (*Agricola*

---

[42] On Roman logistics see D. J. Breeze, 'The Logistics of Agricola's Final Campaign', *Talanta* 18–19 (1986–7), 7–28, W. Groenman-van Waateringe, 'Food for Soldiers, Food for Thought', in J. C. Barrett and L. Macinnes, *Barbarians and Romans in North-West Europe*, BAR *471* (1989), 96–107, A. Labisch, *Frumentum Commeatusque. Die Nahrungsmittelversongung der Heere Caesars* (Meisenheim am Glan, 1975), and J. P. Adams, *Logistics of the Roman Imperial Army: Major Campaigns on the Eastern Front in the First Three Centuries AD* (Detroit, Mich., 1976). For an attempt to reconstruct the logistical arrangements of a specific series of operations see J. Peddie, *Invasion: The Roman Conquest of Britain* (London, 1987), 23–46, 180–95. On supply in general see M. van Creveld, *Supplying War* (Cambridge, 1977).

26). This would have been extremely dangerous against an opponent with an army that was more formidable in the open field, since it would have risked having the army defeated in detail. The dispersion implied a confidence that any one of the detachments could hold its own until relief. It suggests that a politically fragmented enemy could not be defeated in one mass, but needed to be attacked individually. The concentration of forces was only attractive in campaigns against an enemy capable of massing a strong army. If the enemy did possess such an army, then it was very dangerous to attempt to attack him with small separate columns, which were intended to combine on the battlefield. When Lucius Apronius sent several separate columns against a Frisian army in AD 28, the result was a disaster with each division being defeated in detail (*Ann.* 4. 73). In 54 BC Caesar had been joined on his march to relieve Q. Cicero's besieged garrison by C. Fabius with one legion, nearly half of the total force (*BG* 5. 46–7). This junction took place long before the Romans came near to the enemy. Concentrating separately marching columns in the face of the enemy was too risky an operation to be attempted with any frequency.

We do have three more detailed descriptions of the order of march adopted by a Roman army, two of which are by Josephus. The first, describing Vespasian marching into Galilee (*BJ* 3. 115–26), was as follows:

  i) Auxiliary light-armed troops and archers sent in advance to repel sudden incursions and to explore suspected ambush sites, such as woodland.

 (ii) A contingent of heavily armed Roman infantry and cavalry.

(iii) Ten men from each century with their own kit and the instruments for marking out the camp.

(iv) Men with tools to straighten the route, level rough places and cut through obstructing woods.

 (v) The baggage of Vespasian and his staff escorted by cavalry.

(vi) Vespasian, his personal bodyguard, and a picked guard of infantry and cavalry.

(vii) The cavalry of the legions.

(viii) The siege train.

(ix) The legates, prefects and tribunes escorted by picked troops.

 (x) The eagle and other standards followed by trumpeters.

(xi) Each legion marching six abreast, accompanied by a centurion and followed by the servants and baggage animals.

(xii) The mercenaries (presumably either *auxilia* or allies).
(xiii) A rearguard of light and heavy infantry and cavalry.

The second account from Josephus is of Titus' army marching against Jerusalem and is virtually identical. Only details are different, for instance the trumpeters preceded the eagles instead of following.

Several points are worth noting, particularly the importance of strong vanguards and rearguards, and especially of scouts sent out ahead of the former. This practice was also noted as being used in the description of the columns of Germanicus in Germany (*Ann.* 2. 16), Crassus in Parthia (Plutarch, *Crassus* 23), and Caesar at the Sambre (*BG* 2. 17). The army of the Empire contained a higher proportion of regular auxiliary cavalry, which was often better trained at scouting than the allied horse of the Republic.

The detailing of a detachment to improve the quality of the road or track followed is interesting. This was most important in making the movement of the siege train and baggage wagons easier. In Pseudo-Hyginus' *De Munitionibus Castrorum* a detachment of sailors, protected by Moorish and Pannonian light troops, carried out this important function, apparently ahead of the main column.[43] The division of the camp followers and baggage into distinct parts corresponding with the parent unit was echoed in Vegetius, who claimed that the servants were even given leaders and standards (Vegetius 3. 6).

The order of march given in Arrian's *Ectaxis* was somewhat different. Arrian intended to fight a battle or at least threaten one, and as a result his army had to be able to deploy into battle order directly from the march. Therefore, there was no mention of men improving the road or being detached to lay out the camp. His account does give a far greater insight into the command structure of an army in the field, revealing this to have been far less rigid than scholars have often claimed. The order of march was as follows:

(i) The scout cavalry led by a local guide.
(ii) Mounted archers and the *ala Auriana* in two ranks (or two bodies).
(iii) The cavalry of the Raetian cohort led by Daphnes.

---

[43] Hyginus, *De Munitionibus Castrorum* 24. Trajan's Column scenes 241–4 show men improving or building a road for the army's advance. The men have hexagonal shields with possibly nautical symbols. These men may be sailors. See F. Lepper and S. S. Frere *Trajan's Column* (Gloucester, 1988), 142–3.

(iv) The combined cavalry of three *cohortes equitatae* under Demetrius.

(v) A vexillation of Gallic cavalry under a centurion.

(vi) Armenian foot archers.

(vii) 3 cohorts of *auxilia* under Lamprocles (4 abreast, standards displayed).

(viii) 1 cohort of Numidians under Verus.

(ix) General's bodyguard of horse.

(x) Legionary cavalry.

(xi) Siege engines.

(xii) The legions, by cohort, 4 abreast.

(xiii) 5 cohorts of *auxilia* under Siculinus the Aplanian with the baggage train.

(xiv) An *ala* under its prefect. Another *ala* and the cavalry of a *cohors equitata* were detached to guard the flanks of the column.

Although provision was made in Vespasian's column to reveal and repel any ambush, a major field action was not anticipated. Like Caesar at the Sambre, Arrian massed the baggage of the army at the rear of the column. His enemy was the nomadic Alans, with far greater mobility than his own army. It was therefore important to discover their presence with sufficient time to allow the army to deploy into battle order, hence the emphasis once again on scouting. As the enemy could have appeared from any direction, it was important to protect the flanks of the column. This role was fulfilled by detachments of cavalry. Arrian's column showed the willingness and ability of the Roman army to adapt to the local situation.

One significant difference between these accounts, which cannot be explained by differing tactical circumstances, is found in the dimensions of the column formed by the infantry of the army. In Josephus, these marched six abreast, whereas Arrian's troops used a formation of four files. One Legion, *XII Fulminata* appeared both in Titus' and Arrian's column, so it is possible that, at least in this one unit, but perhaps in the entire army, a different set of drills had been introduced in the late first or early second century. More probably, the difference reflected the apparently unique internal organization of the Cappadocian legions[44] to which the *XII* had conformed when posted to the province.[45]

---

[44] See A. B. Bosworth, 'Arrian and the *Alani*', *Harvard Studies in Classical Philology*, 81 (1977), 217–55.   [45] See Ch. 5, 'Formations'.

The implication from all of the more detailed accounts discussed above is that the cohorts of a legion marched one behind the other, resulting in a very long column.[46] Polybius recorded that, if the army faced attack on the march, the maniples of the legions advanced in three parallel columns, the baggage protected in between (Polybius 4. 40). Such a column was not only able to form up quickly into a line of battle, but was more easily controlled and directed by its commander. It also moved more quickly over the course of a day than a longer column.[47] This is because it more quickly made up any delay. Caesar explicitly states that on one occasion in 55 BC he also advanced with his army formed into three parallel columns ready to deploy into a battle formation of three lines, the *triplex acies* (*BG* 4. 14). It may be that he followed this practice on numerous occasions without mentioning it.

In a long column, not only did the delay itself slow down the army, but the need for each vehicle or unit to wait for those ahead to start moving again, before moving themselves, also imposed a further loss of time. Much must have depended on the quality of the road and the terrain that the army was traversing. The roads built throughout the Empire by the army increased its speed of movement because they provided firm and flat routes for the baggage animals and particularly carts. Whenever possible the baggage moved along a road or track since otherwise its speed was drastically reduced. Men and horses could more easily have moved parallel to the actual road, whilst still keeping pace with the slower moving baggage. It is unlikely that any sizeable Roman army ever moved in a narrow, snake-like column, unless forced to do so by the terrain. Some of the terrain crossed by Cestius Gallus in AD 66, notably the Beth-horon pass, necessitated a very narrow column. The importance placed by Arrian on the commander moving up and down the line of march to regulate the movements of the various units and baggage is significant. Normally the baggage moved on the road and the rest of the army spread out on either side.

According to Vegetius 'the ancients' regularly trained their soldiers

---

[46] Breeze, *Talanta* 18–19 (1986–7), 7–28, suggested that Agricola's army may have formed a column as long as 15.2 km. (10 miles).

[47] See D. W. Engels *Alexander the Great and the Logistics of the Macedonian Army* (Berketer, 1978), 154–6.

in route marches of 32 km (20 miles) in a day.[48] These, it seems, were begun and ended at the fort they garrisoned, and therefore did not involve construction of a marching camp, or the movement of large amounts of baggage. Therefore these figures cannot be used for assessing how fast a Roman army in the field moved. It is now impossible to establish precisely how much and what type of baggage normally accompanied a Roman army. A large proportion of the baggage seems to have been drawn by oxen.[49] There may also have been bullocks moving with the army as a supply of meat.[50] A draught bullock can pull around 180 kg. (400 lb.) at a maximum speed of 4 km. (2.5 miles) an hour, but can only do so over a flat, firm surface, which emphasizes that good roads were absolutely essential for moving baggage. A bullock can only travel at this speed for 7–8 hours a day, because 7 hours (one before and six after work) must be spent grazing and the remainder resting.[51] This meant that, even on the best roads, a single ox-cart could travel for a maximum of between 28 and 32 km. (17.5–20 miles) in a day. In a long column, and crossing uneven terrain on imperfect roads, this total was drastically reduced. Mules and horses, whether as pack or draught animals, moved faster than this, but only small forces could have had enough of these to carry all of their baggage. A large detachment marching *expeditus*, or one with only light baggage, could have moved much more quickly for a brief operation, as was probably the case with most of the punitive expeditions discussed above.

The swiftest method of moving large numbers of men and material was by water. In AD 66 Cestius Gallus sent a vexillation by sea to seize Joppa in a surprise attack. He may also have moved all or part of his army and its supplies from Antioch to Ptolemais and then Caesarea by ship. In AD 15 and 16 Germanicus used both rivers and the sea to advance and withdraw his legions in Germany.[52] The rivers Rhine and

[48] Vegetius 1. 27. Gichon, *PEQ* 113 (1981), 59–60, suggested that Cestius Gallus' army in AD 66 marched an average distance of 25 km. (15 miles) each day. However his calculations are highly conjectural and impossible to prove or disprove.

[49] Wagons drawn by pairs of oxen or mules are depicted on Trajan's Column, scenes 123, 124, 148, 149, 280, 284, 285, and the Column of Marcus Aurelius, scenes 23, 35, 38, 48, 49, 105, 111, 112, 121, 133, 139.

[50] Sall. *Jug.* 29, 90–1, *BG* 7. 17, 56, *BC* 3. 47–8.

[51] G. Wolseley, *The Soldier's Pocket Book for Field Service* (London, 1882), 68, and War Office Veterinary Department, *Animal Management* (London, 1908), 297.

[52] See *Ann.* 1. 60, 1. 63, 2. 5–6, 2. 23–5. On the navy in general see C. G. Starr *The Roman Imperial Navy* (New York, 1941).

Danube gave the units stationed along the frontiers there splendid communications and the ability to shift troops quickly. The Roman Imperial Navy, apart from fulfilling important roles of its own, provided the army with considerable support whenever a campaign occurred near navigable water.

THE MARCHING CAMP

The most characteristic device of the Roman art of war under the Republic and early Principate was the marching camp. At the conclusion of the day's march, legionary troops on the move were assembled at a site, carefully selected in advance, where they were put to work for three hours or more to dig a perimeter obstacle ditch, erect a rampart, assemble a palisade with prefabricated elements and pitch tents.[53]

There are examples of Roman armies which did not follow the practice of constructing a marching camp each day, but normally these occurred in the obviously different circumstances of a retreat, such as that of Paetus in Armenia and Cestius Gallus in Judaea (*BJ* 2. 549–51, *Ann.* 15. 16). According to Tacitus, Petilius Cerialis had not fortified the camp of his army in AD 70 (*Hist.* 4. 72). Overall, the practice appears to have been so normal that Virgil made this almost the first action of Aeneas on arrival in Italy (*Aeneid* 7. 126–9). A large number of marching camps of varying sizes have been discovered by archaeology, the vast majority of these in Britain. As a result of their necessarily temporary nature, the dates of these sites, their garrisons and purposes within a campaign are clearly difficult and often impossible to judge.[54] The wide variety of sizes of these camps, which often do not conform to any known unit size, bears out the suggestion that not only were units often under strength, but also that *ad hoc* 'brigades' or vexillations were common in all campaigns.[55]

For the Republic we have the detailed account of Polybius as to the plan and dimensions of a consular marching camp, but for the armies of later periods the situation is less clear. Due to their temporary nature, archaeology can reveal very little of the internal organization of

---

[53] Luttwak, *Grand Strategy*, 55.

[54] See V. A. Maxfield, 'Conquest and Aftermath', in M. Todd (ed.), *Research on Roman Britain, 1960–1989* (London, 1989), 19–29.

[55] e.g. *BJ* 3. 9, 11, 307 or *Vita* 43, 65, or *Hist.* 4. 24, see Ch. 1, 26–8, Ch. 4 n. 11.

these camps. Psuedo-Hyginus' *De Munitionibus Castrorum* does provide a detailed description of the layout of a camp of a large army, but presents problems of dating and purpose.[56] Although the author does make some allowance for armies of different sizes and proportions, it is difficult to reconstruct such camps, or those of units significantly below strength. Given that no two permanent forts have ever proved to be exactly identical internally, it is likely that marching camps also varied in detail. The various siege camps at Masada give us some idea of the appearance of the more temporary camps of the Roman army. It is especially notable that the cohorts in these camps did not have their full complement of men.[57] *Canabae* have been detected outside many temporary camps and were present at Masada.[58]

According to Corbulo, battles were won with the *dolabra* (Frontinus, *Strategemata* 4. 7. 2). The pick-axe and the marching camp have been presented as the symbol of this mentality and often condemned as approximating to trench warfare.[59] Harmand suggested that a camp's construction took at least three hours.[60] The limits imposed on the army's mobility by its methods of transporting baggage made this less of a burden, yet this does not do anything to counter the claim that the work was useless, since the defences constructed were of little or no military value.[61]

Luttwak has already to some extent countered these claims, pointing out that these camps prevented the army from being harassed by small-scale attacks, provided a sense of normality and security to the troops within them and allowed more effective maintenance of a watch by sentries.[62] The shortcomings of the defences have also been exaggerated. There are many dramatic accounts by Roman historians of camps being attacked and broken into.[63] Yet it is hard to find an account of one being stormed, without the Roman troops having first been defeated in the open field. Indeed, the existence of pickets to give early warning of attacks, and of several gates from which to mount sallies, allowed the army to fight successfully from a camp, even if it never planned to fight in this manner (e.g. *BG* 4. 51). There were very

---

[56] See Ch. 1 n. 7.   [57] See Ch. 1 n. 43.
[58] See Wells, *German Polics of Augustus*, 48, 98, 126, 131, 146, 153, 157, 175, 191, 205, 220, 223, 248, 317.   [59] See Fuller, *Julius Caesar*, 74–5, 86–7.
[60] See J. Harmand, *L'Armée et le soldat à Rome de 107 à 50 avant nôtre ère* (Paris, 1967), 132 n. 240.
[61] Webster, *Roman Imperial Army*, 171, Harmand, *L'Armée et le soldat à Rome*, 129–34.
[62] Luttwak, *Grand Strategy*, 55–7.   [63] e.g. *Agricola* 26, *Hist.* 4. 77.

few instances of a Roman army constructing field fortifications in an open battle, since these would have seriously impaired mobility (*BG* 2. 8, Frontinus, *Strategemata* 2. 3. 17).

A point that Luttwak ignored is that the marching camp not only served to some extent to keep the enemy out, but also kept the Roman soldiers in. Desertion was always a problem in the Roman army. Enemy leaders as separated by time and geography as Jugurtha, Tacfarinas, and Decebalus, recruited their best men from Roman deserters.[64] According to Dio, men were even willing to desert and join the rebels within the city during the siege of Jerusalem in AD 70 (Dio 65. 5. 4). Treaties concluding wars in the second century often seem to have included provision for the return of Roman deserters and prisoners (e.g. Dio 68. 9. 5). According to Tacitus, Corbulo was rare in insisting on the execution of recaptured deserters, but it is noticeable that it is only claimed that he suffered fewer desertions as a result, and not none at all.[65]

All these aspects of the marching camp have dealt with its associations for the Roman soldiers. The comparative weakness of the camp's defences has tended to obscure the effect of these works upon the enemy. Each day, as the Roman army moved, it constructed an almost identical structure at the end of its march. In this way the marching camp symbolized the steady advance of the Roman army. In the discussion of the individual campaigns it was noted that wars were won when the losing side had lost not the ability to fight on, but the will to do so. The Roman emphasis on adopting and maintaining the offensive was intended to attack the collective will of the enemy to fight on. The marching camp was part of this attempt to intimidate the enemy into submission. Combined with the discipline of the Roman marching column, it stressed the order and might of the Roman advance. The overall speed of the Roman approach may not have been that great, but the marching camp displayed its steady progression and helped to suggest that it was unstoppable. The marching camp, although itself a defensive structure, was in a very real sense an instrument of the offensive. It is this aspect of its role that its critics have failed to appreciate, leading them to condemn it as not only a defensive structure, but a bad one. On the contrary it was a means of applying strong moral pressure on the enemy.

---

[64] Sall. *Jug.* 103, *Ann.* 2. 52, *Dio* 68. 9. 5.
[65] *Ann.* 13. 35; see Ch. 6 n. 11.

GENERAL CONCLUSIONS

In all the campaigns discussed, the Roman army adopted the offensive as soon as possible and sought to maintain it until victory had been achieved. When the Roman army abandoned the offensive, as it did after the defeat of Gallus in AD 66, then it was a sign that things had gone badly wrong. Even in this situation it was not long before small Roman forces, such as the garrison of Ascalon, were acting aggressively on a local basis. In all types of warfare Roman tactical doctrine was based upon the offensive. The Roman army sought always to bring the conflict to a decisive conclusion as soon as possible by seizing the initiative and dictating the course of the fighting. A decision was reached when the enemy's will to fight was broken. Wars were never fought simply to control territory, but were always fought against a political entity such as a tribe or state. If the enemy was fragmented politically, then this often required each political subdivision to be beaten in turn. The economic assets of a people, in terms of its crops, cattle and dwellings might be attacked, but the destruction of these by the Roman army was more apparent than real. Such attacks were part of the assault upon the collective will of the people in question to fight. The Roman emphasis on the offensive in all forms of warfare was another aspect of this attempt to dominate the enemy's collective willpower and suggested the inevitability of Roman victory. As on the battlefield, the appearance of force was more important than its reality. The appearance of confidence in an army, shown for instance in its willingness to confront overwhelming odds, lowered the enemy's morale and contributed to final victory.

In practical terms, the campaigns discussed above have shown the ability of the Roman army to fight successfully different types of conflict against very different opponents. It was superior to most armies that it faced in battle in this period. Its skill at siegecraft gave it the ability to take almost any fortification. This skill in 'high intensity warfare', certainly did, as Luttwak pointed out, give it 'escalation dominance' over most opponents.[66] Yet to assert that the Roman army could not cope with 'low intensity' warfare is to go against the evidence. Caesar, Cicero, and Germanicus were all able to use forces of heavily armed, legionary infantry as raiders to attack and completely surprise enemies who habitually fought using the tactics of raid and

---

[66] Luttwak, *Grand Strategy*, 40–1.

ambush. The war with Tacfarinas showed the inherent flexibility of the Roman military system in adapting to the local situation, so that it was eventually able to beat the enemy at its own style of warfare. The organization and discipline of the Roman army, combined with the sound logistical arrangements that allowed it to stay in the field, gave it some advantages in every scale and type of warfare. Therefore to follow Luttwak, and suggest that the expansion of the Empire ended when the Romans encountered peoples whom they were unable to defeat militarily, is to deny the fundamental flexibility of the Roman army.[67]

This chapter has suggested that many of the orthodox opinions about the Roman army and the type of wars which it fought are derived, not from the evidence of our sources, but from our own anachronistic assumptions about warfare. The Romans and their opponents did not base their actions on physical geography in the way that historians have assumed that they must have done. Moral factors were more important than physical in determining the outcome. Warfare in this period may also have been unlike more recent conflicts in many other ways that have not been discussed in this chapter. There is a real need for a full study of Roman warfare.

[67] Ibid. 45–6.

4

The General's Battle

The principles of strategy and tactics, and the logistics of war are really absurdly simple: it is the actualities that make war so complicated and so difficult, and are usually neglected by historians.

(Field Marshal Lord Wavell in J. Connell, 'Writing about soldiers', *Journal of the Royal United Services Institute* (1965), 224)

THE primary purpose of any army is to defeat the enemy in battle. This is true, even if few of its soldiers ever experience battle directly. This section examines the nature of a battle in this period, and looks at the way in which the Roman army did, or did not, function on such occasions. The Roman army possessed a clearly defined hierarchy of officers, at the head of which was the general, who sought to control and co-ordinate the army during a battle. Potentially, this position enabled the general to influence the course of the fighting more than any other individual. This chapter discusses the role of the commander in determining the outcome of a battle.

Many studies have examined the skills of generals in the Roman army, especially those of successful commanders, such as Scipio, Caesar and Pompey. Often these studies have formed part of military histories, which embrace many, or all, periods. Delbrück, in his survey of the art of war from ancient times up to the Napoleonic Wars, contributed much to our understanding of the Roman army and its tactics. Yet the very nature of the study, dealing as it did with the military institutions of many ages, encouraged a tendency to dwell upon those attributes which armies, and especially generals, have in common, regardless of period. The generals who receive individual attention are those who introduced innovations in tactics or organization. The commander's use of strategy and tactics becomes his most important skill, and is compared to that of commanders from all periods of history to assess his overall competence.[1] Since, not only are the principles of strategy and tactics 'absurdly simple', as Lord Wavell pointed out, but they are also in their essence unchanging, such a line of investigation was, and is, understandably attractive. Yet the result is that the differences between the commander's role in armies produced by different societies become obscured by the emphasis on those qualities that they apparently have in common.

Even when historians have written about specific wars or commanders, as opposed to wide-ranging military histories, the tendency has been to judge generals by a set of unchanging martial virtues, chief amongst which is skill in tactics. The title of Liddell-Hart's book, *A Greater than Napoleon—Scipio Africanus*, clearly implies that comparison of commanders, separated in time by more than 2,000 years, is both legitimate and important—and, in a sense, that the role of the general in the Second Punic War was automatically the same in its fundamentals as it was in the Napoleonic Wars.[2] Major-General Fuller believed that the concepts behind the campaigns of Alexander the Great were quite modern, so that 'much could be learnt from his battles, which might be applied to tank warfare'.[3] It is clear that his involvement in the development of armoured warfare between the two World Wars heavily influenced his studies of ancient armies and commanders. For him, Caesar and the predominantly infantry army with which he conquered Gaul, with its extensive use of field fortifications, symbolized the outmoded ideas that had led to the stalemate of the Great War. Alexander's campaigns covered vast areas of the East and involved the aggressive use of cavalry, and so foreshadowed the possibilities of mobile breakthrough offered by armoured warfare, partially realized in the Blitzkrieg of the Second World War.[4] The comparison of historical commanders is nothing new. Livy relates an almost certainly spurious conversation between Hannibal and Scipio, in which they discussed, and compared

---

[1] H. Delbrück, *History of the Art of War within the Framework of Political History*, i (Westport, 1975), esp. 230–4 on Alexander as a military commander; 380–7, where Hannibal and Scipio are compared with each other and Napoleon and Wellington respectively; 565–71 on the generalship of Caesar.
[2] B. H. Liddell-Hart, *A Greater than Napoleon—Scipio Africanus*, (Edinburgh, 1930), esp. 248–80.
[3] Maj.-Gen. J. F. C. Fuller, *The Generalship of Alexander the Great* (London, 1958), esp. the preface, and *Julius Caesar, Man, Soldier, and Tyrant* (London, 1965), 74.
[4] See Introd. and Ch. 3.

themselves to, the great commanders of history, which shows that the Romans themselves could think in these terms (Livy 35. 14).

Both Fuller and Liddell-Hart wrote about many different periods of military history, so that their concentration on those aspects that all warfare appears to have in common is understandable. However historians writing purely about the Roman period have tended to adopt the same approach. Cuff, in an article dealing with Caesar as a soldier, felt that it was legitimate to judge him, not just by the standards of his contemparies Lucullus and Pompey, but by comparison with Napoleon and Wellington.[5] Keppie, in a brief section on Caesar's generalship, dealt largely with his tactical skill and introduction of new equipment, assuming as a matter of course that these were the most important skills of a commander.[6] Leach, in a biography of Pompey, regretted that there was no account of his campaigns comparable to Caesar's *Commentaries*, since this would have allowed us to criticize his use of tactics.[7] Two assumptions are implicit in this approach to the study of generals. The first is that the 'rules of war' and the role of the general are both unchanging throughout military history. The second is that it is the primary task of the historian to judge any commander on this basis, the most important factor in this judgement being a commander's tactical ability.

As in so many other aspects of the study of warfare, it was probably John Keegan, in his innovative *The Face of Battle*, who first cast doubt on the usefulness of this approach.[8] His own study of generals, *The Mask of Command*, attempted to reveal some of the changes in the role of commanders over the centuries.[9] The result was not entirely happy, since the validity of comparisons between Wellington and Grant on the one hand, and Alexander the Great and Hitler on the other, seems questionable given that the last two were both generals and heads of state simultaneously, whilst the others were not. Be that as it may, Keegan made little reference to the generals of the Roman army. However, his approach, looking at what the commander actually did and placing him within the context of the army and society which produced him, seems useful for this study.

---

[5] P. J. Cuff, 'Caesar the Soldier', *Greece and Rome*, 2: 4 (1957), 29–35.
[6] L. Keppie, *The Making of the Roman Army* (London, 1984), 101–2.
[7] J. Leach, *Pompey the Great* (London, 1978), 210.
[8] J. Keegan, *The Face of Battle* (London, 1976), 20–2, 53–77.
[9] J. Keegan, *The Mask of Command* (London, 1987).

This chapter attempts to discover what was distinctively Roman about the generals of the period, rather than to concentrate on their observation of universal rules of warfare. It looks less at the tactics themselves and more at the way in which these were implemented. Most of all, it concentrates on the commander himself, to examine where he was, and what he did, immediately before, during and after the battle, and how far this influenced the end result.

To this end, it may be useful to divide the ways in which a general could influence the success or failure of his army in battle into two categories, namely the skills of generalship and of leadership. Generalship may be defined for our purposes as the way in which a commander sought to direct his army as units of troops to achieve victory over the enemy. This includes the tactics that the general employed, and also the means—through the issuing of orders and communications with subordinates and units—by which these tactics were put into practice. In essence, it is the use of the technical skills required to move an army and fight a battle with it. Leadership may be defined as the way a commander sought to exploit the moral and psychological factors which governed the behaviour of his men. It is how a commander sought to inspire his men to fight harder or endure worse privations in order to beat the enemy. This is much harder to define rigidly, since styles of leadership differ greatly with each individual's character, so that often the absence of a leader's guidance is more obvious than its presence. The division between the two categories is not as great as might be implied, and the two are usually mutually dependent. Confidence in the ability of a commander as a general, providing overall direction, might have inspired confidence in his troops and led them to fight better. Likewise, a good leader would have found his men better equipped to carry out the schemes suggested by his skill as a general. On many occasions, we may find that the general did things that come under both categories at the same time.

For this topic the overwhelming majority of the evidence will be provided by literary sources, including theoretical military treatises such as those of Frontinus, Onasander, and Vegetius, as well as historical accounts of particular campaigns. The depiction of Trajan and other commanders, and of Marcus Aurelius and his subordinates on the monuments in Rome can illustrate aspects of how a general interacted with his men, but the nature of these works prevents us from following the actual activities of the commanders at different

stages of the campaigns and battles. As literature is to be our chief
source, it is worth considering the imbalances inherent in it. First, it is
important to note that the evidence is not spread evenly over the
period. For the late Republican period, we have the Caesarian *corpus*,
written either by the commander himself or other officers who served
under him. Added to this, we have Appian's *Civil War*, and Plutarch's
Lives of such commanders as Marius, Sertorius, Sulla, Pompey,
Crassus, Caesar, Mark Antony, and Brutus. There are also Suetonius'
Lives of Caesar and Augustus and some of the letters of Cicero, most
notably the account of the battle of Forum Gallorum written by
Sulpicius Galba (Cicero, *ad Fam.* 10. 30). As a result, for the decades
of the late Republic, we have a wealth of information, either written by
commanders themselves, or biographies of generals, which concern
themselves with what they actually did as individuals.

For the Empire the evidence is far poorer. Tacitus provides a
reasonable amount of detail about the campaigns of Agricola,
especially the battle of Mons Graupius. The *Annals* and *Histories*
provide us with other pockets of information scattered throughout the
first century. However, it is only in the *Jewish War* of Josephus that we
have a level of detailed concern with the doings of the commander in
any way comparable to Caesar's *Commentaries*. For the second century,
the situation is much worse. Apart from the *Ectaxis* of Arrian, there are
only brief anecdotes from the *Epitomes* of Dio, usually concerning the
emperor on campaign. As a result our evidence is heavily slanted
towards the first part of our period, and without that detail, it is
unlikely that the picture of the whole would be anywhere near as
coherent. Therefore it is vital to attempt to discover any differences
between the behaviour of the commander in the late Republic
compared to the rest of our period. These in fact were few and
insignificant, but for the second century, after Arrian, our sources are
so poor that massive changes may have occurred and gone unrecorded.

One genre of ancient literature that deserves separate mention is the
military manual, such as those written by Onasander, Frontinus, and
Vegetius. Campbell has recently argued that these manuals did serve a
practical purpose, as several of their authors claimed.[10] Yet his
discussion, following those of scholars who have criticized these
manuals, concentrates on tactics as the most important skill of a

---

[10] J. B. Campbell, 'Teach Yourself how to be a General', *JRS* 77 (1987), 13–28,
appendix on battle tactics, 28–9.

commander, providing an appendix, in which he attempts to list the known tactical innovations of the Principate. In this he follows the tendency to view tactics as the most important aspect of generalship, which, as we have seen, has dominated all scholarship concerning generals. Campbell admits that, not only do the military manuals not deal with this aspect of the commander's role, but most Roman historians also avoid detailed discussion of tactics. Both historians and the writers of theoretical works instead dealt more with the general's skills as a leader. Leadership was, and is, an art which cannot be taught by a rigid set of rules, and this helps to explain why the ancient manuals seem so unsatisfactory to modern eyes, forced as they were by their subject matter to be vague. It is always difficult to tell the extent to which any theoretical treatise reflected actual practices, and so this study uses evidence from these sources only where it appears to confirm practices described in the historical accounts of actual campaigns.

THE GENERAL AND HIS STAFF

War is the continuation of policy by other means

(Clausewitz, *On War* 1. 24)

Who were the generals of the Roman army? Almost without exception throughout our period, the general was also provincial governor or a *consul*. Under the Republic and in some provinces under the Principate, this meant a *proconsul* or *propraetor*. Under the Empire he was normally a legate of the emperor. Smaller armies might have been led by a legate of the governor, before Augustus, and a legionary legate or auxiliary prefect afterwards.[11] Whatever his actual title, he was a member of the Roman élite following a career or *cursus* that saw him holding a succession of roles, some essentially civilian in nature, others with the army. As provincial governor, he combined both the civil and the military roles, administering the province or leading an army as the

---

[11] Examples of small independent armies are common in Josephus. e.g. under legionary legates: 1,000 cavalry and 2,000 infantry under Trajan, *BJ* 3. 289; 600 cavalry and 3,000 infantry under Cerealis, *BJ* 3. 310; an unknown number of horse and foot under the same man, *BJ* 4. 552: under tribunes: 1,000 cavalry and 6,000 infantry under Placidus, *BJ* 3. 59; 1,000 cavalry under the same man, *BJ* 3. 144; 500 horse and 3,000 foot again under Placidus, *BJ* 5. 419; the prefect Antonius commanded an *ala* and a cohort at Ascalon, BJ 3. 12. For the importance of mixed vexillations in general see Ch. 1.

situation required. The result of this was that the commander, representing both military and political authority in the area, normally knew the political aims of any war that he was to fight. Having clear objectives for a conflict was an advantage, making it easier to see clearly what was needed to achieve victory.[12]

Most provincial governors, and therefore most generals, seem to have been in their early forties.[13] There were exceptions: Germanicus' subordinate in Germany in AD 14, Caecina, had already served forty years in the army (*Ann.* 1. 65). Germanicus himself, along with his father Drusus and uncle Tiberius, all had accelerated careers that gave them command of armies when still in their twenties. Titus, who succeeded to the command of the army in Judaea when his father became emperor, was only 29 at the siege of Jerusalem. Although members of the imperial family and commanders produced by the civil wars can provide exceptions, most men served in several capacities with the army before being given a command. In the more formal career structure of the Empire, this involved service as a *tribunus laticlavius* with a legion for perhaps one to three years, and later a spell as a legionary legate, the commander of a legion. There is considerable dispute as to how much an individual's success in such a career, and his chances of going on from it to achieve one of the major army commands were dependent on military ability.[14] What is clear is that the degree of military knowledge to be gained from this service, particularly that as a tribune, depended to a great extent on the individual's inclinations.[15] There was no system of formal training as soldiers, no military college, at any time in Rome's history, so that in this sense all Roman commanders were amateurs.

Some authors have gone further and, because of this amateurism have claimed that 'the natural conclusion is that Roman armies and the

---

[12] For senatorial service in the army in general see R. E. Smith, *Service in the Post-Marian Roman Army* (Manchester, 1958), 59–66, 73–4, and A. von Domaszewski, *Die Rangordnung des römischen Heeres*, 2nd edn. B. Dobson (Cologne, 1967), 'Senatorische Offiziere', 172–84.

[13] J. B. Campbell, 'Who were the *Viri Militares?*' *JRS* 65 (1975), 11–31, esp. 16–17.

[14] E. Birley, 'Senators in the Emperor's Service', and 'Promotion and Transfers in the Roman Army: Senatorial and Equestrian Officers', *The Roman Army*, Papers 1929–1986 (Amsterdam, 1988), 75–114, where the view is that the individual's merit was assessed from an early age. Contrast J. B. Campbell, *JRS* 65 (1975), who plausibly doubts the existence of any rigorous assessment system in the process of promotion.

[15] Tacitus, *Agricola* 5, claimed that Agricola made better use of his service than most tribunes, but this may be merely a conventional compliment.

Roman system did not require too much of their generals'.[16] According to Fuller, the Roman army, being predominantly infantry, was a comparatively simple instrument to use and required of the commander nothing more than a basic knowledge of drill.[17] Messer argued that Roman generals achieved a fairly consistent level of mediocrity, other than exceptional individuals such as Caesar.[18] All these authors agree that the best officers in the Roman army came lower down the command structure, in the form of the 'professional' centurionate.[19] I believe that the emphasis placed by scholars on amateurism and lack of ability amongst Roman commanders rests heavily on anachronistic assumptions of what a general should be.

For our purposes the general's 'staff' may be divided into two sections, namely that element which aided his direction of the army, including administration, the issuing and receipt of orders and information etc., and secondly the fighting troops of his bodyguard. More is known about this second element. Caesar had a bodyguard of 900 cavalry at the beginning of the Civil War (*BC* 1. 41). Most commanders seem to have drawn on the *auxilia* for this unit as did Caesar.[20] Not only did these men act as personal bodyguards, but they also formed an élite reserve force at the commander's immediate disposal (Arrian, *Ectaxis* 22–3; *Hist.* 5. 16). In this respect the *singulares* can be considered in the same way as any other unit in the army. Commanders also seem to have had personal bodyguards following them everywhere. In the rout at Dyrrachium, Caesar attempted to stop one of his standard bearers from running away. The man cut at Caesar with his sword and would have wounded him, had not one of Caesar's attendants cut off his arm (Appian, *BC* 2. 62; Plutarch, *Caesar* 39). Whether these men were drawn from the ranks of the *singulares* is unknown.

We can do little more than guess at the composition of the commander's 'staff' proper. Titus seems to have had centurions seconded from their units in his immediate following and Arrian had both centurions and decurions close to him (*BJ* 6. 262, *Ectaxis* 22). We

---

[16] F. E. Adcock, *The Roman Art of War under the Republic* (Harvard, 1940), 101.

[17] Fuller, *Julius Caesar* 74–5.

[18] W. S. Messer, 'Mutiny in the Roman Army in the Republic', *Class. Phil.* 15 (1920), 158.   [19] Delbrück, *History of the Art of War* 429–36.

[20] e.g. Petreius *BC* 1. 75, Germanicus *Ann.* 2. 16, Titus *BJ* 5. 52; for bodyguards in general see M. P. Speidel, *Guards of the Roman Armies: The Singulares of the Provinces* (Bonn, 1978).

know that many officers did serve away from their units in the retinues of magistrates and commanders, but it is impossible to do more than guess at their precise function. For instance, would a general have sent an order to a subordinate via an officer such as a centurion or merely have used one of his bodyguard as a messenger? It might have been useful for an officer, with a better appreciation of the situation than a ranker, to carry orders, since the recipient could have questioned him about the general's intentions. However, only once is the identity of the messenger revealed, when Otho sent his orders for his generals to advance at the First battle of Cremona by a Numidian courier (Plutarch, *Otho* 9). In this case the orders were written rather than verbal, the instructions plain, and their implementation left to his commanders. Similarly, the *officium* of a governor included numerous *beneficiarii*, drawn normally from the legions, but we do not know whether any or all of these were used to control an army on the battlefield.[21]

A general could also have called upon more senior officers, legates, tribunes, and prefects, to perform a role in his immediate retinue. The only thing that does seem clear is that there was no standard complement for a general's staff, other than the *singulares*. Therefore its effectiveness depended on the commander's own abilities and the qualities of the officers that he had chosen. Many in his following were either his clients, whom he wished to reward, or men recommended to him by friends, who might have similar intentions (Pliny, *Epistulae* 2. 13. 1–3). Caesar had his finest subordinate in Gaul, Labienus, recommended to him by Pompey. Other recommendations were less fortunate, for instance Publius Considius who had made a name for himself under Sulla, but proved incompetent (*BG* 1. 21). The general's staff was thus an improvised, temporary body, capable of development under an able man, but not automatically efficient. Some men may have served on the staff of successive governors, but there was no institutionalization of the means of controlling an army during

---

[21] See N. B. Rankov, 'The Beneficiarii Consularis in the Western Provinces of the Roman Empire', D.Phil. thesis (Oxford, 1986), and E. Schallmayer and others *Der römische Weihebezirk von Osterburken I. Corpus der griechischen und lateinischen Beneficiarier Inschriften des Romischen Reiches* (Wurttemburg, 1990) on the *beneficiarii* in general. An inscription from Samothrace dated to AD 165 lists the staff of a *proconsul*, but the staff of a *legatus Augusti* may well have been much larger, J. H. Oliver, 'A Roman Governor Visits Samothrace', *AJP* 87 (1966), 75–9.

our period.[22] This was to be the case until the early nineteenth century and significantly limited the size of armies.[23] It seems unlikely that a Roman commander's staff could have effectively controlled a very large army, even under the best of commanders. Tiberius did not feel himself capable of controlling ten legions in Pannonia (Velleius 2. 113). This was not a significant disadvantage, since few if any of the military situations facing the Roman army in this period required them to field armies larger than 40–50,000 men, and the forces involved in most battles were a good deal smaller.[24]

RECONNAISSANCE AND INTELLIGENCE

> The whole art of war consists in getting at what lies on the other side of the hill, or, in other words, in deciding what we do not know from what we do.
>
> (Wellington, *The Croker Papers* (1885), iii. 276)

The gathering of intelligence has always played a vital role in any military operation. The urge to see the 'other side of the hill' became even more important as armies developed logistical systems allowing them to stay in the field for longer periods of time and to manœuvre seeking an advantage over the enemy before joining battle.[25] In the ancient world, when armies were small and compact in comparison to the large areas of country a campaign might cover, the simple need to find the enemy was of paramount importance. In 53 BC Quintus Cicero was unaware of the presence of a raiding band of several thousand German cavalry, until their attack came out into the open ground in front of his camp (*BG* 6. 37; cf. Plutarch, *Lucullus* 25). Normally, in Caesar's day, Roman armies attempted to patrol the area around themselves thoroughly enough to prevent such surprises. The presence of Ariovistus' army was discovered when it was 37 km. (23 miles) away from Caesar's vanguard, a distance of at least one day's march (*BG* 1. 41). Except in very mountainous terrain, reconnaissance was primarily carried out by the cavalry. Under the Republic, Rome's

---

[22] The provincial *officia* were clearly organized, but it is unclear if any part of this was given a battlefield role, Rankov, 'The Beneficiarii Consularis', 33–96.

[23] M. Van Crefeld, *Command in War* (Harvard, 1985), Ch. 2.

[24] There are few reliable figures for the size of armies. According to Caesar, *BC* 3. 88–9, Pompey commanded 47,000 men at Pharsalus. There is no evidence for any permanent unit larger than a legion, which suggests that very large armies were not contemplated. [25] See Ch. 2.

allies provided this section of the army, so that the degree to which scouting was important in native warfare greatly affected how good these horsemen were at this task. Under the Principate, the *auxilia* steadily became more regimented and the better-trained cavalry could normally have been expected to perform the reconnaissance role efficiently. There were also units of *exploratores*, whose primary function was the gathering of intelligence.[26] Titus in Judaea, and later Arrian in Cappodocia, screened the advance of their army with auxiliary cavalry, who patrolled ahead to discover any ambush.[27]

Once the enemy was known to be nearby, his exact location, strength, and intentions would have been sought to influence the plan of campaign. Much information could have been gained from the local population, if these were at all friendly or neutral. Antony was warned by local civilians of the presence of Pompey's army near to his camp, which had been concealed by the latter's refusal to allow his men to light camp fires. Information could also be gained from enemy captives or deserters. Caesar and Vespasian amongst other commanders seem often to have interrogated prisoners themselves.[28] Even the appearance of captives and deserters could have been used to estimate how well supplied the enemy was and the level of his morale.[29]

A picture of the enemy could have been gained from these sources, but the best way to find out anything about him was, and has always been, to go and look. Whenever close to the enemy, cavalry patrols kept him under observation, so that for instance in 57 BC, Caesar's scouts immediately reported the withdrawal of the Belgae, although this occurred at midnight, making it clear that patrols were maintained day and night (*BG* 2. 11). The disorderly way in which armies of Germans or Gauls moved made this observation simpler,[30] so that it was comparatively easy for Caesar to follow the Helvetii for a fortnight

---

[26] K. R. Dixon and P. Southern, *The Roman Cavalry* (London, 1992), 138–40, for brief comment on the role of cavalry in intelligence gathering. On reconnaissance and *exploratores* in general see M. P. Speidel, 'The Captor of Decebalus', *Roman Army Studies*, i (Amsterdam, 1984), 182, and '*Exploratores*: Mobile Elite Units of Roman Germany', *Epigraphische Studien*, 13 (1983), 63–78. On the institutionalization of intelligence from the mid-2 cent. onwards see N. B. Rankov, 'M. Oclatinius Adventus in Britain', *Britannia*, 18 (1987), 243–9, see Ch. 3, 'The Order of March'.

[27] *BJ* 3. 115–26, 5. 47–9; *Ectaxis* 1.

[28] *BG* 8. 7; *BC* 1. 66; Josephus, *BJ*. 3. 142–3, 3. 318. The last passage emphasizes the danger of the captive giving false information.

[29] e.g. *African War* 44–6, where the behaviour of captured Caesarian troops is used to illustrate the morale of his army.   [30] e.g. *Ann.* 2. 11; see Ch. 2, 45–8, 57.

at a distance of 8–10 km. (5–6 miles) (*BG* I. 15). The general had to deduce what reports of the enemy's activity revealed of his actual intentions. Thus, when the movement of troops around Pompey's camp at Pharsalus, and particularly the reflections from their shields, was reported to Caesar, he concluded that Pompey planned to give battle, and consequently gave the order for his own army to prepare (Plutarch, *Pompey* 68). A cloud of dust betrayed the movement of any large body of men in all except the coldest or wettest conditions.[31] Apparently, a high, thin cloud of dust suggested the movement of cavalry, and a more dense, lower cloud that of infantry or transport.[32] At Pharsalus, which may have been fought on an untypically dry plain, Pompey was able to deduce that his left flanking cavalry had been defeated by the direction of the cloud of dust thrown up by their hooves (Plutarch, *Pompey* 72).

When two opposing armies were close together, not only could a general observation be maintained, but specific patrols could be made to look for weaknesses in the enemy's defences that might be exploited.[33] Caesar personally made two reconnaissances of Gergovia before mounting an initially successful attack on a weak spot in the Gallic line, which was discovered in the second patrol (*BG* 7. 36, 7. 44). Whenever an assault on a town or fortification was planned, a reconnaissance was first carried out, usually by the commander himself.[34] In this case, the high risk of failure and loss of life, inherent in the assault on any strong position, and the amount of time and labour involved in siegeworks, made the responsibility for gaining the information on which to base planned operations too great for the commander to delegate. During the younger Crassus' attack on a Gallic camp in 56 BC, scouts sent out earlier reported a weakness in the defences at the rear of the Gallic position (*BG* 3. 25–6). In Judaea in AD 66 Cestius Gallus was unable to take a strong hilltop position held by the Jews until a way around the flank was discovered and the position turned (*BJ* 2. 511–12). Another strong position held by the Treveri was taken in the same way in AD 70 by Cerialis (*Hist.* 4. 71).

---

[31] *BG* 4. 37; *BC* 3. 36; *African War* 12; Plut. *Pompey* 72; App. *BC.* 2. 55; Onasander, *The General* 6. 8.

[32] H. Whitehouse, *Battle in Africa 1879–1914* (Camberley, 1987), 35.

[33] *BG* I. 21, 2. 17, 4. 21; *BC.*2. 24, 3. 38, 3. 41; App. *BC* 2. 104.

[34] *BG* 5. 36; Josephus, *BJ* 4. 92, 5. 52–3, 5. 258–62, 7. 190; *Dio* 68. 31. 3 for instances of Roman commanders personally reconnoitring enemy positions.

In the last two incidents it was the discovery of an alternative route around the enemy position that brought victory. It was important to gain as much knowledge as possible regarding the terrain over which an army planned to move or fight. In Spain in 49 BC both Caesar and Afranius sent officers with a party of cavalry to reconnoitre the terrain over which the armies planned to march. Caesar's patrol discovered a previously unknown route and his army was able to steal a march over their opponents the next day (*BC* 1. 66). In Africa in 46 BC, Caesar halted his advance over a line of hills in order to survey the terrain (*African War* 38). The Romans may not have rationalized the topographical information into the same form of maps as would be understandable to the modern mind, but it is clear that they understood the importance of terrain, and sought to exploit it to their advantage. The reconnaissance of dead ground or terrain, such as woods, that might have concealed troops, seems to have been standard practice. Scipio's cavalry in 48 BC discovered the concealed army of Domitius Calvinus, when they heard the neighing of some horses. Instead of the whole army falling into a trap, only two *turmae* were caught (BC 3. 38). At Forum Gallorum, Antony's army concealed in a marsh was betrayed to Pansa by the swaying of reeds and the gleam of equipment (Appian, *BC* 3. 67).

One incident from the Gallic Wars, which seems to bring out many of the aspects discussed so far is worth study in some depth.

That same day the patrols brought word that the Helvetii had stopped at the foot of a hill eight miles [13 km.] from Caesar's camp, whereupon he sent a party to reconnoitre the hill and find out what the ascent was like on the farther side. They reported that it was quite easy. Shortly after midnight he explained his plans to Labienus, his second-in-command, and detailed him to climb to the summit with two legions, taking as guides the men who had reconnoitred the ground. In the early hours of the morning Caesar himself marched towards the enemy, following the route by which they had proceeded, and sending all the cavalry in front. They were preceded by a patrol under the command of Publius Considius, who was reported a first-class soldier, and had served under Sulla and later under Crassus.

At daybreak Labienus was actually in possession of the summit, while Caesar was not more than a mile and a half [2.5 km.] from the enemy's camp; and he learned afterwards from prisoners that neither his own approach nor that of Labienus had been observed. But suddenly Considius galloped up and said that the hill Labienus had been sent to occupy was held by the enemy; he knew this, he said, because he had recognized their Gallic arms and the crests of their helmets. Accordingly, Caesar withdrew to a hill close by and formed his line of battle. Labienus had been instructed not to engage until Caesar's force was seen close to the enemy's camp, so that they might be attacked on all sides at once. After occupying the hill, therefore, he was waiting for Caesar to appear, without offering battle. (*BG* 1. 21–2)

Although this operation ended in failure, the procedure followed by Caesar's army would be familiar in principle to any modern army. This procedure may be broken down into the following stages:

1. Caesar received reports on the Helvetii's location and intention (i.e. camping for the night) from routine patrols.
2. Another patrol was sent out with the specific intention of exploring the terrain along the route to the enemy camp, and particularly the ease of ascent on the reverse slope of the hill behind the enemy camp (and therefore invisible from it).
3. Using the information gained from both of the above reconnaissances, Caesar formulated his plan of an attack from two directions on the enemy camp.
4. Caesar then briefed the man who would lead the outflanking force to seize the high ground above the Gallic camp. This job was entrusted to his best subordinate, Labienus, who then briefed his own officers.
5. Labienus led out his command and was guided along the same route followed by the previous day's patrol (2) by men who had taken part in it. He succeeded in reaching his objective without being discovered, and following his orders waited for Caesar's approach.
6. Later Caesar followed him using the same route which the patrol had established was free from any obstacles.
7. Caesar advanced in the normal way, with his cavalry leading the column to spring any ambush, and cavalry patrols even further ahead. These reported that Labienus had failed to take or hold his objective.
8. Caesar, unwilling to be attacked whilst in column of march, withdrew to the nearest suitable defensive position and formed a hasty line of battle. As a result of this delay the Helvetii were able to march away unmolested on the next morning.

Several points deserve emphasis in this process. First the vital importance of gaining both specific and general information about both the enemy and the terrain, before planning and whilst putting into practice any operation. The one attempted by Caesar was particularly complicated, involving a combined attack by two columns converging on the enemy after a long night march. At least two patrols were made before the operation was decided upon and planned. During his advance to meet Labienus, Caesar sent more patrols forward to discover any changes in the situation. Both Roman columns followed the route reconnoitred by the earlier patrol, so that not only did they not get lost, but no previously unknown obstacles, such as rivers or dense woodland, delayed or impeded the march. The second point deserving emphasis is the report, made to Caesar by Publius Considius, that the Gauls were in the position held by Labienus. The vital importance of intelligence concerning the enemy and the terrain in any operation made the commander very dependent on the quality of the officers leading his patrols, and of the horsemen who served under them. Considius panicked, or was mistaken, and his report halted the whole operation. As mentioned earlier, it seems to have been very common for a commander to go out to reconnoitre personally, especially if the information sought would affect a major operation. Not only would the general have felt more confident in relying on his own judgement of the situation, but knowledge of his own intentions allowed him to seek specific information required by his plans.

One factor in this operation which would not be comprehensible to a modern army is the complete inactivity of the Helvetii, who failed to discover either of the Roman columns and marched on the next day as if nothing had happened. Either their patrolling was very poorly performed, or they had not bothered to mount any at all. Against other armies, the Romans did not enjoy this luxury. At Carrhae, almost all of Crassus' scouts were captured or killed by the Parthians (Plutarch, *Crassus* 23). Therefore, if a commander chose to accompany a patrol personally, it could be dangerous. Titus was cut off by a sudden Jewish sally whilst making an appreciation of the defences of Jerusalem (*BJ* 5. 56). On another occasion he only escaped when his horse had been killed by mounting another horse whose rider had been pulled down (Suetonius, *Titus* 4). At the siege of Hatra, a trooper standing next to Trajan as part of a patrol was struck by an arrow (Dio 68. 31. 3).

Apart from the risk that the enemy would capture or kill the patrols or prevent them from gaining the information they sought, there was also the danger that the enemy would attempt to feed them false information. A high proportion of the stratagems included in

Frontinus, and to a lesser extent in Onasander, concern ways of convincing the enemy that you plan to do one thing, before doing another (Frontinus, *Strategemata* 2 and 8). Before his attack on Gergovia, Caesar ordered his camp followers to be given helmets and a semblance of armour and to ride mules and pack horses, converging at one spot. A few real cavalrymen were sent around the flanks and in advance to add to the impression of a large body of cavalry moving towards one point in the Gallic defences. The Gauls, unable to penetrate the disguise at that distance, shifted their reserves towards this perceived threat. Caesar attacked elsewhere and initially achieved a great success (*BG* 7. 45). In Armenia, Corbulo was to conceal the size of his army by massing the troops of two legions and placing them under a single eagle.[35] These ploys often appear very obvious, but it seems that anything more complicated may not have succeeded in giving the enemy the desired impression. The art of command, as a result, included the skill of being able to see the 'other side of the hill' yourself, whilst preventing the enemy from discerning your own real strength and intentions. In this respect an important skill of generalship involved reconnaissance and intelligence. The development of units of *exploratores*, specifically dedicated to this role shows that the gathering of intelligence was considered important and necessary by the Romans themselves.

DEPLOYMENT AND FORMING A LINE OF BATTLE

> Sabinus, having failed to foresee what might happen, now got excited and ran to and fro arranging the cohorts; but even this he did nervously and in a way which showed that he was at his wit's end—as generally happens to those who are compelled to make decisions when a battle has actually begun.
>
> (Caesar *BG* 5. 33)

In the incident discussed in the last section, Caesar briefed Labienus on the projected operation as soon as he had formulated his plan. It seems to have been normal practice, whenever there was time, for a commander to hold a *consilium* before battle. Caesar did so on board ship before attempting to land in Britain (*BG* 4. 23), and in the field

---

[35] *Ann.* 13. 38, cf. *BG* 5. 50, *BC* 3. 38, where the size of marching camps were altered to give a false impression of an armies size.

before launching the attack on Gergovia (*BG* 7. 45). The practice was certainly followed throughout our period, and *consilia* are frequently mentioned in Josephus' account of the Jewish War.[36] Those present at the *consilium* seem to have varied, depending on the situation and size of the army. Invariably the legates were present, the tribunes were often included, and prefects and centurions, particularly the *primi ordines*, might have been.[37] What is clear, is that the commanders of all the major sub-units of the army, be they legions or collections of auxiliary *alae* or cohorts, were included.

The officers present often seem to have expressed opinions on the tactical situation and recommended certain courses of action. Probably under the Republic, when for instance an inexperienced commander such as Cicero in 51 BC deliberately took experienced *legati* with him, their advice may well have been followed.[38] What is important to note is that almost invariably the commander is represented as having the final decision after the other officers had spoken, and he might reject all their suggestions. The only exception to this is Caesar's account of the *consilium* called by Sabinus and Cotta, including their tribunes and senior centurions, when their camp was attacked in late 55 BC (*BG* 5. 28–9). The impression given by the passage is that Caesar had not clearly appointed one of the legates as commander of the garrison. It is possible that in wishing to avoid personal responsibility for a major disaster, Caesar concentrates on the divided command to explain the defeat. He was still indirectly responsible, if it was his own failure to appoint an overall commander that precipitated disaster, but the blame was more distant. Whether Caesar's account of this debate is accurate or not, it does not change the general conclusion that the commanders' *consilium* was not normally a forum for debate, not a 'Council of War' as the term is often translated. Rather it was more akin to the Orders or 'O' Group of the modern British army, at which a commander explains his plan and issues orders to his subordinates. We do not know whether the commander's orders were written or verbal, or perhaps a combination of both.[39] At the *consilium*, the general

---

[36] *BJ* 3. 161–2, 4. 366–78, 5. 491–502, 6. 236–243, cf. in the Civil War of AD 69, Plut. *Otho* 8–9.

[37] *BG* 4. 23, 5. 28–31, 7. 45, *BC* 2. 30, *BJ* 3. 162, 4. 366–78, 5. 491–502, 6. 236–43.

[38] D. Stockton, *Cicero* (1971), 231.

[39] The *memorandum* from Vindolanda shows that some information and advice might be written down, see A. K. Bowman and J. D. Thomas, 'New Texts from Vindolanda', *Britannia*, 18 (1987), 125–42 = *Tab. Vindol.* ii. 164.

explained his plan and issued direct orders to his subordinates. In a large army, these men might then have gone and held lesser *consilia* with their own immediate subordinates, explaining their own command's role in the operation. Onasander described this process as follows:

The General should communicate his orders to his higher officers and they should repeat them to the officers next below them who in turn pass them to their subordinates, and so on to the lowest, the higher officers in each case telling the orders to those below them. (*The General* 25. 2)

These orders would have included such aspects as the unit's position, objectives, and information about friendly units to their flanks or rear and an assessment of enemy intentions. In forming his plan of action, the commander was of course exercising his skills in generalship, but it should not be forgotten that at the *consilium* it was also his qualities as a leader that could inspire confidence in his subordinates and, through them, the rest of the army.

One of the most significant elements within a commander's orders would have dealt with the formation that the army was to adopt. The order of battle of an army varied according to the individual circumstances and terrain. In 49 BC, Caesar fought an action on a hillock below the town of Ilerda. Although the top of the hill was relatively flat, the sides were too steep for units to move on, so that only three cohorts on either side could be put into line. In most large-scale actions the terrain was more open and level, so that more of the army could be put into the line. Terrain still had its uses. A hilltop position, for instance, gave an advantage to a unit charging downhill (*BG* 1. 24–5). Since Roman armies were often significantly smaller than their enemies, it was often important to secure the army's flanks on some obstacle. In AD 60 Suetonius Paulinus placed his army in a defile with a wood at his back to protect his flanks and rear. Arrian planned to form his battle line against the Alans with a hill at each flank (*Ectaxis* 12). If necessary, and if time permitted, a position could be strengthened with ditches and earthworks, if nature had not provided such defences. Sulla at Chaeronea dug trenches to protect his flanks from the more numerous army of Mithridates (Frontinus, *Strategemata* 2. 3. 17). Caesar once strengthened his position when facing the Belgians in a similar manner (*BG* 2. 8).

In open battle the protection of the flanks was normally a task performed by the cavalry. Horsemen were always more mobile than men on foot and so more able to turn to face or manœuvre against any threat to the wings. Because of the speed of their mounts, both in advance and retreat, cavalry were also inherently less stable than infantry, less suitable for the central body of an army.[40] The formation adopted by Suetonius Paulinus against Boudicca (Fig. 1) provides an illustration of what in general outline may be taken as a 'typical' battle order. The auxiliary cavalry were divided between the two wings. The centre was formed by the infantry, in this case auxiliary cohorts on either side of the legionaries. Agricola's formation at Mons Graupius (Fig. 2) provides an example of a variation on this basic pattern. Again cavalry formed both wings, but here they were supported by more *alae* behind the main line. The centre was formed by 8,000 auxiliary infantry, with the vexillations of several legions in reserve, in front of the army's camp.

The arrangement of legionary and auxiliary infantry seems to have varied considerably. Agricola placed the *auxilia* in the front line, which mounted his main attack, as did Petilius Cerialis in AD 71 (*Hist.* 5. 17). In Spain in 49 BC, Afranius formed his infantry up with the cohorts of five legions in two lines in front of a single line of predominantly

Fig. 1. Plan of the deployment of the army under Suetonius Paulinus in AD 60

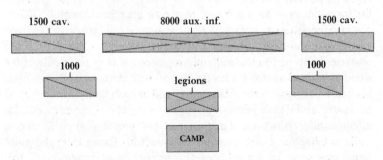

Fig. 2. The formation of the Roman army at Mons Graupius in AD 84

[40] See Ch. 5, 'Cavalry against Cavalry'.

Spanish *auxilia*. Suetonius Paulinus and Arrian both formed their *auxilia* on the flanks of the legions. Crassus in Gaul in 56 BC did the reverse, placing his allies in the centre of the line with the legionaries on their flanks (*BG* 3. 24). Under the Principate the majority of auxiliary infantry seem to have been close-formation, armoured troops whose tactical role differed little, or not at all, from that of the legionaries, so it seems that their position in the line was not dictated by any specific role, but varied according to circumstances.[41]

Arrian's battle order against the Alans provides us with the most detailed account we possess of the planned deployment of any Roman army (Fig. 3). His flanks rested on high ground, each defended by auxiliary heavy infantry, supported by light infantry, archers and artillery firing over their heads from the slopes behind them. The centre was composed of *Legio XV Apollinaris* and part of *Legio XII Fulminata*, formed in a single line of cohorts each eight ranks deep. Behind these was a single rank of infantry archers, with horse-archers behind them, both firing in support over the heads of the infantry. The remainder of the cavalry was massed in reserve to guard the two flanks. The ultimate reserve was provided by the general's own *singulares*. The enemy army on this occasion was a tribe of Alans, whose sole tactic consisted of a headlong charge by a mass of heavily armoured horsemen, and Arrian's formation was designed solely to counter this threat. The main infantry line was so solid that providing the troops remained steady, the Alans would be unable to break it. The fire support of archers and artillery was intended to ensure the infantry remained in place and kept in a steady formation by deterring the Alans from coming too close. The cavalry was ready to ward off any threat to the flanks and to pursue the enemy once he had been driven off. Arrian's formation was appropriate for a single tactical situation, namely facing an exclusively cavalry army with one containing a high proportion of infantry. It should not be taken as evidence of changes in the tactical practices of Roman forces throughout the Empire in the second century AD.[42] Rather it should be seen as a sign of the flexibility of the Roman system, that using essentially the same mixture of forces, they could develop a method of successfully opposing very different types of armies.

---

[41] See Ch. 1.

[42] e.g. M. P. Speidel, *The Framework of an Imperial Roman Legion*, Fifth Annual Caerleon Lecture (Cardiff, 1992), 14–19, or E. Wheeler, 'The Roman Legion as Phalanx', *Chiron*, 9 (1979), 303–18.

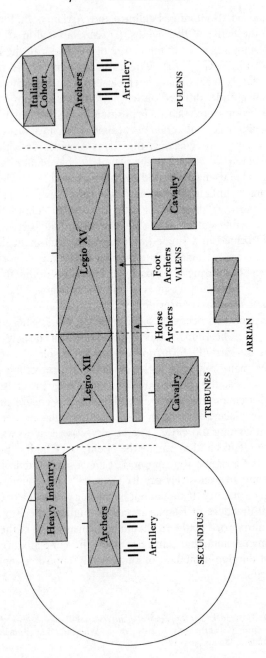

Fig. 3. Arrian's formation against the Alans

In all the Roman deployments discussed so far, a high proportion of the army was kept initially in reserve behind the first line of battle. I have found only one occasion on which a Roman army deployed its units in a single line. This was in 46 BC when Caesar in Africa was faced by an enemy force consisting primarily of cavalry and light infantry which so significantly outnumbered him that he felt it necessary to extend his line at the expense of its depth (*African War* 13). In the engagement, Caesar came close to defeat and was only saved by a desperate charge (*African War* 17). At Forum Gallorum, Pansa may have formed his cohorts into a single line whilst waiting for his two other legions to arrive (Cicero, *ad Fam.* 10. 30. 3). On all other occasions where the army's formation is recorded the battle line was always formed by at least two lines of cohorts (*BG* 1. 49, 3. 24), and the *triplex acies* of three lines was the most common of all formations.[43] At Pharsalus, to counter the threat posed by the mass of cavalry on Pompey's left flank, Caesar added a fourth line behind *Legio X* drawn from one cohort from each of the third lines of the other legions in the army. There is some suggestion that the first and second lines worked together very closely, being mutually supporting. When the Younger Crassus discovered a weak spot in the enemy camp he was attacking in 56 BC, he attacked it not with men from his second line, but with cohorts that had been left to guard his own camp (*BG* 3. 26). When a fresh enemy force attacked Caesar's army, engaged with the Helvetii in 58 BC, the first two lines were left to continue fighting the main enemy body, whilst the third was drawn off to meet the new threat (*BG* 1. 25). In the battle against Ariovistus later the same year, the Germans began to outflank the Roman left. Again it was the third line of cohorts that was used to counter this (*BG* 1. 52). At Pharsalus, Caesar specifically ordered the third line only to engage on his signal (*BC* 3. 94). The implication is that the second line quickly became involved in combat soon after the first line met the enemy. As a result it either could not be withdrawn and redeployed at all, or would in doing so have seriously weakened the army's front line. Therefore the possession of a third line gave the commander a reserve that could be more easily channelled to meet any sudden threats. On some occasions he arranged to have even more of a reserve than this, and placed whole legions behind the main line.[44]

---

[43] e.g. *BG* 1. 24, 1. 52, *BC* 1. 41, 1. 83, 3. 88–9, *African War* 81.

[44] *BG* 1.24, 2.8, where in each case Caesar posted his two least experienced legions behind the main line.

If the three lines were formed in each sector by individual legions, the normal arrangement seems to have been to have four cohorts in the first line, and three each in the second and third (*BC* 1. 83). Caesar reduced the last line to two cohorts in his deployment at Pharsalus mentioned above. Vegetius gives the formation of the *antiqua legio* as essentially in two lines (Vegetius 2. 4–14). The first line was composed of (from right to left) the First, Third, and Fifth cohorts, with the Second and Fourth slightly behind in the intervals between the other units. The second was made up of the Sixth, Eighth, and Tenth, with the Ninth and Seventh supporting them. The best troops appear to have been the units on the flanks of the formation, especially the first cohort on the right. The suggestion that the first cohort was normally in the front line of a legion is supported by an incident at the first battle of Cremona, when *Legio I Adiutrix* overran the first line of *Legio XXI Rapax*, capturing its eagle. *I Adiutrix* was in turn driven back, losing many *signa* and having its legate, Orfidius Benignus, killed by the supporting lines of the Vitellian legion (*Hist.* 2. 43). The implication is that the first cohort, which carried the eagle, was in the first line of the legion. The placing of the best cohorts on the flanks of the legion's formation, described by Vegetius, mirrored the common practice of placing the best troops on the flanks of the army's battle line. At Pharsalus, Caesar placed the veteran *Legio X* on the right, reinforcing them with a fourth line, and held his left with the equally experienced *VIII* and *IX* combined as one formation, since both were heavily depleted by casualties (*BC* 3. 89). The imperial practice of sometimes entrusting the flanks to the *auxilia* may well show the high degree of confidence felt in this arm of the service.[45] Caesar's combining of the weakened *VIII* and *IX* at Pharsalus shows that even if there was a standard formation for the cohorts of a legion, this could be set aside when the conditions of campaigning rendered it unsuitable.

A cohort of 480 men would have covered an area of 146 by 6.4 m. (160 by 7 yards), if deployed in three ranks. A cohort of 800 men covered about 247 by 6.4 m. (270 by 7 yards).[46] It is however, difficult to calculate the area occupied by a legion, even assuming it was at full strength, because we have no information on how large the intervals between the cohorts were. Arrian planned for his legionary line to remain static when attacked by the Alans and so formed the cohorts in one continuous block. Once the enemy had been forced to withdraw,

---

[45] See Ch. 1.   [46] See Ch. 5, 'Formations'.

the legions were to divide up into their separate cohorts, leaving gaps in the line. This allowed first the cavalry to pursue, passing through the gaps, and then the infantry themselves to advance (*Ectaxis* 27). If the legions had attempted to advance in one solid block, they would have moved slowly and their officers would soon have lost control over their men, making manœuvre impossible. The reason for this is that it is inordinately difficult to march in a perfectly straight line. A minor shift in direction by an individual within a formation will be transferred to the other members, resulting in a more significant cumulative shift in the unit as a whole. This can be shown by watching any large-scale military parade, such as the annual Trooping of the Colour by the Household Brigade at Horseguards' Parade in London. During any such ceremony, the parading troops will stop on numerous occasions to dress their ranks, minor irregularities having appeared. Although the manœuvres in such parades are often highly complex, they are being performed by troops with an exceptionally high standard of drill on a perfectly flat parade ground. Anyone with a knowledge of drill will realize how much more difficult it is to march across broken, soft, or boggy ground, compared to a drill square. The irregularities of the ground will soon cause the ranks to become ragged and any forward movement will almost inevitably be subject to a gradual drift to the left or right. Going up or down a slope will tend to make this drift more pronounced as individuals instinctively try to take the easiest path. The longer a line is, the more difficult its movement will be. More irregularities in the ground will be encountered, slowing sections of the line down and gradually breaking it up. If the officers do not frequently halt the line to dress the ranks, then the unit will swiftly become disordered, making it less able to respond to orders, and therefore to manœuvre. The result is that a formation with a narrower frontage will move quicker than a wider unit. Judging from the experience of armies in the seventeenth, eighteenth, and nineteenth, centuries, a frontage of about 500 men is the maximum practical, if a unit is to move in formation. About half that number would seem to be closer to the ideal.[47]

This tendency of units to drift gradually to left or right, instead of advancing in a straight line, which may have been even more pronounced if the Romans also suffered from the tendency of Greek hoplites to edge to the right (Thucydides 5. 71), meant that units

---

[47] J. Weller, *Wellington in the Peninsula* (London, 1992), 23–7.

advancing on parallel courses would have tended to converge. If the intervals between the units were not large enough, then the formations would collide, causing disorder, the units losing their separate identity. The result would have been a mob of men, incapable of manœuvre or changing formation.[48] This was normally the result when massed columns composed of numerous regiments were adopted in the nineteenth century. MacDonald's Corps at Wagram in 1809, Soult's divisions at Alburea in 1811, and D'Erlon's corps at Waterloo in 1815, were all employed in large formations composed of combinations of battalions in initially separate units. After only a comparatively short advance on all these occasions, the battalions merged into a large disordered mob, incapable of reacting to the changing tactical situation, so that all were defeated with heavy losses.[49]

Intervals between units were therefore essential if the army planned to move even a short distance. The size of these intervals seems unlikely to have been larger than the frontage of the unit itself and may have been significantly less. This would give a maximum frontage of 1,125 m. (1,230 yards) for a legion with three cohorts of 480 men and one of 800 in its front line. Normally the frontage must have been a lot less. Most scholars seem to have assumed that although the legion advanced with intervals between its cohorts, it fought as a solid continuous line.[50] If this was not so, then it is claimed that an enemy charge would have flooded through the gaps in the Roman line causing this to collapse. This theory ignores the fact that for the enemy army to have advanced, it must also have had intervals between its units. We shall find later that there is considerably more evidence for the battle line being more open and fluid during combat than has normally been suggested.[51]

Under the Republic, legions had no legate as a permanent commander, so that it was normal before an army's deployment for the general to allocate officers to command these units.[52] In the battle against

---

[48] This seems to have happened to the Pompeian cavalry at Pharsalus, see Fuller, *Julius Caesar*, 237–8.

[49] See Weller, *Wellington in the Peninsula*, 175–81 on Alburea, and J. R. Elting, *Swords around a Throne* (London, 1988), 536–7.

[50] For a convenient summary of the arguments on this question, see T. Rice Holmes, *Caesar's conquest of Gaul* (Oxford, 1911), 587–99.

[51] See Chs. 4 and 5.

[52] See Smith, *Service in the Post-Marian Army*, 62–6.

Ariovistus in 58 BC, Caesar placed his five *legati* and his *quaestor* in charge of each of his six legions (*BG* 1. 52). In very large armies there might have been another level of officers between the commander-in-chief and the commanders of legions or groups of *auxilia*. The normal practice seems in this case to have been to divide the army into a centre and two wings. At Pharsalus, Pompey commanded the left of the line, Metellus Scipio the centre, and Afranius the right. Caesar had placed Antony on the left, Cnaeus Domitius in the centre, and Publius Sulla on the right. Since Caesar himself spent most of the battle on the right, Publius Sulla's command may have been little more than nominal (*BC* 3. 88–9). However, had Caesar moved elsewhere along the line, Sulla would have resumed full responsibility for the area. At Chaeronea, Sulla controlled the right, Galba and Hortensius the centre and reserves, and Murena the left flank (Plutarch, *Sulla* 17).

Arrian's *Ectaxis* provides us with an example of the command structure in an Imperial army (Fig. 3). On the rising ground to the right, a mixed force of Armenian archers, artillery and the Italian cohort was all under the command of the commander of the latter unit, the prefect Pulcher. On the hill to the left, a comparable force of auxiliary heavy and light infantry and artillery was led by Secundius. Valens, legate of *XV Apollinaris*, not only commanded his own legion, but all troops on the right of the army. This included the horse and foot archers behind his legion, the massed reserve cavalry covering the right flank and Pulcher and his whole command. Similar authority over the left of the army was vested in the tribunes of *XII Fulminata*, presumably led by the *laticlavius*, if he was present. This command included the legion, the cavalry behind it and the auxiliary 'brigade' or 'battle-group' of Secundius. In overall command of the army was Arrian himself, or Xenophon as he chose to describe himself in the *Ectaxis*.

Having considered the deployment of the army, it is useful to examine the actual tactics used by the general to achieve victory, since the commander's objectives would have influenced his actions during the battle. Even in defence, it seems to have been rare for the army to be static, and normally it counter-attacked. Suetonius Paulinus did this against Boudicca in AD 60, despite being heavily outnumbered (*Ann.* 14. 37). Arrian planned to advance in pursuit of the Alans once their initial charge had been defeated (*Ectaxis* 27–9). The emphasis on adopting and maintaining the offensive apparent in Roman strategy was thus equally dominant in the armies' tactics.[53] In general terms, the most common aim in battle was either to break or outflank the enemy's line. His remaining forces could then be easily 'rolled up' by attacks on their flank, resulting in a complete rout. The Roman emphasis on maintaining a high proportion of the army in reserve ensured that there was normally a body of fresh troops on hand to exploit the situation if the enemy's line had been turned or broken. Breaks in the opposing line were or were not created, depending on the relative fighting skills of the troops facing each other. The general could not really plan for this, only exploit it. He could however, have planned to outflank his opponent. At Pharsalus, Pompey hoped to outflank Caesar's right wing with his far more numerous cavalry. When these were driven from the field, his own left was in turn threatened by Caesar's right, leading him to hold his men back (Appian, *BC* 2. 79). These outflanking manœuvres occurred on the battlefield itself, but as we have seen in the section on reconnaissance, columns could be sent on a long march, out of the enemy's view, to strike against his rear or flank. This was attempted by Labienus against the Helvetii in 58 BC, and used successfully by Cestius Gallus in Judaea in AD 66 and Petilius Cerialis near Trier in AD 70.[54] The latter, in a later battle, sent two *alae*, led by a Batavian deserter, on a long outflanking march to attack Civilis in the rear (*Hist.* 5. 18). Marius concealed a force of 3,000 men behind the lines of the Teutones, to fall on their rear (Plutarch, *Marius* 20). These were led by Marcellus who, since Marius had no way of communicating with him, was ordered to engage on his own initiative. Frontinus records more cases of outflanking manœuvres in his *Stratagems* than of any other type of operation (Frontinus, *Strategemata* 2. 3. 1–24).

As with so many of the other skills of generalship, the art lay in achieving such surprises whilst preventing the enemy from doing the same thing to you. Roman armies were themselves very susceptible to attacks in the flank. In AD 69 the defection of a Batavian *ala* resulted in the army of Munius Lupercus being rolled up from the flanks (*Hist.* 4. 18). Only the quality of the legionaries, and their being deployed in depth, prevented a complete rout on this occasion, and gave the withdrawal some semblance of order. In the battles against the Helvetii and Ariovistus in 58 BC, the existence of unengaged reserves, in both

---

[53] See Chs. 3 and 5.   [54] *BG* 1. 21–2, *BJ* 2. 511–12, *Hist.* 4. 71.

cases the third line of the legions, allowed the Romans to fight off threats to their flanks (*BG* 1. 25, 1. 52).

One aspect of warfare which appears with great frequency in the sources for the late Republic, but not in those for the rest of our period, is the tendency for armies to remain in very close proximity with one or both sides offering battle, but without fighting actually taking place. This was certainly a feature of most warfare for centuries before our period and it may simply be that it continued, but is not mentioned in the less detailed sources for the Principate.[55] Armies often manœuvred close to each other with no actual fighting beyond the odd skirmish taking place. Caesar followed the Helvetii at a distance of 8–10 km. (5–6 miles) for a fortnight before attempting an attack (*BG* 1. 15). The campaign in Spain in 49 BC consisted of as much manœuvring as fighting. Caesar camped 2 miles from Ariovistus in 58 BC, and for five days led out his army, formed it into a line of battle and offered to fight. Apart from a little skirmishing, the Germans refused to engage (*BG* 1. 48). In the next year, the Belgae camped only 3 km. (2 miles) from the Roman army, and for several days both sides deployed holding strong positions. Neither side was willing to attack the other, so eventually the Belgae were forced to disperse because their supplies ran out (*BG* 2. 7). Later in the Gallic Wars, the Gauls surrounding the camp of Sabinus daily offered battle, which the Romans refused to join (*BG* 5. 17). In 52 BC, on different occasions, both Caesar and Vercingetorix offered battle from a strong position, which the other refused to attack (*BG* 7. 19, 7. 53).

In the Civil War, the practice seems to have been common. At least twice in the Spanish campaign of 49 BC, both Caesar and the Pompeians formed up in battle order, facing each other, but did not actually engage (*BC* 1. 41, 1. 83). Often the distance mentioned between the two camps of the opposing armies is 3 km. (2 miles) (*African War* 75), although on one occasion this was initially as great as 6 miles before the Caesarian army advanced (*BC* 3. 37). On one occasion in 46 BC, the opposing armies drew up only half a kilometre (a quarter of a mile) apart, without actually fighting. Hirtius commented that to be this close without fighting was considered exceptional (*African War* 61). Many more instances of armies facing each other

[55] For Greek parallels see W. K. Pritchett, *The Greek State at War*, ii (1974), 147–55.

without fighting occur in the first century BC.[56] In a civil war, there could clearly have been a political advantage in allowing the enemy to start the fighting. Shorter-term advantages could also have been sought, as for instance in 48 BC, when Curio's army faced that of Varus in Africa. Varus attempted to encourage the former Pompeian soldiers in the Caesarian army to desert (*BC* 2. 27). Another factor to be considered in fighting another Roman army was that if the opposition drew up close to their own camp, they would receive the significant advantage of supporting artillery fire from the ramparts (*BC* 3. 55).

The most common reason for a confrontation without actual fighting seems to have been that one or both armies had adopted a very strong position, which the other side was unwilling to attack. In 57 BC Caesar and the Belgae formed up on the high ground either side of a valley containing a marsh. If either side was to attack the other, it would not only have faced a strong defensive position, but would have done so in a disordered state from having crossed the obstacle.[57] In Africa in 48 BC, Curio and Varus faced each other from the heights on either side of a valley, this time with a stream running through it, which again both sides waited for the other to cross. Sometimes, as in the latter case, one side attacked anyway.[58] In 56 BC, Crassus felt that his army had been made confident enough by the Gallic refusal to fight for him to storm their camp (*BG* 3. 24). The refusal to come out of your camp, and at least form line of battle, even if you did not actually fight, seems to have normally been taken as a sign of low morale. In 48 BC Scipio had faced the army of Domitius outside his camp, but was unwilling to engage. According to Caesar:

he suspected that on the following day he would either be forced against his will to fight, or, if he stayed in camp he would be utterly disgraced . . . and so he followed his reckless advance with an ignominious withdrawal. (*BC* 3. 37)

Later in 46 BC, the same commander was to draw up outside Caesar's camp without provoking the latter to battle, and so told his army that this was a sign that the enemy was demoralized (*African War* 30). The Cimbri and Teutones seemed to have similarly condemned

---

[56] *BC* 2. 27, 3. 41, 3. 55, 3. 85; *African War* 30, 41–2, 75; Plut. *Lucullus* 15, *Brutus* 45, *Marius* 16–19, 33; App. *BC* 1. 45, 4. 107, 4. 121.

[57] *BG* 2. 8–9, cf. *BG* 7. 19, 7. 53, *BC* 3. 37.

[58] *BC* 2. 33, *Spanish War* 28, *BG* 1. 50, 3. 24, App. *BC* 4. 107.

Marius' army, when it remained in camp without fighting, suggesting that this was not purely a Roman idea (Plutarch, *Marius* 16–18).

An army that had challenged its enemy to battle and had seen them decline, might therefore have expected to have an advantage in morale. In itself this was unlikely to ensure success in battle, but it gave it a slight edge over its opponents. Much of the manœuvring before battle seems to have been intended in a similar way, to build up gradually your own army's morale, by giving it small victories in minor skirmishes, whilst detracting from the morale of the opposition. Implicit is the assumption that the campaign would be decided by a major battle. The military treatises of Frontinus, Onasander, and Vegetius concentrated heavily, in discussing strategy, on when and where to fight a battle.[59] They recommended avoidance only so that a more suitable occasion might be found in future, perhaps when the enemy had been worn down. Put simply, their doctrine was always to fight with as many advantages over the enemy as possible. The general secured these advantages by a combination of skills. His ability as a general allowed him to manœuvre himself into a favourable position and force the enemy to fight there. His skills as a leader were needed to ensure that his army fought the ensuing action in as confident a mood as possible. The situation is summed up by an anecdote concerning Marius in the Social War. Publius Silo, an enemy commander, faced a strong position held by Marius, and criticized him for not leaving it to fight in the open.

'If you are a great general, Marius', he said, 'come down and fight it out.'

Marius replied, 'If you are, make me' (Plutarch, *Marius* 33).

CEREMONY AND THEATRE

> As to speeches—what effect on the whole army can be made by a speech, since you cannot conveniently make it heard by more than a thousand men standing about you?
>
> (Wellington, in Keegan, *The Mask of Command*, 143)

Unless his army was subjected to a surprise attack, which gave him no time, a Roman commander normally addressed his army before any engagement (Suetonius, *Caesar* 55; *Hist.* 4. 33). With his army

---

[59] Frontin. *Strategemata* 2. 1–2; Onos. *The General* 31–2; Veg. 3. 9–13.

struggling to form up to meet the sudden Gallic onslaught at the Sambre in 57 BC, Caesar rode along the hastily formed line, speaking briefly to those troops not already engaged (*BG* 1. 20). Like some of the measures mentioned earlier, a commander's speech did not in itself raise his men's morale enough to guarantee victory, but it was one further way of giving them a slight advantage (Onasander, *The General* 1. 13).

Historians normally seem to have assumed that the general addressed the whole army at the same time.[60] With smaller forces this may have been possible, but with most armies this was impractical, unless the commander relied on the essence of his speech being passed on to the men who could not hear. In a discussion of the oratory of Alexander the Great, Keegan provides some figures for numbers in crowds addressed, which may give us some useful guidelines.[61] Abraham Lincoln addressed 15,000 men at Gettysburg, but was badly heard, whilst Gladstone habitually spoke to crowds of 5,000–6,000 people, albeit usually indoors. Most Roman armies were larger than the 5,000 men that Keegan suggests as the maximum that could be clearly addressed in the open. At Thapsus, Caesar seems to have ridden along the lines speaking to the units in turn (*African War* 75). Both Civilis and Cerialis were depicted by Tacitus as doing this in AD 70 (*Hist.* 5. 16–17). Dio described Suetonius Paulinus speaking to each of the three bodies, into which his 10,000 man army had been divided, in turn (Dio 62. 9–11). Finally, in his address at Lambaesis, Hadrian spoke to each of the units present at the exercise individually (*CIL* VIII. 18042). Although this was not actually a speech made by a commander before or after a battle, it is probably the only military speech which we possess whose text is at all reliable. It seems safe to conclude that the convention of giving a single speech to the whole army, common in most histories, is no more than a literary device. Rather, the army either marched past the commander or he rode amongst it, addressing smaller sections at one time.

By convention the historian normally composed a suitable speech to put into the mouth of a commander before battle, so that we have no text of a pre-battle speech as accurate as Hadrian's address at

---

[60] e.g. Caesar and Pompey at Pharsalus, App. *BC* 2. 50–4; Titus in AD 70, *BJ* 7. 6; see M. H. Hansen, 'The Battle Exhortation in Ancient Historiography. Fact or Fiction?', *Historia*, 42. 2 (1993), 161–80.

[61] Keegan, *Mask of Command*, 54 ff.

Lambaesis. Often the type of appeals attributed to commanders sound plausible, for instance Tacitus' description of Cerialis in AD 70:

Then he found appropriate arguments to spur the courage of the various legions, calling the men of the Fourteenth the Conquerors of Britain. Galba, he added, had owed his elevation to the lead given by the Sixth, and in the coming battle the men of the Second would earn their new standards and new eagle. Riding further along the ranks towards the garrison of Germany, he stretched out his hands in an appeal to them to recover at the cost of the blood of the enemy a river frontier and a camp rightfully theirs. There was a general shout of mounting enthusiasm. (*Hist.* 5. 16)

The blunt sentiments attributed to Suetonius Paulinus in Tacitus' account of the Boudiccan revolt likewise sound right (*Ann.* 14. 35), as does the joke which Tacitus gave to Agricola before Mons Graupius: 'These are the greatest runaways of all the Britons—which is the reason they have survived so long. (*Agricola* 34–5).

All three speeches mentioned above were greeted by cheering and acclamation by the men, and this seems to have been an important element in the relationship between the commander and his troops. There were enough other occasions when the men reacted to a general's speech for us to assume that this was normal.[62] Usually, this seems to have taken the form of general cheering, but on occasions an individual spoke from the ranks to the commander. At Pharsalus the veteran *primus pilus*, Crastinus, turned to Caesar and said, 'General, today I shall earn your gratitude, either dead or alive' (*BC.* 3. 91). Individual soldiers felt free to bring trophies to the commander after engagements, and by this action asked for praise and reward.[63] During the siege of Avaricum, Caesar claimed that he went around the siege lines asking each legion in turn whether they were finding the work too arduous and offering to abandon the siege if this was the case, but the men begged him not to give up. This same message was repeated via the centurions and tribunes later in the day (*BG* 7. 17). Later in the same siege, the army was faced by a strongly positioned Gallic force, and the soldiers clamoured to be led against the enemy, so that Caesar made a speech to explain why he did not do so (*BG.* 7. 19). There were other instances of commanders having problems restraining their armies when near the enemy.[64] Discipline in the Roman army

[62] *BC.* 3. 90–1; Plut. *Antony* 44; App. *BC.* 2. 50–2, 53–4; *Ann.* 1. 51; Dio 62. 9–11.
[63] *BJ.* 5. 316, 7. 197; see Ch. 6, 276–81 for a discussion of this.
[64] *BC* 1. 71, 3. 37; *African War* 82; *Hist.* 2. 18.

reflected Roman society and seems to have given the men the freedom to express their opinions to their commanders. In part, the origins of the army in a militia of citizens led by magistrates elected by the same populace that filled the ranks may have been responsible for this.

In many respects, Roman aristocrats behaved in a similar way when commanding an army, as they did in the political environment of Rome, the soldiers filling the role of the plebs. The same sort of theatrical gestures might be made by a commander in an effort to persuade his men. Plutarch described Lucullus attempting to regain control of his army in Asia by going around the camp from tent to tent and in tears, begging his men to follow him (Plutarch, *Lucullus* 35). Caesar took an oath not to shave or cut his hair until he had avenged the troops lost under Cotta and Sabinus (Suetonius, *Caesar* 67). Commanders appear at their most theatrical during mutinies, when it must be admitted that an army is more like a crowd than at any other time, whether it was Caesar confronting the mutinous *Legio X* and addressing them as *Quirites* or Germanicus offering to let the mutineers cut his throat in AD 14 (Suetonius, *Caesar* 70; *Ann.* 1. 33–48).

Several of the rituals associated with the giving of battle have a strong element of theatre about them. The normal signal seems to have been the raising of a red *vexillum* outside the commander's tent as an order for the troops to arm and equip themselves.[65] The commander himself then appeared wearing the red commander's cloak.[66] Before Carrhae, Crassus made the mistake of wearing a black cloak, which was taken as a bad omen by his men (Plutarch, *Crassus* 23). The auspices were normally taken before a campaign and, if time and the situation permitted, each battle. It is difficult to estimate how much such ceremonies meant to the individual soldiers. Frontinus believed that a commander ought to be able to dispel any fear amongst his troops resulting from apparently adverse omens (Frontinus, *Strategemata* 1. 12. 1–12). On Trajan's column, the Emperor is several times depicted performing the *suovetaurilia*, the only occasion he appears in civilian rather than military dress.[67] Such religious ceremonies—Caesar performed a *lustratio* of the army on 21 March 46 BC (*African War* 75) as did Brutus and Cassius before Philippi (Appian, *BC* 3. 89)—as well as formal parades, such as the pay-parade before

---

[65] *Spanish War* 28; *Hist.* 2. 41; Plut. *Pompey* 68, *Brutus* 40, *Antony* 39.
[66] *BG* 7. 88; Plut. *Lucullus* 28, *Antony* 44.   [67] Scenes 8, 53, 103.

Jerusalem in AD 70 and Hadrian's review at Lambaesis, were in a sense very similar to the conduct of politics and state religion at Rome. The general, like the priest or magistrate he might also be, had a more prominent role in the ceremony, but still officiated as one citizen amongst the many, who witnessed, and in a passive sense, took part. Such displays served to show the troops their commander in his dominant role, but also to emphasize their bond to him, and their unity of purpose.

Just how important the religious element of these ceremonies was to the men in the ranks is difficult to judge. As far as we can tell, Roman soldiers did not seem to fight any less well when the situation prevented the proper rites before battle from taking place, as must often have been the case when the fighting was brought on by a sudden or surprise attack. Helgeland, in one of the few studies to examine the formal religion of the army, argued that these practices served to identify the soldier and his unit with Rome's destiny.[68] He claimed that the marching camp took on the same religious significance as the city, if anything being more traditional in its ritual practices. For him, the rites before battle, like the environment of the camp, were familiar and reassuring to men anxious about what was to come. Yet in another way, the peculiar ceremonies and rituals before a battle emphasized the very novelty of the experience that the men were about to undergo.

THE GIVING OF BATTLE

> He (Marius) imagined that he was the commander in chief in the war with Mithridates and then behaved just as he used to do when really in action, throwing himself into all sorts of attitudes, going through various movements, shouting words of command and constantly yelling out his battle-cry.
>
> (Plutarch, *Marius* 45)

Once the army had been deployed on the battlefield and the commander had issued his orders and spoken to the men (and it must always be remembered that this would take several hours, and even longer with a very large army) he then gave the signal for battle. In Caesar's army, this seems to have taken the form of a gesture with the general's personal standard, or more often the sounding of a horn. The signal made by the trumpeter with the general was then repeated

---

[68] J. Helgeland, 'Roman Army Religion', *ANRW* II 16. 2, 1470–505.

by all the musicians with the other units along the line and the army moved forward.[69] Judging from its use well into the gunpowder period, the high-pitched sound of the horn or trumpet has the best carrying power of any instrument used for military signalling, although repetition of the signal was necessary to co-ordinate a line which might cover several miles in frontage. The process is best described by the author of the *African War* in his account of Thapsus. Caesar was reluctant to advance:

He was bawling out constantly that he did not approve of engaging in battle by an impromptu sally, and repeatedly checking the line from advancing, when suddenly a trumpeter on the right wing, yielding to pressure from the troops and without Caesar's orders, began to sound the call to charge. This was taken up by all the cohorts and they begun to advance on the enemy, but the centurions faced about and vainly attempted to restrain their men, urging them not to engage without their commander's orders.[70]

Given that often an army had stood facing the enemy for hours or even days, it is not surprising that the men were nervous and tense, and that such accidents could occur. According to Plutarch, Brutus sent written orders to each of his legates and other officers at Philippi to begin the advance. Due to the length of the line, these orders arrived at different times, added to which some units advanced as soon as they saw others moving, throwing the whole line into disorder (Plutarch, *Brutus* 41). Again, given the tense situation and the inexperience of the army, this confusion is understandable.

Once the army had begun to advance, the commander was faced with the choice of where to position himself to have the greatest influence on the action. Essentially, he had three options. First, he could find a point in the rear to observe the whole battle, directing his reserves as required. Second, he could fight in the front rank, inspiring his army by sharing the same risks as an ordinary soldier. Finally, he could stay close to, but behind the line, directing the fighting from this position and moving around the battlefield.

1. *'From Behind'*

As the battle of Mons Graupius was about to begin, Agricola sent away his horse and took up his position on foot, in front of the legions at the

---

[69] *BG* 3. 24, 7. 27, 7. 45, 7. 62; Plut, *Pompey* 70; App. *BC* 2. 78.
[70] *African War* 82; see Ch. 5, 191–2.

rear of the line. He was to remain there until the Caledonian army had been broken, when he remounted and organized the pursuit of the enemy (*Agricola* 35–7). The gesture of sending away his horse, thus telling the army that he would stay and, if necessary die with them, was once again a piece of theatre. Caesar did the same in the first battle he fought in Gaul, against the Helvetii (*BG* 1. 25). Spartacus went further and publicly killed his horse as the battle was about to begin (Plutarch, *Crassus* 11. 6). Caecina in Germany in AD 14 had his own horse and those of other officers given to the best fighters in the army, before mounting a desperate attempt to break through the surrounding Germans (*Ann.* 1. 66). If the commander appeared confident in this way, and in his general demeanour, then there was a chance that the men would become more confident. Dismounting did however deprive the commander of mobility and, by lowering him, reduced the amount he could see and in turn how many of his men could see him.

At Mons Graupius (Fig. 2), Agricola opened his attack by sending four Batavian and two Tungrian cohorts, supported on each flank by cavalry, against the enemy centre. The attack made good progress initially, but then began to bog down. The Britons on higher ground began to envelop the Roman line. Seeing this Agricola sent in four *alae* of cavalry from the reserve against the enemy flanks and rear. The infantry pushed on, presumably supported by the rest of the auxiliary foot, and the British army began to break up and retreat. Agricola ordered the army to pursue and personally rode around directing this. During the battle, we thus have Agricola making three main decisions.

1. He ordered the attack by the six cohorts of infantry.
2. He sent in his reserve of four *alae* against the enemy outflanking movement.
3. He ordered the pursuit.

Agricola's skill as a general was exercised in ordering the main assault and committing his reserves to support this and then mount a pursuit. His position behind the main line gave him the ability to watch the movements of both his own and the enemy army. What could he have seen? Without knowing the dimensions of the battlefield, we cannot be too precise, but the figures given in the Victorian *Artillerist's Manual* on recognition distances provide us with a useful guide:[71]

---

[71] Whitehouse, *Battle in Africa*, 35.

1,700 yards [1,550 m.]—masses of troops can be recognized.
1,300 yards [1,190 m.]—infantry can be distinguished from cavalry.
1,000 yards [900 m.]—individuals can be seen.
  700 yards [640 m.]—heads, crossbelts etc can be distinguished.
  500 yards [450 m.]—uniforms recognized, reflections from weapons.
  250 yards [225 m.]—officers recognizable, uniforms clear.

These figures are based upon 'good eyesight', possession of which should not always be taken for granted in a commander. At Philippi, Cassius was unable to make out the identity of approaching horsemen because he was short-sighted, so sent an officer to see who they were (Plutarch, *Brutus* 43). Even if his eyesight was good, the commander's view might have been obscured by the terrain. In Africa in 46 BC, Labienus was unable to see an outflanking move made by Caesar's army because his view was obscured by a large farmhouse (*African War* 40). At Alesia, Caesar rode to some higher ground to observe the battle more clearly (*BG* 7. 85). Even if the commander had a good observation point, the distances involved must often have meant that he saw the armies as masses whose identity might be unclear, especially in a civil war, when uniforms were similar. We have seen how Publius Considius mistook Labienus' legions for Gauls in 58 BC (*BG* 1. 22). Such mistakes were by no means uncommon. At Gergovia, the Aedui were mistaken for hostile Gauls, despite their having bare right shoulders as a mark of distinction (*BG* 7. 50). In AD 70 the Batavians were to mistake the rallying men from the cohorts they had routed for a fresh army (*Hist.* 4. 77).

Nevertheless, despite the risks of confusion, a commander who positioned himself to the rear on the best observation point available, stood a better chance of observing the battle as a whole from there, than in any other position. He was then able to direct the reserves (which as we have seen, normally formed a high percentage of the army's total strength) to where they were most needed, as Agricola had done at Mons Graupius. Sometimes a specific manœuvre by reserves, planned beforehand to deal with an anticipated situation, could have been ordered by a signal. Caesar did this at Pharsalus to order his fourth line to advance to face the Pompeian cavalry and later to commit the third line (*BC* 3. 93–4). Normally, the range of possibilities for where the reserves might be required, prevented this from being feasible, and a messenger would have been sent to order the troops to move. A 1914 Military Manual gave the speed of dispatch riders as 'ordinary—5 m.p.h. [8 k.p.h.]; rapid—7 to 8 m.p.h. [11–13 k.p.h.]; urgent—10 to 12 m.p.h. [16–19 k.p.h.].'[72] Further delay in the delivery of the message was imposed by the time taken to find the right unit and commander for whom the orders were intended. There were then further delays, whilst it was put into effect, and all the time the risk of its being intercepted. Not only that, but the commander could never have been sure that the messenger had got through at all. Communications were made difficult at Carrhae when several messengers between Crassus and his son were delayed or intercepted by the Parthians (Plutarch, *Crassus* 25–6). Distance in this case prevented Crassus from actually seeing what was going on. The result of these delays between the commander issuing an order and its being carried out meant that it was important for him to anticipate the course of the battle and dispose his reserves accordingly. At Pharsalus, Pompey was unable to see the cavalry attack mounted by his left, because of the dust thrown up by the hooves. He had to guess from this dust cloud that his men had been beaten, and on the basis of this assumption stopped his infantry from advancing and being enveloped by Caesar's right (Appian, *BC* 2. 79). If the commander was static, it at least made it easier for reports sent to him to be delivered, since messengers knew where to go.

Observation of an action from the rear by the general is most commonly recorded during assaults on towns. In AD 9 Tiberius sat on a platform to watch the attack on Seretium. According to Dio he did this

not only to watch the battle, since this would encourage his men to fight with more spirit, but also to be able to throw in support at the critical moment, if the need arose. In fact . . . he was holding a part of his force in reserve for this very purpose. (Dio 56. 13)

He kept the attack going by committing reserves as the men became tired, and was eventually successful. At Jerusalem in AD 70, Titus twice watched an attack on the Temple from the captured fortress of Antonia. Not only was he able to commit reserves as required, but he was also there 'so that none of the brave might go unnoticed and unrewarded, nor any of an opposite character escape the penalty, but that he who had power both to punish and to reward might be a spectator and witness of all'.[73] The confined and intensive nature of an

[72] Whitehouse, *Battle in Africa*, 17.
[73] *BJ* 6. 133–4, 6. 245; see Ch. 4, 'Close to the Front Line' and Ch. 6, 'Rewards and Morale'.

assault into a town allowed the commander to fulfill both these roles from the same position. On a wider battlefield, it is unlikely that a commander, such as Agricola at Mons Graupius, was in a position to witness any individual acts of courage by his men.

Once the battle had begun, the general stationed at the rear could not have influenced the course of events as a leader. As a general, his main role was to direct the army and particularly its reserves. His vantage point allowed him to view the battle as a whole and better judge how to use these. He would have had difficulty in judging the morale of any of his own or enemy units doing the fighting, other than in obvious cases of flight or pursuit.

2. *'In Front'*

The second position open to the commander was the exact opposite of directing from the rear. This was when the commander took up position in the front rank of one of the units of his army, and fought there as an ordinary soldier for the whole battle. The only clear instance I have found of this practice in our period, is that of Marius at Aquae Sextiae in 102 BC. According to Plutarch (*Marius* 20), Marius sent officers along the line reminding the men of their orders, whilst 'he was himself visible in the front rank, putting into practice the advice which he had given to his soldiers, for he was in as good training as anyone and in daring, he far surpassed them all'.

During the battle, Marius fought like a legionary and cannot have issued any orders until it was over. Indeed, as the battle lines closed, he can have seen little more than the men immediately around him. His attention would have been almost exclusively focused on fighting the individual enemies who were attempting to kill him. Marius did not fight in the front line at the second battle of the campaign at Vercellae, and his reason for doing so at Aquae Sextiae should be put into context. The Ambrones and Teutones were part of the great confederation of migrating tribes that had not only defeated, but virtually destroyed successively the armies of five consuls sent against them in the last decade. These barbarians had gained an aura of invincibility, a powerful fear acting on his men's minds. Before this battle, Marius had kept his army near the enemy without fighting to get his men used to their wild appearance (*Marius* 16). Although well trained, his army lacked experience and the confidence that this provided. Fighting with them in the front rank was the final gesture, in its way as theatrical as Caesar or Agricola sending away their horses. It proved to his men that Marius was confident enough of victory to stake his own life on it, and in this way Marius sought to inspire them. Once the battle had begun, he could at best have influenced the men immediately around him. In the situation, he chose this action and left the direction of reserves to his subordinates. That he did not do so in later, or indeed in earlier battles, clearly suggests that it was an exceptional decision made necessary by the times.

There are other instances of Roman generals actually fighting hand-to-hand, usually in desperate situations, for instance Caesar at the Sambre in 57 BC and Cotta at Atuatuca in 54 BC (*BG* 2. 25, 5. 33). There are non-specific references to both Drusus and Germanicus seeking personal combat with enemies in Suetonius (Suetonius, *Gaius* 3, *Claudius* 1). In his youth, during the Social War, Pompey led a cavalry charge and, riding out in front of his men, struck down an enemy champion causing the rest to flee before he or his men reached them (Plutarch, *Pompey* 7). Although Plutarch records other combats between Pompey and individual enemies in Spain, in each case he was attacked and had not sought the combat himself (*Pompey* 19, 35). In 29 BC Crassus claimed the right to dedicate the *spolia opima* after killing the Bastarnian king, Deldo, but Dio's account of this suggests that he did so during the pursuit after, rather than during, the battle (Dio 51. 24). Titus fought on several occasions, when cut off, or leading his *singulares* in a charge at a critical point during the Jewish War.[74] In all these cases, it seems that the commander chose, or was forced to fight for a short time. What he had not done was to position himself in the front line with the intention of fighting the entire battle from this position. Instead he attempted to inspire the men at a particular point of the line, before moving on elsewhere.

A commander who chose to fight throughout a battle automatically lost the ability to direct his reserves or indeed issue any orders for the duration of the action. Given that reserves formed a high proportion of the total army on most occasions, it was therefore rare for the Roman commander to lead from the front, after the manner of Alexander the Great. Onasander specifically condemned the practice on the basis not only of the risk to the commander, but also on the grounds that he had much more important things to do (Onasander, *The General* 33. 6). What a commander might do was to join in the fighting for a short time

[74] *BJ* 3. 487, 5. 66, 87, 82, 486–7.

at a critical point, but leave it and move elsewhere as soon as the crisis was over.

3. 'Close to the Front Line'

> The duty of the general is to ride by the ranks on horseback, show himself to those in danger, praise the brave, threaten the cowardly, encourage the lazy, fill up gaps, transpose a unit if necessary, bring aid to the wearied, anticipate the crisis, the hour and the outcome.
>
> (Onasander, *The General* 33. 6)

It seems clear that subordinate officers, such as legates, tribunes or prefects, placed in control of a section of the line, were expected to stay close to the fighting, riding around encouraging their men and directing reserves. When fighting Ariovistus, the reason Caesar gives for placing his five *legati* and his *quaestor* in command of one legion each was 'that every soldier might know that there was a high officer in a position to observe the courage with which he conducted himself' (*BG* 1. 52). The implication is that these officers were close enough to the fighting to be able to see this. The commander-in-chief could likewise move around, close to the fighting, with the distinction that he was not restricted to any one section of the line. He could closely direct the movement in one area, but then move elsewhere leaving direction of that sector to the subordinate officer placed in charge before the battle. At Pharsalus, Caesar seems to have spent most of the battle close behind the right wing with *Legio X*. He gave two signals after the advance had begun, firstly to the fourth line which only covered the right flank, and secondly, to the third line which supported the entire front (*BC* 3. 93–4). From the accounts we have of the battle, all the major tactical moves occurred on this flank, which explains why Caesar spent the whole action there.

Roman commanders were often depicted during battles as riding around their lines, encouraging and urging on both the reserves and those men in the front line actually facing the enemy. At the Sambre in 57 BC Caesar rode along the line that his army was attempting to form. He spoke to *Legio X* and gave them the signal to attack. Moving to the right wing, where *Legio XII* were in danger, he took a shield from a man in the rear ranks and moved to the front, yelling encouragement to the troops and speaking to the centurions by name. When the enemy had been driven back a short distance, he altered the formation of the *XII* and the nearby *VII* (*BG* 2. 20–6). Even when not actually fighting, he must often have been very close to his own forward troops, and therefore the enemy. When their army was ambushed in 54 BC, Sabinus panicked and rushed about nervously arranging the cohorts, whilst Cotta: 'did everything possible to save the army, calling upon the men and encouraging them as their commander-in-chief might have done, and fighting in the ranks like a soldier' (*BG* 5. 35).

The army was drawn back into a circle, so the commanders could see all of it and more easily encourage the men. Later Cotta was wounded whilst cheering on the units, and finally fell fighting (*BG* 5. 36-7). At Gergovia, Caesar was actually with *Legio X* and able to stop them pursuing the enemy too far. He was unable to affect the units he was not actually with, because his horn signal was ignored (*BG* 7. 47).

A similar style of command, with the general moving around close behind the front line is apparent in the Civil War from 49-46 BC.[75] At Carrhae in 53 BC, Crassus, seemingly stirred out of his lethargy by the news of his son's death, rode around the square of the army, encouraging the men not to be demoralized (Plutarch, *Crassus* 26). At Philippi, Antony, Octavian, and Brutus are all described going around their armies urging the soldiers on and in the case of the former, shaking hands with them (Appian, *BC* 4. 126; Plutarch, *Brutus* 41). This very forward style of command seems still to have been common under the Empire. Both Germanicus and Caecina in Germany in AD 14-15, seem to have directed actions from very close to the fighting.[76] In AD 69 Antonius Primus rode around the Flavian army in the bright moonlight at the second battle of Cremona, urging his men on (*Hist.* 3. 24). Cerialis is depicted during the revolt of Civilis as riding around the battlefields, directing the units personally in one sector, leading charges and then moving off to direct another part of the line (*Hist.* 4. 77, 5. 20-1). In Judaea, Titus is frequently attested near to, or involved in, the actual fighting, particularly around Jerusalem.[77] Dio described how one of the commanders in Domitian's Dacian War ordered his men to have their names and units marked on their shields, to allow him to recognize the brave, which suggests that he planned to lead from near the front (Dio 67. 10). Arrian does not tell us whether he planned to move during the battle against the Alans, although he planned to be active on the march, directing the column. Overall, there

---

[75] e.g. *BC* 1. 45; *African War* 16, 18, 58, 81, 83; Suet. *Caesar* 56; App. *BC* 2. 104.
[76] *Ann.* 1. 51, 65, 20-1.
[77] *BJ* 3. 487, 5. 82-4, 287-9, 311-6, 486-7, 6. 70.

is no evidence to suggest that the static command style of Agricola at Mons Graupius superseded the more mobile and active Republican style epitomized by Caesar. Instead, the character of the individual commander and the situation determined the commander's style, with most choosing the mobile, Caesarean method.

What did the commander so close to the front actually see and do? The author of the African War supplies an instructive anecdote concerning a battle in which Caesar's small legionary force was being worn down by a combination of cavalry and light infantry under Labienus.

Labienus was riding up and down in the front line bare-headed, cheering on his own men as he did so, and occasionally addressing Caesar's legionaries like this: 'What do you think you're doing, rookie? Little fire-eater aren't you? Are you another one whose had his wits fuddled by his nibs' fine talk? I tell you, he's brought you into a desperate situation. I am sorry for you.' Then a soldier said, 'I am no raw recruit, Labienus; I'm a veteran of the Tenth.' 'I don't recognize the standards of the Tenth,' Labienus replied. 'You'll soon be aware of what sort of man I am,' said the soldier. As he spoke, he threw off his helmet, so that he could be recognized by Labienus, then seized his javelin and flung with all his might. He drove it hard, full into the chest of Labienus' horse and said, 'Let that show you, that it's a soldier of the Tenth who attacks you.' (*African War* 16)

If Labienus was within *pilum* range, then he must have been as close as thirty metres to the enemy line. He was seeking to encourage his men by cheering them on and by simply showing himself to be confident of success, and unafraid of the enemy, as proven by his bare head. Except in civil wars, it seems unlikely that Roman commanders normally addressed the enemy. The sequel to the incident is equally instructive. Caesar rode along his line, both rearranging the units and urging the men on to one last effort. In a sudden controlled charge, he managed to drive off the enemy and return to his own camp (*African War* 17). Commanders seem to have had no difficulty riding along behind their own front lines or riding through them. Caesar was able to join the front ranks of the *XII* at the Sambre (*BG* 2. 25). As described above, Labienus could get to the front of his own army in Africa. In 43 BC at Forum Gallorum, the legate Sulpicius Galba clearly directed his men from near the front. His wing began to be outflanked by Antony's cavalry, so, according to his own account:

I began to retreat and to put out my light-armed troops to oppose the Moorish cavalry, to prevent their attacking our men from the rear. Meantime, I became aware that I was surrounded by Antony's troops and that Antony himself was some distance behind me. In a moment I galloped up to the legion of recruits which was coming from the camp, slinging my shield behind me. The enemy were close upon me, and our men were eager to hurl their javelins. I was only saved by a stroke of good luck, for my own men quickly recognized me. (Cicero, *ad Fam*. 10. 30)

Galba had thus not only ridden to the front of his own line, but through the enemy's as well, so that Antony, the opposing commander, who was directing the battle from close behind his front line, was actually behind him. Realizing this and being recognized by the enemy, Galba fled back through the lines and was almost killed by his own men. In a civil war, the distinctions between the uniforms of the two sides must often have been minimal, but this incident and those referred to above point to two conclusions concerning the environment of an ancient battle. First, it seems clear that there were normally gaps in the battle lines between friendly units, suggesting that the intervals necessary to allow the units to move, as discussed above, remained after the fighting had begun. Second, they suggest that there were frequent lulls in the fighting when the opposing lines were very close, but not actually in contact. Battlefields seem then to have been quite open and the fighting fairly fluid.

It may seem implausible that someone could accidentally ride through two opposing battle lines without noticing. Even if the enemy wore similar uniforms to friendly troops, would not the direction they were facing have revealed their identity? The evidence from military history as a whole suggests that the confusion of battle is so great, and individual participants so disorientated that they lose all sense of direction and identify units on their appearance rather than the direction of their movement. At the battle of Fuentes de Onoro in 1811, the French mounted an attack on a British-held position. One of the units in the French army, the Hanoverian Legion, wore red jackets like the British defenders, rather than the more usual blue. The Hanoverians were mistaken for a friendly unit by the defenders, who allowed them to come close and fire a short range volley into them. On the point of success, a participant described what happened to the Hanoverians.

The 66th regiment, having been sent to support the Hanoverians, who were in the fighting line, mistook them in the smoke for an English battalion, and fired a volley into them, while our artillery, equally misled by the red coats, played on them with grape. I must do the brave Hanoverians the justice to say that, placed as they were between two fires, they endured them for a long time without recoiling a step, but after losing 100 men killed and many wounded, the battalion was compelled to retire, passing along one side of the village. Another regiment, which was entering the village at that moment, seeing the red coats on their flank, supposed that the position had been turned. (*The Memoirs of Baron Marbot* (London, 1988), ii. 161–2)

Other instances of similar confusion could be mentioned.[78] It seems clear that the confusion of battle is often so great as to make individuals leap to illogical conclusions. Even without the added problem of powder smoke, Caesar's men mistook the Aedui for hostile Gauls at Gergovia. There was no reason for them to expect hostile Gauls to appear in that position, the confusion was due entirely to their similar appearance (*BG* 7. 50). Galba may well have not realized that he had crossed his own line and entered the enemy's, in the same way that the enemy soldiers could at first have taken him for one of their own commanders or messengers riding along the lines.

A commander close behind or in the front line was always at risk from missile fire, which made the common gesture of removing his helmet a dangerous one.[79] We have seen how Labienus had his horse killed by a thrown *pilum*. Caecina's horse was killed whilst he was riding along his line in Germany, and he was only saved by the sudden approach of some men from *Legio I* (*Ann.* 1. 65). In 54 BC, Cotta was struck full in the face by a sling stone, whilst encouraging his men (*BG* 5. 35). In 43 BC the consul Pansa was hit by a thrown javelin and mortally wounded. His colleague Hirtius was killed in the fighting near Antony's tent when storming the latter's camp (Appian, *BC* 3. 39, 3. 71). The open nature of the battle line also allowed individual enemies, keen to make a name for themselves, to seek out the commander and attack him (*BC* 2. 33). Plutarch records two occasions when Pompey was singled out and attacked by lone enemy horsemen (Plutarch, *Pompey* 19, 35). At the battle outside Rome, Sulla, riding his conspicuous white charger, was chased by enemy horsemen and only escaped because his own horse was faster (Plutarch, *Sulla* 29). In AD 70 Cerialis ran a great risk of being intercepted by the enemy as he rode

---

[78] e.g. at Vitoria in 1813, the British 71st Foot mistook an attacking French column for an allied Spanish unit, and were driven back when the enemy fired, see C. Hibbert, *A Soldier of the Seventy-First* (London, 1975), 87. At First Manassas in 1861 a Union battery was taken when it mistook approaching enemy regiments for friendly troops, see P. Griffith *Rally Once Again: Battle Tactics in the American Civil War* (Marlborough, 1987), 173.   [79] *African War* 16, App. *BC* 2. 104, *Ann.* 2. 21.

from one part of his army to another (*Hist.* 5. 20). Commanders who led from close behind the battle line thus ran a far higher risk of injury than a static commander like Agricola.

Whilst moving around his line, the general was engaged chiefly in two things, neatly fitting in with the roles of generalship and leadership. As a general he lacked the overall battlefield view of the commander in the rear. However, in the area immediately around him, he could see far more clearly what was going on. He was able to estimate the morale of both his own men and the enemy. At Pharsalus, Pompey is supposed to have decided, from the contrast between the steady silence of the enemy and the noise and confusion of his own men, that his men could not be trusted to keep formation in a charge, so ordered them to meet the enemy at the halt (Plutarch, *Pompey* 69). Not only the appearance of troops, but the noise that they made could be used to judge how well things were going (*Hist.* 4. 18, *Germ.* 3). From a closer position, the general could assess the situation more easily and adjust his dispositions. At the Sambre and again in Africa we have seen that Caesar went along the line altering the formations and positions of his units. If the commander did this himself, he might speed up the process and could anyway be sure that his orders were interpreted correctly.

The other way of reacting to or exploiting a situation was in the use of reserves. A commander fighting in the front rank could not have issued any orders to these, but one close to or in the front line, but not actually fighting, could have done so. At Gergovia in 52 BC Caesar stayed with *Legio X* and sent orders to Titus Sextius in camp to bring up his cohorts and cover the retreat of the other legions.[80] In Spain in 49 BC he ordered up *Legio IX* from the reserve to support the main line which he was himself encouraging (*BC* 1. 45). Once again, if the orders were sent by messenger, it was important that the instructions to the reserves of what to do and where to go should be very clear. Sometimes it might have been desirable to send a senior subordinate to lead the troops up and make sure they did what was required (*BG* 7. 86, 87). Otherwise, the commander himself might have gone and either led the troops up to the right position or actually charged with them.[81]

Although the commander could see better what was actually

---

[80] *BG* 7. 49; cf. *BG* 7. 67, 70, 86, 87; *BC* 3. 65; *BJ* 4. 73, 5. 84, 287.
[81] *BG* 7. 87; Plut. *Sulla* 19; *Ann.* 1. 51, 2. 20; *BJ* 5. 287–9.

happening in the area of the battlefield around him by being close to the front, he was unable to see what went on elsewhere. It was important for him to be ready to move to each section of the field as a crisis threatened. Fighting against Pompey, Sertorius began by commanding his right wing personally, but hearing from messengers that his left was in trouble, he rode to the point, rallied his men, and counter-attacked to beat the enemy (Plutarch, *Sertorius* 19). It is important to remember that all along the line there were subordinate officers acting in a similar way to the commander himself. In 58 BC in the battle against Ariovistus, Caesar's left was threatened by the Germans. 'Publius Crassus, who was in charge of the cavalry and better able to move about and see what was happening than those in the fighting line' saw this threat and ordered the third line to relieve the left (*BG* 1. 52). The commander either needed to be able to 'read' instinctively a battle and anticipate each crisis or to have reliable subordinates who could cope with most situations. Normally a combination of the two seems to have ensured success.

We have seen the commander as a leader, riding around encouraging his men by his confidence and cheering them on. Another vital aspect of leadership could only have been exercised from near the front line, namely the need to act as a witness to the behaviour of individuals. At the end of a campaign and perhaps after each battle, a parade was held at which the commander decorated, rewarded, and promoted individuals for gallantry.[82] Josephus described the parade held after the fall of Jerusalem in AD 70:

A spacious tribunal having accordingly been constructed for him (Titus) in the centre of his former camp, he here took his stand with his principal officers, so as to be heard by the whole army . . .

He accordingly gave orders to the appointed officers to read out the names of all who had performed any brilliant feat during the war. Calling up each by name he applauded them as they came forward, no less exultant over their exploits than if they were his own. He then placed crowns of gold upon their heads, presented them with golden neck-chains, little golden spears and standards made of silver, and promoted each man to a higher rank; he further assigned them out of the spoils silver and gold and raiments and other booty in abundance.[83]

---

[82] For the importance of the commander as witness and rewarder of bravery, see Ch. 6, 'Rewards and Morale'.

[83] *BJ* 7. 6–16; on *dona* in general see V. A. Maxfield, *The Military Decorations of the Roman Army* (London, 1981).

Throughout his work Josephus emphasizes that the Roman soldiers were more eager to display their bravery when their commander, who could praise and reward them, was present.[84] It was to their general, that soldiers brought and presented their trophies and captives (*BJ* 6. 163, 7. 197–9). As mentioned earlier, Caesar put his *legati* and *quaestor* in charge of his six legions in 58 BC, so that there were witnesses to individuals' behaviour (*BG* 1. 52). Throughout the Gallic Wars, it is emphasized that troops were expected to fight more bravely when it was their commander himself and not a subordinate who watched their actions.[85] Dio mentioned a general under Domitian, one Julianus, who ordered his men to inscribe their own and their centurions' names on their shields, so that he could recognize those who had shown bravery or cowardice (Dio 67. 10). It is difficult to imagine that the commander can ever have been close enough to read the writing on shields, but at least the men may have felt that they were individually conspicuous, even if this was not so.

The commander could only have acted as a witness in this way, if he moved around and stayed close to the front of a battle. From this position he had a better chance of assessing the situation and directing his reserves accordingly, than a man in the front rank or at the rear. The position was dangerous, perhaps more so than being in the front rank, since the commander could be singled out by opponents. The disadvantage was that a commander in the middle of things did not enjoy the overall view of someone watching from the rear.

DEFEAT AND DISASTER

What did the commander do if things started to go wrong? Initially, he could send reserves to a threatened spot or go there himself and perhaps join in the fighting to inspire his men. Once his troops started to run away, the general might try and stop them. In Asia, Lucullus once was able to rally his fugitives, turn them around and drive back the enemy. He still had the men punished, despite their success (Plutarch, *Lucullus* 15. 6–7). Many commanders are reported as having seized a standard or fleeing standard-bearer in an attempt to stop the rout, and re-form the men. Caesar did this at Dyrrachium and, in his own account, failed to stop the rout and was left holding a *signum* (*BC* 3. 69). Appian and Plutarch both report a story in which one of the

---

[84] *BJ* 5. 311–16, 6. 133–4, 142–6, 245.   [85] *BG* 3. 14, 6. 8, 7. 62.

standard-bearers slashed at Caesar with his sword, and Caesar only escaped being wounded because one of his attendants severed the man's arm with a blow (Plutarch, *Caesar* 39, Appian, *BC* 2. 62). After this action, it was the standard bearers that Caesar punished and demoted, for abandoning the symbols of their units' pride (*BC* 3. 74). In Africa, Caesar is supposed to have been more successful, turning a *signifer* around and saying, 'Look, that's where the enemy are' (Plutarch, *Caesar* 52). He not only stopped the standard-bearer but caused many of the fleeing men to gather around the standard. Sulla is said to have rallied enough men around a standard to hold back Mithridates' army until reserves came up and won the day (Plutarch, *Sulla* 21). In AD 69 Antonius Primus is said to have actually killed a cavalry standard bearer, whom he could not stop from riding away, and, taking the standard himself, rallied about 100 troopers (*Hist.* 3. 17). If a commander could gather even such a small band, he might have been able gradually to stop the rout (Suetonius, *Augustus* 10; Plutarch, *Antony* 8).

The contrasting behaviour of the ambushed Cotta and Sabinus seems to provide us with an example of how a commander should and should not behave in the face of disaster (*BG* 5. 33–7). Sabinus panicked, dashing about the army, spreading his obvious nervousness. He was killed after ordering his tribunes and senior centurions to follow him to negotiate with Ambiorix. Clearly this was how a commander should not behave. Cotta seems to have acted in the way that Romans considered proper. He began by riding around the line, encouraging the men and leading individual units in charges. Whilst he was doing this, he was wounded by a sling-stone and was finally killed fighting against the last Gallic rush.

If the army were not surrounded, then the commander was not expected to fall fighting, even though he had been beaten. In Spain, Pompey was pursued by enemy horsemen and only escaped by abandoning his horse, leaving the enemy to argue over its expensive trappings (Plutarch, *Pompey* 19). Rosenstein, in his study of the political effects of a military defeat on an individual's career, suggests that it was far more important for a commander to display personal *virtus*, than for him to be actually successful.[86] He contrasts Polybius' account of the disaster at Trasimene, in which Flaminius is shown as helpless and confused, with the later version in Livy, where he rides

---

[86] N. Rosenstein, *Imperatores Victi* (Berkeley, 1990), 114–51.

around encouraging the men and is finally killed fighting hand-to-hand (Polybius 3. 84. 6, Livy 22. 6. 2–4). Sallust has little good to say of Catiline, apart from praising the *virtus* that he displayed, leading his army and dying heroically (Sallust, *Bellum Catilinae* 60). Rosenstein's conclusion was that as long as you displayed personal courage and did not flee before your army did, and did not surrender, then it could be considered acceptable to run away.[87]

Rosenstein could find no examples of defeated commanders being prosecuted for lack of technical military ability. A general's career did not suffer as long as he had displayed personal *virtus*.[88] The general showed *virtus* by displaying physical courage in fighting the battle from close behind the front line, setting an example to and inspiring his men. Even when actually defeated, *virtus* did not allow the Roman commander to surrender or admit that Rome had lost the war. Rosenstein was surprised that the technical skills of a defeated commander were never questioned at Rome;[89] influenced by the orthodox view of a commander's role, he looked for technical ability in the use of grand tactics. But the real technical skill of a Roman commander was the ability to direct the small detail of a battle. The commander did this by staying close to the fighting and directing his reserves as the situation required, whilst at the same time encouraging his men by his presence. Leadership and the close direction of units were both vital aspects of *virtus*, exercised simultaneously. Therefore criticism of a commander for failing to show the *virtus* expected of a member of the Roman élite, involved a criticism of a man's technical skill as a general as well as his personal courage.

The importance attached to the unwillingness of Roman commanders to surrender is interesting. In the chapter on 'The Campaign', it became clear that a war was normally decided when the victor had destroyed the enemy's will to fight on, rather than his ability to do so.[90] In this context the refusal to admit defeat contributed to eventual success in the conflict. As in so many other aspects of warfare in this period morale and the appearance of confidence were of more importance in determining the outcome of events, than the reality of force and its practical results.

---

[87] Outside civil wars, it was rare for a defeated Roman commander to commit suicide. Varus is the only definite example of this from our period, Velleius 2. 119. 3.

[88] Rosenstein, *Imperatores Victi*, 6–53. [89] Ibid. 92–113.

[90] See Ch. 3.

VICTORY

You have won a great battle, and the enemy are in full retreat; run
after him; hammer him with guns, charge him with cavalry, above
all things pass around his flanks, and keep pushing him and
hitting him from morning until night. His forces will soon cease
to be an army.

(Lt. Gen. Sir Garnet Wolseley, *The Soldier's Pocket Book for
Field Service* (London, 1882), 335)

Having remained static throughout the battle of Mons Graupius, once
the Britons began to flee, Agricola called for his horse and rode around
organizing the pursuit and urging his men on (*Agricola* 37). After a
defeat, an enemy army is highly vulnerable and the victor normally
enjoys a massive advantage in morale over him. Yet after the enormous
stress of battle, with its combination of fear and physical exertion, it
has throughout history proved difficult to persuade troops to move in
pursuit of the enemy. Even Napoleon, who always sought to destroy
the enemy army after beating it in battle, seldom managed to mount a
concerted pursuit on the night after a battle. It was thus vital for the
commander, who was himself suffering from the same lethargic sense
of relief after the fear of the battle, to force his men to move and
exploit the enemies' weakness. A large-scale, concerted pursuit was
always a mark of Roman warfare, attempting to turn each victory into a
decisive rout (Suetonius, *Caesar* 60). It was much easier to send troops
who had been in reserve, and were therefore fresh, after the enemy,
and as we have seen Roman armies always tended to keep a high
proportion of their strength in reserve.[91] Under the Empire at least, a
commander might hope to have a force of well-trained and disciplined
cavalry to send hunting after the enemy. The use of cavalry in this vital
role should be seen as a sign of their importance in the Imperial army,
not of their ineffectiveness during the battle. Roman pursuits were
organized affairs whenever possible. After Forum Gallorum in 43 BC,
Antony's army, straggling back from a victory, was turned on by a force
of twenty fresh cohorts, force-marched to the area by Hirtius, and
suffered severely (Cicero, *ad Fam.* 10. 30. 4). Arrian planned to keep
all his infantry and half his cavalry as a formed reserve, whilst the other
half pursued the fleeing Alans, in case of the appearance of any new
threat (*Ectaxis* 27–9).

---

[91] See Ch. 4, 'Deployment and Forming a Line of Battle'.

Apart from attempting to destroy the enemy army, the successful commander had also to look after his own troops. Caesar spent several days after defeating the Helvetii in attending to his numerous wounded and dead (*BG* 1. 26). In Italy in 43 BC Antony sent his cavalry out in the night to bring in his wounded left on the battlefield (Appian *BC* 3. 70). During his Parthian campaign Antony went around to visit and speak to the wounded men in the days after a battle, which Plutarch claims helped to keep his men's morale high (Plutarch, *Antony* 43). If a man felt that he would be cared for if wounded, and had some chance of surviving, then he was more likely to risk his life. In Dacia, Trajan on one occasion had his own clothes cut up into bandages to cope with the large number of wounded, another theatrical gesture to encourage good morale in the army (*Dio* 68. 8. 2).

As mentioned before, the commander might choose to decorate men after a battle. He could also punish units or individuals who had misbehaved. Titus had a cavalryman executed for abandoning his horse to the enemy, whilst a legionary *eques*, who had been captured, but had boldly escaped, was expelled from his unit for surrendering in the first place (*BJ* 6. 154–5, 6. 359–62). These were gestures, similar to cutting up his clothes for bandages or visiting the wounded, and formed part of the system of reward and punishment by which the commander encouraged his army to behave in the way that he desired.

CONCLUSION

Earlier in this chapter I referred to the almost universal judgement of scholars that the success of the Roman army had little to do with the abilities of its commanders. This view seems to have been based upon the anachronistic assumption that the most important skill of a general was his use of grand tactics. In this study we have seen that most Roman commanders were very active before, during and after a battle. Before the battle, the general might personally have been involved in the gathering of intelligence, and was certainly concerned with its interpretation. Combining this knowledge of the enemy and ground with that of his own situation and aims, the general was then faced with the decision whether or not to fight a battle, and if so where and when. All the time both he and the opposing commander were seeking to give their armies every possible advantage in the coming engagement. Once he had decided to give, or had been forced into giving, battle, the commander as a general had to issue clear orders, covering unit dispositions and objectives, whilst as a leader he had to inspire the courage of his men. In battle a few commanders stayed well to the rear, directing the fighting by messengers or signals, whilst a very few fought in the front rank as ordinary soldiers, hoping to inspire their men by taking the same risks as they did. Most stayed close to the fighting without actually taking part, encouraging their men and directing their reserves as the situation required. In each sector of the line, subordinate officers were behaving in a similar way, but the general was not tied to any one unit or area, and so could move to wherever a crisis threatened. This mobile style of command required the general to be able to guess where he would be most needed at different stages of the battle, no simple task, which in itself suggests that Roman commanders were not wholly lacking in ability. After the battle, the main task was to make full use of success in the case of victory, pursuing and destroying the enemy's further ability to fight, or to salvage as much as possible of his army in the case of defeat. Overall, the commander's ability must have had a major influence on the result of a battle, since he played an important role at every stage of the action.

The universally harsh judgement of scholars regarding the ability of Roman commanders rests on the fundamentally anachronistic assumption that grand tactics were the general's most important skill. Few battles involving the Roman army were decided by subtle tactical moves. In 58 BC Caesar defeated both the Helvetii and Ariovistus in battles that were simple head-on clashes between the opposing lines. In the Civil War of 49–45 BC the decisive battles were comparatively simple affairs. Pharsalus saw an attempted outflanking attack by Pompey, but both Thapsus and Munda were simple collisions between the opposing armies. Both the later Battles of Philippi were similarly unsubtle affairs, as were the major engagements in AD 68–9. Yet in all these battles, the victorious Roman commanders were very active behind the battle line, encouraging their men and deploying reserves as the situation required. Victory came when a break made in the enemy line could be exploited by reserves to roll up the rest of his army. A high proportion, often the majority, of a Roman army was positioned behind the main line in reserve at the commander's disposal, to allow him to exploit breaks in the enemy line and plug gaps in his own. Only a commander able to move around the battlefield could properly assess where these reserves could best be deployed. The highly organized command structure of the Roman army did not, as the orthodox view suggests, take control away from the general, but did the exact opposite and concentrated it in his hands. The technical skill of the Roman general lay not in the sweeping moves of grand tactics, but in paying close attention to the detail of small unit tactics, directing his units, especially the reserves, in response to the changing situation on the battlefield. This role could best be performed by a commander who kept close to the fighting, without becoming personally involved in it.

The Roman general played a vital role in determining the success of his army. How far was a Roman commander prepared and trained for his job? Did his upbringing and periods of subordinate military service make up for his lack of formal military training, as this would be understood in modern armies? The ability to 'read' a battle and direct reserves accordingly could only have been learnt by experience. Service in subordinate ranks or as a *contubernalis* of another commander could contribute towards this experience. The upbringing of a member of the Roman élite and his pursuit of a political career required him to deal with and 'lead' people for most of his adult life. It is unsurprising that many commanders interacted with their soldiers in the same way that a magistrate dealt with the *plebs* at Rome.

The upbringing and social environment of the Roman aristocrat gave him a clear image of what the 'good commander' was like. Above all else he should possess courage or *virtus*. First, he must possess the moral courage to take and stick to decisions affecting the army. Second, he must possess the physical courage to expose himself in the front line, encouraging and directing his men. *Virtus* was the most essential attribute of the Roman aristocrat, a virtue that his upbringing had taught him to admire above all else. Not all would have possessed it, but the standards of Roman society meant that most did to some degree. Aristocratic *virtus* seems to have been divorced from actual killing in our period. Some commanders did choose to fight and were praised for it, but it was more important for the general to direct and encourage his men, rather than to fight in the same way as one of them.

It is noticeable that a *novus homo*, such as Marius, behaved in basically the same way when commanding an army as a *nobilis* such as Metellus. Similarly Labienus, a member of the *domi nobiles*, led in essentially the same style as Caesar or Pompey. Sallust attributed a speech to Marius in which he emphasized his own military experience, compared to his rivals who relied on their family name, rather than personal ability, in seeking election (Sallust, *Jug.* 85. 5–43). The implication was that these men failed to display the military qualities expected of a Roman senator. Roman commanders were expected to be capable of performing the active role required of them in battle.

This has implications for our understanding of Roman society in general, and in particular the nature of competition amongst the élite. A senator was expected to display *virtus* when given a military command. This included technical skill as well as personal bravery. If a man failed to display this, then his political career suffered. He was also liable to prosecution brought by another member of Rome's élite. There was no formal procedure to train commanders or to punish those who had failed, but the system did encourage ability. This might suggest that in other fields of political activity personal ability was vital for further success. This ability might not have been of the kind that modern commentators would expect to find in a particular role, in the same way that the general's role was peculiar to the Roman army. It was in the interest of the state to have able men in important magistracies, but the methods of ensuring this might well be unique to Roman society.

5

The Unit's Battle

Le combat est le but final des armées et l'homme est l'instrument premier du combat.

(Col. Ardant du Picq, *L'Études sur le Combat* (Paris, 1914), 1)

A la Guerre, les trois quarts sont des affaires morales, la balance des forces réalles n'est que pour un autre quart.

(Napoleon, *Observation sur les affaires d'Espagne*)

HAVING looked at the battlefield role of the general and his immediate subordinates, in this chapter I shall examine the fighting from the perspective of the individual unit, the cohort or *ala*. There have been many studies of the unit tactics of the Roman army, often in conjunction with the examinations of generalship discussed in the last chapter. Delbrück attempted to explain in detail how the legion, based on the maniple and later the cohort, worked in battle, dealing with equipment, formations, and tactics.[1] Other scholars have adopted a similar approach, whilst differing on the minutiae of these aspects.[2] The ancient sources were often ambiguous or silent concerning points of minor tactics, allowing room for debate. Most scholars, such as Keppie, have assumed that ancient authors believed that their audience had full knowledge of these aspects of military practice, and so did not deal with it. They have not considered the possibility that ancient authors did not consider tactics to have been important.[3] Von Domaszewski doubted that the battle tactics of the legions of the Principate could ever be reconstructed, given the lack of technical detail in the literary sources after Caesar.[4] Recently, Speidel attempted

---

[1] H. Delbrück, *History of the Art of War*, i (Westport, 1975), 412–28.
[2] e.g. Maj.-Gen. J. F. C. Fuller, *Julius Caesar: Man, Soldier and Tyrant* (London, 1965), 85–91, or T. Rice Holmes, *Caesar's Conquest of Gaul* (Oxford, 1911), 587–99.
[3] L. Keppie, *The Making of the Roman Army* (London, 1984), 96.
[4] A. von Domaszewski, 'Die Fahnen im römischen Heere', *Aufsätze zur römischen Heeresgeschichte* (Darmstaat, 1972), 1.

to fill in the gaps in the literary evidence by using information concerning unit organization derived from inscriptions and the excavation of fortress sites.[5] Like those scholars who had relied exclusively on literary evidence, he assumed that the imperial legion followed a standard method of operation, or battle-drill. This is an understandably attractive assumption, since a coherent picture will only emerge if the isolated scraps of evidence are treated as indications of a single tactical drill. Thus all these scholars have suggested that the legions and *auxilia* always deployed in standard formations, or attacked in a certain number of lines. When our sources clearly describe Roman units using different tactics, then it is concluded that by this date all units in the army had replaced their old battle-drill with this new method of operation. Therefore Wheeler claimed that the formation used by Arrian's legions in Cappadocia was the standard tactic of all legions under Hadrian, having replaced the *triplex acies* of Caesar's day.[6] Speidel was unwilling to go this far, but did believe that the equipping of half of the Cappadocian legionaries with javelins instead of *pila* showed that all legions by the 130s AD had a similar division of weaponry.[7] There is no reason to believe that the Roman army did not adapt its tactics, formations, and equipment to local circumstances.[8] Any investigation of tactics must consider why these were adopted, and how they worked or did not work, in the context of the local situation, and not try to devise a tactical formula that can then be applied to all situations.[9]

The way in which scholars have discussed tactics, and generals' use of them, has tended to encourage them to view cohorts and *alae* as units in every sense of the word. They became single entities, which moved and fought as one block, automatically following orders, instead of collections of individuals, capable of acting for themselves and affected by human instincts. A general moved these units which, like pieces on a chessboard, had certain unvarying capabilities and limitations, in such a way as to defeat the opposing commander. This

---

[5] M. P. Speidel, *The Framework of an Imperial Legion*, Fifth Annual Caerleon Lecture (Cardiff, 1992), see Ch. 1.

[6] E. Wheeler, 'The Legion as Phalanx', *Chiron*, 9 (1979), 303–18.

[7] Speidel, *Framework* 15 n. 18.   [8] See Ch. 1.

[9] For a discussion of the method of studying tactics, see P. Griffith, *Rally Once Again: Battle Tactics in the American Civil War* (Marlborough, 1987), App. 1, 193–6, who emphasizes the need to understand both the technical and psychological aspects of combat.

dehumanized view of battles made their study more palatable to scholars.[10] Yet this approach does not explain what happened in a battle and why it happened. What actually happened when two or more opposing units of infantry or cavalry encountered one another? Adopting this approach, the only important differences between troops were in their equipment, formation, or training. The morale of the units, both as composite bodies and as individuals, was seldom dealt with, save in the vaguest sense, such as describing some troops as 'veterans' and some as 'raw'. As with the studies of generalship, the result is a blurring between periods of history, the assumption being that for units as for commanders there are certain factors common to all periods of history, which explain success or failure in battle.

There has been an alternative approach to the study of the Roman army in battle, which in many respects is the opposite of the study of unit tactics. This has been to examine the equipment, armour, and weapons of the individual soldier and try to deduce from these the manner in which he fought. Todd studied warfare amongst the early Germans on the basis of changes in weaponry, using this as a guide to the fighting techniques of individuals.[11] This approach, based as it is around pieces of equipment, has understandably been most common amongst archaeologists, who have produced much of the information about this in recent years. An extreme example of the genre is an article by P. Connolly in which he attempted to explain changes in the design of helmets and swords as results of altered styles of individual fighting.[12] Implicit in his approach were several assumptions, all of which are open to doubt. First it may be questioned whether all changes in such equipment as weaponry and armour were due purely to military and not stylistic or cultural considerations.[13] Second, the concentration on equipment can turn the soldier into an unthinking automaton as easily as the emphasis on unit tactics. The man using a

---

[10] For the historiography of military history in general see J. Keegan, *The Face of Battle* (London, 1976), 53–72.

[11] M. Todd, *The Northern Barbarians* (Oxford, 1987), 140–82. Contrast with E. A. Thompson, *The Early Germans* (Oxford, 1965), 109–49, who dealt more with organization. See Ch. 2, 'The Germans'.

[12] P. Connolly, 'The Roman Fighting Technique Deduced from Armour and Weaponry', in V. A. Maxfield and M. J. Dobson (eds.), *Roman Frontier Studies 1989* (Exeter, 1991), 358–63.

[13] M. C. Bishop and J. C. N. Coulston, *Roman Military Equipment* (London, 1993), esp. 196.

weapon, and subject to extremes of emotion, most of all fear, under the stress of battle, was and is more important than the implement he uses. To assume simply that he is a disciplined Roman soldier and therefore would have continued to carry out the drills taught to him despite the stress of battle, is contrary to our literary evidence. We must understand the behaviour of the man using the weapons and wearing the armour, if we are to understand battles. This is not to say that the studies of weaponry have not contributed much to our understanding of the technical limitations of the military equipment of the period. Connolly's work on the Roman saddle, for instance, has shown us just what a Roman cavalryman was capable of doing.[14] Even so, he did not attempt to use this information to show how several hundred horseman acting as a unit would have behaved.

If neither a concentration on unit tactics, nor on individual fighting techniques allow us to understand battles fully, then it is largely because these approaches do not treat the soldier as a human being, who may not have acted as he was ordered, or trained to do, under the stress of combat. Both are factors that need to be placed into the context of the behaviour of soldiers as men. This approach was suggested by Colonel Ardant du Picq in the nineteenth century, who argued that any study of warfare must be based on an understanding of the behaviour and morale of soldiers.[15] In his study of ancient warfare, he concentrated on two battles, Cannae and Pharsalus, and sought to explain them in terms of the morale of the participants.[16] This work has made virtually no impact on scholarship on the subject and, undeservedly, is now seldom read. Some of his conclusions may be questionable, and this part of the work, as compared to that dealing with contemporary warfare, is brief and does not deal with some issues, but many of his conclusions, for instance that most men were killed in ancient battles whilst they were running away, still hold good.

John Keegan's *The Face of Battle* has received more attention with its different approach to the study of military history, and most of all of battles. Keegan examined the battles of Agincourt, Waterloo, and the first day of the Somme, and attempted to explain what happened

---

[14] P. Connolly, 'The Roman Saddle', in M. Dawson (ed.), *Roman Military Equipment: The Accoutrements of War*, BAR 336 (Oxford, 1987), 7–27.
[15] Col. Ardant Du Picq, *L'Études sur le Combat* (Paris, 1914), 1–2.
[16] Ibid. 25–43, 45–63.

during these and why. His attention was always focused on the individual participant and his experience of the battle. Keegan's approach has been adopted by several scholars studying hoplite warfare in Classical Greece. Pritchett began by attempting to analyse warfare and battle in this period.[17] Hanson argued that there was not enough information about any one Greek battle to analyse it using Keegan's method, so instead attempted to describe a 'typical' battle, drawing evidence from all accounts of fighting in the period.[18] These studies significantly increased our understanding of hoplite battles, most of all giving an impression of what they were like. The soldier is placed in the context of his tactics and equipment, but most of all is treated as an individual, coping, or failing to cope, with the stress of battle.

The comparatively simple nature of the hoplite battle, in which everything depended upon a single clash between two similarly armed and organized phalanxes, was ideally suited to analysis based on a 'typical' battle. The battles involving the Roman army in our period were far more complicated affairs. They involved many different units and troop types, and were composed of many small clashes between units. Therefore, this type of battle does not lend itself to a chronological examination of a 'typical' action from beginning to end. However, as with Greek warfare, we do not have sufficiently good sources to analyse in detail any one battle. Instead, in this chapter I shall modify Keegan's method of examining a single battle according to different types of combat to include information from all the actions described by our sources.[19] These categories will be, 'Skirmishing and Missile Fire', 'Close-Order Infantry against Close-Order Infantry', 'Cavalry against Infantry', and 'Cavalry against Cavalry'. Single combat and the actions of individuals will be dealt with in the next chapter, dealing with individual motivation. Each section will attempt to combine a discussion of the behaviour of individual soldiers with the technical side of fighting.

---

[17] W. Kendrick Pritchett, *The Greek State at War*, iv (Berkeley, 1985).

[18] V. D. Hanson, *The Western Way of War: Infantry Battle in Classical Greece* (New York, 1989), and *Hoplites: The Classical Greek Battle Experience* (1991), esp. J. Lazenby, 'The Killing Zone', 87–109.

[19] Keegan, *The Face of Battle* 92–107, 144–94, 247–58. For Waterloo the categories were 'Single Combat', 'Cavalry versus Cavalry', 'Cavalry versus Artillery', 'Cavalry versus Infantry', 'Artillery versus Infantry', 'Infantry versus Infantry'.

FORMATIONS

Before discussing the various types of combat which went to make up a battle, it is worth examining what can be reconstructed of the formations used by Roman units. In the last chapter, the deployment of the army as a whole was discussed, and several points made about the way in which a body of men moved across country.[20] To recapitulate, it is important to recall several of them. First, a unit of men will not move in a perfectly straight line when advancing over a battlefield. As a result, there had to be intervals between units if these were to maintain their integrity and so be able to manoeuvre following the orders of their officers. The intervals between separate cohorts and *alae* must therefore have been quite large.[21] Smaller gaps must have been kept between the centuries or *turmae* of the unit itself in order to allow it to change formation, front or direction of march, if and when required. Therefore a line of cohorts was not actually a solid, continuous line of men. Even the lines of the individual cohorts comprising it had small intervals between their centuries. When units became crowded together, so that these intervals disappeared, it was a sign that things were going badly wrong, as will be discovered later.[22]

Second, the width of a formation affected its speed of movement. It is impossible for men moving across country to maintain a perfectly straight line. This was made worse by any irregularities in the ground. Therefore a wide, shallow formation—which would have encountered more obstacles and have been subject to the deviation in direction of more individuals—had to stop to dress ranks more often than a narrower formation, otherwise the formation would have broken up and no longer responded to orders. Therefore a narrow-fronted formation moved significantly faster than a wider one. The quality of the unit's drill and discipline also affected this. A poorly drilled unit would have lost its order more quickly when moving in a wide formation, than a well-drilled one. It is no coincidence that Greek hoplites in the fifth century, who, apart from the Spartans, were not normally well drilled and trained, formed and moved in phalanxes

---

[20] Ch. 4, 'Deployment and Forming a Line of Battle'.
[21] The Byzantine manual, *Maurice's Strategikon*, 12. 17, recommended gaps of 30–60 m. (100–200 feet) between each *meros*.
[22] *BG* 2. 25, 5. 43, *Ann.* 2. 21, 14. 37.

eight ranks or more deep.[23] Similarly, the ill-trained infantry of Revolutionary France abandoned the shallow, wide-line formation of the Ancien Régime and replaced it with a narrow-fronted column.[24] A deep formation has often been the sign of poorly drilled troops.

The problems of moving a body of men across a battlefield and keeping them in an ordered body that was responsive to command, is one of the practical considerations in determining the formation used. The other practical factor involved, namely the need to employ the unit's weaponry in the most effective way, to some extent conflicted with this. Some missile weapons could have been fired or thrown over several ranks of men and still have been effective. Arrian in Cappadocia formed his infantry with the fifth to eighth ranks throwing javelins over the heads of the men in front of them. Behind these was a ninth rank of foot archers and a tenth of horse-archers, firing over the men in front of them (*Ectaxis* 17–18, 21). A formation using long spears or pikes might have been able to reach the enemy with the weapons of more than one rank.[25] However, Roman legionaries and most auxiliaries were primarily swordsmen. The killing zone of a sword extended only a metre or so from the body of the user. (The killing zone is the area in which a weapon is capable of inflicting physical injury on the enemy.) If a cohort of swordsmen aimed to kill or wound the maximum number of the enemy, then it would have aimed to have as high a proportion of its men as possible in contact with the opposing unit, and therefore in the front rank of its formation. In short, it would have deployed in a single rank, or perhaps two ranks, if it was considered desirable to have men behind to replace any casualties. One of the reasons that neither the Romans nor any of the armies that they faced did deploy in this manner was the practical difficulty of moving and manœuvring a formation as wide as a single or double rank.

Practical considerations were not however the only factors affecting formation. Shallower lines, especially those of a single rank, would have only worked if all the men composing them were uniformly brave.

---

[23] Pritchett, *The Greek State at War*, i (1971), 134–43. The Spartans and the better-drilled mercenaries of the 4th cent. might deploy 4 deep.

[24] Keegan, *The Face of Battle* 32–3.

[25] Polybius 18. 29; see also V. D. Hanson, *Western Way of War* 84–5.

The seventeenth-century military theorist, Raimondo Monteuccoli, explained what happened if a unit deployed in a single line attempted to attack the enemy.

When a troop is formed as a hedgerow (i.e. in a single line) even though the brave soldiers, who are normally in the minority, proceed resolutely to the fray, the others, who are normally in the majority, remain behind. And so, over a distance of 200 paces, one sees this long rank thin out and dissolve. Great breaks occur in it, which miraculously encourages the enemy.[26]

Any ranks behind the first in the formation, by their sheer physical presence, prevented the men in the front rank from running away. Greek military theorists thought it best to place the bravest men in a phalanx in its front and rear ranks. Those in front kept the formation advancing, and actually fought. Those in the rear stopped the others from fleeing (Asclepiodotus, *Tactics* 14. 6; Xenophon, *Mem.* 3. 19). Under extreme stress, man seems to have been, and still is, by nature subject to the herd instinct. Even on the modern battlefield, the tendency of men under fire to bunch together has often been noted, even when this made them more of a target.[27] S. L. A. Marshall, who studied the behaviour of the American soldier during combat in the Second World War and Korean War, concluded that the most important factor in keeping a soldier actively fighting against the enemy was the close proximity of his comrades.[28] Deep formations kept the men moving and allowed them to attack as a body. The physical presence of the men behind the front rank helped to keep these from fleeing from any perceived threats. In the same way that better-drilled troops could have manœuvred in wider, shallower formations, a unit with higher morale could have adopted a shallower formation on the battlefield than a less confident unit. It partially countered the urge of its members to flee from any threat by qualities of leadership, confidence, and discipline, so that it had less need to rely on the physical presence of the rear ranks, to hold its members within its formation.[29] Once again, a shallower formation, when successfully used, could be the hallmark of a good unit.

---

[26] T. Barker, *The Military Intellectual and Battle* (Albany, NY, 1975), 92.

[27] W. Trotter, *The Instincts of the Herd in Peace and War* (London, 1947).

[28] S. L. A. Marshall, *Men against Fire* (New York, 1947), 42.

[29] Both Vegetius 3. 15, and the author of the *Strategikon*, 2. 6, 12. 11, recommended deeper formations for less reliable troops.

With these considerations of the factors affecting formations in mind, we may now turn to the evidence for those used by the Roman army. It is easiest to start with the infantry, since there is more information concerning their formations, vague and contradictory though it often appears to be.

We have two conflicting versions of the area which an individual soldier was supposed to occupy in the ranks of a legionary line, both from outside our period. Polybius, in a passage comparing the relative merits of the legion and the pike phalanx, claims that each legionary was allotted 180 cm. (6 foot) frontage and 180 cm. (6 foot) depth, as opposed to the phalangites 90 cm. (3 foot) by 90 cm. (3 foot) (Polybius 18. 28–30). The space allotted to the Roman, conforms with the normal order of Asclepiodotus, which he viewed as only appropriate for a column of march, and it does seem a very loose order for the battlefield (Asclepiodotus, *Tactica* 4). Pritchett has cast doubt on the text of this portion of Polybius, especially the numbers, arguing that the pikeman occupied less than the 90 cm. (3 foot) that was allotted to him by Polybius (*The Greek State at War*, i (Berkeley, 1971), 144–54). Our other version of the space occupied by a single legionary is given by Vegetius, who appears to be using a source describing the Republican army at this point, since he refers to lines of *hastati*, *principes*, and *triarii* (Vegetius 3. 14, 15). He gives the frontage for a single man as 90 cm. (3 foot), and the depth as 2 m. (7 foot) (including 30 cm. (1 foot) occupied by the man himself). The depth was required to allow a man room to throw his *pilum* without striking the man behind. The 90 cm. (3-foot) width would seem to have allowed a man sufficient space to fight with his sword, whilst still being close enough to his comrades on either side to feel reassured by their presence. Compared to eighteenth- and nineteenth-century armies, the space allotted is quite generous. British Infantry of the Napoleonic Wars were allowed only 53 by 81 cm. (21 by 32 inches) deep, in which to perform the complicated motions necessary to load and fire a musket.[30] Vegetius' figures for the area normally occupied by a legionary seem more plausible than those of Polybius, but it is not possible to prove that he is correct for our period. Even if his figures are correct, then some legionaries, at some periods in some provinces, may have fought in significantly looser order, such as the Pompeian legionaries in Spain in 49 BC (*BC* 1. 44). There does not appear to be

[30] J. Weller, *Wellington at Waterloo* (London, 1992), App. 1.

any suggestion in our sources that a Roman infantryman in mêlée normally occupied more or less space than any of their opponents in our period.

The evidence for the number of ranks that a cohort normally formed is apparently contradictory. At Pharsalus, Pompey deployed his legions in lines ten ranks deep (Frontinus, *Strategemata* 2. 3. 22). Josephus twice mentions Roman infantry deployed in lines three deep. In the first instance, Pontius Pilate surrounded and attacked a crowd with such a line (*BJ* 2. 173). In the second, a line formed by three ranks of infantry, had a fourth rank of archers, and a further three of cavalry behind them (*BJ* 5. 131). When the army marched in column, its men were formed six abreast (*BJ* 3. 124). If we assume that Josephus did not mention these figures because they were deviations from a normal practice, which he assumed that his audience was familiar with (and this does not seem an unreasonable assumption), then he is clearly describing a system of drill based on multiples of three. A column six abreast, could have wheeled to form a line six deep and perhaps closed ranks from the looser marching order to form a line three deep. Vegetius seems to lend some support to a drill book based around threes and sixes in his description of the battle line (Vegetius 3. 15). He gives figures for the space occupied by lines of men, three and six deep, preferring the latter for its extra solidity, and also allowed for a ten deep line in exceptional situations.

However, in Arrian's army in Cappadocia the legions and cohorts appear to have employed formations based around multiples of four. His men marched in a column four abreast and then formed up eight deep to counter the expected Alan charge.[31] The depth of this formation was intended to allow the infantry to withstand an attack by enemy heavy cavalry, suggesting that they might have deployed in a shallower array, perhaps a line four deep, to face enemy infantry. Hellenistic military manuals described formations based around multiples of four ranks, as did the fifth-century Byzantine manual, *Maurice's Strategikon*, which preserved Latin commands and seems to have been heavily influenced by the practices of the earlier Roman army (*Strategikon* 12. 9–11). It may be that the system of drill described by Josephus had been replaced by an alternative system by the time of Arrian's Cappadocian campaign. Just as plausibly, individual legions

---

[31] *Ectaxis* 4, 5, 15–17.

may have had their own systems of drill, based on local requirements or purely on unit tradition.[32]

Such as it is, the evidence suggests that a cohort of legionaries or auxiliaries normally fought in a line three or four deep, and might have deployed six or eight deep if facing cavalry, in a confined space, or of questionable morale. Pompey's use of a ten-deep formation at Pharsalus was made possible by his superior numbers, but made necessary because his men were of significantly lower morale and less experienced than Caesar's troops (*BC* 3. 87, 3. 92). At Cannae, the unusually ill-trained and inexperienced Roman legions were deployed far deeper than was normally the case (Polybius 3. 113). When facing Pharnaces in 48 BC, Domitius formed a Galatian legion of questionable morale and loyalty in an exceptionally deep formation. In the event this made little difference, and the unit was routed by the first attack (*Alexandrian War* 39).

There is no evidence explaining the order in which the centuries of a cohort, and the *contubernia* within the centuries, were arranged to make up the unit's formation. If a unit had to advance a long distance towards the enemy (and armies often deployed several miles apart),[33] then it might have moved in a more manœuvrable, narrow-fronted column, before deploying into line near the enemy. Local circumstances might have dictated whether a cohort then deployed all its centuries in a single line, or echeloned to right or left, or perhaps with them in more than one line. Speidel suggested that each century, forming a four-deep line, was deployed one behind the other, giving the unit a width of 20 files and a depth of 24 ranks.[34] Such a formation might have been necessary to assault enemy fortifications, especially through a breach in the wall. On the battlefield, it is likely that only troops of highly dubious morale needed to be formed in such depth. Unless a unit formed in such a way could rely on frightening the enemy purely by its dense appearance, causing them to flee before it had contacted them, then it would have performed poorly in actual contact. Only the front rank of the unit could have employed their swords, whilst the majority of men would not even have been able to throw their *pila* without severe risk to the ranks in front of them.

---

[32] In the 18th cent. the British army had no standard drillbook until 1788. Prior to that a battalion's drill had been dictated by its colonel. See M. Glover, *Peninsula Preparation* (Cambridge, 1963), 116–22. Also see Ch. 3, 'The Order of March'.

[33] Ch. 4, 'Deployment and Forming a Line of Battle'.

[34] Speidel, *Framework*, pp. 20–2.

Where did the officers of the century stand in its formation? Centurions were expected to lead from the front. Whenever anything went wrong, they suffered a disproportionately high casualty rate.[35] Perhaps the centurion stood slightly ahead and to the right (the right being the natural side of offensive action) of the front rank. The *pilus prior*, commander of the cohort,[36] may have been stationed away from his century, perhaps near the centre of the line of the entire cohort. Speidel has plausibly argued that the *optio* of the century stood behind the rear rank.[37] From this position he could have used his long *hastile*, which was his staff of office, to control the men in front of him. The officers of the Byzantine army described in the *Strategikon*, used their staves to prod any soldier breaking the silence of the battle line, and also could stop any man from attempting to flee from his position. Livy described Gallic leaders at Mutina in 193 BC attempting to prevent the men in the rear ranks from fleeing by striking them with their spear shafts, forcing them onwards (Livy 35. 5. 10). In the eighteenth and nineteenth centuries, the sergeants in many European armies carried spontoons or halberds, polearmes of negligible value in contemporary warfare, so that using the long staff of these laterally, they could push their men on, physically preventing them from running away.[38] Once again this practice can explain the desirability of forming poor troops in a deeper formation, with fewer men in each rank. The *optio* at the rear of such formation had fewer men to force into position and might therefore have prevented the unit from running away for a longer period.

Cavalry formations are even more obscure than those of the infantry. The *Strategikon* claimed that 'the Ancients', which may well mean the Roman army of some period, formed their cavalry four deep (*Strategikon* 2. 6). Josephus recorded a line of horseman, three ranks deep, deployed behind an infantry formation (*BJ* 5. 135). In his *Tactica* Arrian deals largely with the tactics and formations used by a double *turma* of 64 men (*Tactica* 18. 2). On cavalry formations for larger units he recommends generally that these should be considerably wider than they were deep, but does not go into any greater detail (*Tactica* 16–17). Even so a very deep formation might be employed to break through an enemy line (*Tactica* 17. 3). An individual horseman must have occupied

---

[35] e.g. *BG* 6. 40, 7. 50–1, *Ann.* 12. 38; see Ch. 6, 'Part 1 (c) Leadership'.
[36] Ch. 1, 'Unit Organization: Theory and Practice'.
[37] Speidel, *Framework*, 24–6.   [38] Keegan, *The Face of Battle*, 185.

a space at least a metre wide, even if deployed in a line knee to knee, and perhaps had a depth of 4 m. (12 foot).

Other formations, such as the wedge, might have been used by both infantry and cavalry. Vegetius defined a wedge as being wider at the rear than at the front (Vegetius 3. 19). These formations seem to have had a specific battlefield function and can probably best be understood in the context of an examination of combat.

SKIRMISHING AND MISSILE EXCHANGE

A high proportion of soldiers both in the Roman army and in the armies of its opponents, carried some form of missile weapon. The legionaries had their *pila*, and most auxiliaries, both cavalry and infantry, who were not specifically archers or slingers, carried several javelins.[39] Depending on the local situation, a Roman army might also have had support from artillery, usually light bolt-shooters, the scorpions, but occasionally heavy stone-throwing engines.[40] Ammianus Marcellinus, writing of battles in the fourth century, left a vivid picture of battles in which the air seemed to be full of volleys of missiles.[41] In our period, most authors seem to have assumed that a battle at least began with an exchange of missiles.[42]

Before discussing the tactical role of troops with missile weapons, it is worth discussing the ranges and attributes of those available. The weapon with the shortest range was the *pilum*. Designed to concentrate all its force behind a small head for maximum penetration of armour and shield, this was thrown in the last stages of a legionary charge, and so will be discussed in the section on infantry combat. Its maximum range was about 30 m. (100 feet).[43] Most javelins were lighter than the *pilum*, having shorter but broader iron heads. These had reduced powers of armour penetration, but greater range, perhaps as much as twice that of a *pilum*. Javelins might have been thrown by close-order

---

[39] Bishop and Coulston, *Roman Military Equipment*, 48–53, 65–9, 79–81, 112–15, 123, 206–9.

[40] Scorpions: *BG* 2. 8, *Ann.* 1. 56, 2. 20, *Ectaxis* 19, Trajan's Column scenes 104–5, 163–4, 165–7, 169; Heavy stone throwing engines: *Hist.* 3. 22.

[41] e.g. at Strasbourg 16. 12. 21–54.

[42] e.g. Appian, *BC* 2. 78 describing Pharsalus.

[43] Based on trials carried out under Napoleon III, J. B. Vechère de Reffye, 'Les Armes d' Alise', *RA* 2 (1864), 342, and more recently in M. Junkelmann, *Die Legionen des Augustus* (Mainz, 1991), 188.

infantry or cavalry during a charge, or used by loose-order troops, who did not close with the enemy.[44]

Estimates have varied as to the effective range of the composite bow used by Roman archers.[45] Vegetius claimed that archers should train by shooting at a target some 200 metres away (Vegetius 2. 23). The same French trials under Napoleon III that gave the estimate for *pilum* range, estimated the range of the Roman bow to have been 165–175 m. (175–190 yards). Other modern studies have given various estimates for ranges. Bivar suggested a maximum range of 250 yards [230 m.] and an effective range of 100 yards [90 m.], Collingwood of 250 and 150 yards [230 and 150 m.] respectively, whilst McLeod reduced effective range to 55–65 yards [50–60 m.].[46] Later Arabic and Saracen Manuals, dealing with horse-archers, claim that a proficient archer ought to be able to hit automatically a target 90 cm. (3 feet) in diameter at 70 m. (75 yards) range.[47] A horse-archer normally used a less-powerful bow than a foot archer, and thus had a shorter range. This is because the archer standing on his own feet can achieve better balance than a man on horseback, so that the strength and weight of his whole body contributes to the bow shot. A horse-archer has to rely upon the strength of his torso and arms.

One of the main reasons why opinions have varied so widely on the effective range of Roman bows is that the skill of the archer was and is far more important in determining this than the technology of the bow. Unlike firearms or weapons such as the crossbow, which store chemical or potential energy and, by releasing this, propel their missile, a bow converts the bodily strength of the firer into a force propelling the arrow. This skill is much harder to learn than the use of a firearm, which has only to be loaded and aimed to be effective. This partially explains why muskets replaced bows, that in most respects out-performed them, when armies expanded and became regular in

---

[44] *Germ.* 6, Arrian, *Tactica* 40. 9, 41–2.

[45] On archery in the Roman army see J. C. Coulston, 'Roman Archery Equipment', in M. C. Bishop (ed.), *The Production and Distribution of Roman Military Equipment. Proceedings of the Second Roman Military Equipment Research Seminar, BAR* 275 (Oxford, 1985), 230–348.

[46] Ibid. 290 for a discussion of ranges, in which he wisely avoids being too dogmatic. The most conservative estimate comes from W. McLeod, 'The Range of the Ancient Bow', *Phoenix,* 19 (1965), 1–14, esp. 8.

[47] J. D. Latham and W. F. Paterson, *Saracen Archery: A Mameluke Work, c. 1368* (London, 1970).

the seventeenth century.[48] In military history, periods in which archers have enjoyed great success, such as that of the English longbowmen in the Hundred Years War, have usually been due not to technological advances in types of bow, but simply because a large number of better-quality archers were available than had been the case before.[49] This is not to say that the technical quality of an archer's bow made no difference at all. A composite bow, which was certainly used as a war bow by the Romans even if self bows were used for practice, combines several types of wood and sinew in tension with each other. This gave more force to the arrow fired, than a self bow of the same draw strength. The Romans deployed archers, who used good quality bows, in specialist units, so that a reasonably high level of skills might have been expected.[50]

These archers, like those today, used the Mediterranean release. In this, the bow is held in the left hand, the arm stretched out straight. The right hand holds the string, one finger above the flight of the arrow, and one or two below. The right hand is drawn back to the chest or the chin, before the string is released. Since the bow string passes close to the inside of the left arm, a bracer, or leather arm guard, is worn to prevent bruising. Arrows varied in type, but included often the short, narrow-headed type (known in the Middle Ages as the bodkin point) which were intended to penetrate armour, acting on the same principles as the *pilum*.[51] Except at very close range, even these arrows might not have penetrated both shield and armour to wound the target. When archers fired at Roman legionaries, or other similarly well-protected troops, far more arrows that hit caused wounds rather than fatalities. At Carrhae in 53 BC, the Parthian arrows failed to penetrate the Roman shields and armour, but caused many wounds to the unprotected legs and right arm (Plutarch, *Crassus* 25. 4–5). At Dyrrachium in 48 BC, a fort garrisoned by three cohorts of Caesar's legionaries endured a heavy assault, supported by especially heavy concentrations of archers. Most of the garrison were wounded, and four centurions from one cohort lost their eyes (*BC* 3. 53). Once again, the legionaries wore armour and carried shields that protected their bodies, and helmets that covered all their heads apart from their face.

---

[48] J. Keegan, *The Mask of Command* (London, 1987), 168–71.
[49] J. Bradbury, *The Medieval Archer* (Woodbridge, 1985), 71–115.
[50] For the tactical use of bows and their distribution see Coulston, 292–8.
[51] Coulston, 'Roman Archery Equipment', 282.

Arrow wounds to the limbs, and perhaps to the face, did not necessarily incapacitate a man immediately, nor would a man have been knocked over by an arrow hit except at very close range.

The use of the sling by the Roman army is less clear than its use of archers. Caesar had Balearic slingers with his army in Gaul, and Tacitus makes several vague references to *funditores*, but there were no known cohorts of slingers under the Principate.[52] *Glandes* have been found at many sites, and unarmoured slingers appear on Trajan's Column, but the only definite reference to the use of slings by an auxiliary cohort, appeared in Hadrian's address at Lambaesis to the *Cohors VI Commagenorum Equitata*.[53] How many men, in how many units, used the sling during our period is unclear. Like the bow, proficiency with the sling could only have been achieved by constant practice. Unlike an arrow, a sling stone could not be seen in flight, and so avoided. In addition it did not need to penetrate a piece of armour, especially a helmet, to incapacitate the target. A blow from a sling stone on a helmet might well have given the wearer concussion (Celsus, *De Medicina* 5. 26, 7. 55). The slinger could therefore be more dangerous to armoured targets than an archer. The range of the sling is, like that of the bow, difficult to estimate.[54] Anecdotal evidence suggests that some slingers could fire effectively further than some archers, but more usually their range was not more than, and probably less than, that of an archer. Once again, much depended upon the skill of the firer, and for effectiveness, on the amount of protection worn by the target.

There were two options open to any troops employing missile weapons. One was to aim at individual targets, singling out an enemy soldier and firing at him. The alternative was to attempt to land as many missiles as possible within a wider area. In this case, the aim was not to hit specific targets, but to land so many missiles around the area in which a unit was positioned that some enemies were bound to be hit. Effectively, the firer was shooting at a unit rather than an individual. In

---

[52] *Ann.* 2. 20; for the use of slings by the Romans see W. B. Griffiths 'The Sling and its Place in the Roman Imperial Army', in C. van Driel-Murray (ed.), *Roman Military Equipment: The Sources of Evidence. Proceedings of the Fifth Roman Military Equipment Conference, BAR* 476 (Oxford, 1989), 255–79, esp. 267–74.

[53] *CIL* VIII. 18042, Trajan's Column scenes 167, 177, 185–6.

[54] Griffiths, 'The Sling in the Roman Imperial Army' 261–5, discussed the sling's range, but did not allow for the drop in performance inevitable in battlefield conditions.

some cases the second method was the only option available. When Titus formed a fourth rank of archers behind three of legionaries, or Arrian in Cappodocia had a ninth rank of bowmen behind eight of legionaries, these men could have had little or no opportunity of seeing their target. They would have been firing blind, over the heads of the men in front, hoping to drop their arrows down from a high trajectory onto the general area occupied by the enemy (*BJ* 5. 135, *Ectaxis* 25–6). When the enemy was close order-troops, formed into a dense block of men, it might be expected that a reasonably high proportion of missiles would have struck the target. Yet at Carrhae, around 10,000 horse-archers fired at a very dense body of Roman foot for most of a day, at least once replenishing their ammunition. The result was 4,000 Roman wounded, some of whom may have been injured in hand-to-hand combat (Plutarch, *Crassus* 28). In the fort at Dyrrachium, mentioned above, 30,000 arrows were supposedly found after the action within its perimeter. Even assuming that none of the Roman wounded had been struck in close combat, then the Pompeian archers were firing about 40 arrows for each hit achieved.

The degree by which battlefield conditions reduced the effectiveness of weaponry was, and is, much larger than is normally believed. Brigadier General Hughes carried out a study into the effectiveness of smoothbore artillery and muskets in the eighteenth and nineteenth centuries, and estimated that in most battles, fewer than 5 per cent of the musket balls fired actually hit and incapacitated the target.[55] In part this was due to the tendency of troops to fire at long ranges, at which their muskets were inaccurate. Even so, in ideal conditions, with exceptionally well-drilled infantry firing at point blank range (about 20–30 metres) at a very dense target, no more than 25 per cent of the rounds fired resulted in a casualty.[56] American army studies into the nature of combat during the Second World War and Korean War, may help to explain why such a high proportion of men failed to hit the target.[57] These discovered that even in highly trained and experienced units during the Second World War, only a maximum of 25 per cent of soldiers present in a firefight, actively participated in it, by firing at the enemy.[58] This estimate included men who did not aim, but merely

[55] Brig.-Gen. B. P. Hughes, *Firepower: Weapons effectiveness on the battlefield* (London, 1974), 127, 133, 164–6. [56] Ibid. 81–3.
[57] Marshall, *Men against Fire*, and *Infantry Operations and Weapons Usage in Korea* (London, 1988). [58] Marshall, *Men against Fire*, 51–4, 65.

fired off a few shots in the general direction of the enemy. Although
the best units had 25 per cent of active firers, the average over the
whole army was around 15 per cent, figures which seemed to be
reflected amongst the enemy. Awareness of this problem in Korea
increased the number of firers to around 50–55 per cent of a unit, but
this still included a high proportion of men who did not aim at the
enemy, but fired wildly.[59] The remainder of the men shared the
danger of the firefight, but could not actually participate. When men
were deployed in close-order formations, it is implausible to suggest
that the majority of men did not fire at all, since this would clearly have
been noticed by their officers. What it does suggest is that most men
never aimed at the enemy, but fired generally in his direction. It might
be thought that when the enemy target was a close-order block of men,
and the range was not great, then a reasonably high proportion of
missiles might be expected to strike the enemy somewhere. Yet the
eighteenth- and nineteenth-century evidence suggests that this was
not so, and that such a target could be surprisingly easy to miss for the
archer or slinger shooting without aiming. Given that the three cohorts
at Dyrrachium, referred to above, were protected by ramparts, a ratio
of one hit per 40 missiles may actually have been rather good.

On the open battlefield it seems that archers, who could fire over the
heads of ranks in front, did not perform well in formed bodies, and
were unable to defend their own frontage (i.e. they could not stop an
enemy charge on their position by their own fire). Against cavalry, who
could charge quickly and thus reduce the number of arrows fired at
them, this is not surprising, even though horsemen made better targets
than infantry (*African War* 29). Arrian kept his archers behind a dense
block of legionaries in the centre of his line in Cappadocia, whilst even
on the flanking hills, archers were stationed behind close-order,
auxiliary, heavy infantry (*Ectaxis* 12–14, 18). It was a common practice
to station light infantry and archers in support of cavalry, as will be
discussed in a later section, but invariably once the enemy had routed
this cavalry, the supporting infantrymen were quickly cut down.[60]

When fighting Mithridates, Roman legionaries were ordered to
charge more quickly than normal in an attack on archers, to minimize

[59] Marshall, *Infantry Operations*, 59–63, estimated that 12–20 per cent actively aimed
at the enemy and took initiative in attacks, 25–30 per cent fired but did not individually
play an active role in the firefight.
[60] *BG* 7. 36, 7. 80, *BC* 2. 34, *African War* 61, 66; see Ch. 5, 'Cavalry against Cavalry'.

the amount of time spent under fire. The Romans sacrificed their ordered ranks to do this, but easily routed the enemy, who fled before contact (Plutarch, *Lucullus* 28; cf. Xenophon *Hell.* 4. 3. 29). Roman legionaries were well protected by helmet, armour, and shield from arrows, but it seems that even 'barbarian' infantry, protected in most cases only by shields, could still sweep archers away by a quick charge. In AD 15, Arminius led a charge against Germanicus' archers, which broke through them and was only stopped by their supporting close order auxiliary units.[61] In Thrace in AD 26, a cohort of archers successfully inflicted losses on the rebel Thracians at long range. Moving closer, they were routed with heavy loss by a sudden Thracian charge (*Ann.* 4. 47). Dio commented that Roman archers in Britain in AD 60 were similarly at high risk when the Britons were allowed to come closer (Dio 62. 12. 4).

Yet in Judaea, both Titus and Vespasian used their archers and slingers to stop Jewish sallies, before they could contact the bodies of heavy infantry guarding the siege-works. In one instance mentioned above, the archers formed the fourth rank of a formation with three ranks of infantry in front and three of cavalry behind them (*BJ* 5. 135). On other occasions, the archers and slingers were protected by earthworks and supported by artillery (*BJ* 3. 207, 5. 263). On each occasion, many Jewish attacks were stopped before they had contacted the Roman line, simply by the weight of missiles directed at them. However, a cohort of archers in the open would not have fired any fewer arrows at the approaching Jews, than one protected by infantry or behind a rampart. In each case the difference seems to have been that the archers did not run away when the enemy came close. In the first case this was because they were in the middle of the formation and so prevented from doing so by the ranks behind, in the others because they were protected by fortifications. Might it then be, that the reason these archers were able to beat back an enemy charge was not that they had hit more of the enemy with their arrows, but because they did not flee when the enemy came close? The latter were prevented from closing with them, even if they had attempted to do so, by the infantry to their front and the fortifications respectively.[62]

---

[61] *Ann.* 2. 17, cf. 1. 51 where a German attack quickly broke through the *leves cohortes* or light troops.

[62] See Keegan, *The Face of Battle*, 95–6, for a discussion of the confrontation between cavalry and archers protected by stakes at Agincourt.

On the open battlefield, the enemy could normally have approached the archers freely, and so these seem usually to have fled. Archers normally appear supporting other troops and were often stationed behind them, firing over their heads.[63] As such, they were especially useful supporting heavy infantry against cavalry, as we shall see in the section dealing with this. If they were stationed ahead of the main line, it was normally as skirmishers, with other slingers and javelin men, who might have weakened the enemy, but could not close with him, and would have withdrawn before any charge (*Ann.* 1. 51).

Last of all we come to discuss artillery, since as crew-served weapons whose power is derived from technology and not strength of body, they are somewhat different. The smaller bolt-shooters, or scorpions, most commonly appeared on the battlefield. These weapons significantly outranged any other missile weapon and fired a heavy bolt with greater force. In Africa in 46 BC, a scorpion on the walls of Leptis fired at a *turma* of Pompeian cavalry demonstrating outside. Whether by aim or chance is unclear, the bolt hit the commander of the *turma* and went through his body to pin him to his horse, causing the rest of his unit to flee in panic (*African War* 29). In an attack on a rampart in Germany in AD 15, light *ballistae*, with archers, laid down a barrage on the German fortification, picking off the most conspicuous leaders (*Ann.* 2. 20). One of the skeletons buried at Maiden Castle was found with the iron head of a bolt fired by one of these machines still embedded in his spine.[64] Even at long range the momentum of one of these bolts could normally have expected to penetrate both shield and any armour. The numbers hit may actually have been few, since, unlike the stone throwing engines, only a single man could have been hit with each shot, but the moral effect on those around must have been enormous. In Africa, the shooting of the leader of the *turma* led to its immediate flight. Josephus graphically described the gruesome effects that engines could have on their targets (*BJ* 3. 245–7). Men were killed horribly, at distances at which only those armies possessing engines themselves could have hoped to reply. Like archers, artillery was used largely to support other troops, often positioned behind them or in fortifications.[65]

---

[63] *Ann.* 1. 56, 2. 17, 2. 20.

[64] R. E. M. Wheeler, *Maiden Castle, Dorset* (1943), 352, nos. 52 and 53.

[65] *Ann.* 1. 56, 2. 20, *Ectaxis* 19, *BJ* 5. 263. On Roman artillery and its effectiveness see E. W. Marsden, *Greek and Roman Artillery: Historical Development* (Oxford, 1969), 86–98, 164–8.

CLOSE-ORDER INFANTRY AGAINST
CLOSE-ORDER INFANTRY

On the battlefield the real enemy is fear and not the bayonet or bullet.

(Robert Jackson, in S. L. A. Marshall, *Men against Fire*,
(New York, 1947) 36)

Cavalry could play a very important role in battles of this period. In armies formed by people such as the Sarmatians or Parthians, it was the only significant arm. However in most battles, the decisive action was the clash, or often a series of clashes, between the opposing close-order or heavy infantry. Only infantry could both take and hold any position. It is to this aspect of combat that we now turn. Unlike a battle between Greek phalanxes, there was not a single clash between the entire infantry of both sides. Rather, the numerous cohorts comprising the Roman army might have each been involved in one or several small-scale clashes with a section of the enemy. The results of all these combined to decide the action. It is important, whilst discussing each type of combat, to bear this in mind and to consider the wider picture of the battle, discussed from the general's perspective in the previous chapter.

Many battles might only occur after the opposing armies had stood, watching each other for hours, or even days, before any fighting occurred.[66] Alternatively, the Romans might have been advancing into the German forests or across the Armenian or Mesopotamian deserts, waiting for the sudden burst of yelling from the woods, or clouds of dust, that signalled an enemy attack. Whatever the circumstances, in most cases the men would have known that a battle was imminent or at least probable. This was a time for nervousness. Anyone who has ever had to wait before a known, unpleasant experience, be it only a trip to the dentist, will be familiar with this fear, albeit to a much lesser degree. The desire to get it over with as soon as possible appears to be normal when confronted with such an experience.[67] This could lead to confusion. At Thapsus, a *cornucen* gave in to the urgings of the troops,

---

[66] Ch. 4, 'Deployment and Forming a Line of Battle'.
[67] J. Baynes, *Morale: A Study of Men and Courage* (London, 1967), 63.

and sounded the advance before Caesar had ordered it (*African War* 82).

If the army had marched any distance, then the order was first given for the men to prepare for battle. The army marched bareheaded, unless threatened with immediate attack, so helmets were donned and tied into place. If the army was camped nearby, then all baggage would have been left there, otherwise the troops would also have downed packs, probably leaving these for the servants to guard (*BG* 1. 24, *African War* 12). Shields were pulled from underneath their leather covers, showing the brightly painted unit insignia. In Caesar's army it was normal to fix crests onto helmets and wear decorations in battle (*BG* 2. 21). According to Plutarch, Taxiles realized that Lucullus and and his army were planning to fight, because they were wearing their finest equipment (Plutarch, *Lucullus* 27. 5). The men on Trajan's Column and the Adamklissi Metopes do not wear crests, so perhaps this practice had been abandoned by the early second century. We know that the army was paraded to witness the sacrifice and hear a commander's speech, but we can only guess at the way in which the soldiers as individuals prepared for battle. Probably, there were practical considerations, such as checking that armour fitted, that a sword had a good edge and had not been rusted by rain into the metal fittings of the scabbard. Perhaps others would have made their wills, or taken a vow to an honoured deity.

1. *The Advance*

> Defeat in battle starts always with the eyes.
>
> (Tacitus, *Germania* 43)

> They (the Parthians) have, it seems, correctly observed that the sense of hearing has the most disturbing effect on us of all our senses, most quickly arouses our emotions and most effectively overpowers our judgement.
>
> (Plutarch, *Crassus* 23)

Let us begin with our cohort deployed in a line, three or four deep, stretching, if at full strength, for 145 or 110 m. (160 or 120 yards). In most respects it does not matter that much if the cohort was legionary or auxiliary. If it was in the front line, then the enemy may have been no more than half a kilometre away.[68] If the Romans were on the

---

[68] Ch. 4, 'Deployment and Forming a Line of Battle'.

defensive, then the line would remain stationary, beginning its charge when the enemy had come close enough to reach with a volley of *pila*.[69] Pharsalus was one of the very few occasions when a defending Roman line remained stationary (*BC* 3. 92). When the Romans were advancing to meet the enemy over a longer distance, then units in the first line would repeat the general's trumpet signal with their own *cornus*. The *pilus prior* in charge of the cohort (or the prefect if it was an auxiliary unit) may well have attended the local commander's or even the commander-in-chief's *consilium* and been given his orders there.[70] A unit from the second and third lines might have acted on its own initiative to attack a local enemy breakthrough, but more probably received orders from a dispatch rider, or even have been led into action by the commander himself.[71]

The fifth-century *Strategikon* records Latin drill commands, although few Byzantine soldiers would have spoken the language (*Strategikon* 12. 14). The antiquity of these commands is difficult to estimate, but it is at least possible that the order given for the advance was similar to the ones used in our period.

Silentium. Mandata captate. Non vos turbatis. Ordinem servate. Bando sequate. Remo demittat, bandum et inimicos sequare.

(Silence. Follow orders. Do not get into disorder. Hold your ranks. Follow the standard. Do not leave the standard and pursue the enemy.)

The emphasis on keeping the ranks in order and keeping silent was certainly reflected in our period. At Pharsalus, Caesar's men expected the Pompeian line to charge to meet them, and so accelerated and prepared to throw their *pila*. Perhaps they were 55 m. (60 yards) from the Pompeian line, assuming that the normal charge distance was about the same as *pilum* range. Even this close to the enemy, the Caesarian cohorts stopped and reformed their ranks, as soon as they realized that the Pompeians had not moved (*BC* 3. 92–3). The normal practice was clearly to keep the ranks in as good order as possible, keeping everyone moving forward, and only accelerating into a run for the last 30 metres, so that most of the men arrived at the enemy lines in a group, not a scattered mob of individuals. As mentioned above, this order could be sacrificed if the enemy were archers or slingers, the

[69] *BG* 1. 25, 2. 23; Plut. *Marius* 19; *Ann.* 14. 37.
[70] Ch. 4, 'Deployment and Forming a Line of Battle'.
[71] Ch. 4, 'The Giving of Battle'.

legionaries running to cover the killing zone of the enemy weapons, to minimize the number of missiles received. Some auxiliary and allied units may not have possessed the discipline necessary to keep their ranks strictly in order during the advance.[72]

Indeed, it seems that a slow, steady advance was difficult to achieve. The instinct, due to nerves and fear, to get the thing over with as soon as possible, encouraged most men to run towards the enemy. Over a distance their formation broke up, simply because some men ran faster than others. A looser formation allowed those not relishing the prospect of fighting to hang back.[73] It may be that the wedge formations that Tacitus said made up a German battle line were not a deliberate ploy, but a natural result of this process.[74] The faster and bolder spirits formed the narrower front, whilst the bulk of the less keen warriors hung back, waiting to see what happened. Caesar claimed that Gallic and German infantry could advance very quickly (*BG* 1. 52, 2. 23). Apart from their tendency to move at a run, they carried less weight of armour and equipment than Roman troops, to slow them down. Josephus claimed that speed and dash were also the hallmark of attacks by the Jewish rebels (*BJ* 6. 17–18). Most Celtic and German tribes seem to have formed fairly deep formations.[75] The pressure from the rear ranks may have ensured that, even if their order became ragged during a speedy advance, they still arrived as a fairly dense group. There are interesting parallels in Greek hoplite warfare. The Spartans, who alone were trained and well disciplined, were the only ones to advance in step, slowly and in silence (Thucydides 5. 70). The phalanxes of other states usually advanced at the double, their ranks ragged and their men noisy.[76]

One of the most important aims of any advancing unit, was to intimidate the enemy facing them both by its appearance and the noise that it made. A frightening appearance was based on two aspects. The first was the visual impression of the group. Large numbers of men advancing, even if most were in the rear ranks of the formation and so

---

[72] Tacitus referred to instances of the poor discipline of auxiliary units, *Ann.* 4. 47–8, *Hist.* 2. 22.

[73] See Ch.5 n. 26 for the Raimondo Montecuelli passage.

[74] *Germ.* 6; see Ch.2, 'The Germans'.

[75] *BG* 1. 25, 52, where both the Helvetii and the Germans are descibed as forming a phalanx.

[76] Thucydides 4. 96, Xenophon *Hell.* 4. 3. 17; see also V. D. Hanson, *The Western Way of War*, 135–51.

unable actually to fight, presented an intimidating sight. The armies of Mithridates contained many units of questionable morale and combat value, but even these helped to present a façade of overwhelming numbers and strength.[77] The appearance of individuals was likewise intended to intimidate the enemy. Many German and Parthian warriors piled their hair on the tops of their heads to make themselves seem taller (*Germ.* 38, Plutarch *Crassus* 24). Some Celtic warriors stiffened their hair with lime and combed it up to increase their apparent height. Plumes on a helmet likewise made a man seem taller (Plutarch, *Marius* 25; Polybius 4. 23). The bearskins worn by the Brigade of Guards, and the helmets worn by policemen today, employ the same principle, adding to a man's height to make him seem more impressive.

Added to this frightening appearance, was the use of noise. Many European tribes used the Celtic trumpet, the *carnyx*, in battle.[78] The Parthians used

hollow drums of stretched hide to which bronze bells are attached. They beat on these drums all at once in many parts of the field and the sound produced is most eerie and terrifying, like the roaring of wild animals with something of the sharpness of a peal of thunder. They have, it seems, correctly observed that the sense of hearing has the most disturbing effect on us of all our senses, most quickly arouses our emotions and most effectively overpowers our judgement.

(Plutarch, *Crassus* 23)

As recently as the Korean War, UN troops commented on how frightening was the Chinese tactic of preceding and accompanying an attack with bugles, shepherd's horns, drums, and rattles, especially at night.[79] Added to these sounds were human cries and yells. Many German tribes used the *baritus*, which Tacitus described as follows:

By the rendering of this, they not only kindled their courage, but, merely listening to the sound, they can forecast the issue of an approaching engagement. For they either terrify their foes or themselves become frightened, according to the character of the noise they make upon the battlefield; and they regard it not merely as so many voices chanting together, but as a unison of valour. What they particularly aim at is a harsh, intermittent

---

[77] Plut. *Sulla* 16. In practical terms these unreliable troops may have been a hindrance, getting in the way of the good fighters.

[78] Polyb. 2. 29. 5–6, described the numerous horns and trumpets in the Celtic army at Telamon.   [79] Marshall, *Infantry Operations*, 133.

roar; and they hold their shields in front of their mouths, so that the sound is amplified into a deeper crescendo by reverberation. (*Germ.* 3)

According to Ammianus Marcellinus, writing after our period, the *baritus* began as a low murmur and gradually increased in volume (Ammianus 16. 42). Some tribes may have chanted a phrase or their name as a battle-cry. Plutarch described the Ambrones in 102 BC, who attacked

> clashing their arms together rhythmically, and all leaping up together in the air, often shouting their name 'Ambrones! Ambrones!' either as encouragement to themselves or to strike terror into the enemy by making themselves known.
>
> (Plutarch, *Marius* 19)

On one occasion, in the Batavian revolt of AD 70, Civilis' army was supported by the women of the tribe, adding their own shrieking to the war cries of the warriors (*Hist.* 4. 18, *Germ.* 7–8). According to Tacitus, the Britons defending Mona in AD 60 were urged on by wild, black-robed women carrying torches, and cursing Druids (*Ann.* 14. 30). In all passages describing barbarian warriors in ancient literature, we must be aware that the stereotype of the savage warrior, more beast than man, was very influential.[80] Nevertheless, all the evidence does seem to suggest that these peoples did advance in a noisy manner, and it does not take much imagination to believe that the approach of such an army must have been an intimidating sight.

Polybius, described the Roman legionaries advancing at Zama, 'shouting their war-cry, and banging their weapons on shields as is their custom' (Polybius 15. 12). This custom does not seem to have still been common in our period. In Caesar's commentaries, the raising of the war-cry was always associated with the volley of *pila* and final charge into contact, suggesting that the shout began no more than 55 m. (60 yards) from the enemy.[81] During the assaults on towns described by Josephus, the Romans raised a shout, blew their trumpets and hurled *pila* and fired arrows, at the last stage of the assault.[82] At Jotopata, Josephus ordered his men to stop their ears to prevent them being terrified by the sudden, enormous noise (*BJ* 3. 259). Arrian's infantrymen were to remain silent until the enemy came close, and

---

[80] Plut. *Marius* 16. On one occasion Josephus compares the attacking Jews to savage beasts, *BJ* 5. 85–97.　　　　　　[81] *BG* 6. 8, 7. 88, *BC* 3. 93, *Spanish War* 30.

[82] *BJ* 3. 259, 266, 4. 20.

then raise a terrific shout.[83] In his description of the defeat of Boudicca in AD 60, Dio emphasized the contrast between the noisy barbarian advance and the silent Roman line:

Thereupon the armies approached each other, the barbarians with much shouting, mingled with menacing battle songs, but the Romans silently and in order until they came within a javelin throw of the enemy. Then, while their foes were still advancing against them at a walk, the Romans rushed forward at a signal and charged them at full speed, and when the clash came, easily broke through the opposing ranks. (Dio 62. 12. 1–2)

A slow, steady, silent advance may actually have been much more intimidating than a noisier, quicker charge. It was certainly more difficult to achieve, and probably only possible with highly disciplined troops. It is always easier to cope with fear when doing something, rather than passively enduring it. Confronted by an approaching enemy body, which could not actually be fought until it came closer, the instinct was to try to do something about it, even if this were only to shout. The urge to get the thing over with in the same way instinctively quickened the advance. In a sense, a quick pace, accompanied by loud war-cries at the beginning of an advance, was a symptom of fear as much as a means of frightening the enemy. A slower, silent advance suggested imperturbability, even if this was only a façade. In the Dio passage above, he mentioned that the Britons, despite his description of a disorderly advance, met the Romans at the walk. It may be that, when their intimidating charge had failed to make a visible impression on the Roman line, the Britons' confidence began to ebb, and their advance slowed down. Certainly, the Roman charge quickly routed their front line, perhaps even before it reached them.

2. *The Pila Volley*

The Roman advance was normally a silent, steady affair. Perhaps the only human noises, above that produced by armour and equipment, were the voices of the *optiones* behind the line reprimanding or striking any men who spoke, and trying to keep the ranks straight with their staves. Closer to the enemy, perhaps as close as 30 metres, a signal was given to prepare to throw *pila*. It is unclear if this was a verbal order, or a signal on the *cornu*, the unit's horn. Each soldier drew back his *pilum* in his right hand. The 1.8 m. (6 feet) separating ranks allowed him to

---

[83] *Ectaxis* 25, cf. Plut. *Antony* 39, where Antony's infantry shouted and clashed their weapons to frighten the Parthians' horses.

do so without striking the men behind. On another signal, he would have hurled his slim, 2 m. (7-foot) weapon at the enemy. This was clearly intended to be an ordered drill carried out under command. At Pharsalus, Caesar's cohorts halted and reformed, when they had already levelled their *pila* for throwing (*BC* 3. 93).

The exact dimensions of *pila* varied, but on average they were about 2 m. (7 foot) long, with a small head joined to the wooden shaft by a long thin iron shank. On the most complete example, the head was 5 cm. (2 inches) long, the shaft 55 cm. (22inches).[84] If a *pilum* penetrated a shield its soft shank was intended to bend. The barbs on the point made it difficult to draw out the *pilum*, and its weight prevented the shield from being used properly. An enemy was forced to abandon his shield and fight unprotected (*BG* 1. 25). Marius experimented with an alternative method of achieving the same aim by weakening the joint between the wooden shaft and iron shank. He replaced one of the two iron bolts which pinned the two component parts of the weapon together with a wooden pin. The wood snapped on impact, causing the shaft to hang down at right angles from the head (Plutarch, *Marius* 25). As well as depriving the enemy of his shield this quality of the *pilum* made it impossible for the enemy to re-use the weapon, by throwing it back at the Romans.

The *pilum* had a more lethal function than merely to render an enemy's shield useless. All of the weapon's weight was concentrated behind its small pyramid-shaped head. This gave it great power to penetrate armour and shield. When a *pilum* punched a hole in an enemy shield its narrow shank followed easily behind the head, driven by the weight of the heavy shaft. The length of this shank gave it the reach to strike the man behind the shield. Modern experiments with reconstructed weapons have shown them capable of piercing 30 mm. (1 inch) of pinewood or 20 mm. (¾ inch) of ply, when thrown from a distance of 5 m. (16 foot).[85]

Maximum range was 30 m. (100 foot), but better armour penetration could have been achieved closer to the target, as the tests referred to above showed. The limited range of the *pilum* was one reason why the Romans did not normally use deep formations. When each legionary occupied 2 m. in depth, then the men in the eighth or ninth rank of a formation had to throw their *pila* 16 and 18 m. (56 and 63 feet) respectively, before clearing their own front rank, let alone

---

[84] Bishop and Coulston, Roman Military Equipment, 50.   [85] Ibid. 48.

reaching the enemy. By that stage the *pila* would have been on the downward trajectory and so a severe danger to the men in the front ranks of the Roman formation. Greater ranges could have been achieved throwing downhill onto the enemy.[86] In Polybius' day, each legionary carried two *pila*, one lighter than the other. Only one relief from an early first-century AD tombstone depicts a legionary holding two *pila*, compared to the many from our period that show auxiliary soldiers with two or more javelins.[87] Josephus described legionaries as carrying only one *pilum* (*BJ* 3. 95). It is difficult to see how a man could have had time to throw more than one *pilum*, when both he and the enemy ranks were approaching over a distance of, at most, 30 metres at a run. Yet if a man threw one *pilum* and kept the other for a subsequent charge, where could he have held it? Auxiliary infantry were sometimes depicted holding light javelins behind their shield.[88] Yet even if a legionary could have gripped his *pilum* in his left hand, whilst still holding the grip of his shield boss, its weight, added to the already heavy *scutum*, would have made this very difficult to use in combat. Two *pila* may have been carried on campaign as a reserve, but only one seems likely in battle. In 58 BC Caesar claimed that the advance of his own men and the approaching Germans was so fast that they had no time to throw *pila* (*BG* 1. 52). At the first battle of Cremona in AD 68, two opposing lines meeting on the high road did not throw *pila*, but fought hand-to-hand, perhaps because they had met suddenly (*Hist.* 2. 42). If soldiers marched carrying two *pila*, probably tied together, this might explain why it was difficult to throw them if time was short.

There are recorded occasions when an individual aimed his *pilum* at and hit a specific target. In 54 BC, one of two centurions fighting outside the rampart of Cicero's besieged camp, threw his *pilum* at a Gaul, wounding him so that he collapsed (*BG* 5. 44). Soon afterwards a Gallic javelin pierced the centurion's shield and stuck in his sword-belt, whilst another knocked his sword out of place. In Africa in 46 BC, one of Caesar's legionaries flung his *pilum* at Labienus and killed his horse (*African War* 16). Vegetius claimed that soldiers should practice throwing their *pila* by aiming at a post (Vegetius 1. 14). In a three- or

---

[86] *BG* 1. 25, 3. 2, 4. 23; *Alexandrian War* 75; Plut. *Marius* 19–20.
[87] Polyb. 6. 23. 9–11, see P. Connolly 'The Roman Army in the Age of Polybius', in Gen. Sir John Hackett, *Warfare in the Ancient World* (London, 1989), 162 for a discussion of this.
[88] W. Selzer, *Römische Steindenkmaler, Mainz in römischer Zeit* (Mainz, 1988), no. 271.

four-rank formation, most of the men were able to see partially where
the enemy were, but it is unclear whether in these circumstances the
men were expected to aim at specific targets, or simply at the mass of
the enemy. The comments made in the section on missile fire would
have applied here. Even if the men were supposed to aim at the enemy,
most under the stress of battle would not have done so, and indeed
many would have missed the target altogether. In 52 BC Caesar
claimed that *Legio XII* managed to kill or disable all of the enemy front
rank with its volley of *pila*.[89] The claim may not have been literally
true, but it is clear that a volley of *pila* delivered at close range could be
very effective. In practical terms many of the enemy would have been
disabled or at least lost shields. In terms of morale, the shock might
have been even more serious and led to a quick enemy flight.[90] All the
above would be true, even if no more than a quarter or a third of the
pila actually struck the enemy.

If the advancing Roman cohort was opposed by other legionaries,
then it would have received a volley of *pila* in reply. Many infantry
carried javelins or some form of missile weapon, lighter than a *pilum*,
and seem to have thrown these during a charge (*Germ.* 6). Most
auxiliary infantry had javelins and may have thrown them before
contact. The Batavian and Tungrian cohorts at Mons Graupius were
described by Tacitus as fighting with swords and shields, suggesting
that if they did have javelins or spears, then they had already thrown
them (*Agricola* 36). Most javelins could have been thrown significantly
further than *pila*, but had less penetrating power. The reason that most
armies employed these, rather than the more effective *pila*, may in part
be due to this. If a *pila* volley was not to be wasted, it had to be
delivered at very close range (Plutarch, *Pompey* 32). Yet the instinctive
urge during the approach to the enemy was to counter fear by acting.
One way of doing so was to hurl a missile at the enemy, even if he was
too far away to be injured. Polybius' legionaries, who advanced noisily,
had lighter *pila* to throw before the heavier volley, allowing the latter to
be thrown at a closer range. Certainly, a volley of *pila* seems to have
been more devastating than any other missile barrage, which may

---

[89] *BG* 7. 62. A similar claim was made regarding the first volley fired by the British
Guards at the Swiss Guards at Fontenoy, Hughes, *Firepower*, 81–3.
[90] *BG* 1. 25, 2. 23, 7. 62; Plut. *Pompey* 32; Dio 62. 12. 2.

suggest that most missiles were hurled when out of effective range by nervous soldiers.[91]

Whatever missiles were striking the unit, its men almost certainly went into a crouch, heads bowed, as if walking into the wind, which seems to have been the timeless posture of the infantryman advancing under fire. Practically, a bowed head meant that a man presented his helmet top and not his face to missiles, and the crouch allowed him to cover more of his body with his shield. Churchill noticed his own troop of Twenty-First Lancers bowing their heads at Omdurman in 1898, and remembered reading that the French Cuirassiers at Waterloo had done the same.[92] In the grave finds on the site of the battle of Wisby in 1361, many skulls were found with holes from crossbow bolts in the top of the *cranium*, suggesting that these men had been hit whilst advancing in a crouch.[93]

3. *The Charge*

> So vigorous was the shouting on both sides, the discharge of javelins and the subsequent engagement, that our men almost lost confidence. In fact, in the shouting and the engaging at close quarters—the two aspects of a battle which are most effective in terrorizing an enemy—the sides were on even terms.
>
> (*Spanish War* 31)

From the eighteenth century onwards it has been very rare for infantry from European armies to meet for hand-to-hand combat on the open battlefield. Invariably, before two lines met, one or the other gave way and fled, or a close-range firefight resulted.[94] Most troops in this period had some form of firearm, which allowed them to fight at a distance, and possessed no armour, which may explain their reluctance to cross bayonets. In our period the vast majority of heavy infantrymen used close-combat weapons, swords or spears, carrying only a few missile weapons, which would quickly have been exhausted. Did this mean that units normally closed and fought hand-to-hand?

The Roman advance was a slow, steady affair, culminating in two

---

[91] See Hughes, *Firepower* 164–6.
[92] P. Ziegler, *Omdurman* (London, 1973), 149.
[93] B. Thordeman, *Armour from the Battle of Wisby 1361*, i (Stockholm, 1939), 190.
[94] See P. Griffith, *Military Thought in the French Army, 1815–51* (Manchester, 1989), 118–20, and *Rally Once Again*, 140–5, also D. Winter, *Death's Men* (London, 1978), 109–10 on the Great War.

massive shocks to the enemy morale, a close-range volley of heavy *pila* and a sudden charge by men, now released to run and yell. It was as much intended to intimidate as a quicker approach by wilder, noisier barbarian infantry. Quite often the enemy gave way very quickly under such an attack. Dio's description of the quick collapse of the Britons' front line in AD 60 has already been mentioned. In AD 14 Germanicus led the *Legio XXI Rapax* in an attack which swiftly routed the Bructeri, Tubantes, and Usipetes in a single charge (*Ann.* 1. 51). The following year Caecina mounted a sudden sally from his surrounded camp, which again swiftly routed the Germans with heavy loss (*Ann.* 1. 68). Twice in AD 68 Tacitus described Othonian infantry scattering inexperienced enemy foot at the first charge (*Hist.* 2. 12–13, 26). In AD 26 Sacrovir's inexperienced rebels were similarly quickly routed, apart from the body of heavily armed gladiators (*Ann.* 3. 46). Sudden collapses in the face of an enemy charge were not restricted to inexperienced Roman troops. In 48 BC Mark Antony led *Legio IX* in an uphill charge that routed the Pompeians immediately (*BC* 3. 46). In the same year, Domitius commanded a Galatian legion that fled before a charge of Pharnaces' army (*Alexandrian War* 40). In AD 70 both legionary and auxiliary cohorts quickly collapsed in the face of Batavian charges (*Hist.* 4. 20, 33). In these cases, it is not clear from the sources whether or not the losing side actually met the attackers and fled after a short spell of fighting or whether they fled before the enemy reached them.

On other occasions, it is clear that the intimidating appearance of the enemy, and how determined they appeared to be, led to one side's morale collapsing, so that they fled before the two lines met. The Roman combination of shocks, the *pila* volley, and the sudden charge often seems to have so destroyed the enemy's morale that they ran away before any fighting actually occurred. Caesar recorded several occasions in Gaul when this was so, and a Roman charge panicked the enemy before it had actually met them.[95] In 54 BC, a sudden charge from Caesar's camp panicked the Belgic attackers, causing them to flee, dropping their weapons. Some men in this force may have been defeated by the Romans at the Sambre, three years before, which may partially explain their sudden collapse.[96] Caesar's men similarly routed

[95] *BG* 3. 6, 19, 5. 34, 6. 8, 7. 62.
[96] *BG* 5. 51; there are many other instances of a Roman charge putting the enemy to flight before it had reached them, e.g. *Ann.* 4. 24, 47; *BJ* 6. 394–5; Sall. *Jugurthine War* 74; Plut. *Lucullus* 30, *Pompey* 32.

Egyptians and other Roman troops by the physical shock of a volley of *pila* and the moral one of a sudden charge of screaming men.[97] In Spain in 45 BC, Caesar's own men fled before an enemy assault. Two centurions temporarily held them in check, but when these were killed by the enemy, the flight continued (*Spanish War* 23).

Roman units could also be put to flight by the frightening appearance of a barbarian charge, despite the bonds of discipline. The remnants of Cotta and Sabinus' army fled before the final Gallic charge in 54 BC, when only a few men died fighting and most in attempting to reach their camp. These troops had suffered casualties and fought for a long time in a hopeless position, so that this is less surprising (*BG* 5. 37). In AD 20 Tacfarinas surrounded the Roman garrison at Pagyda, probably a legionary cohort, commanded by Decrius. The cohort fled before the enemy advance, despite Decrius himself attempting to inspire them by charging at the enemy alone. Decrius was killed fighting, and the cohort later decimated for cowardice.[98] Both Mark Antony and Octavian decimated legionary cohorts, and fed the survivors on barley rather than wheat. The punishment was inflicted on units which had fled before an enemy charge.[99] When Cestius Gallus approached Jerusalem in AD 66, the Jews mounted an attack despite it being the sabbath. The Jews charged with such fury that they broke through the Roman ranks, probably of *Legio XII Fulminata*, who lost their eagle and suffered heavy loss (*BJ* 2. 517–519; Suetonius, *Vespasian* 4). Josephus mentioned other occasions when Jewish sallies, often led by a very few exceptionally bold men followed at a distance by a larger crowd, broke formed Roman units by the appearance of their charge.[100] On one of these occasions, Josephus described how another group of Jews,

perfectly fresh, sprang forth with such impetuosity that their rush was comparable to that of the most savage of beasts. In fact not one of the opposing line awaited their charge, but, as if struck by an engine, they broke their ranks and turned and fled up the mountainside.

---

[97] *BC* 2. 34, 3. 51, *Alexandrian War* 17; for shock action in general, and the difficulty of achieving it see Griffith, *Rally Once Again*, 140–5.

[98] *Ann.* 3. 20, cf. Sall. *Jug.* 38, 58 where a Numidian surprise attack panicked Roman troops.

[99] App. *Roman History* 10. 26 Octavian at Promona; Plut. *Antony* 39 Antony at Phraata.

[100] *BJ* 3. 233, 5. 54, 85, 473–85.

Titus was abandoned by this line, and, according to Josephus, stayed with his staff and *singulares* to fight the Jews. These chose to bypass the men standing against them, and pursue and kill the men running away (*BJ* 5. 85–97). Roman working parties, although protected by a few pickets of formed and equipped men, seem to have been especially vulnerable to sudden panic in the face of an assault.[101] Probably scattered men, many of whom might have stood to face a charge when in the security of a group, or when prevented from fleeing by men around standing firm, would instinctively flee from the threat of an enemy charge.

On other occasions a unit attacking a stationary defending body might not have turned and run, but was unwilling to close with it. Roman troops showed reluctance to disembark from boats and attack the Britons when Caesar landed in 55 BC, and when Suetonius Paulinus attacked Mona in AD 60, moving only after a few individuals had set an example (*BG* 4. 25, *Ann.* 14. 30). After the battle of Orchomenus, Sulla's men attacked the enemy camp, but hesitated in the face of a dense body of the enemy standing with drawn swords in one of the gateways. A tribune, Basillus, charged alone at these men and killed one, whereupon the rest of the Romans followed and the enemy was beaten (Appian, *Roman History* 12. 50). During an attack on a breach in one of the walls of Jerusalem, most of the Romans hesitated and only twelve men, led by a Syrian auxiliary, Sabinus, tried to enter the city. Sabinus was killed and the other eleven killed or wounded and the attack petered out (*BJ* 6. 54–67). Another brave man, the centurion Julianus, attempted to spur on a flagging Roman attack on the Temple by charging alone against the enemy, who at first fled before him. He was killed and the Romans fled before a Jewish charge (*BJ* 6. 81–92). In these situations, where men were hesitating, heroic examples by individuals could stop hesitation and lead to a successful attack. Alternatively the individuals might be killed and the attack fail, or degenerate into a rout.

On one occasion outside Jerusalem, the Jews mounted a sally.

But while their own advance was abnormally spiritless, they found the Romans drawn up in stouter array than usual, with their bodies and armour so completely screening the earthworks . . . and each man's heart braced to die rather than quit his post.

---

[101] *BJ* 3. 468, 5. 75–84, 284–8; cf. Plut. *Sulla* 21; *Spanish War* 23.

Most of the Jews hesitated and did not close with this line. The few that did were outnumbered and killed, so that the attack failed (*BJ* 6. 15–22). This was the danger with any hasty advance. If the enemy was not frightened into giving way by their approach, then the attackers might have begun to lose confidence. Any quick advance disordered the ranks and led to the unit becoming scattered, as the faster and bolder raced ahead of the slower and more cautious. As confidence ebbed, this loose formation allowed the less eager to slow down and not close with the enemy. A few of the bolder men might have reached the opposing line, but in such small numbers that they could have made no impact upon it, whilst the enemy, outnumbering them, was encouraged. It may have been this effect that Pompey was hoping to cause at Pharsalus when he ordered his infantry not to advance, but to meet Caesar's charge at the halt (*BC* 3. 92–3). According to Caesar, he hoped to preserve his own men's close formation, whilst scattering the enemy's line, by forcing him to charge double the normal distance. His own men were strenghened against the fear engendered through passively awaiting an assault, by being formed exceptionally deeply. In the event, Caesar's men possessed the experience and discipline necessary to halt and re-dress their ranks during the charge, and so arrived in reasonable order.

It is difficult to know how a rout, caused by a frightening enemy advance, began. Perhaps the men in the front rank turned to run, but they cannot have actually fled until the ranks behind them gave way. If a few men in the rear rank turned to run, the *optio* behind the Roman line might have stopped them, but if many or all fled, then he could have done little. Movement and disorder in the ranks of a Greek phalanx were said to be a sign of imminent collapse (Appian, *BC* 2. 78; cf. Thucydides 5. 10. 5). It is in this context that we should view the *cuneus* or wedge formation. This was considered especially effective in breaking through the enemy line.[102] A narrow-headed formation was very manœuvrable and could advance quickly, whilst still retaining order, yet if it actually met the enemy its advantages would have been dubious. The depth of the formation prevented many of the men in the rear ranks from using their *pila*. In hand-to-hand fighting only a few men in the front rank were actually able to fight and these might have

---

[102] *BG* 6. 40, *Ann.* 14. 37, *Hist.* 4. 19; Arrian recommended a very narrow, deep column for cavalry seeking to break through an enemy line, *Tactica* 6–7, 17.

been outnumbered by the enemy.[103] Yet an approaching wedge, moving quickly, but remaining a dense block, must have been an intimidating sight. Not only that, but its arrow shaped head made it seem to be aimed at part of the line. The individuals in that part of the line, and probably to a fair distance either side, might have seen the attack as somehow personally targeted at them. The instinct was to edge to one side, to let others in the formation meet the enemy instead. This shuffling and movement in the ranks could have caused disorder and led to panic. If the wedge was intended to beat the enemy before it reached them, then it made more sense as a formation. The counter measure, known as the 'pincer', suggested by Vegetius to oppose a wedge seems to support this view. This was to have a body of very reliable troops formed in a 'V', lapping round the wedge on either side. Once the wedge was enveloped its defeat was certain, but only very good troops had the confidence and discipline to face its charge (Vegetius 3. 19).

4. The Collision

It is difficult to estimate just how many charges were decided without the two sides actually meeting. Certainly it does seem that the most decisive clashes were over very quickly, with little or no actual fighting. Yet if neither side gave way, what actually happened? Broadly speaking there have been two interpretations of the nature of the resultant clash.

The first interpretation has largely been championed by some, but not all scholars, who have examined Greek hoplite warfare.[104] Greek sources sometimes speak of a hand-to-hand combat as *othismos*, 'the shoving'. According to Lazenby:

none of the earlier sources gives any clear indication how the 'shoving' was accomplished, but Thucydides, in saying of the Thebans at Delion, that 'they followed up little by little as they shoved', makes it sound very like the inexorable 'heave' of a well-drilled pack on the rugby football field. The famous story of a Epameinondas' cry for 'one more pace' at Leuktra

[103] M. Markle, 'The Macedonian Sarissa, Spear and Related Armour', *AJA* 81 (1981), 323–39, attempted to explain the effectiveness of the wedge, but failed to consider the morale of the men in the wedge and in the unit under attack.

[104] V. D. Hanson, *The Western Way of War*, 152–9, 171–84, Lazenby, 'The Killing Zone', 87–109. Pritchett, *The Greek State of War*, iv. 65–76, references to *othismos* in Greek sources are Herod. 7. 225. 1, 9. 62. 2, Thucy. 4. 43. 3, 4. 96. 2, 6. 70. 2, Xen. *Hell.* 6. 4. 14. For a more detailed discussion of the *othismos* see A. K. Goldsworthy, 'The *Othismos*, Myths and Heresies: The Nature of Hoplite Battle', *War in History*, 4.1 (1997), 1–26.

(Polyaenus 2. 3. 2) also sounds like the kind of thing the leader of a rugby 'pack' might shout.[105]

According to this argument the ranks behind the first leaned their broad hoplite shields against the backs of the men in front and pushed them forwards. The men in the opposing front ranks would have been firmly pressed together and unable to fight properly. The combat was decided by which ever side pushed the hardest, perhaps the phalanx with the most ranks.[106] The losers would have been pushed back, and knocked down, leading to a swift massacre of stunned and prone men, and flight of the survivors. The frequent resolution of combat by pushing would then be seen to explain the tendency for Greek phalanxes to be very deep formations, even up to fifty ranks. Several writers did in fact claim that the rear ranks of a Macedonian phalanx pushed the men in front of them onwards.[107]

Yet none of these authors claim that this pushing was the decisive factor in a phalanx's success, and in all accounts of battles it is claimed that the opposing front ranks actually fought each other with their weapons. Hanson was forced by this to divide the fighting into two phases, in the first of which the front ranks fought each other. Afterwards pressure from the rear ranks forced the two front ranks together and the phalanxes pushed at each other like rival packs of forwards.[108] In earlier sections, I have argued that the use of deep formations, especially by poor-quality troops, can be explained without assuming that mêlées were pushing matches. The rear ranks prevented those in front from running away by their physical presence, rather than forcing them on to the enemy. The exceptional success enjoyed by the Thebans using very deep formations, may have employed similar principles to the wedge, frightening one section of the enemy line with a more personal attack (Xenophon, *Hell.* 6. 4. 12–14, 7. 5. 24). Even if the clash between Greek phalanxes was in fact a pushing match, then there is no evidence to suggest that this was true of battles involving the Romans. The Roman *scutum*, with its prominent central boss, was not well adapted for pushing the man in front, since it would

---

[105] Lazenby, 'The Killing Zone', 97.

[106] V. D. Hanson, *The Western Way of War*, 68–71 claimed that the hoplite shield was well designed for pushing the man ahead, but according to Xenophon, *Cyropadaedia* 7. 1. 33, the Egyptian shield was better adapted for this. The Greeks did not copy this shield design, which in itself suggests that battles were not pushing matches.

[107] Polyb. 18. 30. 4; Asclepiodotus, *Tactica* 5. 2; Arr. *Tactica* 12. 10; Ael. *Tactica* 14. 6.

[108] V. D. Hanson, *The Western Way of War*, pp. 160–93.

have applied pressure very unevenly. It was very effective for striking an enemy and unbalancing him.[109] Polybius actually said that the rear ranks of a Roman formation were useless for practical purposes once at close quarters (Polybius 15. 13. 3). The evidence also suggests that the Romans deployed in comparatively shallow formations, which does not suggest that pushing by the rear ranks played a vital role in a mêlée.

How many ranks of a formation took an active part in the fighting? In a Macedonian phalanx the points of the pikes of the first five ranks projected beyond the front of the formation (Polybius 18. 29–30). An enemy had to fight his way past five points at intervals of about 90 cm. (3 feet) before he reached the leading pikeman. The long spears used by Greek hoplites may well have allowed men in the second, and perhaps even the third, rank of a phalanx to jab at the enemy over the shoulders of the men in front. Roman infantry were primarily swordsmen and the length of a sword precluded men from any rank behind the first from joining in a mêlée. It has been suggested that, during a long combat, fresh men from the rear ranks of a Roman formation gradually advanced through the intervals between the men in front and replaced the tired soldiers fighting the enemy in the front rank.[110] This would only have been possible if Roman infantrymen occupied a frontage of 1.8 m. (6 feet) as claimed by Polybius, which I have already argued seems highly unlikely. It is also difficult to see how this replacement could have been accomplished whilst in physical contact with the enemy. None of our ancient sources refer to any process of this nature. The idea seems to have arisen out of a desire to explain the existence of ranks behind the first. It is similar to the rugby scrum theory invented by scholars to explain the presence of the apparently useless rear ranks in a Greek phalanx. In the section on formations I have already discussed the many other factors which forced units to deploy in depth.

If two lines met in our period, it was not for a great scrummage, but for a period of fighting with the weaponry each soldier carried. The speed at which each side was moving is unclear. It may be that if both sides' approach appeared to be steady, then each would have slowed down

---

[109] *Agricola* 36, *Ann.* 2. 14, 14. 36–7.
[110] See Connolly, 'Roman Army in the Age of Polybius', 162 and Fuller, *Julius Caesar*, 91–2.

and not have run to meet each other. Even if they were moving quite slowly, the noise of shields striking each other, combined with wild war cries, must have been enormous. To this would soon be added the sound of blades striking each other, shield and armour, or flesh. A witness of a cavalry sword fight at Waterloo described the sound of swords meeting each other, and armour, and helmets as like 'a thousand copper smiths working together'.[111]

A combat between two units became inevitably a collection of fights between individual soldiers in the opposing front ranks. To understand these we must look at the behaviour and equipment of the individual soldier. We shall begin by examining in some detail the defensive and offensive equipment of the Roman soldier.

The first item to consider is the shield or *scutum*. Throughout our period legionaries seem to have carried curved, semi-cylindrical shields, whilst auxiliaries employed flat shields.[112] At the beginning of our period, and for much of the Republic, legionary shields were normally oval. According to Polybius the legionary shield measured 120 cm. (4 foot) in length by 75 cm. (2.5 foot) in width. It was made of two layers of wood glued together. The outer surface was covered first with canvas and then with calfskin, and the top and bottom edge protected by iron binding. In the centre was an iron boss strong enough to deflect missiles and blows from weapons (Polybius 16. 23). The only example of a shield from this period was found in 1900 at Kasr el-Harit in Egypt.[113] Originally identified as Celtic, the shield is almost certainly Roman, and matches Polybius' description closely. The shield is 128 cm. (4 foot) long and 63.5 cm. (2 foot) wide. It was constructed from three layers of birch wood strips, the centre layer vertical and of the widest strips, the others horizontal and narrower. The layers were glued together and covered with lamb's wool felt. The overall thickness was just under a centimetre at the edges, rising to 1.2 cm. around the centre. The shield had a wooden boss and a wooden spine, running vertically above and below this to the rim, which was nailed to the front. The shield was held by a horizontal hand grip behind the boss. There was no evidence of metal binding around any part of the edges.

---

[111] R. Holmes, *Firing Line* (London, 1986), 163.
[112] See Bishop and Coulston, *Roman Military Equipment*, 206–9.
[113] See W. Kimmig, 'Ein Keltenschild aus Aegypten', *Germania*, 24 (1940), 106–11.

The use of plywood in the shield's construction gave it greater strength and a lighter weight than an identically sized shield formed by a single piece of wood. The increased thickness around the boss gave the shield strength in the centre, making it harder to penetrate or shatter. The thinner edges of the shield possessed a flexibility allowing them to bend rather than break under cuts to the side. Further strength was provided by the leather covering stretched over the shield's surface which gave it further flexibility and added to its cohesion. A reconstruction of the Kasr el-Harit shield suggested that its protective qualities were very good, but showed that it must have been very heavy, as much as 10 kg. (22 lb.).[114]

Oval shields continued to be used by some legionaries until the end of our period. A fragmentary leather shield cover found in the legionary fortress of *II Augusta* at Caerleon seems to have been intended for a shield measuring 115 cm. by 66 cm. Both the top and bottom of this shield were curved and the sides may have been curved or straight.[115] However rectangular shields become far more common for legionaries from the early days of the Principate.[116] A third-century example of this type of shield was found in the collapsed Tower 19 at Dura-Europus.[117] Construction was similar to the el-Farit shield with three layers of wooden strips glued together. The back was reinforced with a system of wooden strips acting as bracing, and both front and back were covered with a thin layer of red dyed kid. The shield was 102 cm. (3.3 foot) long and 83 cm. (2.75 foot) wide, 66 cm. (2 foot) wide across the chord of the arc. It lacked a boss, but had a horizontal wooden handgrip 2.5 cm. thick, glued into place and lashed with rawhide to make it doubly secure. It had no metal binding, but a strip of leather was folded over the edges and sewn into place. Unlike the el-Harit shield, the Dura *scutum* was of uniform thickness of 5 mm. There does not seem to be any good reason to suggest that it was an item of antiquated or parade equipment, but it is possible that shields

---

[114] See P. Connolly, *Greece and Rome at War* (London, 1981), 131. For a discussion of this shield see Bishop and Coulston, *Roman Military Equipment*, 58–9.

[115] See C. van Driel-Murray, 'A Fragmentary Shield Cover from Caerleon', in J. C. Coulston (ed.), *Military Equipment and the Identity of Roman Soldiers*, BAR 394 (Oxford, 1988), 51–66.

[116] See Bishop and Coulston, *Roman Military Equipment*, 81–2.

[117] M. I. Rostovtzeff, A. R. Bellinger, C. Hopkins, and C. B. Wells (eds.) *The Excavations at Dura-Europus: Preliminary Report of the Sixth Season of Work, October 1932—March 1933* (1936), 456–66.

of the early Principate had thicker centres like the el-Harit example.[118] It is also likely that most shields possessed a metal binding in iron or bronze, since pieces of this are common finds in Roman military sites from the first two centuries AD. A reconstruction of a shield based on the Dura *scutum*, but with an added metal boss and binding weighed 5.5 kg. (12 lb.). If the same size shield was made thicker in the area around the central boss, then the weight would increase to 7.5 kg. (16.5 lb.).[119] Even this higher figure is still 25 per cent lighter than the bulky el-Harit shield. It may be that this was the reason for the rectangular pattern substantially superseding the larger, oval republican shield. The rectangular shield offered good protection, but was lighter to carry in battle, and, of as great or greater importance, on the march. It is possible that its adoption was a direct result of the creation of a professional army which insisted on a soldier carrying the bulk of his equipment personally.

Only one substantially complete auxiliary shield has survived in the archaeological record. This find was associated with the first-century AD fort at Doncaster.[120] The shield was 125 cm. long and 64 cm. wide (about 4 foot by 2 foot), with straight sides and a curved top and bottom. It was almost certainly constructed of three layers of wood glued together, and was of a uniform thickness, about 10 mm. An iron boss was positioned slightly above the centre of the shield board. A reinforcing iron bar, 80 cm. long, ran vertically along the back of the shield, curving out behind the boss to form a vertical handgrip. Other auxiliary shields and all legionary shields from our period seem to have had horizontal handgrips.[121] The shield was covered in leather on both sides and lacked any sign of a metal binding around the edge. In size the Doncaster shield was closely comparable to the el-Harit example, but unlike the Egyptian shield it was completely flat. A reconstruction suggested that the Doncaster shield was almost as heavy, at 9 kg. (20 lb.), but it also appeared to be well balanced, making it easier to use than its weight might suggest (see Fig. 4).[122]

---

[118] See Connolly, *Greece and Rome at War*, 233, Bishop and Coulston, *The Western Way of War*, 149–51. The original excavators believed that the shield's location with a store of other types of equipment indicated its use by a unit within the garrison, Rostovtzeff and others, *Excauations at Dura-Europus*, 439–40.

[119] Connolly, *Greece and Rome at War*, 233.

[120] P. Buckland, 'A First Century Shield from Doncaster, Yorkshire', *Britannia*, 9 (1978), 247–69.   [121] Ibid. 260.   [122] Ibid. 259.

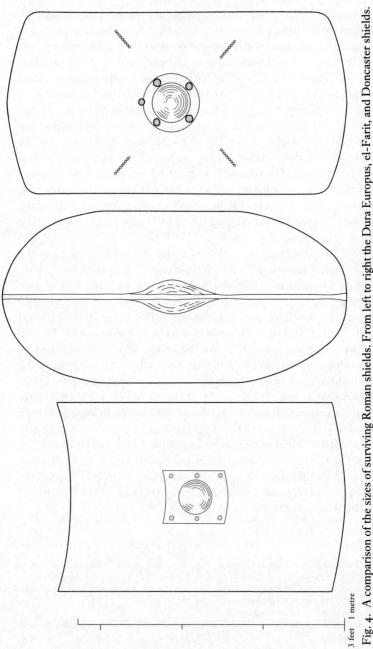

3 feet 1 metre

Fig. 4. A comparison of the sizes of surviving Roman shields. From left to right the Dura Europus, el-Farit, and Doncaster shields. The scale on the left = 3 ft. The scale on the right = 1 m.

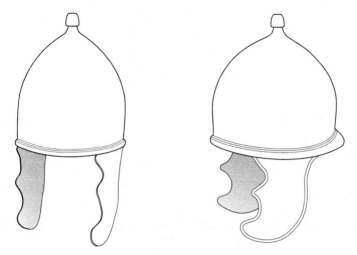

Fig. 5. A bronze Montefortino helmet of the type in common use in the first century BC

The next item of defensive equipment to consider is the helmet. The Roman infantry helmet invariably left the face and ears exposed, since a soldier had to be able to see and hear to understand and follow orders.[123] At the beginning of our period the Montefortino helmet was probably the most common type employed by Roman legionaries, as it had been for several centuries.[124] These bronze helmets have a tall bowl often surmounted by a crest knob, wide cheek pieces, and a narrow, stubby neckguard (see Fig. 5). By the end of the first century BC the Coolus pattern helmet comes into widespread use. Coolus helmets have a lower bowl than the Montefortino types, wider cheek pieces, and a wider peak or neckguard projecting straight out at the rear (see Figs. 6 and 7). They also have a strip of metal fixed to the front of the helmet as a brow guard to protect against cuts to the front

---

[123] The Corinthian helmet worn by most Greek hoplites in the 5the cent. enclosed and protected both face and ears, but prevented a man from hearing orders and reduced his visibility. The Spartans, who alone at this period were drilled and disciplined and therefore able to be given orders by their officers, wore a more open helmet in order to hear these, V. D. Hanson, *The Western Way of War*, 71–5.

[124] See Bishop and Coulston, *Roman Military Equipment*, 60–1, and Connolly, *Greece and Rome at War*, 133. On the development of helmets see Robinson, 13–81, esp. 26–7.

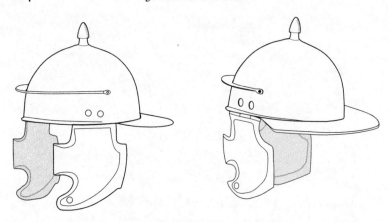

Fig. 6. Bronze Coolus helmet (Russell Robinson's type E), early first century
AD

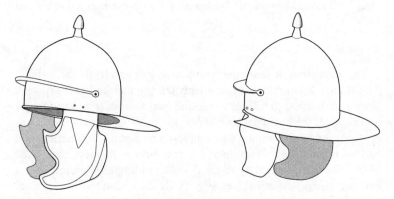

Fig. 7. Bronze Coolus helmet (Russell Robinson's type G), mid-first century
AD

and top of the helmet. The bowls of many Montefortino and Coolus
helmets from the early Principate were manufactured by the process of
spinning, leading to structural weaknesses in the metal, which may
explain this added protection.[125] However the trend towards greater
protection for the top and front of infantry helmets is continued in the
Imperial-Gallic (see Fig. 8) and Imperial-Italic (see Fig. 9) types which

---

[125] Bishop and Coulston, *Roman Military Equipment*, 191.

over the course of the first century become the dominant types. These have thick brow guards and in later examples strengthening cross bars on the helmets top. The other notable development in these patterns is the wider neckguards, placed below the level of the brim. Thick ribs around the section leading down from the bowl to the neckguard offered further protection to the back of the neck. Separate ear guards were fitted running from the cheek pieces to neckguard. Throughout our period there is a clear trend towards greater protection for the front and top of the helmet, and the rear and neck. This may not be a

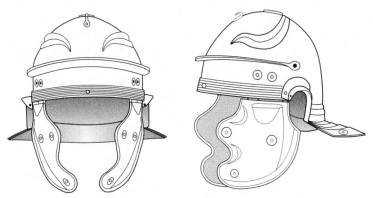

Fig. 8. Iron Imperial Gallic helmet, mid-first century AD

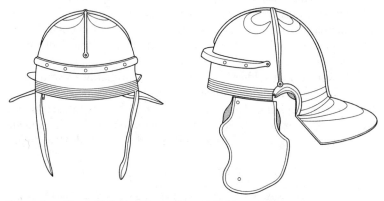

Fig. 9. Iron Imperial Italic helmet (Russell Robinson's type G), early second century AD, based on an example found at Hebron

response to encountering enemies employing particular weapons, but a long term desire to achieve optimum protection for the most vulnerable areas.

There were three types of body armour worn by Roman infantry in our period, mail, scale, and segmented. Mail armour was flexible and offered good protection, but was very heavy. A mail shirt might weigh as much as 12–15 kg. (26.5–33 lb.), varying with length, and the bulk of this burden was carried by the shoulders.[126] A belt, or belts, helped to spread out this weight, although modern re-enactors have found that this gives the soldier a pot-bellied appearance.[127] Scale armour was less flexible than mail, and easier to penetrate, but was worn frequently. Its use may have been due to availability (it was easier to manufacture than mail), but the ability to polish this type of armour to a high sheen may also have appealed to a soldier wishing to look impressive. Roman mail cuirasses, and many made of scale, had doubling on the shoulder giving extra protection to this area. Segmented armour, conventionally described by the modern phrase *lorica segmentata*, was the most advanced type of armour employed by Roman infantrymen. It may have been used exclusively by legionaries. There is certainly no evidence for its use by the *auxilia*.[128] This consisted of a series of iron bands, linked by leather straps on the inside, which covered the stomach, chest and shoulders. The curved shape and 'soft', untempered metal of the bands spread, and so helped to absorb, the force of a blow.[129] Reconstructed cuirasses have weighed in at 9 kg. (20 lb.), and the metal plates spread this weight more evenly than mail armour.[130] Like the other types of armour, the segmented cuirass gave greatest protection to the shoulders. The shoulder bands of *lorica segmentata* also made a man's shoulders appear to be broader, and his chest seem wider, making him look more impressive to the enemy.

The Roman foot soldier in this period was primarily a swordsman, although it is possible that some units of the *auxilia* used spears for hand to hand fighting. *Pila* were only used in mêlées in exceptional circumstances (*BG* 7. 88). At the beginning of our period the Roman short sword, the *gladius*, was most often of the so-called Mainz type.

---

[126] Connnolly, *Greece and Rome at War*, 133, 231.

[127] D. Peterson, *The Roman Legions Recreated in Colour Photographs* (London, 1992), 52–3.   [128] See Bishop and Coulston, *Roman Military Equipment*, 206–9.

[129] See ibid. 190 n. 33.   [130] Connolly, *Greece and Rome at War*, 233.

These were between 40 cm. (16 inches) and 55 cm. (22 inches) long and taper from about 5.4 (2 inches) to 7.5 cm. (3 inches) width at the hilt. These blades have triangular points between 9.6 and 20 cm. (3.75–8 inches) long. During the first century AD these swords were replaced by the Pompeii type, which have shorter points. These were between 42–50 cm. (16.5–20 inches) long, with straight blades 4.2–5.5 cm. (1.75–2.25 inches) wide.[131]

Both the Mainz and the Pompeii pattern of *gladius* were well-balanced weapons that could be used to cut as well as thrust. Tacitus and Vegetius laid great stress on the Roman's use of the *gladius* for thrusting rather than slashing. A thrust was certainly more likely to deliver a fatal wound, than a cut (Vegetius 1. 12). According to Tacitus, Suetonius Paulinus in AD 60 ordered his men to knock over the Britons by striking them with their shield bosses, and then to stab them on the ground (*Ann.* 14. 36–7). He also described the Batavians at Mons Graupius striking the enemy with shields and then stabbing them in the face, contrasting this with the ineffective slashing technique of the Britons (*Agricola* 36). Connolly, basing his argument around equipment patterns, attempted to describe the Roman technique of sword fighting, emphasizing the use of the Mainz type of *gladius* for thrusting.[132]

There is ample evidence for men using their *gladii* to cut. The depiction of Roman soldiers fighting, on monuments such as Trajan's column and the Adamklissi *Troepaeum Triani*, show them using a wide variety of cuts and thrusts, which suggests that we should not believe that all soldiers followed a rigid drill in combat. Both underarm and overarm thrusts, and overarm cuts are depicted.[133] One legionary on the Adamklissi metopes appears to be holding his *gladius* stabbing downwards like a dagger, with his thumb on the pommel. More probably he is holding the sword normally, but has inverted his hand at the wrist to thrust downwards, like the lunge of a modern fencer.[134] A

---

[131] See Bishop and Coulston, *Roman Military Equipment*, 53–4, 69–74. They point out on p. 69 that the word *gladius* is not specific to the short swords used by Roman infantry. However this meaning of the word has entered into such widespread usage that I have chosen to employ it in this sense in this chapter.

[132] Connolly, 'Roman Fighting Technique'.

[133] Underarm thrusts, Trajan's Column scenes 310–11, metopes 21, 22, 23, 27, 36, 39; overarm cuts, scene 250–1, metope 17. A swordsman thrusting underarm could protect most of his body behind his shield, but his thrust could easily be parried by his opponents shield. The frequency with which this stroke appears on the metopes is probably partially explained by the enemies' lack of shields. [134] Metope 19.

modern fencer stands with his right foot forward, his body turned in profile to his opponent to present as small a target as possible. In this position he can put all his body weight behind the lunge with his sword in his right hand. According to Vegetius, the Romans taught a sword-drill that similarly required a man to have his right foot forward (Vegetius 1. 20). In battle, a man had his left foot forward, so that he could protect as much of his body as possible with his shield. If he had attempted to lean into a thrust, to add his own weight to the blow, he would have exposed his sword arm and much of his right side. Therefore he could not get as much weight behind a thrust as a fencer.

The shield was the most important piece of defensive equipment. For some of Rome's enemies, such as the German and Gallic tribes, it was the only defensive equipment possessed by the majority of their warriors. The Roman *scutum* was also a weapon of offence. Earlier we noted descriptions of Roman soldiers striking their opponents with their shields to unbalance them and then stabbing them with their swords (*Ann.* 14. 36–7, *Agricola* 36). At the naval battle off Massilia in 49 BC, a certain Acilius boarded an enemy ship and had his right arm cut off by a sword, 'but still kept hold of his shield with the other hand and struck his enemies in the face with it until he drove them all back and got possession of the ship' (Plutarch, *Caesar* 16). The Adamklissi monument shows a legionary punching an opponent's face with the boss of his shield, and stabbing him in the stomach (Metope 23). The shield was held in the left hand by the horizontal grip behind the boss, allowing the soldier to punch at his opponent. As he stood with his left foot forward, a man could get much of his body weight behind this punch. Added to this was the considerable weight of the shield itself, between 5.5 and 10 kg. (12–22 lb.), making a blow delivered in this manner easily enough to unbalance, or even knock down, an opponent. The thickness and weight of a Roman shield made it more effective as a weapon, and gave a greater ability to stop blows. Such a shield was more difficult to move quickly to parry an opponent's attack. Normally the *scutum* was held out horizontally in front of a man. The soldier stood behind it in a slight crouch, his left leg towards the enemy, and his right side turned away. This is the fighting stance depicted on Trajan's Column, the Adamklissi metopes, and the relief from Mainz. The shield covered a man's torso, the top of his legs, and the bottom of his face. The helmet protected the top half of the head, whilst its cheek pieces covered more of the face. The only parts of the body exposed to the enemy were the legs, principally the left, the right arm, and parts of the face. A shield was difficult to penetrate and behind that remained the protection of body armour. P. Connolly suggested that the Romans would have fought against opponents armed with slashing swords, like the Celts, in a very low crouch, trying to get in under their opponents guard.[135] There is no evidence to support this conclusion, and his suggested stance looks both impractical and awkward. If a man fought in this manner, he gained little benefit from his shield, and left his head, shoulders and the top of his back exposed to downward cuts, which is exactly the sort of attack the Celtic long sword was best suited to. Even for a man wearing helmet and armour, such a stance would have been suicidal.

Having looked at the equipment of the individual, we must now consider how he fought. Can we assume that all men in the front rank of a unit fought in the same manner, or even that they fought at all? Earlier in this chapter, I referred to the findings of S. L. A. Marshall, that at best only 25 per cent of a unit participated in a firefight and many even of these did not properly aim their weapons or actively seek to kill the enemy. Marshall found that it was the same 25 per cent who repeatedly led charges and cleared enemy positions.[136] It is difficult to believe that 75 per cent or more of the men in close combat did not fight at all, but merely stood next to the enemy. What seems likely is that these men fought more with the object of staying alive, than of actively aiming to kill the enemy.

The skeletons discovered at Maiden Castle show that the Romans storming this hillfort had used their swords for cutting as well as thrusting. The type and distribution of wounds on these skeletons conforms closely to the far more numerous finds on the site of the battle of Wisby fought in 1361.[137] There, around 1,200 corpses were discovered, some still wearing armour or mail coifs. Not all wounds would necessarily appear in the archaeological record, which only shows damage to bones, especially cuts. The investigators worked on the principle that a series of closely grouped, deep cuts could only have been inflicted when the individual was defenceless, rather than in the

---

[135] Connolly, 'Roman Fighting Technique'.

[136] Marshall, *Men against Fire*, 50–65, and *Infantry Operations*, 55–63.

[137] Thordeman, *Armour from the Battle of Wisby*, 94–5, 160–94, as do finds from other periods in which edged weapons were used, see S. J. Wenham 'Anatomical Interpretations of Anglo-Saxon Weapon Injuries', in S. Chadwick Hawkes, *Weapons and Warfare in Anglo-Saxon England* (Oxford, 1989), 123–39.

course of actual fighting, which seems plausible. One of the skeletons at Maiden Castle had received nine severe cuts to the head, any one of which would probably have been fatal.[138] Weapon types may have been different at Wisby, compared to those used by the Romans and most of their opponents, but the close similarities with the finds at Maiden Castle, suggest that it is legitimate to generalize about combat in our period from this evidence.

A Roman, standing in the fighting stance discussed above, only exposed certain parts of himself to enemy attack. Very few thrusts, perhaps only those delivered at the end of a running charge, could have penetrated the centre of a *scutum*, whilst its thinner sides were protected from cuts by the brass rim.[139] Not covered by the shield were the legs, particularly the left leg which was nearer the enemy, the right arm and the head. Interestingly it is precisely these areas, the head, the right arm and legs, where the vast majority of the wounds, judged to have been inflicted in combat, occurred at Wisby. If a man had lost his shield to a *pilum*, then he was much more exposed.

Most of the wounds judged to have been fatal or incapacitating occurred to the head. Our literary sources seemed to view thrusts and cuts to the head as very effective.[140] The Roman infantry helmet invariably left the face and ears exposed, since a soldier had to be able to see and hear to understand and follow orders. The face could have been partially covered by the shield and was protected by the helmet's wide cheek pieces, but might still have been vulnerable to a thrust from a sword or spear. Caesar's centurion, Crastinus, was killed at Pharsalus by a sword thrust that entered his mouth and came out at the back of his head (Plutarch, *Caesar* 44). A man cutting with a Celtic long sword or Dacian *falx*, was more likely to hit the top of his opponents head. The finds at Wisby showed far more cuts to the top left of the skull, logically, since this was the side easiest to hit for a right-handed swordsman. The trends in Roman helmet design during our period were towards more protection for the front and top, in the form of thicker peaks halfway up the helmet and strengthening crossbars on the top, along with deeper and broader neckguards. This suggested attempts to protect the head against blows delivered by slashing weapons. The strengthening bars to the top, and the peak in the front,

---

[138] Wheeler, *Maiden Castle*, 352, pl. 12.
[139] Bishop and Coulston, *Roman Military Equipment*, 59, 81–2.
[140] *Ann.* 2. 14, *Agricola* 36; Plut. *Caesar* 45.

would have taken some of the force out of a cut to the top and side (probably the left) of the head. If such a blow missed or was deflected, it would land on the defender's shoulders. The wide deep neckguard of an Imperial Gallic helmet gave some defence against this. More important was the soldier's body armour. All types of Roman infantry armour had especially heavy protection for the shoulders. Even this was unlikely to make the wearer completely invulnerable to this sort of attack. All the different types of armour found at Wisby seem to have been penetrated.[141] To some extent this is an unrepresentative sample, since a mass grave is most likely to be filled by those men whose armour had proved unsatisfactory. Nevertheless, Josephus makes it clear that Roman armour resulted in their suffering far fewer serious wounds and fatalities than their Jewish opponents (*BJ* 2. 508, 3. 198).

Wounds to the arms or legs were far less likely to be serious than cuts to the head, and at Wisby several such wounds are often combined with one serious blow, usually to the head, which probably finally killed the victim. When a Syrian auxiliary, Sabinus, led a small band of men up a breach in one of the walls of Jerusalem in AD 70, he slipped in his moment of triumph. Rising on one knee and protecting himself with his shield he fought off the Jews surrounding him and wounded some of them. After receiving many wounds and losing the use of his right arm, he was finally killed (*BJ* 6. 63–6). In the same siege the Bithynian centurion, Julianus, was surrounded by a crowd of opponents. His armour, shield, and helmet protected him well, but he was worn down by many wounds to his exposed limbs, and eventually dispatched (*BJ* 6. 85–90). Individual wounds to the limbs were more serious on some occasions. One man at Wisby had both his legs cut off below the knees by a single incredibly powerful blow, probably from a double-handed sword or axe.[142] The double-handed, scythe like *falces* used by the Dacians or Bastarnae on the Adamklissi metopes, may well have been capable of delivering such a blow. The Romans on the monument wear greaves and vambraces to protect legs and arms respectively from such blows. Most cuts to the legs or arms would have been weakening to the victim, but not incapacitating. A succession of such minor wounds might have eventually reduced his strength and ability to wound his attacker. The man might then have been killed by a more

---

[141] Thordeman, *Armour from the Battle of Wisby*, 165.
[142] Ibid. 164–5, fig. 170.

serious blow to the head, now that he was less able to defend himself. Alternatively, lesser wounds, especially to the legs, might have prevented a man from escaping when his unit fled.

It seems most likely that the majority of men, the 75 per cent fighting to stay alive rather than kill the enemy, would have delivered such tentative blows, rather than stronger thrusts or slashes to the head, which, whilst more likely to kill, left the right arm more exposed to the enemy. In addition, a man dealing out these stronger strokes with the sword and using his shield aggressively to drive back and overbalance an opponent ran the risk of losing balance himself. We may picture a line of men in contact with an enemy unit, with the majority of soldiers fighting very cautiously, gaining the maximum protection from their shields, watching their opponents, and only occasionally delivering a weaker blow, exposing as little of their right arm and side as possible. A minority of men would fight far more aggressively, attacking their opponent with powerful blows from their *scutum*, and delivering savage thrusts and cuts with their sword.

It also seems likely that it was the 25 per cent or less actively seeking to kill the enemy who were more likely to kill their opponent and step into his place in the enemy ranks. Breaking into the enemy line was the way to begin a rout. In AD 66 in Alexandria, a Jewish formation with a front rank of better-equipped men held out until the Romans broke into this rank, at which point they were routed with heavy losses (*BJ* 2. 494–8). Appian described the opposing lines at Philippi attempting to hack their way into each other's ranks (Appian, *BC* 4. 128). According to Caesar, on one occasion some of his men went as far as to throw themselves against their German opponents dragging aside their shields (and so presumably having dropped their own, and fighting without their protection) to stab at them and break into their lines (*BG* 1. 52). When a man in the front rank was killed, he most likely fell backwards, making it difficult for the man behind to step immediately into his place. It would have taken exceptional nerve to step into the enemy ranks, and they would have made every effort to kill the intruder. If he survived, then the enemies on either side of him would have begun to edge backwards, a movement that might swiftly lead to flight.[143]

[143] See V. D. Hanson, *The Western Way of War*, 160–70 for a description of this process in hoplite battles.

This movement in the front rank or ranks may have been the beginning of a rout, but the men in these positions could not have given way until those behind them had fled. The men in the rear ranks were exposed to many of the same stresses and fears as the men fighting in the front rank, but, unlike them, were inactive, unable to do anything to counter their fears. Nor could they have seen which way the fight was going, if in a deep formation. If the rear ranks refused to give way, perhaps because there were many of them, then a mêlée could have lasted longer than usual (*BJ* 6. 71–80, 136–48). This was not always beneficial and might have resulted in far heavier casualties for the losers. Sometimes an exceptionally deep formation could prevent the men in the front ranks from escaping when things were going very badly, because the men in the rear were unwilling to retreat.[144] Another factor could keep the men in the ranks behind the first from running away even in a shallow formation, namely morale. Ardant du Picq argued that the reason why the Romans could beat barbarian peoples in hand-to-hand combat was that a greater fear had been instilled in their minds than their fear of the enemy. This fear was based on two factors. The first was the fear of the high casualty rate inevitable amongst men who turned their backs when so close to the enemy. The other was the fear of harsh punishment as a penalty for flight, instilled by rigid and draconian discipline.[145] This may have contributed to Roman morale, but other factors, such as leadership and comradeship, were equally important. A full discussion of Roman morale will be attempted in the next chapter. Whatever its origins, the normally high morale and discipline of Roman units allowed them to cope with the fear of combat longer than many of their opponents.[146] On the whole it seems that the Romans were likely to win any actual fighting.

When the broken line turned and fled, it suffered very heavy casualties.[147] Perhaps the sudden release of fear, when the enemy who had been attempting to kill you turned his back, so that he could be struck without risk, turned this emotion into elation and rage. It seems to have been the case throughout history that most men could more

---

[144] *BG* 5. 43, *Ann.* 2. 20, 14. 37, *BJ* 3. 271–5.

[145] Col. Ardant du Picq, *Études*, 15–18.

[146] Tacitus noted how quickly the Germans would withdraw from an attack that had failed to make progress, *Germ.* 6, *Ann.* 2. 14.

[147] Col. Ardant du Picq *Études*, 57–61.

easily kill an enemy who was running away.[148] Perhaps in these circumstances even the 75 per cent of men who did not normally fight actively would have tried to kill any enemy within their reach. An attempt to take a unit's standard could also have led to a particularly vicious fight, when again perhaps a higher proportion of men than usual actively sought to kill. The eagle of *Legio VII* was only saved after a bitter struggle at the second battle of Cremona (*Hist.* 3. 22). At Jerusalem in AD 70, three *signa* were captured by the Jews only after all the men around them had been killed (*BJ* 6. 223–6).

Not all hand-to-hand confrontations seem to have been as decisive as this. Sometimes the losing side were said to have retreated step by step, still facing the enemy. If the latter followed up their advantage and pursued the retiring side, these may then have turned and fled (Appian, *BC* 4. 128; *BJ* 5. 85–97). In some cases neither side could gain an advantage and the two sides would separate, both retiring slightly, but neither willing to follow the enemy. According to Appian, *BC* 3. 68, two veteran legions met without either gaining the advantage at Forum Gallorum in 43 BC: 'when they grew weary they drew apart from each other for a brief space to get their breath back, just as in gymnastic contests and then rushed again at each other.'

Hand-to-hand fighting can never have lasted very long, simply because the physical and emotional strain was enormous. Clausewitz believed that in his day troops were exhausted after 20 minutes close fighting.[149] Major General Fuller suggested 15 minutes for the maximum time that a man could have fought in an ancient battle before becoming exhausted.[150] Probably most mêlées actually took even less time that this. If neither side gained an advantage, then such lulls in the fighting with the two sides drawing breath, separated by only a short distance, must have been common. Subsequent charges made by the unit lacked the force of the first, partially because the men were tired, but also because there were no *pila* or javelins to throw.

It was probably during lulls in the fighting that wounded men from the front rank were replaced and sent to the rear (Appian, *BC* 4. 128). Many of the wounds received in combat, especially to the limbs, were light enough for a man to have continued fighting until such an interval

[148] Keegan, *The Face of Battle*, 103–5, 150–1.

[149] C. von Clausewitz, *On War*, iii, trans. M. Howard P. Paret (Princeton 1949), 291–313.   [150] Fuller, *Julius Caesar*, 90–1.

occurred, or the enemy were routed, and perhaps even in successive combats.[151] Trajan's column depicts a legionary and an auxiliary being led to a dressing station, apparently during a battle.[152] It seems unlikely that men wounded in the front rank during combat attempted to retreat whilst the fighting was going on. To attempt to do so, not only exposed the individual to his opponent, but his pushing to the rear of his own formation, might have led to a rout. It is impossible to quantify the casualties suffered by the victors in a mêlée, or by both sides in an indecisive clash. Only the first rank was at risk from the enemy weapons, that is within their killing zone. The probability that only a few on either side were fighting actively to kill the enemy suggests that losses amongst these might have been very slight.

The length of time which opposing lines might spend disputing the same ground, again suggests that lulls in the fighting were common. Caesar's victory over the Helvetii lasted from midday until evening. Early in the action, the Helvetii had retreated to a hilltop about a mile (1.6 km.) from the Roman position. The Roman line clearly did not follow them in this retreat, as there was a delay before they attacked again (*BG* 1. 25–6). In Spain in 49 BC, two opposing lines of legionaries fought on a narrow spur for five hours, before a final charge by Caesar's men drove the enemy off and allowed them to retreat from their exposed position. Both sides replaced the units in the front line with fresh cohorts, which in itself suggests that there were many lulls when the opposing sides were not actually in contact. In this case, at least some of the fighting also involved missile exchanges. Losses were heavy on both sides. Caesar lost 70 killed and 600 wounded including a *primus pilus*, whilst Afranius lost 200 dead, including 5 centurions, and an unspecified number of wounded (*BC* 1. 45–6). In AD 70 one of the assaults mounted into the Temple Court resulted in heavy fighting, lasting from the ninth hour of the night until the fifth of the day, which brought no decisive result (*BJ* 6. 136–48).

Even if the enemy first line fled before contact, or after a short fight, an attack could still have failed or resulted in stalemate. At the second battle of Philippi, the rout of Brutus' first line panicked the troops in the second and third lines, most of whom fled without fighting (Appian, *BC* 4. 128). On other occasions the men of the second and

---

[151] *BG* 2. 27, Caesar claimed that wounded men fought on, leaning on their shields to rest themselves during lulls. [152] Scene 102–3.

third lines did not become infected with the panic of the men in front of them. At Cremona in AD 68 *Legio I Adiutrix* broke the first line of *XXI Rapax* in its first charge, and captured its eagle. The supporting lines of the *XXI* then drove back the *I*, capturing many *signa* and killing its legate (*Hist.* 2. 43). In the defeat of Boudicca in AD 60 the quick success of the initial Roman charge was followed by long and heavy fighting against supporting units (*Dio* 62. 12. 1–2). Even initial success could then have led to a long drawn-out fight, interspersed with many lulls. Many small-scale, local charges, routs, retreats, and mêlées might have been involved in such fighting, which overall led to a virtual stalemate. The winners in a hand-to-hand combat probably suffered comparatively few casualties. However, if a unit had to charge several times and fight several such combats, then its casualties could have begun to mount, without its ever losing and suffering the heavy losses associated with flight. In AD 60 in such a battle, Suetonius Paulinus' army suffered somewhere between 8 and 10 per cent casualties (*Ann.* 14. 37).

A virtual stalemate could last for hours. At Zela, the veteran *Legio VI* broke through the enemy line, which elsewhere was only being pushed back slowly, and caused the collapse of the whole enemy army (*Alexandrian War* 76). At Munda, after a long, hard fight, it was *Legio X* that broke into the enemy line at one point, causing the collapse of the rest (*Spanish War* 30). The Roman emphasis on deploying troops in several lines ensured that there were always troops available to exploit such a breakthrough and roll up the enemy line.[153] At the Sambre, Caesar's troops on the left achieved quick success, but instead of turning against the remainder of the Belgic line, pursued the enemy to their camp. It was only after a delay that some of these troops were sent back to relieve the beleaguered right, by attacking the enemy in the rear (*BG* 2. 23–7). Attacks by troops approaching the enemy from the rear or flanks could have led to an enemy collapse more quickly than a breakthrough. The Teutones collapsed when a concealed Roman force attacked them in the rear (Plutarch, *Marius* 21). At Mons Graupius the Caledonian army began to break up when Roman cavalry attacked its rear (*Agricola* 37).

---

[153] Mithridates was similarly able to pour reserves into a breach made in one section of Triarius' line and roll up the entire army, App. *Mithridatic Wars* 12. 89.

In infantry combat the most decisive victories seemed to have happened quickly. If neither side achieved a breakthrough in the early stages of an attack, then a stalemate normally resulted. Many units charged, and drove the enemy back a short distance, either after fighting or by delivering a shock to their morale. The fighting was punctuated by many long periods of inactivity, when neither side was willing or able to advance. Even the victors in these local encounters suffered a few casualties, whose numbers mounted with each successive clash. Overall the army might suffer a comparatively high loss, before a breakthrough was achieved somewhere. If reserves could be sent into the resultant gap, then the enemy would probably have been defeated with heavy loss. Alternatively some external force from the flanks or rear might precipitate an enemy collapse at lesser cost.

The tactics of Roman infantry were fundamentally aggressive, emphasizing the offensive above all else. Pompey's decision at Pharsalus, to order his infantry to meet the enemy charge at the halt, has no parallel elsewhere in our period. Even in battles where they were heavily outnumbered, as in the defeat of Boudicca, the Romans' defence was based on counter-attack. Surrounded and outnumbered in 53 BC, Cotta and Sabinus' cohorts repeatedly attempted to close with the enemy and drive them off (*BG* 5. 33–5). The aim of closing with the enemy was to deliver two terrific shocks at close range, the physical one of a volley of *pila* and the moral one of a charge by yelling men. Shock action of this sort was the best and quickest way of reaching a decisive result in the encounter, routing the enemy before contact or after only a short burst of fighting. His weapons required the legionary to get very close, first to throw his *pilum*, and then to reach the enemy with his short sword. In the previous chapters we have seen that, at army level, Roman strategy and tactics were dominated by the principle of the offensive. Even when heavily outnumbered, the aim was normally to defeat and destroy the enemy army. To achieve this his line had either to be outflanked or penetrated at one point and then the remainder rolled up. The enemy army was then destroyed in a concerted pursuit. Even in a defensive action the occupation and possession of particular pieces of terrain was seldom of significance, unless it offered some advantage in the actual fighting. Adopting the offensive seems to have been the fundamental principle of Roman tactics.

CAVALRY AGAINST INFANTRY

Many of the factors involved in infantry combat also applied to other types of close combat, so that the following sections will be briefer than the last. In our period there were two contrasting styles of cavalry fighting. The first, epitomized by the Parthian horse-archer or Numidian light horseman, was to harass the enemy from a distance, using missiles. Close contact was avoided unless the enemy had been so weakened by fire as to be unable to resist. The alternative tactic was to charge into contact, defeating the enemy by shock action, in the manner of the Parthian or Sarmatian cataphracts. Some cavalry, including many auxiliary units of the Principate, fought using a combination of these styles.[154]

As with infantry combats, an important aspect of a clash between cavalry and infantry was the attempt by both sides to intimidate the other before contact. The appearance of the Parthian army before Carrhae appears to have represented a concerted attempt to frighten the Romans. Drums were beaten from various directions as the army approached. The cataphracts disguised their armour with cloaks and coverings (although perhaps this was a normal measure to reduce their glare and protect the wearer from the sun) and advanced, concealed behind a line of horse-archers. Then at a signal, when nearing the enemy, the cataphracts revealed their armour. Both men and horses were heavily armoured and must have presented a formidable sight. In turn, the Parthians were impressed by the apparent lack of effect that all this had had on the Roman line. Surena judged that his cataphracts would not have broken the Roman infantry in a charge at this stage, which had been his original plan. Instead he used his horse-archers to wear the enemy down (Plutarch, *Crassus* 23–4). On one occasion, during Antony's Parthian campaign, the enemy was so impressed by the disciplined order of a Roman marching column that they refrained from attacking it (Plutarch, *Antony* 39).

Cavalry could naturally have moved faster than infantry, so that an army with strong infantry, but outnumbered in cavalry, always faced the danger of being outflanked. In the last section, we have seen that

---

[154] For cavalry in general see K. R. Dixon and P. Southern, *The Roman Cavalry* (London, 1992), 34–77, and A. Hyland, *Training the Roman Cavalry (Gloucester,* 1993), 13–31, 45–51, 69–165.

an attack from flank or rear was one of the quickest ways of breaking up an army. In Cappadocia, Arrian planned to rest his flanks on two securely held hill positions (*Ectaxis* 12). Fighting the Parthians, the Romans often seem to have advanced in large hollow squares, with troops facing in each direction.[155]

Arrian's account of his army's formation in Cappadocia provides more information than any other source dealing with an action of Roman infantry against cavalry. His opponents were the Alans, a Sarmatian tribe, whose main force in battle consisted of shock cavalry, armed with the *kontos*, a two-handed lance, and at least some of whom were heavily armoured. His formation was therefore designed to counter this threat, and may not have been used against cavalry who fought from a distance. Arrian's legions were formed with the first four ranks armed with *pila*. The first rank placed the butts of their weapons on the ground and held them firmly at an angle of 45° towards the enemy. The three ranks behind the first were to hurl their *pila* when the enemy came close enough and then lean into the men in front, bracing the front rank and the points of their *pila* against the enemy charge. Behind these were another four ranks of legionaries armed with a lighter throwing weapon, probably a javelin such as the *lancea*. If they had been equipped with *pila*, then the men in the eighth rank would have had to throw them 15 m., merely to clear their own formation. Even if these missiles had then gone on to hit and kill an approaching horse or rider, they might not have had sufficient stopping power to prevent the target from being carried by momentum into the front rank. Behind the legionaries was a ninth rank of foot-archers, with both horse-archers and artillery firing over the heads of these nine ranks (*Ectaxis* 18–19).

On the flanks a line of close order auxiliary infantry were similarly supported by archers and artillery firing over them. Any rider approaching the legionary line, in the front rank of his formation, was the target for at least three *pila*, four javelins, and an unspecified number of arrows and *ballista* bolts. In addition, once the enemy came within range, the Roman soldiers were to raise their war-cry in unison (*Ectaxis* 25; Plutarch *Antony* 39). Arrian believed that the moral shock of this great shout, and the physical shock of the barrage of missiles, would be enough to stop the enemy before they had reached the Roman line (*Ectaxis* 26).

---

[155] Plut. *Crassus* 23, *Antony* 42; *Ann.* 13. 40.

If a galloping horseman had in fact been able to strike the Roman line, then his mount would have been impaled by its own momentum on the *pilum* of the man in the front rank. Yet this same momentum, given that the armoured horse and rider might have weighed something in the region of a ton, would have led the horse to collapse on to, and knock over, the man in the Roman front rank, and probably several of those behind him. Therefore, if charging cavalry had relied upon causing a physical shock, that is actually colliding with their enemy, then the results would have been mutually catastrophic to the opposing front ranks. This did not happen, largely because a horse, particularly a ridden horse, will not in normal circumstances collide with a solid object if it can stop or go around it. A dense line of men, especially one tipped with the points of spears or *pila*, would have appeared to have been a solid object. This was the principle on which the Napoleonic formation of the square was based.[156] If the infantry remained in their places in a dense block, then the cavalrymen's horses either stopped short of the square or rode around it. One of the very few occasions on which a steady square was broken was at Garcia Hernandez in 1812. On this occasion one of the leading cavalrymen, a Heavy Dragoon of the King's German Legion, was killed close to the French square. Both horse and rider were shot and killed in mid-stride, but momentum and a nervous reaction kept the horse moving, so that it finally toppled over on top of the French infantry, dragging men down with it. This dead horse had done what no living animal and rider could have done, and actually struck the face of the enemy square, creating a gap and allowing the rest of the unit to enter.[157] Therefore had the Alans continued their charge despite the barrage of missiles, and been able to bypass the resultant barrier formed by their own fallen men and horses, they would have still have been unable to break the Roman line, providing that the legionaries stayed where they were. Halted in front of the line, they would have suffered further casualties from arrows and javelins, without achieving anything. Tacitus described how some Treveran *turmae* were stopped in this way in front of a steady line of praetorian cohorts in AD 68 (*Hist.* 2. 14). In AD 70, loyal Roman cavalry similarly refused to charge home on a solid line formed by the rebel Batavian cohorts (*Hist.* 4. 33).

The conclusion must be that the main force of a cavalry charge on an infantry line was not physical but moral. The cavalry had to

---

[156] Keegan, *The Face of Battle*, 154–160.   [157] Ibid. 155-6.

persuade the infantry to run away before they had reached them, frightened by their appearance and noise. A man, unless of exceptionally strong nerves or very familiar with horses, would normally instinctively move out of the way of a galloping horse. Add to this instinctive fear of the galloping horse, a rider, impressively armed and equipped, and the fear inspired by a cavalry charge may be understood. Outside Jerusalem in AD 70, a lone horseman, Longinus, charged a dense Jewish line. He was able to break into it, almost certainly because the Jews immediately in front of him instinctively tried to shuffle out of the way (*BJ* 5. 312–13). Arrian's infantry were formed so deeply that the men in the front rank were prevented from running away by the physical presence of the men behind and to the sides. Scattered infantry could suffer very heavily if caught in the open by a cavalry charge. When in 49 BC Petreius ordered his cavalry to attack those of Caesar's men who had been fraternizing with his own troops, only the few who managed to form up in a dense knot survived (*BC* 1. 75). In Gaul, in 53 BC, three cohorts, some veterans and servants had been surprised whilst foraging by a group of German cavalry. The veterans formed up in a dense wedge and charged the cavalry, who parted to let them through. The three inexperienced cohorts were surrounded and all killed (*BG* 6. 40). During an abortive Jewish attack on Ascalon in AD 66, a Roman *ala* inflicted heavy losses on the Jews who had run away in the face of its charge. When dense knots of more determined Jews deterred the cavalry from charging home, these were broken up by missiles (*BJ* 3. 12–21). The Jewish rebels seldom seem to have been able to stand in the face of Roman cavalry charges and so suffered heavily from these on numerous occasions during the Jewish War.[158] Skirmishing troops normally fought in a fairly loose and open order as a protection from enemy fire. This made them exceptionally vulnerable to cavalry, since very few individuals would have stood against charging horsemen. As a result skirmishers charged by cavalry and, unable to escape or shelter behind other troops, suffered extremely heavy losses and even annihilation.[159]

When a cavalry charge against a steady body of formed infantry ended in a line of horsemen halting a few metres, or even less, away from the foot soldiers, the type of weapon used by each side became of

[158] *BJ* 2. 512, 3. 22–8, 3. 488, 4. 57–61, 419, 434–6.
[159] *BG* 7. 80, *BC* 1. 55, 70, *African War* 61, 66.

great importance. The front rank of Arrian's legions in Cappadocia presented a solid row of *pila* points 60–90 cm. (2–3 feet) ahead of them. No horseman armed with a sword, or short spear would have been able to strike at these legionaries without exposing himself and his mount to the sharp heads of the *pila*. A cavalryman armed with a long, two-handed kontos, as many of the Alans were, had an extra reach allowing him to stab at the legionaries from far enough away to be immune from *pila* thrusts. Therefore, even if the initial charge had failed to contact, cavalry using the *kontos* could have walked their horses close enough to the infantry line to fight a combat on terms very favourable to themselves. They might have been able to cause sufficient casualties to break the infantry. Arrian had made sure that the Alans were unable to fight in this way. The constant barrage of missiles from the javelin men in the rear ranks, the foot- and horse-archers behind, and the artillery, prevented the Alans from lingering close in front of the legionary formation. This highlights the importance of having plenty of supporting missile troops when fighting Parthian or Sarmatian cataphracts with their heavy armour and long lances.

If cavalry did not attempt to charge infantry, they might have employed missile fire to beat them. All that was said in the section on missile fire will be as applicable here. In addition it is important to note how difficult it was to shoot from a moving horse. Anyone who has done any shooting will know how difficult it is to hit a moving target, or a stationary target when the firer is moving. Thus, whilst the speed of his mount made a horse-archer or javelin-man a difficult target to hit, its irregular motion also made his own aim uncertain. In short, to use an anachronistic term, a horse was an unstable gun platform. Saracen manuals dealing with horse-archery recommended that the best time to fire from a galloping horse was when it was in mid stride. The archer was also to fire very quickly, even as many as three arrows in 1.5 seconds.[160] Such a high rate of fire could not have been maintained for any length of time, since not only would the archer's arm have got tired, but his ammunition would quickly have been exhausted. A horse-archer would have ridden towards an enemy formation firing straight ahead. Then, when within effective range, he would have swung to the right (since a right handed man cannot fire to the right when mounted) and ridden parallel to the enemy formation, shooting

---

[160] Latham and Paterson, *Sarasen Archers*, 142.

off as many arrows as possible, before turning away and perhaps firing a Parthian shot as he retired. In these circumstances each shot could not have been properly aimed, so that the intention was to deluge the general area occupied by the enemy with as many arrows as possible. If the enemy was in a dense formation (and if he was not, then he was vulnerable to a direct charge) then some of these missiles would have been bound to take effect. According to Plutarch, the Roman square at Carrhae was so dense that, even firing from long range, the Parthian archers could not fail to hit it (Plutarch, *Crassus* 24).

The drills described by Arrian for displays of javelin throwing by the Roman cavalry suggest that their basic tactics were similar to those of horse-archers. A cavalryman usually seems to have been supposed to aim each throw during these drills, either at a target, or at the shields of the 'enemy' unit (Arrian *Tactica* 36–7, 41–2). In an all-out charge across the parade ground, which was not carried out in battle equipment, horsemen were expected to throw as many as fifteen, or, in exceptional cases, twenty light javelins, ahead of them (*Tactica* 40. 10–11). Drills carried out in battle order included an individual gallop, during which a man was to attempt to hit three targets, each in a different direction (*Tactica* 42). One formation used was the Cantabrian gallop, in which the horsemen rode in a circle, moving to the right to keep their shields facing the enemy, throwing javelins in turn as men reached the point closest to the opposing line (*Tactica* 40. 1–8). Riders using javelins had to go closer to the enemy than archers, because of their shorter range. A man could carry fewer javelins than an archer could carry arrows, so perhaps this and the necessity of going closer to the enemy might have encouraged greater attempts to aim each throw. The horse's motion still made this difficult, whilst the stress of battle probably meant that only a proportion of the unit attempted to aim at all. A Cantabrian formation resulted in all the missiles, however badly aimed, landing in roughly the same area, if only because each firer was throwing from the same position.

If the enemy infantry possessed some form of missile weapon, or had archers behind them firing over their heads, then their fire at the shooting cavalrymen would have helped further to spoil the latter's aim. Cavalry armed with javelins had to come within range of similarly equipped infantry to shoot effectively, whereas horse-archers did not. However, horse-archers were not able to fire as far as bowmen on foot. At Carrhae, Crassus' legionaries were unable to reply effectively to the Parthian arrows, because there were very few archers and slingers supporting them. When Mark Antony campaigned against the Parthians, he included a far higher proportion of such troops, with the result that his infantry suffered far less. Arrian's army in Cappadocia contained an exceptionally high proportion of auxiliary archers, to protect the heavier infantry from cavalry, showing how the Roman army could adapt to local threats.[161]

The object of shooting at an enemy infantry unit was to weaken it, so that it would be unable to stand up to a mounted charge. On one occasion in 36 BC Roman legionaries came under heavy fire from Parthian horse-archers and were ordered to form a *testudo*. The Parthians mistook the resultant movement in the Roman ranks for disorder, caused by their fire, and charged, expecting the infantry to break before contact. The charge failed when the archers were confronted with a steady line and a volley of *pila* (Plutarch, Antony 45). Roman legionaries were well protected from missiles by their armour and shields. The Parthian arrows caused far more wounds than fatalities at Carrhae, tending to hit exposed limbs (*Crassus* 24. 4). Adopting a *testudo* formation might have covered with shields even these exposed parts of the body and led to virtual invulnerability. The threat of a shock charge by the Parthian cataphracts, prevented the Roman infantry from advancing and driving off the horse-archers at Carrhae. Even so, despite the Romans' lack of an effective reply, the horse-archers' fire failed to weaken the Roman line sufficiently to have allowed a cataphract charge to break it (*Crassus* 27). Outside Ascalon in AD 66 the poorly armoured Jewish rebels were quickly reduced by the javelins of the Roman cavalrymen to a state in which they could not stand up to a charge (*BJ* 3. 13–21). Many Roman *alae* under the Principate carried javelins, but were still armoured and equipped for close combat. Troops of this sort combined the two styles of cavalry fighting. Alternatively a combination of separate shock and skirmishing cavalry, such as the Parthian cataphracts and horse-archers, could act in concert. Caesar's legionaries seem to have been brought close to breaking point in 46 BC by a combination of skirmishing infantry and cavalry (*African War* 12–18). Infantry charges failed to bring the Numidian cavalry into *pilum* range, since they fled quickly, leaving the flanks of the cohort, especially the unshielded right, exposed to javelins thrown by the infantry. Even there, the legionaries were not reduced to

---

[161] Plut. *Crassus* 24, *Antony* 37; *Ectaxis* 12–29; see Ch.1.

the state at which they would have given way before an enemy charge, so that the Pompeians could not decisively defeat them.

In that engagement Roman heavy infantry attempted to charge cavalry, but were unable to catch them because of their speed. Attacks by infantry on cavalry did occur, but were always risky. The advancing infantry unit had to keep its ranks in order, since if the men were not closely packed together they were unlikely to stand up to a mounted counter-charge. At Pharsalus Caesar's fourth line suddenly attacked the Pompeian cavalry. These seem to have degenerated into a single unformed mass after fighting and beating Caesar's cavalry, and were panicked by the sudden appearance of the enemy infantry and their bold approach.[162] The infantry could have inflicted little or no loss on the fleeing enemy. On this occasion it is important to note that very good infantry encountered very poor cavalry. Normally such charges were not so decisive, and indeed most infantry chose to face cavalry at the halt.[163]

CAVALRY AGAINST CAVALRY

Many of the factors already discussed applied equally to combats between two cavalry units. The main difference was that everything happened a good deal faster. Ancient authors depicted cavalry fights as very fluid affairs, with each side alternately advancing and retreating many times before any decision resulted (Dio 56. 32, *Ann.* 6. 35). Only in part was this fluidity due to some cavalry being primarily skirmishers, who fought from a distance and fled if the enemy threatened to come close.[164] The way in which shock cavalry operated ensured that a successful attack could very quickly have been followed by an enforced retreat.

Cavalry could not actually have been pushed forward by the men and horses in the ranks behind, but their physical presence prevented them from turning and retreating. A close formation was therefore

---

[162] *BC* 3. 93, Plut. *Caesar* 45. Fuller plausibly suggested that the Pompeian cavalry had become disordered and were panicked by the sudden appearance of Caesar's men (*Julius Caesar*, 237–8).

[163] On other occasions when infantry charged and drove off cavalry, the former appear to have very good troops, significantly more confident than the enemy, Plut. *Lucullus* 28; *BC* 1. 64; *Alexandrian War* 40; *African War* 75.

[164] e.g. the Numidian light cavalry, Sall. *Jug.* 50. 4; *BC* 2. 41; *African War* 7.

important to prevent an advancing unit's less bold soldiers from
hanging back. As soon as the cavalry began to gallop, the ranks of a
formation tended to loosen, and the men to spread out, because of the
differences in speed and strength of individual horses.[165] This can be
observed by watching any of the 'cavalry charges' staged in Hollywood
Epics. Invariably carried out at, or near, the gallop in order to be
spectacular, a neat line of horsemen in one of these films will swiftly
degenerate into a mob spread over a wide area. If such a mob of
horsemen were attacked, it was very easy for each man to escape by
flight. Therefore it has been standard practice for cavalry throughout
history to advance at a walk or trot and only accelerate into a charge,
when closer to the enemy, so that the formation had little chance of
breaking up, and arrived as a group. Such control over the instincts of
men and horses to press on only came with discipline and practice. A
nineteenth-century British manual suggested that the gallop should
begin 50 yards [46 m.] away from the enemy if infantry, and 150 yards
[137 m.] from a cavalry unit advancing in the chargers' direction.[166]
The same manual discussed what actually happened when two lines of
horsemen charged at each other:

Cavalry seldom meet each other in a charge executed at speed; the one party
generally turns before joining issue with the enemy, and this often happens
when their line is still unbroken and no obstacles of any sort intervene.

   The fact is, every cavalry soldier approaching another at speed must feel that
if they come in contact at that pace, they both go down and probably break
every bone of their body . . . there is a natural repugnance to engage in deadly
strife. How seldom have infantry crossed bayonets! Some authors say never!
. . . Lines advancing to meet each other have shown hesitation at the same
moment, thus:

   In the retreat of our army from Burgos (*in the Peninsula War in 1812*) three
squadrons of French Chasseurs charged some squadrons of our rear guard;
these advanced to meet them; both lines pulled up close to each other and
stood fast, till one Frenchman made a cut at the man opposite him, upon which
both sides instantly plunged forward and engaged; The Colonel of the
Chasseurs was killed, most of his officers wounded and the French were
driven back with heavy loss.[167]

---

[165] Hyland, *Training the Roman Cavalry*, 18, noted that speed tends to excite most
horses.
[166] L. Nolan, *Cavalry: Its History and Tactics* (London, 1853), 279, 281–2.
[167] Ibid. 228–9.

There is no evidence to suggest that cavalry in our period were uniquely able to force their horses to collide with the enemy. Certainly it seems to have been common for even supposedly good-quality and fresh cavalry to turn and flee before the enemy charge had reached them. In 48 BC Curio's cavalry charged their Pompeian opponents, who fled before any fighting had occurred (*BC* 2. 34). In Africa in 46 BC, Hirtius claimed that thirty of Caesar's Gallic horsemen charged and put to flight no less than 2,000 Numidian cavalry, which suggests that the latter fled before any fighting occurred (*African War* 6). Later in the same campaign, Caesar's cavalry quickly gave way before a sudden Pompeian attack, which may again suggest that they fled before the enemy had reached them (*African War* 52). During the Sullan civil war, Pompey led a cavalry charge and rode ahead of his men to kill a lone Gaul, who was likewise in advance of his own unit. The rest of the Gallic cavalry then fled, before Pompey or his unit reached them (Plutarch, *Pompey* 7). Arrian suggested that a very narrow, deep formation should be used to break through an enemy line. Since the horsemen in the rear ranks could not have pushed those in front onwards, this suggests that the enemy facing the line were expected to give way, like those facing a wedge (Arrian, *Tactica* 13).

If neither side was so intimidated by the other as to give way, then the two sides might pull up near each other and then fight hand-to-hand as described above. At Waterloo, some stationary cavalry were seen to open their ranks to allow the charging side to enter, and the mêlée to be fought.[168] Another witness at Waterloo saw two lines of cavalry meet at speed:

> There was no check, no hesitation, on either side; both parties seemed to dash on in a most reckless manner and we fully expected to have seen a most horrid crash—no such thing! Each, as if by mutual consent, opened their files on coming near, and passed rapidly through each other, cutting and pointing, much in the same manner one might pass the fingers of the right hand through those of the left. We saw but few fall. The two corps reformed afterwards, and in a twinkling both disappeared, I know not how or where.[169]

Fighting between cavalry could then have been very brief, but not decisive, or longer, and involved the two sides becoming intermingled. The design of the Roman cavalry helmet may suggest the nature of these fights. Cavalry helmets differ from infantry in two main

---

[168] Keegan, *The Face of Battle*, 149.   [169] Ibid. 150.

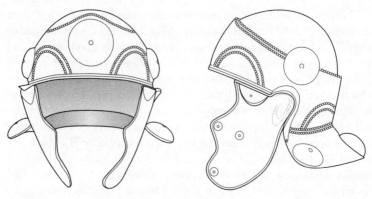

Fig. 10. Iron cavalry helmet (Russell Robinson's type B), based on an example found at Ely in Cambridgeshire

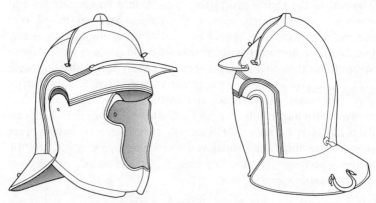

Fig. 11. Iron cavalry helmet (Russell Robinson's type E), based on a find from Heddenheim

features.[170] The first is that the neckguard is very deep, reaching down to close to the shoulders, but not wide, since this would have made the rider likely to break his neck if he fell from his mount (see Figs. 10 and 11). The second difference was that the ears of a cavalryman were invariably covered by his helmet. Usually holes were drilled in the ear piece, or a slight gap retained between this and the rear of the helmet, so that the cavalryman was able to hear orders. The cavalry helmet therefore protected equally well against blows to the side and the back

[170] Robinson, *Armour of Imperial Rome*, 89–106.

of the head. If the Roman horseman expected to be attacked from the side and rear as well as the front, then this suggests that it was common for the two sides in a mêlée to become intermingled. What factors determined the winner in such a combat are unclear, but skill and determination in the actual fighting must have played a part. Equipment might also have been important. According to Plutarch, Crassus' Gallic cavalry were forced to give way in a combat with Parthian cataphracts, in which they suffered heavily, because they lacked armour, but had difficulty wounding their opponents who were heavily protected (Plutarch, *Crassus* 25. 6–8). As with infantry combat, the sheer ability to stay in the fight for a little extra time, derived from discipline and high morale, meant that the enemy often abandoned the fight first.

Once one side gave way, they suffered very heavily, as the other side pursued striking at their backs in the elation and relief of success (*BG* 8. 29, *African War* 40). Even the victorious cavalry had their formation disrupted by becoming interspersed with the enemy during the fighting. Once they began to pursue, the victors became even more scattered, and they and their horses tired. It took time for the unit's officers to restore some semblance of order and re-form the unit's ranks, even if it were highly disciplined. The victors of a cavalry encounter were therefore often highly vulnerable to attack by a fresh enemy unit. In Britain in 54 BC, Caesar's Gallic horsemen often charged the British cavalry and put them to flight. Whilst pursuing them, they were in turn attacked by a fresh unit of enemy cavalry and themselves routed (*BG* 5. 16). At the second battle of Cremona, Vespasian's cavalry, having routed and pursued several Vitellian *alae*, were themselves put to flight by enemy reserves (*Hist.* 3. 16).

It was therefore useful for a side to have kept some of its cavalry units in reserve. If the front line was defeated, then these could charge the pursuers and probably defeat them, assuming that they had not been panicked by the flight of the defeated units.[171] If the front line had driven back and pursued the enemy, then the reserves could advance behind them, so that there was a formed unit with which to counter any fresh enemy. Caesar noted that the Britons did not form their cavalry into a single block, but kept small bodies of reserves

---

[171] *BG* 1. 18 where the rout of one unit of cavalry panicked the rest, and *BC* 3. 93 where the entire Pompeian cavalry on the left flank was defeated by Caesar's 4th line.

positioned around the field.[172] Hirtius believed that it was a common, but dangerous, error for cavalry to crowd together. In one engagement that he described, the Roman units instead: 'took up separate positions and small groups of the men fought by turns, covering one another's flank so that the Gauls could not surround them' (*BG* 8. 18–19).

Arrian planned to divide his cavalry into two halves for the pursuit of the Alans. One half was to chase the enemy, whilst the others were to follow more slowly, so that any enemy reserves or counter-attacks could have been met by a formed body on fresh horses (*Ectaxis* 27–8). The author of the *Strategikon* (2. 1) recommended that cavalry, regardless of their numbers, should always be deployed in at least two lines, so that there was a reserve.

The same manual pointed out that it was not dishonourable for cavalry to take to flight, providing that they returned to the combat (*Strategikon* 3. 11). Cavalry combats could sway to and fro as each side beat the enemy, pursued them, and were in turn beaten and pursued by fresh enemy troops. It may have been difficult for an observer to follow the course of such a fight. Normally the victor was the side that kept a formed, fresh reserve the longest. In 52 BC on several occasions the Romans won a previously indecisive cavalry encounter by committing a final, fresh reserve, usually the German cavalry.[173] In Africa in 46 BC one encounter between cavalry and light infantry swayed back and forth as each side committed new troops, until finally Caesar committed an *ala* which routed the enemy in a charge (*African War* 78).

Most Roman *alae* were as capable of fighting from a distance with missiles as delivering a shock charge, but in the second century AD a number of units intended purely for shock action were formed. Trajan raised the *ala I Ulpia contariorum milliaria* armed with the two-handed lance, the *kontos*.[174] By the Principate of Antoninus Pius other *alae*

---

[172] *BG* 5. 16. The *memorandum* from Vindolanda stated that the British cavalry did not take up fixed positions to shoot. This may simply mean that they were primarily skirmishers, who avoided close contact, but could be a description of a tactic similar to that encountered by Caesar. A. K. Bowman and J. D. Thomas, 'New Texts from Vindolanda', *Britannia*, 18 (1987), 125–42, esp. 135–7 = *Tab. Vindol.* II. 164.

[173] *BG* 7. 13, 7. 67, 7. 70, 7. 80.

[174] *CIL* 3. 4183, 4278, 4341. See J. W. Eadie, 'The Development of Roman Mailed Cavalry', *JRS* 57 (1967), 161–73. Although mistaken in his belief that most *alae* wore non-metallic armour, this is still a reasonable account of the development of cataphracts and lancers.

without the title *contariorum*, such as the *ala I Canninefatum*, were using the *kontos*.[175] Hadrian formed *ala I Gallorum et Pannoniorum cataphracta*, a unit of lancers in which both men and horses were heavily armoured.[176] Horsemen using the *kontos* could not make effective use of a shield, so that the weapon became most effective when combined with the good protection provided by a cataphract's armour.[177] Cataphracts were to form an increasingly high proportion of Roman cavalry over the next few centuries. What were the advantages of this type of cavalry? Clearly their charge was considered to be more powerful than that of ordinary cavalry (*Hist.* 1. 79). The greater weight of men, horses, and equipment cannot have made the shock delivered by their charge heavier, since as we have seen the shock of a cavalry was more moral than physical. The long *kontos* allowed lancers to wound an enemy equipped with shorter weapons first, but once the opponent had got past the point of the lance then the lancer was vulnerable. More important was the visual impression of a charge by lancers, especially cataphracts. The weight of the cataphracts' equipment prevented their horses from charging at anything much faster than a trot. This made it easier to keep a unit together as an ordered block, with all the advantages of close formation discussed above. Their heavy armour offered good protection against most missiles, and might make them appear impressive to the enemy (Plutarch, *Crassus* 23–4). A slow, but steady advance by a dense mass of cataphracts, their armour and weapons gleaming, may have offered a similar type of shock to the enemy's morale as the charge of Roman infantry. The lack of any missile weapons deprived most lancers of the option of hanging back and shooting, which may in turn have inclined them to press home their charge further than other cavalry. Lancers had their disadvantages. They were not as flexible as other *alae*, who could fight at a distance or charge into contact. Cataphracts suffered from the problems of the weight of their armour, which quickly tired their horses and so reduced their mobility. Cavalry solely equipped for shock action were a useful ingredient in an army, especially in battle, but the majority of cavalry needed to be of a less specialized type.

---

[175] See M. P. Speidel, 'Horsemen in the Pannonian Alae', in *Roman Army Studies*, ii. 62–6.　　　　　　　　　　　　　　　　　　　　　　[176] *CIL* 9. 5632.

[177] The best examples of horse armour come from Dura Europus. See Rostovtzeff and others, *Excavations at Dura Europus* 440–3.

Combats involving skirmishing cavalry seem to have taken much longer to be decisive and often produced no definite result. All that was said in the last section on the difficulties of firing from a moving horse applies equally here. When both the shooter and the target were on rapidly moving horses, then the chances of accurate aim must have been slight, and casualties as a result of fire, few. In Africa in 48 BC Curio's outnumbered cavalry became gradually exhausted after repeated attempts to charge into contact with the Numidian light horsemen failed (*BC* 2. 41). In 46 BC Caesar's own cavalry became exhausted, and suffered many wounds to their horses in a similar combat with Numidian cavalry. Caesar was forced to protect his men behind his infantry line, resting them there. After this, they were restored enough to mount a successful charge (*African War* 15–17).

In this second action, the Numidian cavalry were very closely supported by light infantry, a common Numidian tactic (Sallust, *Jug.* 59). Caesar first encountered a similar combination of cavalry and infantry in Ariovistus' army in 58 BC.

The Germans were trained in the use of a special battle technique. They had a force of 6,000 cavalry, each of whom had selected from the whole army for his personal protection, one infantryman of outstanding courage and speed of foot. These accompanied the cavalry in battle and acted as support for them to fall back upon. In a critical situation, they ran to the rescue and surrounded any cavalryman who had been unhorsed by a severe wound. They acquired such agility by practice, that in a long advance or quick retreat they could hang on the horses' manes and keep pace with them. (*BG* 1. 48)

In 52 BC Vercingetorix interspersed archers with his cavalry in skirmishes outside Gergovia (*BG* 7. 36). Later in the same year he used the same tactic outside Alesia. After a long and fluid combat, the Gallic cavalry were routed when Caesar committed a fresh reserve of German horse. With their cavalry gone, the Gallic archers were surrounded and all killed (*BG* 7. 80). During the Civil Wars, both sides frequently interspersed their cavalry with units of archers and light infantry, who invariably suffered heavily if the cavalry were beaten.[178] In the Pharsalus campaign, Caesar employed a special unit of 400 legionaries to act with his cavalry, allowing the latter to drive off far more numerous enemy horse. These men seem to have marched in battle order, without packs, to be ready for immediate action.[179]

---

[178] *BC* 2. 34, *African War* 20, 61, 78.   [179] *BC* 3. 75, 84, see Ch. 1, 18.

Caesar claimed that the German light infantry moved clutching the manes of the horses, being swift enough to keep pace with them. Does this imply that the light infantry also charged and fought interspersed within a cavalry unit's formation? It is difficult to believe that men could have kept up with galloping horses. If, as was commonly the case, one of the two sides in a cavalry charge fled before contact, then the infantry would not have served any useful purpose, being too slow to pursue. If two opposing units of cavalry opened their files and became interspersed, engaging in a standing mêlée, then individual foot soldiers might have been able to enter into this looser mob of horsemen and take part in the fight. Yet archers could have made little use of their bows in the middle of a cavalry formation, jostled by horses on either side. A cavalry unit with foot soldiers interspersed between its files would itself have had great difficulty manoeuvring properly, or adopting any of the skirmishing formations of the type described by Arrian.

It seems more likely that these mixtures of cavalry and infantry were in fact lines in which whole units of infantry were placed alternately to whole units of cavalry. The infantry must have been formed in fairly dense formations, since otherwise they were exceptionally vulnerable to enemy cavalry. In the African War, Caesar on several occasions sheltered his beaten cavalry behind a solid line of legionaries. The cavalry were able to reform and rest their horses, and then successfully charge the enemy.[180] When friendly cavalry fled from an enemy charge, a dense knot of infantry could have provided shelter from pursuit. The pursuers were in a fairly loose formation, and vulnerable to a volley of arrows, *pila*, or javelins from the infantry, whilst probably not in good enough order to charge and break these. Cavalry combats were whirling affairs, with each side chasing and being chased by the other, backwards and forwards for quite long periods of time. Infantry blocks could lend stability in such a combat, being hard to defeat and static, able, unlike cavalry, to actually hold ground. Their fire support, particularly if archers, was very valuable. Only once the enemy had driven off the friendly horse, were his cavalry able to concentrate on the infantry, using the tactics described in the last section. In these circumstances, as with Caesar's troops in Africa in 46 BC, a legionary force, well protected by armour and shields, could have held out for a long time. Poorly protected javelin-men and unshielded archers might

---

[180] *African War* 16–18, 52, 69.

quickly have been reduced by the cavalry's missiles to a state, in which they would have broken before a charge.

It may seem surprising that nowhere in this section have I referred to the Roman cavalryman's lack of stirrups. Throughout this section I have compared the performance of Roman cavalry to the horsemen of nineteenth-century armies. There is a reason for this. Recent work has shown that the Roman saddle supported the cavalrymen well, despite his lack of stirrups.[181] Stirrups would actually have restricted the movements of a man throwing a javelin to the sides. A cavalry charge did not result in the two sides colliding at high speed, so that a horseman did not need to use his stirrups to concentrate weight and momentum behind his lance. There is no evidence to suggest that lack of stirrups reduced the effectiveness of cavalry.

CONCLUSION

Neither the study of tactics nor individual weaponry can adequately explain what happened in a battle of this period, for the single reason that neither takes account of the behaviour of the soldier. Technology imposed limits on the effectiveness of weaponry, but far greater limits were imposed by the performance of the soldier attempting to use them under the stress of battle. The majority of soldiers were, for instance, incapable of aiming calmly at a human target during battle, so that few hits would have been achieved even with the most effective of bows. Similarly tactics depended for their success on the behaviour of the men, who composed the units, attempting to implement them. Even trained and disciplined Roman soldiers could not have been relied upon invariably to follow orders, and might have panicked and run away for no apparent reason. The battlefield was a place of massive confusion, where the participants were subject to enormous stress. It is only by realizing this, and studying battles accordingly, that we can hope to understand the importance of factors such as weaponry and tactics.

Moral, far more than physical, factors were of most importance in determining the course of the fighting. The formations adopted by units were determined far more by the need to prevent soldiers from

---

[181] See Connolly, 'The Roman Saddle' and Hyland, *Training the Roman Cavalry*, 45–51.

running away, than by the practical requirements of manœuvre and weapons usage. The appearance of force and confidence, even if it were only a façade, was more important than the actual fighting power of a unit. An attack failed if the defenders stayed in their position, and appeared to be steady, even if their missile fire had caused few actual casualties. The defenders might have caused the same number of losses by their fire, but lost if they then gave way and ran at the last minute. The appearance of strength was the decisive factor. The vast majority of men were instinctively more prone to avoiding threats to themselves than to attempting to kill the enemy. This was as true of 'wild barbarians' as of 'disciplined legionaries'. Training, discipline, and pride could only partially allow a man to counter this instinctive urge towards flight. Morale was the decisive factor in all fighting, but was inherently unpredictable. To impose structure on the battles of this period, as scholars have invariably attempted to do, is to create an inherently false picture of warfare, and to impose a pattern where there was none. It is also to deny the importance given by our sources, especially those of eyewitnesses such as Caesar and Josephus, to morale. The whole subject of ancient warfare needs to be re-approached from this perspective.

Most battles consisted of very many of the small actions discussed in this chapter. In these, appearance was often more important than actual physical force. The most decisive results were often achieved when one side gave way before an enemy charge had reached them. Cavalry combats were more fast moving and fluid than infantry encounters, as the victors from one mêlée fled before a fresh body of the enemy, who, in turn, were routed by the opposing supports. Infantry, who had driven back the enemy front line, might in turn have been pushed back by their supporting lines. Alternatively a combat might not have resulted in the rout of one side, but their merely retiring a short way, still facing the enemy, or perhaps the two sides parted without either having gained an advantage. Much of the fighting was very tentative and brief in duration, largely because it was so emotionally and physically exhausting. In between these bursts of fighting were long lulls with each side facing the other over very short distances, until one side felt more confident. Casualties in the actual fighting were few for the victors, but could have mounted with each successive encounter. Many missiles were thrown or fired of which only a very few actually wounded or killed anyone. Overall, the scene was massively confusing. Very few men could have had any idea of the grand tactics of the battle, or indeed what was happening anywhere outside their own patch of ground. Within that, very small features could assume immense importance for those involved. The actions of a few individuals, be they the men who pressed ahead when an attack was faltering, or were the ones to fight their way into an enemy formation, or alternatively the few men who first decided to run away, could decide the outcome of an encounter.

Why did the Romans usually win these battles? One factor was certainly their superior organization, at high levels, to most of their opponents, as discussed in the last chapter. Roman command structure and organization made it more likely that a Roman army had reserves available, and the ability to direct them to exploit a break in the enemy line or plug a gap in their own. At a unit level, the Roman army was better equipped and protected than many of its opponents. More important was the training, discipline, and high morale that allowed it to behave as it did. Roman infantry could use shallower formations than other armies. They could advance slowly and in silence and wait until the enemy was almost on top of them before hurling a devastating volley of *pila*. Discipline, fear of punishment, and good morale kept them from running away before an enemy charge, and kept them in a hand-to-hand combat for that little extra time, in which an enemy would have turned and fled. The cavalry of the Principate was likewise highly confident, and, because it was well trained and led, was able to rally more easily after a pursuit or flight and keep its formation.

Finally the dominance of the offensive in Roman tactical doctrine deserves some comment. Cavalry was unsuited to holding ground, because of its tendency to advance and retreat rapidly, and therefore by its nature was an attacking arm. In the section on infantry combat, it was noted that the Roman infantry almost invariably charged to meet their enemy, seeking to overpower him in a short decisive clash. Army tactics were almost invariably intended to defeat the enemy army and then destroy it in a concerted pursuit. In the chapter on strategy, it was suggested that the adoption of the offensive as soon as possible was the basic principle behind Roman action in all types of conflict.[182] The Roman army of our period had its origins in the hoplite-type phalanx of early Rome. Hanson discerned a strong tradition of decisive action, which encouraged armies to meet and fight as soon as possible, in the

---

[182] See Ch.3.

warfare between similar phalanxes in Classical Greece.[183] This same instinct may have contributed to the Roman tradition of the importance of the offensive. In the Second Punic War, the dictator Fabius was exceptional because he avoided direct confrontation with the enemy, which was perhaps the instinctive reaction of most contempary Roman commanders. In most campaigns of our period, the Roman army faced enemies significantly inferior to it in organization, discipline, and equipment. These advantages gave it a good chance of winning any action. Bold, aggressive action could often pay off, again reinforcing the tradition of the offensive. It is interesting to note that, when modern scholars have criticized Caesar as a general, it has normally been for his bold or rash actions. It may be that Caesar simply conformed in this respect to contempary Roman strategic and tactical doctrine, and only seems exceptional when placed in the context of some 'timeless' precepts of the art of war.[184]

The morale of the Roman army deserves some examination, and it is this to which I propose to turn in the next chapter, dealing with the fighting from the viewpoint of the individual.

---

[183] V. D. Hanson, *The Western Way of War*, 135–40, 219–27.
[184] See Ch.4.

6
The Individual's Battle

The morale of the soldier is the greatest single factor in war.

(Montgomery, *Memoirs* (1958) 83)

F OR the vast majority of men the instincts of fear and self-preservation were naturally stronger than aggressive impulses. As a result, the formation of a unit was as much dictated by the need to prevent its members from running away from any perceived threat, as by the practical considerations of manœuvre and weapons' use. Other factors were also of great importance in allowing a soldier to cope with the stress of battle. Leadership, training, discipline, and *esprit de corps* could all have contributed to this. The morale of the soldier, which was the product of all these factors, as well as of those peculiar to the situation, was of crucial importance in determining how he behaved as an individual, and collectively as part of a unit. In many situations the actions of a very few individuals, be they the men who led the way and went forwards when an attack had stalled or the men who hacked their way into an enemy formation, could decide the result of an action. Therefore examination of the individual's motivation is crucial to our understanding of a battle.[1] However, few scholars have attempted to study the morale of the Roman army. MacMullen noted, in an article, that 'an attempt to understand anything so romantic as the soul of a soldier has, I think, yet to be made'.[2] In the same article he discussed the importance of comradeship and *ésprit de corps* in the motivation of legionaries. Otherwise scholars have largely ignored morale. Watson

---

[1] See Ch. 5.

[2] R. MacMullen, 'The Legion as Society', *Historia*, 33 (1984), 440–56, esp. 440; see Ch. 6, 252–7, for a discussion of his conclusions. One article on this subject appeared too late for me to read before completing this chapter, namely A. D. Lee, 'Morale and the Roman Experience of Battle', in A. B. Lloyd (ed.), *Battle in Antiquity* (London, 1996).

and Davies both discussed the training of Roman soldiers, but dealt exclusively with the technical and practical aspects of instruction, ignoring those aspects intended to instill pride in himself and his unit into the recruit.[3] In *The Face of Battle*, John Keegan attacked a passage from Caesar's *Commentaries* for its simplified characterization and treatment of the motivations of the participants.[4] Yet this simplification was moderate compared to modern scholarly treatment of the behaviour of Roman soldiers. Articles by Oakley and Ziolkowski, on single combat and the sacking of cities respectively, fine in other respects, were marred by oversimplification of soldier's motivation.[5]

The study of the morale of any army is a highly complicated subject, embracing the fields of psychology, sociology, and anthropology, as well as history, and thus allowing many different interpretations.[6] In the case of the Roman army, there is a major gap in the sources, caused by the absence of any account of a battle written by an ordinary soldier, describing his emotions and actions. The prominent position allocated to *dona* on many soldiers tombstones, suggests that these decorations were important to the soldiers themselves, but in most respects we can only observe the behaviour of soldiers through the eyes of others.[7] A full study of the morale of the Roman army would require first an investigation of the culture and society that produced its recruits, and in particular its attitudes towards violence and authority.[8] Some of these attitudes were then subject to modification, to a greater or lesser extent, as the recruit underwent training and entered the social environment of the army with its own set of ideals of behaviour. Not only did the social background of recruits to the legions change during our period, but the army also included in the *auxilia* men from an enormous range of cultures and societies, about many of

---

[3] G. R. Watson, *The Roman Soldier* (London, 1985), 31–74, R. W. Davies, 'The Daily Life of the Roman Soldier under the Principate', in *Service in the Roman Army* (Edinburgh, 1989), 41–3.

[4] J. Keegan, *The Face of Battle* (London, 1976), 63–5.

[5] S. P. Oakley, 'Single Combat in the Roman Republic', *CQ* 35 (1985), 392–410. A. Ziolkowski, '*Urbs Direpta* or How the Romans sacked cities', in J. Rich and G. Shipley, *War and Society in the Roman World* (London, 1993), 69–91.

[6] The most accessible, but also highly perceptive, work on morale in general is R. Holmes *Firing Line* (London, 1986). Also worthy of mention are Lord Moran, *The Anatomy of Courage* (London, 1966), and F. M. Richardson *Fighting Spirit: A Study of Psychological Factors in War* (London, 1978).

[7] V. A. Maxfield, *The Military Decorations of the Roman Army* (London, 1981), 47–9.

[8] See A. W. Lintott, *Violence in Republican Rome* (Oxford, 1968), for discussion of the role of violence in the city.

which we possess little or no knowledge. We must then be aware that many aspects of the army's routine and customs may have had very different associations to soldiers from different parts of the empire, of which we are entirely ignorant.[9]

Nevertheless, it does seem possible to discuss some of the factors that might have enabled a Roman soldier to cope with the stress of combat. Some at least of these will be common to many, if not all, armies. It is therefore tempting to fill in the gaps in the Roman sources by analogy with more modern evidence. A little of this can be instructive, but too much would result in reducing the importance of the factors unique to the Roman army and the societies which produced it, resulting in a rather bland study of morale in general. Therefore this chapter is divided into two sections. The first will deal with several of the various factors which contributed to the motivation of the Roman soldier. The second will look at one aspect of his behaviour in much greater detail, seeking to emphasize the peculiarly Roman elements of this. It attempts to discern some of the other cultural traditions included in the army. This section looks at those incidents in which individual soldiers exposed themselves to danger for apparently no greater purpose than to prove their own courage. This includes entering single combat and other acts of bravado. Not only are such practices well attested, and therefore possible to study, but they may allow us to discern a peculiarly Roman form of discipline, rather than simply assuming that discipline in every army has always been fundamentally the same. This may serve to emphasize that any army will always reflect the society (or societies) that produced it, however many similarities it may appear to have with armies of other periods.

PART I: MOTIVATING THE ROMAN SOLDIER

In an earlier chapter it was noted that it is impossible to assess the importance to ordinary soldiers of, for instance, the general's speech and the religious ceremonies that preceded most battles.[10] In one

---

[9] There are many good studies of the morale of specific armies, which may give us an idea of the complexity of that of the Roman army. The study of the US Army in the Second World War in S. A. Stouffer, *The American Soldier* (Princeton, 1949–65), is unrivalled in its detail. For historians, a fine model for any study of morale in a specific army is J. Baynes, *Morale: A Study of Men and Courage. The Second Scottish Rifles at the Battle of Neuve Chapelle 1915* (London, 1967).

[10] See Ch. 4, 'Ceremony and Theatre'.

speech attributed by Josephus to Titus, the latter alludes to a common belief that the souls of soldiers killed in battle whilst displaying heroism received better treatment in the afterlife than those of men who died of old age or disease (*BJ* 6. 46–9). It is impossible to decide on the evidence available, whether such beliefs were common in that particular army at that time, or amongst Roman soldiers in general. How great a role patriotism and belief in the fundamental justice of Rome's cause played in most soldiers' motivation is likewise unknown. We might suspect that the men who fought under Marius to repel the threat posed by the Cimbri and the Teutones to Italy may have been more inspired by patriotism than the soldiers who invaded Britain in AD 43, but this is pure conjecture. Yet in 73 BC captured legionaries offered to join the slave army of Spartacus and fight against Rome (Appian, *BC* 1. 117). Desertions to the enemy were common throughout our period, and this willingness to fight for the enemy suggests that patriotism was not strong in many Roman soldiers.[11]

(a) Training and Discipline

Both Watson and Davies have discussed training, drawing heavily on Vegetius in each case.[12] They have emphasized the practical side of instruction, as Vegetius himself did, pointing out for instance that continual practice in drill and marching was necessary to allow a unit to keep formation on the battlefield (Vegetius 1. 9). Josephus believed that the continual training of the Roman army in peacetime gave them a great advantage over the Jewish rebels, but he also pointed out that the confidence in their own abilities derived from success in earlier campaigns played an equally important part (*BJ* 5. 309–11). Training certainly did attempt to instill a habit of obedience to instructions, which, combined with a fear of punishment, kept a soldier in his place in his unit's formation, instead of fleeing under the stress of combat. There was also a less tangible side to military training. Recruits were dressed in a uniform manner, drilled to obey instructions as a group, and lived together in the same groups.[13] All this reduced the recruit's civilian sense of identity, partially replacing this with a corporate identity as a member of the unit. Civilian attitudes and standards of

---

[11] See J. B. Campbell, *The Emperor and the Roman Army* (Oxford, 1984), 303–14, for a discussion of desertion under the Principate.

[12] See Ch. 6 n. 3.

[13] See Holmes, *The Firing Line*, 31–73, for a good discussion of this process.

behaviour were likewise replaced by those of a soldier, for whom the use of violence was his ultimate purpose.

All professional armies form, to some extent, closed communities with their own customs and standards of behaviour; but the Roman army, more than most, effectively formed its own society. Military garrisons were surrounded by *canabae* supplying most of their needs, and veterans, especially from the legions, settled after their long service in colonies with other veterans.[14] Within such a closed community it was easier for the army to encourage soldiers to adopt its own standards of behaviour. Each stage of a recruit's progress was marked by subtle changes of status, and the complex structure of ranks within the army governed a man's whole career.[15] Within a closed community these subtle changes of status may have gained an importance that civilians outside the system could never have appreciated. If Tacitus is to be believed, many legionary recruits were men who had failed in other walks of life and joined the army as a last resort (*Ann.* 4. 4). These men entered a new environment in the army and were given a status within it which they could increase by fully adopting its customs. Failures in civilian society, these men might have more easily adopted a new set of values, taking pride in belonging to something exclusive, namely their unit.[16] In this way a man was given far more self-confidence and a greater sense of his own importance. It is important to realize the nature of this closed community, and the great significance of minor distinctions in status to those within it, when we come to discuss *dona* or military decorations later in the chapter.

(b) Unit Cohesion

In a real sense, the army formed an isolated community within society, and the distinction of being a Roman soldier may have been a source of pride to its members, even if many outside the army held the ordinary *miles* in contempt.[17] Within the army, subdivisions into units provided the soldier with something closer and more tangible on which to focus his loyalty. During the mutiny of the Pannonian legions in AD 14, the

---

[14] MacMullen, *Historia*, 33 (1984), 440–56; see also Alston, *Soldier and Society*, 39–52.

[15] See Watson, *The Roman Soldier*, 75–92 on promotion, and R. W. Davies 'Joining the Roman Army', in *Service in the Roman Army*, 3–30.

[16] Holmes, *The Firing Line*, 49–50.

[17] Campbell, *The Emperor and the Roman Army*, 9–13 on attitudes towards soldiers.

mutineers at one point intended to amalgamate their three legions into one, but this move failed because each soldier wanted the single unit to take on the name and traditions of his own corps (*Ann.* 1. 18). In 48 BC Curio led legions that had recently surrendered to Caesar. Despite appeals by their old commander to desert to the enemy, these units remained loyal and fought well, being defeated rather than surrendering (*BC* 2. 28, 34–42). Thus even in the disturbed circumstances of mutiny and civil war, loyalty to the legion was very strong in most soldiers, more so than political considerations. Caesar's flattery and special treatment of *Legio X* not only ensured its loyalty to him, but made it one of the most effective units under his command. Many of the legions of the early Principate remained in existence for centuries, preserving the traditions of earlier battles. In AD 69, Antonius Primus encouraged the men of *Legio III Gallica* by reminding them of their successes under Corbulo and Mark Antony. Some of the men in the unit in 69 may have actually served under Corbulo, but the battles under Antony, over a century earlier, could only have been familiar to them from unit tradition (*Hist.* 3. 24). Such traditions emphasized the unit's successes and set standards of courage and steadfastness that soldiers in the present-day unit might have felt obliged to live up to. Many of the unit's parades and ceremonies, especially those involving the standards, served the purpose of emphasizing the soldier's place within this greater entity. The standards, as the symbols of the unit, were the strongest focus for this pride, and consequently their loss was a great disgrace, whilst the capture of enemy standards was a clear sign of success.[18] In such a system, it did not matter whether one legion was any better than another. If its soldiers believed that it was, then they would have fought better as a result. Rivalry between units was exploited by Roman commanders to make each unit perform better.[19] However, pride in a unit could in extreme cases result in hostility towards members of other units. In AD 68 brawling and even open fighting between legionaries and the élite Batavian cohorts occurred on several occasions.[20] In this case the *ésprit de corps* that made the Batavians so effective in battle also produced disciplinary problems within the army. In the last chapter it was noted that the appearance of

---

[18] On the cult of the standards see J. Helgeland, 'Roman Army Religion', *ANRW* II. 16. 2, 1473–8, and C. Renel, *Cultes Militaires de Rome; les enseignes* (Paris, 1903).

[19] *BJ* 5. 502–3, cf. *ILS* 5795 for a description of a competition arranged between auxiliaries and marines.   [20] *Hist.* 1. 64, 2. 28, 2. 68.

confidence in a unit, its capacity to seem solid and steadfast in defence and unstoppable in attack, was often more important in determining the outcome of the fighting than the physical fighting power of the units. In this context the soldiers' belief and pride in their unit as something special, as a corps of particular prowess, could have encouraged this confidence, which might have been decisive.

Unit *esprit de corps* was fostered in many ways. In his formal address to troops from the province of Africa, delivered at Lambaesis and subsequently commemorated there, Hadrian showed a detailed knowledge of the peculiar situation of each unit.[21] He knew that *Legio III Augusta* was under-strength because one cohort had been detached for service with the *proconsul*, whilst a vexillation of one cohort, strengthened by a draft of four men from the other *centuriae* of the legion, had been posted away two years before. He also mentioned that the legion was normally scattered in a number of small outposts, which prevented it from drilling together. Having acknowledged all these difficulties, and at the same time shown his knowledge of and interest in the conditions of the unit, Hadrian went on to praise the legion's manœuvres without reservation. In a similar way he told a *cohors equitata* how difficult it was for a unit of their type to mount an impressive display of drills after an *ala* had performed, but then went on to say that the unit had manœuvred so well that it required no excuse.

The names and titles of the units of the Roman army often emphasized their distinct identity. Many used titles granted as battle honours for conspicuous service, in the same way that individual soldiers might be decorated and record this proudly on their tombstones. *Legio XIV* became *Martia Victrix* after its distinguished part in defeating the rebellion of Boudicca. Other units were named after particular emperors. *Legio XXX* was raised by Trajan and named *Ulpia Victrix* for its performance in the wars of his reign. Some legions became *Claudia Pia Fidelis* or *Pia Fidelis Domitiana* through loyalty to these emperors during attempted rebellions by provincial governors.[22] Many auxiliary units had titles incorporating the name of an emperor. The most common titles were *Augusta*, *Flavia*, *Ulpia*, and *Aelia*.[23] A variety of other titles were awarded to units of the *auxilia* as

---

[21] *ILS* 2487, 9133–5.

[22] On legion's titles see Campbell, *The Emperor and the Roman Army*, 88–93.

[23] For battle honours in general see Maxfield, *Military Decorations*, 218–35.

battle honours. A unit could receive a premature grant of Roman citizenship, which was received by individuals on discharge in the normal course of events. *Cohors I Brittonum milliaria* was honoured in this way for its service in Trajan's Dacian wars.[24] A grant of citizenship gave tangible legal advantages to the recipients, but most awards carried no practical benefits. Units received the titles of *torquata* or *bis torquata*, *armillata*, or *coram laudata* (abbreviated *C.L.*). A single unit might amass a whole series of such awards. The cohort of Britons granted citizenship by Trajan eventually became *cohors I Brittonum milliaria Ulpia torquata p.f. (pia fidelis) c.R. (civium Romanorum).*[25] In the vast majority of cases we do not know what incident won the unit its title, but it is likely that each generation of new recruits was well instructed in the details of a unit's distinguished service. Titles were still listed long after all the men who had participated in gaining them had been discharged.[26]

A unit's name emphasized its distinct identity. Many of the parades and ceremonies performed by a unit helped to increase the sense of identity felt by individual soldiers to this collective body. The third-century *Feriale Duranum* records the festivals celebrated in one year by *cohors XX Palmyrenorum* at Dura Europus.[27] Most of these festivals were associated with members of the imperial family, even ones like Germanicus who can have had little relevance to third-century soldiers. Only three out of forty-one recorded festivals had distinctly military associations, the day of *honesta missio* (demobilization) and the two days *rosaliae signorum*, when the standards were decorated. Yet the exact purpose of these occasions was in many respects less important than the frequency with which the unit met as a body for a formal parade, and probably a sacrifice to commemorate a festival. The annual dedication of an altar to *Iuppiter Optimus Maximus* (*IOM*), which has left traces outside several forts in Britain, increased the sense of

---

[24] *CIL* 16. 160. On auxiliary awards of citizenship see Maxfield, *Military Decorations*, 227–32.
[25] See P. A. Holder, *Studies in the Auxilia of the Roman Army from Augustus to Trajan*, *BAR* 70 (1980), Chs. 2–3.
[26] Awards of citizenship only affected those soldiers currently serving with a unit. However the title *civium Romanorum* was usually retained long after these men had left, when the unit would have been composed of non-citizens. See Maxfield, *Military Decorations*, 218 n. 1.
[27] See A. D. Nock, 'The Roman army and the Religious Year', *Harvard Theological Review*, 45 (1952), 187–252. Also Campbell, *The Emperor and the Roman Army* 99–101, and *RMP* 117.

corporate identity felt by a soldier for his unit.[28] The course of a year was marked by festivals celebrated as a group. Some units also performed religious devotions to deities outside the official calendar as a collective whole. In the Temple of Bel at Dura Europus there is a wall painting showing *cohors XX Palmyrenorum*, headed by its commander and standard, sacrificing to three Palmyrene gods.[29] At Carvoran *cohors I Hamiorum* made a collective dedication to *Dea Sura*.[30] Therefore a man's relationship to Rome's official deities and to other native gods could be defined through his membership of his corporate body, further enhancing his identification with his unit. Groups of officers of the same rank might also make group dedications to specific deities, emphasizing the sense of collective identity of a section within the unit.[31]

The Roman army was divided into many units, and the men within these units were divided into many different ranks or grades. Since it was a common practice in the Roman world to worship the spirits or deities (the *genii*) of places, things or groups of people, it is unsurprising that cults of the *genius* of many of these divisions within the army came to be worshipped.[32] Dedications were made to these *genii* privately by individuals, and formally by the group as a whole. There were cults of the *genii* of centurions, *optiones*, and *signiferi*, again emphasizing the close bonds felt by a corps of officers.[33] It was common for a man to bequeath his property to comrades of the same rank.[34] The most commonly worshipped *genii* of units were those of legionary *centuriae*. Many of the dedications to these were made by a centurion and his *principales*. Next to his century, his legion seems to have had the greatest emotional appeal to the ordinary legionary, and dedications to the *genius legionis* are frequently attested in the epigraphic record.[35] The prevalence of the cults testify to the degree to which a Roman soldier's sense of identity was bound up with his unit.

[28] Helgeland, *ANRW* II. 16. 2, 1495–6. For the altars at Maryport and Birdoswald see D. J. Breeze and B. Dobson, *Hadrian's Wall* (London, 1987), 259–60.

[29] Nock, 199–200.　　　　　　　　　　　　　　[30] *RIB* 1792 = *CIL* 7. 75.

[31] e.g. a dedication by *decuriones, duplicarii*, and *sesquiplicarii* to Juppiter Dolichenus, see M. P. Speidel, 'Horsemen in Pannonian Alae', *Roman Army Studies*, ii (Amsterdam, 1992), 62–6, esp. 62–3.

[32] See M. P. Speidel, 'The Cult of the Genii in the Roman army and a New Military Deity', in *Roman Army Studies*, ii. 353–68.

[33] Centurions *CIL* 3. 7631; *optiones* 13. 6566; *signiferi AE* 1927, 89, 1958, 303.

[34] See M. P. Speidel, 'Colleagues as Heirs', in *Roman Army Studies*, ii. 129–30.

[35] See Speidel, *Roman Army Studies*, ii. 355–7.

The century seems to have been the most important subdivision of the legion. It was the one with which the soldiers themselves most closely identified, and used to describe themselves on inscriptions.[36] This group, of at most 160, but normally 80 men, lived in the same barrack block in a fort and drilled and marched together in the cohort's line. It was thus a smaller community in which the behaviour of individuals could be observed easily, forcing them to conform to group norms. Even more intimate than this was the *contubernium* of eight men. These men lived and ate together in a small tent on campaign or in a pair of small rooms in a barrack block, and seem to have stood next to each other in the unit's formation.[37] Modern studies have suggested that the bond between such small groups of soldiers is so great that, more than anything else, the desire not to lose face in the eyes of this small group and the fear of not showing as much endurance in the face of danger as his comrades, helps a soldier to cope with the stress of battle and prevents him from running away.[38] At the Sambre in 57 BC, and in Britain in 55, Caesar noted that his men fought well in spite of being formed up at random, rather than in their proper units, which implies that men were expected to perform better when surrounded by their comrades (*BG* 2. 21, 4. 26).

(c) Leadership

The bonds of comradeship might have kept a man with the group of his unit and deterred him from running away, but this would not have encouraged him to advance ahead of this group on his own initiative. Yet in many situations it was vital for success in the fighting to have men who were willing to act on their own, to advance ahead of the main body when an attack had stalled, or to force their way into the ranks of the enemy formation. Once these men had set such an example, the mass of the group might have followed and the enemy have been driven back. It was important to have leaders who were willing literally to deserve the name and go on in advance. The example set by a commander and his immediate subordinates of moving around close to the fighting could inspire men to such acts of

---

[36] See MacMullen, *Historia*, 33 (1984), 446, and M. P. Speidel, 'The Names of Legionary Centuriae', *Arctos*, 24 (1990), 135–7.

[37] Vegetius 1. 26, says that recruits took formation according to their place on the unit's nominal role.

[38] Marshall, *Men against Fire*, 42–9, Holmes, *Firing Line*, 272–4, 290–315.

courage. Most of all the officers of the cohort or *ala* were expected to provide this type of leadership. When the Germans launched a surprise attack on Cicero's camp in 53 BC, the centurion Sextus Baculus rose from his sick bed and, with a small group of other centurions, held the gateway of the camp until the (initially panic-stricken) recruits had been rallied. Outside the camp a detachment of recruits had been cut off by the enemy, but many were able to escape, covered by a heroic, sacrificial stand by their centurions (*BG* 6. 38, 40). Throughout Caesar's *Commentaries* the courage of his centurions is continually emphasized.[39] At Jerusalem in AD 70 a centurion, Julianus, charged single-handedly across the Temple Court when the Romans around him had begun to give way, hoping to inspire these men to return to the fray. In the event he was killed and the Roman retreat became a rout (*BJ* 6. 81–92). This incident emphasizes that the inevitable corollary of such an aggressive style of leadership was a high casualty rate amongst the leaders exposing themselves in this way.[40] Yet a conspicuous display of courage by an officer did not always persuade his unit to follow. In Africa in AD 26, the garrison of Pagyda fled before the Numidian advance, despite the heroic example set by its commander, Decrius, who was abandoned and cut down by the Numidians. We do not know enough about this particular cohort to discover the reasons for its misbehaviour, but it is at least possible that Decrius, although a brave man, was not enough respected by his men for them to follow him (*Ann.* 3. 20). It is important to note that decisive leadership in a critical situation may not always have been provided solely by those men whose rank formally marked them out as leaders. At Jerusalem in AD 70 it was an ordinary auxiliary, Sabinus, who came forward to lead the way into the breach, when the rest of the army was hesitating (*BJ* 6. 54–67). At the second battle of Cremona two unnamed men, who were presumably ordinary *milites*, managed, at the cost of their lives, to put out of action an enemy engine, allowing the Flavian advance to continue (*Hist.* 3. 23).

---

[39] e.g. *BG* 5. 44, 7. 47, 50; *BC* 1. 46, 3. 53, 91, 99; *African War* 45–46.

[40] At Pharsalus Caesar lost 200 men, which included 30 centurions, 0.8 and 6.25 per cent of the total respectively, *BC* 3. 99. Even higher losses would occur amongst centurions as a result of a defeat, for instance 46 out of the 700 fallen at Gergovia, *BG* 7. 51, cf. *Ann.* 12. 38, both Sabinus and the two soldiers at Cremona were also killed, which emphasizes the cost of bold leadership.

(d) The Rewards of Service

The formal rewards of service, such as donatives, decorations, and promotion will be discussed later, since these are closely linked with the question of conspicuous displays of courage. In this section I intend rather to look at the question of the unofficial rewards that a soldier might have gained from a campaign, in the form of booty.

Josephus noted that the booty gathered by the Roman soldiers in the sack of Jerusalem in AD 70 so flooded the Syrian market that gold was devalued throughout the province (*BJ* 6. 317). After the same conflict there was a similar glut of slaves on the market, leading many soldiers to accept only the surrender of prisoners who would be worth something, and kill everyone else (*BJ* 6. 384, 414). When a city was stormed, Roman soldiers seem normally to have killed, raped, and plundered freely, and could make sizeable profits.[41] There was little that the general and his officers could have done to control the behaviour of their men, once dispersed into the streets and houses of a town, even if they had wanted to stop this. In 57 BC Caesar withdrew his men from the town of the Atuatuci, which had surrendered, since he felt that he could not have controlled his men once darkness had fallen (*BG* 2. 33). Similarly in 49 he did not allow his men to enter Corfinium at night, since he felt that he would be unable to control his men once they had entered its darkened streets (*BC* 1. 21, cf. 2. 12). Hirtius emphasized Caesar's achievement in preventing his army from plundering Hadrumentum, when he established a camp outside (*African War* 3). The capture of an enemy camp could similarly have offered a concentration of plunder (Appian, *Mithridatic War* 12. 82). At Gergovia, Caesar claimed to have warned his legates at his *consilium* to prevent their men from advancing too far in the hope of gaining plunder. In the event this happened (*BG* 7. 45).

There seem to have been many opportunities on campaign for soldiers to steal or loot, opportunities of which, in the main, they seem to have taken advantage.[42] Caesar noted in 54 BC that his Gallic cavalry

---

[41] See Ziolkowski, 'Urbs Direpta', 69–91, who suggests that the Polybian model of an ordered Roman sack is a myth, intended to emphasize the level of control a Roman commander had over his troops. However he fails to consider fully the emotional state of troops storming a city which must have affected their behaviour.

[42] For an understanding of the possibilities of theft of property and food on campaign I would recommend *The Autobiography of Sergeant William Lawrence, A Hero of the Peninsula and Waterloo Campaigns*, ed. G. N. Banks (London, 1987).

were vulnerable to sudden British chariot attacks, when they scattered into small parties to ravage and plunder the land (*BG* 5. 19). In the next year he was afraid that his men would suffer cumulatively heavy losses if he used them to ravage the land of the Eburones, since the legionaries would be tempted to split up into small groups to search for plunder, making them vulnerable to ambush (*BG* 6. 34). In Britain in AD 51 the Silures ambushed and destroyed two auxiliary cohorts that had been lured into a trap by the prospect of plunder (*Ann.* 12. 39). Even on the battlefield, men might take the opportunity to loot captives and the dead. At the Sambre the servants and camp-followers in the army ran out behind Caesar's advancing line to plunder the dead and wounded left in its wake (*BG* 2. 24). Tacitus noted that the servants and camp-followers were especially prominent in the sack of Cremona in AD 69 (*Hist.* 3. 33). In the collapsed siege mines at Dura Europus, Roman auxiliaries were found to have worn pouches, containing considerable amounts of coinage, under their mail armour. One Roman, who had been killed or mortally wounded by a blow before the tunnel collapsed, was found with his corselet drawn up about his chest. The excavators suggested that he had attempted to divest himself of his uncomfortable armour to ease his suffering. Alternatively it may be that someone, whether friend or enemy, had dragged the man's armour up in order to steal his purse.[43]

Tacitus believed that the suppression of Vindex's rebellion had given the Rhine armies a taste for easily gained booty and glory, and that this helped to precipitate the civil war in AD 68–9.[44] Certainly, Roman soldiers seem to have taken every opportunity to profit from their surroundings. In extreme cases this could lead to total disobedience of their officers. When Pompey first landed in Spain, a party of his soldiers discovered a hidden hoard of gold, and for several days the rest of the army ignored orders and dispersed to dig for other buried treasures (Plutarch, *Pompey* 11). At Jerusalem in AD 70, some Jewish deserters were discovered to have swallowed their gold coins, both to get them out of the city and prevent their being stolen by their

---

[43] M. I. Rostovtzeff, A. R. Bellinger, C. Hopkins, and C. B. Welles (eds.) *The Excavations at Dura-Europus, Preliminary Report of the 6th Season of Work, 1932–1933* (New Haven, 1936), 192–7.

[44] *Hist.* 1. 51; Isaac *The Limits of Empire*, 381–3, claimed that the troops welcomed war because they did not profit as much from peace. See also W. V. Harris, *War and Imperialism in Republican Rome, 327–70 BC* (Oxford, 1986), 102–4. Even if this is true it need not mean that on the battlefield itself soldiers were motivated by desire for plunder.

captors. The result was a gruesome massacre as first the Arabs in the army, and then the legionaries and auxiliaries, started to cut open the prisoners' bellies, searching amongst their entrails for coins. Titus severely reprimanded the troops, but was unable to prevent some recurrences of this practice (*BJ* 5. 548–54). Yet even in recent times, most armies have looted on campaign.[45] It seems unlikely that greed for booty can have motivated many of the acts of courage in battles or sieges, even if there were some soldiers who would have taken any opportunity for profit that the situation offered. Without personal accounts, we cannot know how important the prospect of loot was in motivating the Roman soldier to fight in battle.

Soldiers on campaign may have carried all their worldly possessions in their baggage. Caesar contrasted the behaviour of the legionaries of Cotta and Sabinus in leaving their units to fetch treasured possessions, when the order had been given to abandon the army's baggage, with that of Cicero's men, who, in the same year, allowed their belongings to burn, rather than abandon their positions on the camp's wall to fight the fire (*BG* 5. 33, 43). As a commander Caesar clearly believed that, although their possessions were important to his men, other considerations could be more important when the men were properly led. Caesar's opinion may tell us how a Roman senator and general believed that Roman soldiers should behave, but the soldiers themselves may have had quite a different view.

(e) Drink

Hanson claimed that Greek hoplites habitually drank heavily to ease their pre-battle tension.[46] Keegan commented on this same practice in the armies at Agincourt, Waterloo, and the Somme.[47] Roman soldiers received a daily ration of *acetum* or sour wine (often beer in the northern provinces), but for most Mediterranean peoples wine was a staple part of their diet. There are no references to Roman soldiers drinking to combat pre-battle tension.[48] In 97 BC the Roman garrison of Castulo in Spain was very prone to drunkenness and this allowed the Celtiberians to mount a successful surprise attack on their quarters

---

[45] Holmes, *The Firing Line*, 353–5.

[46] V. D. Hanson, *The Western Way of War*, 126–31.

[47] Keegan, 114–15, 183–4, 245, 333, cf. Holmes, *The Firing Line*, 244–25, 332.

[48] There are references to Rome's enemies drinking before battle and actually fighting whilst drunk, *Ann.* 1. 65, *Hist.* 4. 29.

(Plutarch, *Sertorius* 3). After Dyrrachium Caesar allowed his army to plunder Gomphi, where they found vast quantities of wine. As a result their march away from the city is said to have resembled a drunken orgy, which produced a marked improvement in morale (Plutarch, *Caesar* 41). Tacitus mentioned a disturbance in Rome in AD 68 caused by drunken praetorians (*Hist.* 1. 80). Once again in default of better evidence, it is impossible to know whether or not soldiers prepared themselves for battle with 'Dutch courage', but it seems quite possible that they did.

(f) The Limits of Courage

The mass suicide of the *sicarii* at Masada in AD 73 is the most famous incident from our period of men's unwillingness to surrender. It was unusual in that it included their families, but by no means unprecedented (*BJ* 7. 389–401). In 54 BC the last remnants of the troops of Cotta and Sabinus managed to reach their camp and hold out until nightfall, after which they all committed suicide (*BG* 5. 37). Whilst fighting the Frisians in AD 47, 400 Romans were cut off in a failed attack and defended themselves in the villa of an auxiliary veteran, Cruptorix. Fearing treachery if they surrendered, all of these men also took their own lives (*Ann.* 4. 73). In both these cases the consequences of surrender would have been at best enslavement, but might have led to torture and death.[49] In Jerusalem in AD 70 a party of Romans was trapped in a burning portico by a feigned Jewish retreat:

The last survivor of them, a youth named Longus, shed lustre on the whole tragedy, and . . . proved himself the bravest of all. The Jews, as well from admiration of his prowess as from their inability to kill him, besought him to come down to them, pledging him his life; his brother Cornelius, on the other hand, implored him not to disgrace his own reputation or the Roman army's. Influenced by his words, he brandished his sword in view of both armies and slew himself.[50]

Later in the siege a legionary cavalryman was captured by the Jews, but managed to escape. Titus wished to execute the man, but relented when the soldiers appealed for his life. Instead he publicly dishonoured

---

[49] *Ann.* 1. 61, for the description of the fate of Varus' men in AD 9, or Trajan's Column scene 117, showing the torture of Roman prisoners by Dacian women.

[50] *BJ* 6. 186–7, cf. 6. 280, where two leading Jews threw themselves into the fire rather than surrender.

the man, dismissing him from the legion and confiscating his arms.[51] Once again we may have an example of a soldier not conforming to the pattern of behaviour expected of him by his commander. His comrades on the other hand did not disapprove of the man's actions in the same way as their commander. In AD 66, the garrison of Jerusalem, an auxiliary cohort under Metilius, agreed to surrender and gave up its arms and baggage on condition that their lives be spared (*BJ* 2. 450–4). In AD 70 the garrison of Vetera, largely elements of *Legio V Alaudae* and *Legio XXI Rapax*, agreed not only to surrender and give up their baggage, but to join the enemy, an action of which Tacitus clearly disapproved (*Hist.* 4. 60). On both occasions the surrendering Romans were massacred, which helps to explain why troops were often reluctant to capitulate. The reluctance of victorious soldiers to take prisoners was sometimes understandable. The only Roman casualty in the final storming of Jotapata was a centurion, stabbed in the groin by a Jew who had pretended to surrender to him. After this the Romans took no prisoners (*BJ* 3. 333–5). Caesar's centurion, Scaeva, pretended to surrender at Dyrrachium, but then killed one of the men who had rushed forward to capture him, and cut the arm off the other (Appian, *BC* 2. 60). In general surrender was far more common during civil wars, when the consequences were less severe, than when fighting foreign enemies.

It is important to remember that there was neither a typical Roman soldier, nor a typical unit. The difference between the legions and auxiliary units is obvious, but less obvious are the differences between individual units of supposedly the same type. The quality of a unit's leaders is an important point of difference, but all the factors discussed above, as well as others, such as the local situation, the unit's previous experience and, above all, chance, varied from unit to unit, making each one unique. These factors combined to produce morale and it is this that explains differences of performance in combat between apparently identical units. Where morale was high the unit would perform well. Where it was low it would perform badly. Judging from

---

[51] *BJ* 6. 359–62, cf. 6. 153 where a cavalryman whose horse had been captured was executed as an example; also App. *BC* 2. 93–4 where Caesar threatened to disband *Legio X* after a mutiny. The men begged him to decimate them instead, and Caesar relented in the same way that Titus refrained from executing this cavalryman after his comrades' appeal. For theatrical gestures by commanders see Ch. 4, 'Ceremony and Theatre'.

the high level of success achieved by Roman units on the battlefield the average was quite high.

PART 2. BRAVERY AND BRAVADO

In the course of a battle there were many occasions when it was important for one, or a few, individuals to push on ahead, or cut their way into an enemy formation, in order to achieve victory. Yet there were also many incidents when individual Roman soldiers chose to expose themselves to danger for no apparent practical military purpose, for instance to fight in single combat with lone enemies. These displays of individual bravery seldom did more than prove the individual's courage. However this type of action by Roman soldiers has seldom been commented upon by scholars. This is perhaps because individual displays of this kind do not conform to the traditional view of the disciplined Roman soldier, whose strength lay in his ability to act as a group. Messer suggested that the frequency of mutiny in the Roman army indicated that discipline was not as rigid as the traditional view suggests, allowing room for individual initiative on and off the battlefield.[52] Certainly soldiers seem to have exercised the right to make their feelings known to their commanders, without this being thought detrimental to discipline.[53]

Before discussing the evidence for these displays of courage, it is important to place them in perspective. These incidents were recorded in our sources primarily because they were exceptional, and the behaviour of the individuals involved surpassed that normally expected from soldiers. In the last chapter the importance of a close group of men in encouraging its members by the ties of comradeship and by herd instinct, and by physically preventing them from running away by the pressure of the ranks behind, was discussed as a major factor in preventing the men from flight. S. L. A. Marshall's findings suggested that only a small proportion of men, the 'natural fighters', actively fought and sought to defeat and kill the enemy.[54] It was the counterparts to these men in the Roman army who were willing to fight aggressively outside the group. The vast majority of Roman soldiers

---

[52] W. S. Messer, 'Mutiny in the Roman Army: The Republic', *Classical Philology*, 15 (1920), 158–75.

[53] See Ch. 4, 'Ceremony and Theatre', and Ch. 6 n. 51.

[54] Marshall, *Men against Fire*, 50–65.

were unwilling to leave the physical and mental security of the group to fight alone against the enemy. Therefore these acts of conspicuous courage only ever involved a very small proportion of soldiers, and did not prompt whole units to rush forward to seek glory without orders. Rather in the many pauses and lulls in any battle, and even more so in a siege, when both sides were in close proximity, but not actually fighting, a very small proportion of men chose to risk their lives in a conspicuous display of their own courage.

Single Combat and Individual action

> And there went out a champion out of the camp of the Philistines named Goliath, of Gath ... and he stood and cried out unto the armies of Israel, and said unto them, why are ye come out to set your battle in array? Am not I a Philistine and ye servants of Saul? Choose you a man for you, and let him come down to me. If he be able to fight with me, and to kill me, then will we be your servants: but if I prevail against him and kill him, then shall ye be our servants and serve us.

> (*1 Samuel* 17: 4–9)

Oakley has plausibly argued that the Romans frequently engaged in single combats under the Republic, especially in the third and second centuries BC. He believed that the changed attitudes to war, and the limits imposed on aristocratic individualism by the institutions of the Principate, caused this practice to die out.[55] He noted that, except perhaps in the earliest periods of Rome's history, these duels were never intended to decide the outcome of a battle or war by replacing massed fighting. There were two occasions from our period when such a combat was proposed. Marius is said to have refused to fight a leader of the Cimbri, whilst Plutarch claimed that Antony challenged Octavian to meet him in personal combat to decide the outcome of the war, but that the latter prudently refused.[56] Instead these combats merely offered a proof of the personal courage of participants, bringing them *gloria*, which in the case of aristocrats, could be turned into

---

[55] Oakley, *CQ* 35 (1985), 392–410, esp. 397–8, 408–10. I do not intend to deal with the single combats fought in Rome's earlier history in this chapter, since Oakley deals with this comprehensively.

[56] Marius, Frontin. *Strategemata* 4. 7. 5; Octavian, Plut. *Antony* 62. With many earlier duels the context in which they occurred is unclear. Did, for instance, the semi-mythical victor in eight single combats, C. Siccius Dentatus fight any of these to decide a battle without mass fighting? Val. Max. 3. 2. 24; Pliny, *HN* 7. 102, 22. 9; *Gell.* 2. 11. 2.

political capital when they returned to Rome. In an earlier chapter I discussed the attitude of Roman commanders towards fighting, arguing that most avoided combat. When they did actually fight, either because they had been attacked, or because they had joined a unit hoping to inspire its men, it was not the actual fighting and killing that was important, but the courage that they displayed in the face of danger.[57]

The single combats, and other similar individual actions in our period did not involve aristocrats, but men from lower down the social scale.[58] It is not always easy to define what was a single combat, and what was not. Keegan pointed out:

that all infantry actions, even those fought in the closest of close order, are not, in the last resort, combats of mass against mass, but the sum of many combats of individuals—one against one, one against two, three against five. This must be so, for the very simple reason that the weapons which individuals wield are of very limited range and effect.[59]

Oakley claimed that the fight between Volusenus and Commius in 51 BC 'almost amounted to a formal duel', yet this occurred as part of a cavalry mêlée between two groups of horsemen.[60] For the purposes of this study, we are only concerned with those occasions when individuals chose to fight away from the physical and moral support of their comrades. In this case the fight between Commius and Volusenus would not qualify, since both men were leading groups of followers. The evidence for this type of individual action is almost purely literary. A few inscriptions give details of notable incidents in a soldier's career, for instance M. Valerius Maximianus, who, as prefect of an *ala* during the Marcommanic Wars, personally killed the leader of a German tribe.[61] Without further evidence, it is impossible to know

---

[57] See Ch. 4, and also J. Harmand, *L'Armée et le soldat à Rome de 107 à 50 nôtre ère* (Paris, 1967), 397–8.

[58] This was also true of some earlier duels, for instance two involving Roman cavalrymen in the Second Punic War, Livy 23. 46–47, 25. 18.

[59] Keegan, *The Face of Battle*, 100.

[60] *BG* 8. 48; see Oakley, *CQ* 35 (1985), 397.

[61] *DONATU QUODMANU SUA DUCEM NARISTARUM VALAONEM INTERMISSET*, *AE* 1956, 124, cf. the Tiberius Claudius Maximus inscription, *AE* 1969/70, 583, see M. P. Speidel, 'The Captor of Decebalus', in *Roman Army Papers*, i. 173–87.

whether he performed this deed whilst acting alone, or at the head of his unit.

The fullest complete account from our period of a duel of this nature is provided by Josephus (*BJ* 6. 169–79). At this period in the siege of Jerusalem, the defenders' positions and the attackers' siege lines seem to have been relatively close, presumably within earshot.

In the course of these days a Jew, named Jonathan, a man of mean stature and despicable appearance, undistinguished by birth or otherwise, coming forward opposite the tomb of the high priest John, and addressing the Romans in much opprobrious language, challenged the best of them to single combat. Of those in the adverse ranks at this point, the majority regarded him with contempt, some probably with apprehension, while others were influenced by the not unreasonable reflection that it was wise to avoid a conflict with one who courted death; being aware that men who despaired of their lives had not only ungovernable passions but also the ready compassion of the Deity, and that to risk life in an encounter with persons whom to defeat were no great exploit while to be beaten would involve ignominy as well as danger, would not be an act of bravery, but of recklessness. For a long time, no antagonist came forward and the Jew continued to rail at them as cowards—for the fellow was supremely conceited and contemptuous of the Romans—until a trooper of one of the *alae* named Pudens disgusted at his language and arrogance and perhaps also thoughtlessly presuming on his puny stature, leapt forward, and was otherwise gaining on his adversary in the encounter, when he was betrayed by fortune: for he fell, whereupon Jonathan sprang upon him and dispatched him: then, trampling on the corpse, brandishing his bloody sword and with his left hand waving his buckler, he shouted lustily to the army, glorying over his prostrate foe and jeering at his Roman spectators: until in the midst of his dancing and buffoonery, Priscus, a centurion, bent his bow and transfixed him with an arrow, calling forth from the Jews and Romans simultaneous cries of a contrary nature. The victim, writhing in agony, fell upon the body of his foe illustrating how swift in war is the nemesis that overtakes irrational success.

On two other occasions Josephus explained the deaths of heroic Romans as being caused by their accidentally falling or slipping.[62] Several other points of detail are worth noting. First, neither of the rival combatants were distinguished individuals, but ordinary soldiers, whilst Priscus was a centurion, perhaps of the *auxilia*. Pudens was a cavalryman from an *ala*, though presumably dismounted in this instance. The importance of his branch of the service will be referred

---

[62] The Syrian auxiliary, Sabinus, *BJ* 6. 54–67, and the centurion, Julianus, *BJ* 6. 81–92.

to later, here it seems worth noting that his presence might suggest that cavalrymen were expected to participate in some of the highly dangerous activities of a siege, even though their horses could not have been used.[63] Furthermore the challenge issued by Jonathan had no significance for the campaign as a whole, only for the participants, though its result may have affected the morale of the observing armies. Neither combatant was forced to fight, but each chose to do so, to display his own courage and prowess. The finale, when Jonathan was shot by Priscus, would have been a shameful act for the heroes of the *Iliad*, yet here the Romans seem to have approved of it.

An incident, similar in many respects, is described by the author of the *Spanish War*. Here Antistius Turpio met Quintus Pompeius Niger after the former had issued a challenge to the Caesarian army. At this time the rival armies were each fortifying positions only a short distance from the other. The passage is incomplete but it is evident that the author was fully conscious of heroic parallels. He compared the two champions to Achilles and Memnon, described their fine arms, and the impression is that his account was to be very full.[64] Yet neither participant, though Niger was an *eques* from Italica, was a leading member of the opposing armies, and their combat was a test of personal courage not related to the outcome of the war.

Single combats could also occur just before two battle lines were about to meet. During the Social War of 89 BC:

> Just as the two armies were coming together to an engagement, a Gaul of enormous size advanced and challenged any Roman to single combat. A Moorish solider of short stature accepted the challenge and killed him, whereupon the Gauls became panic stricken and fled. (Appian *BC* 1. 50)

Note again that at least the Roman participant is an ordinary soldier, although it is unclear if he was a horseman or an infantryman. The combat does not seem to have been formally intended to decide the issue, although in fact its result does so. Like the encounter between David and Goliath, this was a case of the apparently small and weak overcoming the strong and boastful, in a moral story familiar from the folklore of many cultures.[65] As such it contrasts with the later account

---

[63] At the assault on Jotapata, groups of dismounted cavalrymen led the three assault columns, *BJ* 3. 254. See pp. 275–6 for the cavalry ethos.

[64] *Spanish War* 25; for the heroic parallels, cf. the account of Munda, where the author quotes Ennius, *Spanish War* 31.

[65] See Oakley, *CQ* 35 (1985), 408–9.

in Josephus of the fight between Jonathan and Pudens. In that duel, it was the small and undistinguished Jonathan, who was boastful. His victory was accidental, and was followed immediately by his own death.

There are many instances of heroic behaviour by Caesar's soldiers in his *Commentaries*, and occasionally of their non-Roman opponents.[66] However, during the many open battles described in these works there are no instances of single combat.[67] In his description of the siege of Cicero's camp, Caesar does give an account of a display of courage by two centurions, which did not seem to serve any practical purpose (*BG* 5. 44). The two men, Titus Pullo and Lucius Vorenus, were rivals for promotion and prestige within the unit. Pullo first left the fortification, calling out to the other that this was the time to prove who was bravest. Vorenus followed because he did not want to lose face.

Pullo stopped a short way from the Gauls, hurled his spear and transfixed one of them who was running forward from the ranks. The man fainted from the wound, and his comrades covered him with their shields, at the same time showering missiles upon Pullo and preventing him from advancing further. His shield was pierced by a javelin, which stuck in his sword belt; and as the blow knocked his scabbard out of place, he could not get his hand quickly to his sword when he tried to draw it, and was surrounded by the enemy while unable to defend himself. His rival Vorenus ran up to rescue him in his distress and all the Gauls immediately left Pullo, who they thought had been mortally wounded by the javelin, and turned upon Vorenus. Vorenus drew his sword and fighting hand-to-hand, killed one of his assailants and drove the rest back a little; but pressing on too eagerly, he stumbled down a steep slope and fell. It was now his turn to be surrounded, but Pullo came to his aid; both of them escaped unhurt and after killing a number of the enemy, returned to camp covered with glory.

This incident has much in common with more formal single combats. The two centurions may have improved the morale of their watching men by this display, showing that the Gauls were not as formidable as they might seem, but the main significance of their actions was personal. The Gauls were not individual heroes on the

---

[66] e.g. *BG* 4. 25, 5. 35, 7. 50, *BC* 3. 69, 74; the courage of a Gaul at Avaricum is singled out, *BG* 7. 24.

[67] In the *African War* an old soldier of Legio X during a lull in the action aimed his *pilum* specifically at Labienus and killed his horse (16), and later a veteran of the Fifth defeated an elephant by himself, cutting off its trunk (84). Neither incident seems to have been motivated by the same spirit of conspicuously displaying courage, which moved individuals to fight single combats.

same footing as their Roman opponents, but nameless masses, less noteworthy than even the irrationally successful Jew, Jonathan. The actual act of killing these opponents is represented as of less importance than the rivalry of the Roman pair in showing courage in the face of danger.

It is, however, in Josephus that we find the fullest accounts of single combat in the environment of battle, all from the Jewish War. The first comes from a description of the skirmishing around Jerusalem (*BJ* 5. 312–16).

Thus, when in the course of these days, the Jews were arrayed in stout force outside the walls and both armies were as yet engaged in distant combat with javelins, a certain trooper, Longinus, leapt out of the Roman line and dashed into the midst of the Jewish phalanx. Breaking their ranks by his charge, he slew two of their bravest, piercing one in front as he advanced to meet him, and transfixing the other through the side, as he turned to flee, with the spear which he drew from his comrade's body; he then escaped unscathed to his own lines from the midst of the enemy. His valour gave him distinction and led many to emulate his gallantry . . . Titus, on the other hand, cared as much for his soldiers' safety as for successes, and, pronouncing inconsiderate impetuosity to be mere desperation and valour only deserving of the name when coupled with forethought and a regard for the actor's security, he ordered his troops to prove their manhood without running personal risks.

This anecdote follows a passage describing the different motivation for the two sides. Chief amongst those given for the Romans is the presence of Titus with the army.[68] Not only does his presence incite his men to the heights of valour, but his command was enough to control this valour, directing it to the higher purpose of winning the war. There are several aspects of the passage that have been noted already. Longinus was from the ranks of an *ala*. His opponents were unnamed, nondescript Jews, similar to the Gauls who were cut down by Pullo and Vorenus. The action was one of pure bravado having no affect on the campaign as a whole.

Another anecdote from the same siege is similar in several respects (*BJ* 5. 161–3).

Among other incidents, a trooper from one of the cohorts, named Pedanius— when the Jews were at last repulsed and being driven down into the ravine— urging his horse at top speed along their flank, snatched up one of the flying foe, a youth of sturdy frame and in full armour, grasping him by the ankle; so

[68] See Ch. 4.

far did he stoop from his horse, when at the gallop, and such muscular strength of arm and body did he display. Carrying off his captive like some precious treasure he came with his prize to Caesar. Titus expressed his admiration of the captor's strength.

Again the participants were fairly humble, the Roman was a horseman, as were both Pudens and Longinus, and it was to his commander that he brought his prize. The deed was a display of personal prowess, and, in the sheer act of taking a prisoner rather than killing his foe, displayed contempt for the enemy. The Jew was briefly described as a youth of sturdy frame and in full armour, but was clearly not represented as the equal or rival of the Roman. At the siege of Machaerus a similar incident occurred when an Egyptian soldier, Rufus, whose unit is unclear, picked up an armoured Jew, Eleazar, and brought him to his general (*BJ* 7. 196). Both Longinus and Pedanius carried out their respective deeds on horseback. In an open battle a horseman could have advanced far more quickly to capture or kill an enemy than a man on foot, and then just as quickly retreated. Given the comparatively short ranges of contemporary missile weapons, a galloping cavalryman could have reached safety very quickly. This was certainly one reason why we should expect this type of action to be more commonly performed by a cavalryman than an infantryman. Pudens, a trooper from an *ala*, fought his duel on foot. Might it be that the ethos of some or all cavalry units stressed individual action far more than their infantry counterparts? I shall return to this question in the next section.

Head-Taking

One aspect of the behaviour of Roman soldiers that seems relevant at this point is the decapitation of slain enemies, in order to take the severed head as a trophy. This appears more in sculpture than literature. In several scenes on Trajan's Column, clearly recognizable auxiliary soldiers are represented holding the heads of opponents they have killed. In two of the scenes a pair of auxiliary soldiers, all having different devices on their shields, offer severed heads to Trajan, who, at least in the second case, clearly reaches out his arms to accept the trophies.[69] In a frenzied battle scene an auxiliary soldier, still clutching between his teeth the head of an earlier victim by its hair, turns on another opponent.[70] Later, an auxiliary is depicted climbing a ladder

[69] Scenes 57–8, 183–4.   [70] Scene 60.

during the assault on some fortifications, holding in his shielded left arm a severed head, whilst striking the enemy with the weapon in his right hand.[71] Finally, in one of the many scenes in which legionaries construct a camp, two heads, impaled on poles, stand next to the structure.[72] This has been interpreted variously as showing that the place had previously been a Dacian stronghold, that auxiliary troops had earlier fought an action here, or finally that the legionaries themselves followed such practices. Even if the last interpretation is correct, the weight of evidence suggests that the practice was associated more with the *auxilia* than with the legions. Other reliefs confirm this. On the Great Trajanic Frieze three soldiers again present severed heads to Trajan.[73] These men wear mail and scale, and carry hexagonal shields, and are almost certainly cavalrymen. Finally, on metope 7 of the Adamklissi monument, a horseman wearing scale brandishes the head of an opponent, whose dismembered trunk sinks in the background.

The reliefs from Rome might be dismissed as unrealistic, depicting the *auxilia* as wild barbarians who fought for Rome, rather than against her. Tacitus on several occasions emphasizes the wildness of some auxiliary troops (e.g. *Ann.* 2. 46, *Hist.* 2. 22), and describes the Batavians as 'like weapons and armour, only to be used in war' (*Germ.* 29). If so, it might be a little odd to associate such a practice so closely with the emperor, whose glories were being commemorated. The depiction of the practice on the far less-romanticized reliefs at Adamklissi confirms that at least some individuals or units practised the head-taking.

Furthermore, the taking of heads appears twice in literature. In the *Spanish War* Caesar's troops erected a trophy adorned with the severed heads of their foes (*Spanish War* 32). The men involved seem to be legionaries, although it is possible that these were Gauls of the *Legio V Alaudae*. According to Livy in 214 BC the consul Gracchus ordered his men to cut off the heads of enemies whom they had killed, and keep

---

[71] Scenes 302–3.

[72] Scene 140; see F. Lepper and S. S. Frere, *Trajan's Column* (Gloucester, 1988), 101–2. At Newstead skulls were found buried in pits associated with the forts destruction, which may mean that the cavalry garrison of the fort followed this practice, see D. J. Breeze and B. Dobson, *Hadrian's Wall* (London, 1987), 114.

[73] A. M. Leander Touati, *The Great Trajanic Frieze* (Stockholm, 1987), nos. 67, 70, 71.

these as proof of their valour (Livy 24. 15). His men included many ex-slaves recruited in the desperate times after the initial Roman defeats following Hannibal's invasion of Italy. Therefore it could be argued that the origins of these units encouraged practices that were normally alien to the Romans. During civil wars, enemy leaders were often decapitated and their heads brought to commanders,[74] in the same way that Tiberius Claudius Maximus presented the head of Decebalus to Trajan.[75] This appears to have been chiefly to prove that they were dead, and gave something to parade in Rome, or in front of the army, in default of a live captive.

The ritual decapitation of slain enemies seems to have been fairly general amongst northern European peoples (Strabo, *Geog.* 4. 4. 4–5), but was most especially associated with Gallic tribes.[76] It seems that the head had great significance in Celtic religion as the seat of understanding, and source of human strength; the rather gruesome evidence for this comes from the skull porticoes at such shrines as Roquepertuse and Entremont.[77] Both Diodorus and Strabo attest, probably both using Poseidonius as a source, the high value the Gauls placed on heads taken by themselves or their ancestors from notable enemies. The latter states that the Romans had abolished this practice, logically enough, since the prevalence of head-hunting within a province would have done little to keep the peace, but clearly some soldiers or units still practiced it (Strabo, *Geog.* 4. 4. 5).

Does such evidence as we possess for the martial traditions of any individual tribe or people suggest that single combat was of great importance? If so, might this tradition have been maintained within the Roman army by auxiliaries recruited from this race? Diodorus claimed that it was normal for battles between Gallic peoples to be preceded by individual encounters between champions (Diodorus 5. 29. 2). Indeed, sometimes it seems that battles were decided by these encounters without recourse to mass combat. Such combats might have been heavily ritualized, with great importance being attached to the symbols of victory.[78] It seems to have been common in many primitive societies

---

[74] App. *BC* 1. 71, 2. 46, 105.
[75] Lepper and Frere, *Trajan's Column*, 176–9.
[76] Polybius 3. 67; Livy 10. 26, 23. 24; Diodorus 5. 29. 2–5.
[77] M. J. Green, *Dictionary of Celtic Myth and Legend* (London, 1992), 116–118.
[78] M. R. Davie, *The Evolution of War: A Study of its Role in Early Societies* (Yale, 1929), 136–46 on head-hunting, 147–59 on the importance of glory and trophies.

for battle to take this form, with only a few of the armed men actually fighting, whilst the remainder on both sides merely watched. Often the women, children, and the old also observed from a distance.[79] In many respects, this type of battle is close to the Homeric pattern. The Irish literature, such as the *Táin Bó Cúailnge*, describes similar battles in which only named heroes meet. Although written down in the eighth and ninth centuries, these tales seem to have their origin in earlier La Tène Celtic society.[80]

It is noticeable that in neither Polybius nor Caesar is there any hint of the Gauls fighting in anything other than masses.[81] Caesar's emphasis on the role played by the chariot in British warfare might suggest that the tradition of heroic single combat was still important in warfare amongst the Britons (*BG* 4. 33). A chariot, even more than a horse, provided a means for a warrior to move quickly towards the enemy, dismount to fight a duel and then retire to safety. It was the weapon of the warrior aristocrat, like the heroes of the *Iliad*, or of Irish literature. Yet it must be admitted that these vehicles were then deployed in large numbers against the massed Roman troops, skirmishing rather like light cavalry. This might be an occasion when a Roman observer misunderstood the real significance of the behaviour of the enemy, interpreting it instead by the standards of his own culture.

The evidence then, appears to be contradictory, with, on the one hand, the tradition of single combat between champions and, on the other, the descriptions in the historical sources of massed, if ill-organized, armies. Is it possible that single combat between champions had been a feature of an earlier Celtic culture, but did not reflect contemporary military practices in the armies that faced the Romans? As seems to have been the case in the Roman army, the practice of single combat could have continued even when it no longer in itself decided the outcome of battles. Either it preceded battles, or occurred during the lulls in the massed fighting. It would have been very difficult and dangerous for a man to have paused to decapitate a fallen enemy during a hand-to-hand combat between two masses of men. Therefore the taking of a head as a trophy could only have occurred in

---

[79] See D. R. Morris, *The Washing of the Spears* (London, 1965), 37–9 on the Bantu; cf. Ch. 2.
[80] See K. H. Jackson, *The Oldest Irish Tradition* (Cambridge, 1964).
[81] See R. Pleinor and B. G. Scott, *The Celtic Sword* (Oxford, 1993), 21.

massed combat once the enemy had started to run away. When individuals met away from their units in single combat, it was far easier for the victor to decapitate his beaten foe.

In Josephus' accounts of individual displays of courage, three of the Roman participants were clearly auxiliary cavalrymen, Longinus, Pudens, and Pedanius. Rufus, the soldier who captured Eleazar at Machaerus, was described as a native of Egypt, but which type of unit he served in is unclear. In the case of the cavalrymen, we clearly have men who have been produced by a non-Roman society, although these men will have come into some contact with Roman ideas after joining their unit. In their own cultures the concept of what a warrior or soldier was, and how he should behave, may well have been very different from Roman ideas on the subject. Cavalrymen received higher pay than infantrymen, and often owned slaves. Many units, especially in Gaul, had their origins in the semi-professional warrior followers of Gallic nobles.[82] These men formed the very warrior class in Celtic society for whom such displays as single combat, and the taking of trophies, such as heads, from defeated enemies were important. Even men from lower down in society, who joined the army, may have aspired to warrior status, and sought to behave accordingly. Roman army equipment gave a soldier a helmet, sword, and corselet, which in Gallic or Germanic society was normally only possessed by a chief or notable warrior. If a man from this society was dressed as a chief, might he not then have tried to behave as one, indulging in single combat and taking the heads of his enemies as trophies of his prowess? The Romans had their own tradition of single combat, so that such displays were not wholly alien to them, and could be commended and rewarded. Tacitus claimed that the *comites* of a German noble competed in deeds of valour with each other for rewards of equipment, and for status and prestige within the group (*Germ.* 14). Germans serving in the Roman army may have looked upon its system of reward and promotion in the same way. For the auxiliary soldiers themselves, performing an act of conspicuous courage, and being decorated for this, may have had very different implications, and associations, connected with warrior status, to a Roman legionary performing a similar deed, or to the Roman commander rewarding them both. The symbols of success might have been different. Roman soldiers

---

[82] See Ch. 2; see also N. Roymans, *Tribal Societies in Northern Gaul* (Amsterdam, 1990), 40 on tribal *comites*.

certainly might strip the corpse of a defeated enemy of its equipment and insignia, as Pompeian troops did to the bodies of two of Caesar's centurions, killed in Spain in 45 BC (*Spanish War* 23), whereas it might have been more important for a Celt to decapitate his beaten opponent. Both cultural traditions encouraged boldness in soldiers, even if the importance of this to the soldiers themselves was very different.

Rewards and Morale

The importance of the general as the observer, and rewarder, of acts of courage was discussed in Chapter 4 on the General's Battle. In many of the incidents discussed in this chapter, the Roman participant actually brought the symbol of his success, be it an enemy captive, or a severed head, to his commander. After the siege of Jerusalem, Titus rewarded the men who had displayed conspicuous courage in three ways: with an extra share of the booty, with promotion, and with the award of *dona* (*BJ* 7. 14–16). Increased pay earned by promotion and the reward of plunder were doubtless welcomed by the soldier, as were the unofficial opportunities for loot. Yet for many men the award of a decoration may have been more important. In 47 BC Metellus Scipio refused to give gold *armillae* to a cavalryman because he was an ex-slave, so the man's commander, Labienus, gave him a reward of gold instead. The cavalryman rejected this, but was overjoyed when Scipio replaced this with silver *armillae* (Valerius Maximus 8. 14. 5). In this case the prestige attached to the decoration, as a proof of valour, was far more important to its recipient than financial gain. Many men mention that they had been decorated on their tombstones, which also suggests that considerable pride was taken in decorations.[83]

The actual award of decorations involved a very public ceremony, at which the achievements of individuals were greatly stressed. These formal parades occurred either at the end of a campaign, or after a battle. The ritual seems to have changed little from Polybius' day.

The general assembles the troops and calls forward those he considers to have shown exceptional courage. He praises them first for their gallantry in action and for anything in their previous conduct which is particularly worthy of mention and then distributes gifts . . . these presentations are not made to men who have wounded or stripped an enemy in the course of a pitched battle or at the storming of a city, but to those who during a skirmish or some similar

---

[83] See Maxfield, *Military Decorations*, 47–9.

situation in which there is no necessity to engage in single combat have voluntarily and deliberately exposed themselves to danger. (Polybius 6. 39)

Earlier (6. 22) he explained the *velites'* wearing of wolf skins or similar decorations on their helmets 'which serves both to protect and to identify the soldier; this enables the officers to recognize the man and to observe whether or not he shows courage.'

Earlier in the chapter, the extent to which the Roman army formed a separate society was noted. Men who were decorated for acts of valour gained higher status within this closed community. Their decorations were the physical signs of this. The ties of comradeship, and the habit of obedience, helped to prevent most men from running away under the stress of combat. The decorated men had proved that they could do more than this, and act alone, going on ahead of the rest. The formal parade and award of *dona* ritually confirmed their increased status within the community of the army, and especially their own units. It was a ceremony in which all of this community, from the commander to their comrades, participated to honour them. The decorations were awarded not merely for displays of courage such as single combat, in which the participant deliberately chose to prove his manhood, but to the men who were prepared to lead the advance in difficult situations. The first men over the wall of an enemy town received the *corona muralis*, as well as other lavish rewards, and sometimes promotion.[84] What all recipients had shown was a willingness to take individual aggressive action, to advance alone to attack the enemy, whether this meant pushing on with an attack when others were hesitating, or going out individually to attack an enemy during a lull in the fighting.

In a few of the encounters discussed in this chapter, the Romans' opponent was given a name and described as a character. The author of the *Spanish War* described both Antistius Turpio and Quintus Pompeius Niger, placing them on an equal footing, like the Homeric heroes to whom they were compared.[85] Jonathan, the Jew who challenged any Roman to meet him, was of small stature and undistinguished reputation. This was not a case of a 'David and Goliath' story, when the apparently small and weak was able to defeat the proud and strong. Jonathan was not the equal of his opponent, won only by accident, when the Roman fell, and was immediately

---

[84] *BG* 7. 27, 47, *BJ* 6. 53, *Hist.* 3. 22.
[85] Oakley, *CQ* 35 (1985), 402, 408.

afterwards shot by the centurion Priscus. Eleazar, the leading Jew at Machaerus, was shown offering no resistance to his captor, Rufus, and despite his bravery was not the equal of the victor. The Gauls killed by Pullo and Vorenus, and the Jews cut down by Longinus, or captured by Pedanius, were neither named, nor described in any detail. These fights are not represented in our sources as the meetings of equals, like the clashes between the heroes of Homer, Virgil, or of Irish literature, or even some of the single combats in earlier Roman history.[86] Instead the enemy was merely an obstacle for the Roman hero to overcome, in order to display his courage and prowess. It does not seem to have been the actual act of killing the enemy that was held up for praise and reward, but the courage shown in the face of danger. This was emphasized when Pedanius and Rufus did not deign to kill their opponents, but bodily picked them up and brought them as trophies to their commanders. In this case the implication was that the Roman was so superior to his enemy in skill and courage that he did not need to actually fight and kill him. Off the battlefield, personal prowess could be displayed without an enemy at all. A Batavian soldier, Soranus, left an inscription in which he proudly recounts an incident when he impressed Hadrian by swimming the Rhine and displaying his skills as an archer.[87] There was no enemy present, and Soranus displayed skills of little practical use in battle. In this incident, as in the conspicuous displays of courage during a battle, it was the personal skill and boldness of the Roman soldier that was important, and was praised and rewarded. These displays involved actions that the majority of the man's comrades could not, or would not, have copied, but which perhaps represented how they believed a good soldier should behave.

The awards of *dona* to senatorial and equestrian officers seem to have conformed to established scales, rather than being linked to particular exploits.[88] Awards made by the commander to individual soldiers, who had displayed conspicuous bravery, created a far more personal relationship. When Tiberius arrived to take command of the army in Germany in AD 4, he was greeted by cheering soldiers. Individuals called out to him, reminding him that they had served together before, or that he had decorated them (Velleius 2. 104). The general not only rewarded courage, but punished cowardice. In this

---

[86] e.g. the duel between the Horiatii and Curiatii, Livy 1. 25–6, or Marcellus and Britomartus, Plut. *Marcellus* 7.   [87] *ILS* 2558, cf. Dio 69. 9.
[88] See Maxfield, *Military Decorations*, 145–209.

role the relationship between soldier and commander was also very personal.[89] Many punishments were aimed at an individual's or unit's pride, lowering their status within the closed community of the army. Symbolic humiliations, such as ordering a unit to sleep outside a camp's rampart, or to be fed on barley instead of wheat, or dismissing a man from his unit, must be seen in this context.[90] Titus' public decision, after the fall of Jerusalem to send *Legio XII Fulminata* to Cappadocia, instead of returning it to its Syrian garrison, conforms with this pattern. This was a punishment awarded because of the legion's failure in battle four years earlier (*BJ* 7. 18). The Roman army's systems of reward and punishment balanced and complemented one with the other. Fear of punishment, together with other factors discussed in Part *1*, helped to prevent men from running away during a battle. The encouragement of boldness through reward helped to motivate individuals to the displays of aggression needed to achieve victory.

Conclusion: Boldness and Discipline

Why then were acts of conspicuous, but apparently pointless, boldness not only permitted, but actually encouraged and rewarded? One reason seems to have been that these actions demonstrated to all Roman observers that the enemy could be beaten. The display of Pullo and Vorenus, charging around outside the ramparts and killing the enemy with apparent impunity, occurred during a siege, when a recently recruited legion, whose men had yet to gain confidence in their own ability to defeat the enemy, was surrounded and outnumbered by an enemy that had already destroyed one Roman army. The centurions' actions demonstrated that the enemy was by no means invincible.[91] In the last chapter, it was noted that confidence was often more important than physical force in deciding the outcome of a charge or fight. These displays of successful valour helped to give the Romans observing them a confidence in their own ability to beat the enemy. In this sense

---

[89] See Ch. 6 n. 51, where both Caesar and Titus passed judgement on individual soldiers or units, but modified these in response to appeals from their men.

[90] On punishment in general see Messer, 'Mutiny in The Roman Army'.

[91] Oakley suggested that a single combat was seen as a struggle between the rival armies in microcosm (*CQ* 35 (1985), 407. In essence this is true, but observers may not always have defined it so precisely.

the displays could have a practical purpose. The reverse was also true. Apart from the duel between Jonathan and Pudens, none of the incidents discussed in this section ended in a Roman defeat. Logic tells us that this must have happened sometimes, and that when it did, the confidence of the enemy must have been increased, and that of the Romans reduced. When the centurion, Julianus, and the auxiliary soldier, Sabinus, both attempted to rally a hesitating Roman line by charging forward on their own, each man was killed by the enemy. In both cases the Roman attacks failed utterly, because their men had lost confidence (BJ 6. 54–67, 81–92).

There was another, more important, reason for encouraging these acts of individual skill and daring. This was connected with the vital role that a few individuals could often play in a battle. Most men on the battlefield coped with fear and were kept in their formations by the physical presence of, and emotional ties to, their comrades. These men moved with the group, but they did not lead an attack whilst their comrades were hesitating, or fight their way into an enemy unit, breaking its ranks and helping to precipitate its collapse. There was a need for men with the boldness to do these things to set an example that the others in the unit might follow. If these men did not set an example by moving forward in such a crisis, then others might set the opposite example by running away, to be followed by the mass of the unit. The balance between advance and flight in a critical situation could be very slight. The role of the individually aggressive and bold soldier was vital for achieving victory, tipping the balance in favour of moving forward. Therefore boldness and aggression in individual soldiers needed to be encouraged. Recognition of the prowess of bold soldiers, which gave them the tangible rewards of promotion, decorations, and plunder, and the less tangible but no less important prize of high status within their unit, encouraged their behaviour. The importance of the general as witness and rewarder of prowess appears again and again in explaining the motivation behind individual acts of courage. Rewarding acts of individual aggression, whether or not they served a wider purpose, encouraged a spirit of boldness in the army as a whole. This helped to provide men willing to act aggressively on their own, when the situation made this a vital prerequisite for the army's success.

Oakley suggested that there was a degree of tension between the confines of discipline, which held a soldier in his position in the ranks, obedient to orders, and the urge of the individual to seek *gloria* by leaving his unit and displaying his prowess as an individual.[92] As he pointed out this was certainly a feature of the Roman national myth of *disciplina*, of the way that the aristocracy liked to believe that their soldiers behaved.[93] There was certainly not a real tension in the actual conduct of soldiers during our period. Rather, discipline and the bold action of individuals were complementary factors in the success of Roman armies. Discipline and fear of punishment, along with comradeship, kept men in their ranks and stopped them from running away. It allowed units to be manœuvred around the battlefield more easily than many of Rome's opponents could manage. When actual fighting began, it might have kept a unit in contact with the enemy for a long period.[94] Yet in itself discipline did not bring victory, although it might have prevented, or at least delayed, defeat. Boldness and aggression, often by a few individuals, was vital in actually beating the enemy and causing him to run away. The rewards and approval given to acts of individual boldness reflected the need to encourage aggression and offensive spirit in soldiers.

Military discipline is not an immutable virtue common to all professional armies. Rather it is heavily influenced by the society that produces the army in question. The discipline of the modern British army is very different from that of a hundred years ago, which in turn was quite different from that of the century before. Roman discipline reflected Roman society, and in many cases became modified by the cultural background of auxiliary soldiers recruited into it. All too often scholars have assumed that the Roman army encouraged absolute, mindless obedience in its soldiers. If this had been so then the acts of individual boldness discussed in this chapter would have been a problem. The evidence shows that this was clearly not the case and that such acts were encouraged and served a useful purpose. The actual descriptions of the behaviour of Roman soldiers on the battlefield should always be examined before making any assumptions on the way that these men should have behaved. It is just as unwise to accept blithely the idealized descriptions of the Roman army given by sources, such as the digression on the Roman army in Josephus (*BJ* 3. 70–109). In this he claimed that 'never have they been known in any

---

[92] Oakley, *CQ* 35 (1985), 404–7.
[93] Ziolkowski, 'Urbs Direpta', 86–9, commented on this view having heavily influenced Polybius' description of the Roman army.
[94] See Ch. 5, 'The Collision'.

predicament to be beaten by numbers, by ruse, by difficulties of ground, or even by fortune' (*BJ* 3. 106–7). Josephus' account of the actual fighting of the Jewish war includes occasions when Roman soldiers were beaten by all of these considerations.[95]

---

[95] e.g. *BJ* 6. 81–92, 177–87, 2. 547–50, 6. 54–67 respectively.

General Conclusions

THE popular image of the Roman army is of an incredibly modern force, highly organized and rigidly disciplined. When the army fought a war, it operated in a very methodical way. It advanced slowly and cautiously, and at the end of each day's march it constructed a large camp, identical to the ones it had built, and would continue to build, on every other night of the march. Piece by piece and day by day an enemy country was captured. A Roman campaign was almost like a siege on a larger scale, the Romans advancing steadily and carefully, entrenching as they went, just like a besieging force digging its way closer to a city. The eventual success of the Roman army rested as little on luck as the successful prosecution of a scientific siege. In battle the army was just as slow and methodical. In all situations a legion would apply a carefully rehearsed battle-drill, the legionaries moving like components of some huge machine. Individual Roman soldiers were mere automata, reduced by the army's brutal discipline to a point where they were incapable of taking independent action. They were led by centurions, grizzled veterans who were experts at implementing the legion's battle-drills. In overall charge were generals, but these, with the exception of the rare natural genius, like Caesar, were unskilled amateurs who had little influence on the course of a battle. The Roman military machine was so perfect that it had no need for the overall direction of commanders. All they had to do was deploy this machine and point it in the right direction. Any enemy army foolish enough to confront this machine would be crushed beneath it.

This picture of the Roman army owes as much to the Hollywood epics as anything written on the subject. The 1960 film *Spartacus* contains a sequence showing a huge Roman army advance to attack. The legions move in a checker-board pattern of units, their formations perfect. The whole army manœuvres and changes formation, apparently without anyone ordering it to do so. The Roman commander is a mere spectator, watching the inevitable Roman triumph. It is a spectacular piece of cinema, and a powerful image, but it owes more to the film's theme of the suppression of the liberty of individuals by brutal and impersonal domination than it does to reality.

Scholarly works on the Roman army have portrayed a force not substantially different from the popular image. Scholars have emphasized its machine-like quality, and the perfection, or near perfection, of its organization.[1] Its strategy and tactics have been seen as methodical and very rigid, allowing it to beat most opponents, but rendering it incapable of defeating others, like the Germans and Parthians.[2] The army's organization and its great discipline have been praised to such an extent that they have become vices which made the Romans incapable of responding to a sudden change in the situation.[3] The Roman army has been seen as peculiarly vulnerable to an enemy fighting a guerrilla war.[4] When archaeologists have discussed the use of Roman weaponry, they have examined the technological limitations on their effectiveness, but have failed to consider the limitations imposed by the psychological state of the man using them. Since the weapons' user was a disciplined Roman soldier it has been tacitly assumed that his emotional state in the heat of battle was not a significant factor.[5]

In this book I have attempted to show that both the popular and the scholarly view of the Roman army is at best highly misleading, and in most cases utterly false. The Roman army was well organized, far more so than any of its opponents in this period. The size and internal structure of its units were tailored to suit the type and scale of warfare most common at that time. The army's organization was not characterized by its rigidness, but, quite the contrary, by its great flexibility. Its units adapted to the local situation. Many were under-strength, a few may have been over-strength. The army's organization was not an inflexible structure imposed for its own sake, but a system to help the army function. Its adaptability was its strength, not a sign that the organization had failed. The Roman army's organization was very good, but not perfect. The army was required to perform many functions in the provinces, many of which had little to do with its combat role. Large numbers of soldiers, and especially officers, served away from their units and were unavailable for active campaigning. Inevitably this reduced the overall effectiveness of their units.

---

[1] See Introd., esp. n. 26.

[2] See E. N. Luttwak, *The Grand Strategy of the Roman Empire* (Baltimore, 1976), 40–6.

[3] e.g. M. Gichon, 'Aspects of the Roman Army in War according to the *Bellum Judaicum* of Josephus', in P. Freeman and D. Kennedy (eds.), *The Defence of the Roman and Byzantine East, BAR* 297 (Oxford, 1986), 287–310, esp. 301–2 'The Achilles' Heel of the Roman army'.   [4] See Ch. 3.   [5] see Ch. 5.

The strategy adopted by many Roman armies on campaign was anything but methodical. Badly supplied and poorly trained Roman armies took the field on many occasions, hoping as much to bluff their enemy into submission by a display of force as to defeat them by actual fighting. Conflicts in this period were not struggles in which the economic strength of a people and their reserves of manpower were decisive factors. Damage to crops and material resources were seldom sufficiently great to have forced a people to come to terms or face starvation. A people lost a war as soon as it considered itself to have been beaten, perhaps through the loss of a battle, the fall of an important city, or an attack, even a symbolic one, on its crops or cattle. One of Rome's great strengths in warfare was her unwillingness to admit defeat even after she had suffered military catastrophe.

The largest section of this book has dealt with the army in battle, which, more than anything else, has been most misunderstood by scholars. The Roman military system was not designed to take responsibility away from the general, but in fact concentrated power in his hands. Roman generals were very active before, during, and after a battle. They received no formal military training, but were prepared for their vital task by their upbringing and by their earlier military service. The mobile style of command practised by most Roman generals, riding around the battle line encouraging and directing their troops, required skills which could not have been taught, only learnt by experience and instinct. Despite the strict discipline of the army, Roman soldiers had to be led, and not simply driven, into battle.

Battles were very fluid affairs with units, especially cavalry, advancing and retiring alternately, frequently without contacting each other. The appearance of force was often far more important than its reality. Units of men armed only with mêlée weapons might run away before they had come into contact with a similar body, intimidated into defeat by their bold appearance. The discipline of the Roman army was a major asset in battle, but it did not prevent Roman soldiers from running away, or from attacking or pursuing the enemy without orders. There were many lulls in the fighting when the opposing battle lines were very close to each other. A small proportion of exceptionally brave and bold men played a major part in determining the outcome of the fighting. These were the men who were willing to fight their way into an enemy formation as individuals, or to lead the way when an attack had stalled. Recognizing the vital role of these men, the Romans encouraged and rewarded individual boldness, even to the extent of decorating men who performed courageous, but utterly pointless, acts of bravado. This type of behaviour was fostered even though it might seem to conflict with the maintenance of strict discipline. The most decisive factor in the outcome of a battle was the individual and group morale of the participants. We need to study this in order to understand warfare.

Roman military doctrine at all levels was dominated by the principle of the offensive. Roman strategy was almost never cautious and often verged on the reckless. Caesar might seem a rash commander by the standards of the 'Great Captains' of history, but his behaviour is in character with most Roman generals. On the battlefield, both units and individuals fought very aggressively. More than anything else this conflicts with the view of a stolid, methodical Roman army.

The Roman army and its methods of operation described in our ancient sources are quite different to those of popular imagination and modern research. The warfare of this period cannot be judged by the standards and principles of modern war. The bulk of the evidence for this book has come from the descriptions of warfare included in the accounts of ancient authors, especially those who witnessed the events they described, such as Caesar and Josephus. These sources provide a wealth of information concerning Roman warfare, much of which remains unexploited. Warfare was the ultimate purpose of the Roman army. To understand the army, and place into context all other aspects of its behaviour, we must gain a better understanding of the Roman practice of war. This book has dealt with some aspects of Roman warfare, but others, notably siege warfare, have been omitted for reasons of space. The plentiful evidence discovered for the questions addressed in this book must suggest the potential for research into other aspects of Roman military practice.

The Roman army was a highly effective military force. The Roman military system did not produce armies and units of a uniformly good quality, but the average was high. In our period the Roman army won the vast majority of the wars it fought. In this book I have discussed some of the occasions when Roman forces marched to disaster, and I have often emphasized the imperfections of Rome's military system. However a greater awareness of the difficulties faced by the Roman army only increases admiration for its achievement.

APPENDIX: LOGISTICS

The organization of a system to supply the army with all its requirements, most of all of food, was essential for its successful operation. The fundamental importance of supplying the army can be confirmed easily by its prominence in Caesar's *Bellum Gallicum*. Caesar refers continually to the need to arrange and secure the food supply of his army.[1] Shortages of food resulting from these arrangements breaking down are used to explain the actions of his own and the enemy armies.[2] The most combat-effective army was useless if it could not feed and maintain itself in the field.

Chapter 3 noted the importance of supply and its influence on the behaviour of armies, but attempted no reconstruction of the army's logistics. The reason for this was a simple lack of evidence. There is not enough solid fact to attempt even confident conjecture concerning the Romans' system of supply in wartime. A little progress can be made by the use of fragments of information concerning the Roman army of earlier and later periods, placed in the context of reliable statistics dealing with the speeds, attributes, and carrying capacities of baggage animals drawn from the experience of armies in the last two centuries. In this section I shall examine this evidence and attempt some very tentative calculations of the amount of baggage accompanying a Roman army in the field, and the number of animals and vehicles needed to carry it. This is of great importance in estimating the speed at which a Roman army might move during a conflict. I make no claim for the accuracy of my figures, precision being impossible with the available evidence. At best I hope to suggest something of the scale and order of magnitude of the problems involved in maintaining the army in the field, as I feel that these are too often underestimated.

There were two basic methods of maintaining an army on campaign. The first was for the force to carry everything it needed with it. All equipment and *matériel*, and all food requirements for both men and animals which could not be provided by foraging were carried in the baggage train. Such an army was

---

[1] *BG.* 1. 16, 2. 10, 38, 4. 7, 5. 31, 6. 10, 7. 10, 32, 8. 3.

[2] e.g. Caesar forced to withdraw to secure food supply, *BG.* 1. 23; Helvetii surrender when food exhausted, 1. 27; Caesar forced to offer battle before supplies run out, 1. 49; Storm wrecks ships and produces food shortage. Romans forced to forage, 4. 29, 31; Poor harvest in Gaul forces dispersal of army's winter quarters, 5. 24; Caesar unable to supply his men for long enough to bring the Suebi to battle, and so abandons German expedition, 6. 29; Vercingetorix aims to defeat Caesar by cutting off his supplies, 7. 14.

not anchored to any base of operations, but was a self-contained entity. If a large army was to operate in this way it required a huge amount of transport, which could only serve to slow its movements. In the nineteenth century a force travelling in this manner was known as a 'flying column'. Alternatively an army could carry less baggage actually with it, and be supplied instead by convoys going back and forth from a major magazine or supply base, usually a city or fortress. This reduced the amount of transport needed by the main force allowing it to move more quickly. However it did require detachments of troops to guard both the base and the convoys going between it and the army from enemy action. As a result the army had fewer soldiers actually available for battle. The number of baggage animals and transport needed by the convoys also increased the further the main army moved away from its base. If the army was to operate over long distances then either the main supply base had to be moved forward or others established along the route to the main body. If the army was advancing along a navigable river, or near the coast then many of its requirements, especially the transportation of grain in bulk, could be moved by water.

The Roman army used both of these techniques either independently or in combination. An army of several legions needed a massive baggage train if it was to move as a flying column, completely independent of a base. That much transport seriously reduced its speed of movement and its chances of out-manoeuvring or surprising the enemy. In Gaul Caesar tended to move slowly with all his transport to the area in which he expected to campaign. There he left the bulk of his baggage, either in a strong camp occupied by one or more of his legions, or in a friendly *oppidum*, usually with a smaller garrison.[3] The main body of the army moved out from this base to engage the enemy, unencumbered by much of its transport and supplied by convoys protected by troops and small garrisons.[4] Alternatively the army formed one or more flying columns which marched *expedita*, taking only essential equipment and the provisions necessary for a short operation. This might have been a punitive expedition planned on a circular route to return the force to the main base by the time its supplies were exhausted.[5] In 54 BC Caesar marched quickly with a small force and little baggage to relieve Cicero (*BG* 5. 46–52). His force was able to feed itself from the stores of provisions in Cicero's winter camp once the Nervii had been driven off. Had Caesar failed to break the siege, then his column would have been in a very difficult situation. Examination of the campaigns discussed in detail in Chapter 3 will reveal Roman armies in the rest of our period acting in a similar manner to Caesar's forces in Gaul.

Although many of our sources mention the influence of supply on an army's behaviour, they never discuss the technical detail of this. Very occasionally we have anecdotal evidence mentioning the amount of transport possessed by an

---

[3] e.g. *BG*. 2. 5, 5. 47, 6. 5, 32–3, 7. 10, 55, 8. 1.
[4] e.g. *BG*. 2. 5, 10, 7. 34.   [5] e.g. *BG*. 6. 5, 33, 7. 10, 8. 1.

army. In 87 BC during his siege of Athens Sulla is said by Plutarch to have required 10,000 pairs of mules to move and support his siege engines. (Plutarch, *Sulla* 12.) To place this immense total into context, at the battle of Chaeronea, fought soon after the fall of Athens, Sulla's army numbered only 16,500 men (*Sulla* 16). Pompey's army in 48 BC was supported by 'many' wagons (Plutarch, *Pompey* 6). Antony required 300 wagons to transport the siege train of his army in the Parthian war (Plutarch, *Antony* 38). Like all numbers given by ancient authors, it is hard to estimate the accuracy of these figures. Even if they are correct, we do not know how typical the size of these supply trains might be. Many other passages refer to the presence of pack animals and draught animals and vehicles with Roman armies in the field, but give little or no specific detail.[6] Baggage animals and carts are depicted on the Columns of Trajan and Marcus Aurelius. Trajan's Column contains several scenes showing two-wheeled carts drawn by either a pair of mules or oxen.[7] Pack mules are also shown.[8] Both two and four wheeled wagons, some with solid and others with spoked wheels, are shown on the Column of Marcus Aurelius. Again these are drawn by teams of two oxen or mules.[9] The depictions of these vehicles are heavily stylized. On Trajan's Column carts identical to the baggage wagons are shown mounting light *ballistae*, which seems unlikely to have been the case in reality.[10] A tombstone from Strasbourg of uncertain date shows a soldier driving a four-wheeled cart pulled either by horses or mules.[11]

This evidence for the type of transport employed by the Roman army does not not tell us the size of a baggage train normally taken on campaign. The first thing to consider in attempting to deduce this is the amount of essential equipment needed by the army, regardless of how it planned to feed itself.

Each *contubernium* of eight men had a mule to carry its tent and heavier baggage. This gave ten mules to each *centuria* and sixty to each cohort. A milliary first cohort with five 160-man *centuriae* possessed 100 mules. This gives a total of 640 mules for a single legion ((9 × 60) + 100). In a marching

---

[6] e.g. at Gergovia Caesar mounts some servants on unsaddled pack horses and mules to disguise them as cavalry, *BG*. 7. 45; Caesar's foraging expeditions are ambushed and many servants and animals lost, *BG*. 8. 10; Caesar's troops requisition wagons and pack animals from villagers to carry the corn produced by a foraging expedition, *African War* 9; Labienus transports his wounded in wagons, *African War* 21; Prolonged campaigns by AD 16 have exhausted the supply of animals available from Gaul, *Ann*. 2.5; Jewish rebels attack Cestius Gallus' baggage train and carry of large numbers of pack animals, *BJ* 2. 521.　　　　　　　　　　　　　　　[7] Scenes 123, 124, 148, 149, 280, 284, 285.

[8] Scenes 367–8.

[9] Scenes 23, 35, 38, 48, 49, 105, 111, 112, 121, 133, 139.

[10] Scene 104. See S. S. Frere and F. Lepper, *Trajan's Column* (Gloucester, 1988), 88.

[11] E. Espérandieu, *Recueil général des bas-reliefs, statues et bustes de la Gaule romaine* (Paris, 1907–66), 7. 5499.

camp, two *contubernia* were always acting as sentries, so that a *centuria* usually pitched only eight of its ten tents. (Hyginus, *De Munitionibus Castrorum* 1) Under some circumstances a legion might have chosen to only take eight tents and baggage mules with it.

Each centurion possessed a personal tent and, given his high status and pay, a considerable amount of baggage and luxuries. This must have required a minimum of one pack mule per officer and probably considerably more, especially for the *primi ordines*. Fifty-nine more mules need to be added, increasing our total to 699. The senior officers of the legion, the legate, tribunes, and prefect will doubtless have carried even greater amounts of personal baggage as well as their sizeable tents. The legion's administration needed to continue when the unit was on campaign, so that at least a proportion of the vast documentation required by the Roman army must have been carried. Then there was the essential equipment, such as immediate reserves of weapons, clothes and boots, the equipment and tools necessary to maintain and repair armour and weapons, and specialist tools and machinery required for building and siege work. The amounts involved are impossible to estimate, but at least some of this equipment will have been too bulky to carry on pack animals and so required wagons. There was also artillery, and here we have the testimony of Vegetius as to the amount carried by a legion. He claims that each *centuria* operated one light bolt-shooter, probably mounted on a cart drawn by two mules, and each cohort a larger stone-throwing engine, presumably carried on a four-wheeled wagon with a team of four or more mules or oxen. (Vegetius 2. 25) This produces a total of fifty-nine two-wheeled carts (or more if the larger-sized first cohort operated a larger number of machines) and ten four-wheeled wagons, requiring at least 158 draught animals. In a campaign where the enemy possessed no strong fortifications, some or all of these engines might have been left behind. Finally there were the other units of the legion, the veterans and cavalry, whose size, internal organization, and allocations of baggage are unclear. Overall it is difficult to imagine a legion requiring less than a thousand animals to carry its essential equipment and baggage.[12]

An even greater amount of transport was required to provide food for the men and fodder for the horses. In extreme cases, such as the campaign of Aelius Gallus against the Nabataeans, an army was forced to carry all its requirements including water (Strabo, *Geog.* 16. 4. 24). This campaign was a greater battle against nature than the enemy, with only seven men being killed in battle and large numbers succumbing to disease and exhaustion. In more favourable climates, an army was able to gain a large proportion of its needs by foraging. This was easiest in the month or so either side of harvest time.

---

[12] For a discussion of this see A. Hyland, *Equus* (London, 1990), 88–9, J. Harmand, *L'Armée et le soldat à Rome* (Paris, 1967), 156, nn. 56–9. Maj.-Gen. J. F. C. Fuller, *Julius Caesar: Man, Soldier, and Tyrant* (London, 1965), 82–3.

According to Josephus all legionaries carried a sickle as part of their basic equipment (*BJ* 2. 95). In the rest of the year it meant searching the towns and villages of the area for herds and flocks, or hidden stores of food.[13] Even in very fertile land at the right time of year, a large army exhausted quickly the land around it and was forced to send its foragers out further and further afield. These small groups of men were always vulnerable to attack.[14]

In attempting to calculate the amount of food a Roman army needed to carry with it, we are faced with a number of problems. The first is that we have no information on the amount of food each soldier was issued as his daily ration.[15] In this period the Roman army operated throughout a large geographical area in regions where the availability and types of food varied, making it likely that the amount and composition of the daily ration was also subject to variation. Some ration scales are recorded for the Roman army of the sixth century AD, which may give us an idea of the size of those in our period. The smallest daily issue recorded is as follows:

3 lb. (1.4 kg.) of bread
1 lb. (0.45 kg.) of meat
2 pints (1 litre) of wine
0.1 pints (5 cl.) of oil

On campaign the bread was often replaced by biscuit (*bucellatum*) and the wine by sour wine (*acetum*).[16] The issue of 3 lb. (1.4 kg.) of bread per day is identical to that recorded by Polybius for the army of the second century BC (Polybius 6. 39). Josephus claimed that each soldier carried on his back three days' bread ration (*BJ* 3. 95). Larger reserves of supplies must have been carried in the baggage train. It is unclear if this regulation was general to the Roman army, or specific to Vespasian's and Titus' troops in Judaea.

If the army was getting its bread ration by harvesting the ripe crops, then 5,000 men needed around 100 bushels of corn each day. It has been estimated that the average yield of fields in Northern Britain in this period was about 10 bushels an acre. Therefore in a week, a legion of 5,000 men would consume

---

[13] e.g. Caesar waits for the crops to begin to ripen before launching his offensive, *BG*. 6. 29; capture of great stores of supplies at Avaricum, 7. 32; capture of stores of grain in surprise attack on the Bituriges, 8. 3; Corbulo's army, after a long desert march, reach cultivated land and harvest the crop, *Ann.* 14. 24.

[14] The need to send foragers further afield each day, *BG*. 7. 16; on the vulnerability of foraging parties, 4. 32, 5. 26, 38, 6. 34, 8. 10.

[15] For the types of food eaten see R. W. Davies, 'The Roman Military Diet', in *Service in the Roman Army* (Edinburgh, 1989), 187–206.

[16] See A. H. M. Jones, *The Later Roman Empire, 284–602. A Social and Administrative Survey* (Oxford, 1986), 447, 629, 1261–2 n. 44 quoting *P. Oxy.* 2046, 1920. The scale of 1 lb. (0.45 kg.) of meat per day is confirmed in *P. Oxy.* 2013–14.

Table 4. *Meat provided by different animals*

Animal	Weight lb. (kg.)	Average lb. (kg.)	Amount wasted (%)
Ox	600–1600 (272–727)	800 (363)	50
Sheep	60–100 (27–45)	70 (32)	45
Pig	100–250 (45–113)	175 (79)	25

the produce of about 70 acres.[17] If an army carried its rations in the form of grain (Suetonius *Galba* 7), or harvested corn from the fields it passed through, it also needed to carry hand mills to grind the grain into flour. The Emperor Caracalla is said to have led the life of a common soldier, grinding his grain ration by hand and then baking it into a loaf (Herodian 4. 7. 5). An army foraging for most of its requirements was able to reduce the size of its baggage train and so move faster, but it did need to stop to forage, to prepare flour, and bake this into bread, all of which imposed delays. Bread will keep good for 4–5 days in warm climate and 7–8 days in cold weather. When flour is baked into bread it gains 30 per cent in weight. Flour is therefore lighter to transport and will keep for a longer period.[18] Biscuit kept better than bread, but was less appetizing.

The meat ration may have been carried in preserved form, but was most often carried 'on the hoof'. Most armies drove large herds of animals with them on the march, often captured from the enemy, confiscated from the native population, or supplied by allies. These animals could be slaughtered to provide fresh meat for the troops.[19] Table 4 is based on Victorian estimates of the amount of meat provided by different animals.[20]

The amount wasted includes the head, offal, and skin. The regular slaughter of animals ensured that the meat issued was healthy. At a ration of 1 lb. (0.45 kg.) a day, a legion of 5,000 men consumed 12.5 oxen, 120 sheep, or

[17] See A. L. F. Rivet, *The Roman Villa in Britain* (London, 1969), 195–7, and S. Pigott, 'Native Economies and the Roman Occupation of North Britain', in I. A. Richmond (ed.), *Roman and Native in North Britain* (Edinburgh, 1958), 1–27.

[18] See Lt.-Gen. Sir Garnet Wolseley, *The Soldier's Pocket Book for Field Service* (1880), 81.

[19] Sall. *Jug.* 29, 76, 90; *BG.* 7. 17, 56; *BC.* 1. 48, 52, 3. 49; *BJ* 4. 436; *Ann.* 14. 24. On the consumption of meat by Roman soldiers in general see Davies, *Service in the Roman Army*, 191–206.

[20] Wolseley, *Soldier's Pocket Book*, 80. Cows might be a few pounds lighter than bullocks.

Table 5. *Carrying capacity of pack animals*

Animal	Load lb. (kg.)	Harness & Pack	Total lb. (kg.)	Speed m.p.h. (k.p.h.)
Horse	152 (69)	48 (22)	200 (91)	3–3½ (4.8–5.6)
Mule	152 (69)	48(22)	200 (91)	3–3½ (4.8–5.2)
Bullock	100–170 (45–77)	30–60 (14–27)	160–200 (73–91)	2–2½ (3.2–4)
Camels	300–480 (136–218)	114 (52)	414–594 (188–269)	3 (4.8)

38 pigs every day. Some units of the *auxilia* may have had cultural restrictions on the eating of all or certain types of meat, in particular pork.

It is now worth considering the attributes of the various baggage animals available to the Roman army. Table 5 gives an idea of the carrying capacity of pack animals.[21]

Camels were only suitable for use in parts of North Africa and Asia. Only shoed animals were useful for long journeys over paved roads. In most conditions the mule was the superior type of pack animal, moving as fast as a man, and carrying as much as a horse, but eating less. They were also less prone to sickness than horses. Pack animals were able to go anywhere a column of men could go. However they required a lot of attention to control them. According to Sir Garnet Wolseley, 'the worst transport, and the most difficult to manage, is that by pack animals'.[22]

It is less easy to provide a definite table for the attributes of draught animals. We can make the most accurate assessment for draught oxen, since their harness differed little in the ancient world from that used in the last century. A draught ox can pull around 400 lb. (181 kg.) of weight at a speed of 2–2½ m.p.h. (3.2–4.0 k.p.h.) for 7–8 hours a day, but not more than 60 miles (96 km.) in a week. The two-bullock carts depicted on Trajan's Column will have carried about 800 lb. (363 kg.), perhaps slightly more or less depending on the ground to be traversed.[23] An ox needs to graze for at least 6 hours after work and one hour in the morning.[24] If it is able to do this and the land provides a good supply of grass then it requires only a small ration of fodder.[25]

---

[21] Ibid. 65–72, and War Office Veterinary Department, *Animal Management* (HMSO, 1908), 297. [22] Wolseley *Soldier's Pocket Book*, 54. [23] Ibid. 68. In the plains of India a 2-bullock cart carried 800 lb. (383 kb.), a 4-bullock cart 1,600 lb. (725 kg.), whilst in Bombay they pulled 700 lb. (318 kg.) and 1,300 lb. (590 kg.) respectively. In Cyprus a 2-bullock cart held 1,000 lb. (454 kg.), but in the mountainous terrain of Afghanistan in 1878–81 the regulation load was as low as 655 lb. (297 kg.). [24] *Animal Management* (HMSO, 1908), 297. [25] Wolseley, *Solider's Pocket Book*, 64. In the Zulu War of 1879 the daily ration for draught oxen of 6 lb. (2.7 kg.) of mealies, or 3 lb. (1.4 kg.) of mealies and 5 lb. (2.3 kg.), of oat hay was only issued when insufficient grass was available. See *Regulations for Field Service in South Africa 1879* (Pittermaritzberg, 1879).

The Romans very clearly made considerable use of wagons drawn by horses and mules, but their efficiency, compared to the draught animals of the last century, is unclear. The Romans seem to have used ox harness for all their draught animals. In this arrangement the animal wore a collar which was attached to the harness at a point on the back of a horse's neck. The collar was set high on a horse's throat rather than resting on its shoulder blades. The harder a horse or mule pulled, the more the collar constricted its breathing and choked it. Until recently it was generally accepted that this reduced drastically a horse's or mule's pulling power. Estimates of the ancient draught horse's pulling capacity set this as low as a third of its modern counterpart. This view has now been challenged by several authors, who argue that ancient harness, although certainly uncomfortable for the horse, did not reduce its power to such a great extent. Without very extensive testing of Roman harness, it is impossible to give a useful figure for the weight a draught could pull.[26] The nineteenth-century evidence is of little value in estimating the loads of Roman horse and mule carts. A fourth-century law restricted the weight to be carried for a post wagon to 1,000 lb. (454 kg.), and a two-wheeled cart to 600 lb. (272 kg.) (*Codex Theo.* 8. 5. 47). In the British army of the last century horses were given a ration of 12 lb. (5.4 kg.) oats and 12 lb. (5.4 kg.) of hay. Mules received 5 lb. (2.2 kg.) oats and 25 lb. (11.3 kg.) of green or 13 lb. (5.9 kg.) of dry fodder.[27]

The army certainly owned a proportion of the animals it employed for draught and pack transport, but very many of these were bought or requisitioned at the beginning of a war.[28] The longer a campaign went on the more animals would perish through disease, over-use, or poor treatment, and these were in the main replaced from civilian stocks (*Ann.* 1. 71, 2. 5). Therefore the type of animals employed by the Roman army was often dictated by what was available locally, rather than which animal was most efficient. The type of agriculture practised in the area, in particular the type of animal used for ploughing, was a vital factor in determining availability of transport.

Not only were transport animals needed to carry or draw an army's supplies and heavy equipment, but even more were needed to carry fodder for these

---

[26] See K. Greene, *Archaeology of the Roman Economy* (London, 1986), J. Spruytte, *Early Harness Systems: Experimental Studies* (London, 1983), 101–7, and G. Raepsaet, 'La Faiblesse de l'attelage antique: la fin d'un mythe?', *L'Antiquité Classique*, 48 (1979), 171–6. For a consideration of army supply in peacetime see J. D. Anderson, *Roman Military Supply in North-East England: An alternative to the Piercebridge Formula*, BAR 224 (Oxford, 1992).

[27] There were many variations on these amounts according to the local situation, see Wolseley, *Soldiers Pocket Book*, 74–5 and *Animal Management* (HMSO, 1908), ch. 10. Mules in South Africa received either 10 lb. (4.5 kg.) of grain or 20 lb. (9 kg.) of oat hay, or half of each, see *Regulations for Field Forces in South Africa 1879* (1879).

[28] See R. W. Davies, 'The Supply of Animals to the Roman Army and the Remount System', in *Service in the Roman Army*, 153–73, esp. 154–6.

animals and the horses of the cavalry.[29] The ability of oxen to remain healthy on a diet of good grass was a major advantage of this type of transport, compensating for their low speed. Additional animals were also needed as spares, complete teams in the case of draught animals, to ease the progress of the baggage train on the march. These were used to relieve the burdens of exhausted animals and assist in carrying the loads up steeper hills. If this precaution was not taken then the army suffered an exceptionally high loss rate amongst its over-worked animals.[30]

We cannot guess the size and composition of the baggage train of any Roman army. We do not know the exact nature and amount of food, water and wine, and miscellaneous equipment carried in any specific campaign. Nor can we estimate with any precision the type of animals and vehicles composing a baggage train. There is a further problem, which reduces the value of theoretical calculations based on the figures we have discussed above. This is simply the fact that we have few, if any, precise figures for the number of men and horses composing the combat units of any army.[31] This being so, we cannot make even the most tentative calculation of the rations needed to supply such a force. We may be able to reconstruct with some accuracy the units included in an army's order of battle, but as we have seen it is unlikely that these units were maintained at their theoretical strength. During a campaign, steady attrition through disease, accident and enemy action reduced the size of all units. An army's animals tended to be even worse affected than its men.[32]

We have even less information on the numbers of slaves and servants, which followed every Roman army and performed a vital support role.[33] Tacitus claims that Vitellius' army in AD 68 had more *calones*, or camp followers, than soldiers (*Hist.* 2. 87). The same is said of the Flavian army at Cremona in AD 69 (*Hist.* 3. 33). A separate section within this body of camp followers may have been formed by the soldiers' wives and children.[34] There were women in the column of Varus' legions in AD 9 (Dio 65. 5. 4). In Caesar's day it was normal for units of Gallic *auxilia* to travel with their families behind them in wagons (*BC* 1. 51). The camp followers may or may not have received an issue of food

[29] In assessing the number of horses used by an *ala* or *cohors equitatae*, it is important to remember that the officers in these units had more than one mount. See Hyginus 16 and Davies, *Service in the Roman Army* 153. Nor should the requirements of army commanders and legionary legates for a supply of good, fresh horses be underestimated.

[30] See Wolseley, *Soldier's Pocket Book*, 72.

[31] For the numbers in armies see Ch. 4 n. 24.

[32] In a single thunderstorm in the spring of 1812 Napoleon's army in Russia lost an estimated 10,000 horses, many through heart failure. See P. Britten Austin, *1812: The March on Moscow* (London, 1993), 61.

[33] See M. P. Speidel, 'The Soldiers' Servants', in *Roman Army Studies* ii. 342–52.

[34] J. C. Mann, *Legionary Recruitment and Veteran Settlement during the Principate* (London, 1983).

from the army. What is clear is that they must have provided for themselves somehow, so increasing the amount of baggage animals following an army.

The study of an army's logistics requires reliable statistics. In the case of the Roman army these are not available. It is possible that, in time, some firm evidence will appear in the form of military documents on papyrus or wooden writing tablets to fill in some of the gaps in our knowledge. At present the only information provided by these dealing with the army's supply of provisions have dealt with peacetime rather than wartime arrangements.

SELECT BIBLIOGRAPHY

ADAMS, J. P., *Logistics of the Roman Imperial Army: Major Campaigns on the Eastern Front in the First Three Centuries AD* (Detroit, Mich., 1976).

ADCOCK, F. E., *The Roman Art of War under the Republic* (Harvard, 1940).

ALSTON, R., *Soldier and Society in Roman Egypt: A Social History* (London, 1995).

ANDERSON, J. D., *Roman Military Supply in North-East England: An Analysis of and Alternative to the Piecebridge Formula*, BAR 224 (Oxford, 1992).

AUSTIN, P. BRITTEN, *1812: The March on Moscow* (London, 1993).

BAATZ, D., 'Recent Finds of Ancient Artillery', *Britannia*, 9 (1978), 1–17.

BAGNALL, N., *The Punic Wars* (London, 1990).

BANTELMANN, A., *Tofting: Eine vorgeschichtliche Warft an der Eidermündung* (Neumunster, 1955).

BARKER, T., *The Military Intellectual and Battle* (Albany, NY, 1975).

BAR-KOCHVA, B., 'Seron and Cestius Gallus at Beith Horon', *Palestine Exploration Quarterly*, 108 (1976), 13–21.

BASSFORD, C., 'John Keegan and the Grand Tradition of Trashing Clausewitz: a Polemic', *War in History*, I. 3 (1994), 319–36.

BAYNES, J., *Morale: A Study of Men And Courage. The Second Scottish Rifles at the Battle of Neuve Chapelle 1915* (London, 1967).

BELL, M. J. V., 'Tactical Reform in the Roman Republican Army', *Historia*, 14 (1965), 404–22.

BENNETT, J., 'Fort Sizes as a Guide to Garrison Types', in C. Unz (ed.), *Studien zu den Militärgrenzen Roms III*, (Stuttgart: Theiss, 1986), 707–16.

BIRLEY, E., *Roman Britain and the Roman Army* (Kendal, 1953).

—— *The Roman Army: Papers 1929–1986* (Amsterdam, 1988).

BISHOP, M. C., 'The Distribution of Military Equipment within Roman Forts of the First Century AD', in C. Unz (ed.), *Studien zu den Militärgrenzen Roms III* (Stuttgart and Theiss, 1986), 717–23.

—— 'O Fortuna: A Sideways Look at the Archaeological Record and Roman Military Equipment', in C. van Driel-Murray (ed.), *Roman Military Equipment Conference 5*, BAR 476 (Oxford, 1987), 1–11.

——, and COULSTON, J. C., *Roman Military Equipment* (London, 1993).

BIVAR, A., 'The Political History of Iran under the Arsacids', in E. Yarshater, (ed.) *The Cambridge History of Iran*, iii. 1 (Cambridge, 1983), 21–97.

BOON, G., *Isca* (Cardiff, 1972).

BOSWORTH, A. B., 'Arrian and the Alani', *Harvard Studies in Classical Philology*, 81 (1977), 217–55.

BOWMAN, A. K., and THOMAS, J. D., *Vindolanda: the Latin writing-tablets* (Britannia Monograph 4; London, 1983).

—— 'New Texts from Vindolanda', *Britannia*, 18 (1987), 122–42.

—— 'A Military Strength Report From Vindolanda', *JRS* 81 (1991), 62–73.

—— *The Vindolanda Writing-Tablets* (*Tabulae Vindolandenses* ii) (London, 1994).

BRADBURY, J., *The Medieval Archer* (Woodbridge, 1985).

BRANDON, S. G. F., 'The Defeat of Cestius Gallus in AD 66', *History Today*, 20 (1970), 38–46.

BREEZE, D. J., 'A Note on the Use of the Titles *optio* and *magister* below the Centurionate during the Principate', *Britannia*, 7 (1967), 127–33.

—— 'The Organization of the Legion: The First Cohort and the *Equites Legionis*', *JRS* 59 (1969), 50–5.

—— 'The Career Structure below the Centurionate during the Principate', *ANRW* II. 1 (Berlin, 1974), 438–51.

—— 'The Logistics of Agricola's Final Campaign', *Talanta*, 18–19 (1986–7), 7–28.

BREEZE, D. J., and DOBSON, B., 'The Roman Cohorts and the Legionary Centurionate', *Epigraphische Studien 8, Sammelband* (Dusseldorf, 1969, 100–24.

—— *Hadrian's Wall* (London, 1987).

BRUNAUX, J., and LAMBOT, B., *Armament et guerre chez les gaulois* (Paris, 1987).

BRUNT, P. A., *Italian Manpower, 225 BC–AD 14* (Oxford, 1971).

—— 'Conscription and Volunteering in the Roman Imperial Army', *Scripta Classica Israelica*, 1 (1974), 90–115.

BUCKLAND, P., 'A First-Century Shield from Doncaster, Yorkshire', *Britannia*, 9 (1978), 247–69.

BURN, A. R., '*Hic Breve Vivitur*—Life Expectancy in the Roman Empire', *Past and Present*, 4 (1953), 2–31.

CALLWELL, C. E., *Small Wars* (HMSO, 1906).

CAMPBELL, D. B., 'Auxiliary Artillery Revisited', *Bonner Jahrbücher*, 186 (1986), 117–32.

CAMPBELL, J. B., 'Who were the *Viri Militares*?', *JRS* 65 (1975), 11–31.

—— 'The Marriage of Soldiers under the Empire', *JRS* 68 (1978), 153–66.

—— *The Emperor and the Roman Army* (Oxford, 1984).

—— 'Teach Yourself how to be a General', *JRS* 77 (1987), 13–29.

——'War and Diplomacy: Rome and Parthia, 31 BC–AD 235', in J. Rich and G. Shipley (eds.), *War and Society in the Roman World* (London, 1993), 213–40.

CAPRINO, C., *La Colonna di Marco Aurelio: Illustrata a cura del Commune di Roma* (Rome, 1955).

CHEESMAN, G. L., *Auxilia of the Roman Army* (Oxford, 1914).

CLAUSEWITZ, C. VON, *On War*, ed. and trans. M. Howard and P. Paret (Princeton, 1976).

COLLEDGE, M., *The Parthians* (London, 1967).

CONNELL, J., *Wavell, Scholar and Soldier* (London, 1964).

—— 'Talking about Soldiers', *Journal of the Royal United Services Institute* (1965), 221–4.

CONNOLLY, P., *Greece and Rome at War* (London, 1981).

—— 'The Roman Saddle', in M. Dawson (ed.) *Roman Military Equipment: The Accoutrements of War*, BAR 336 (Oxford, 1987), 7–27.

—— 'The Roman Army in the Age of Polybius', in Gen. Sir John Hackett, *Warfare in the Ancient World* (London, 1989), 149–68.

—— 'The Roman Fighting Technique Deduced from Armour and Weaponry', in V. A. Maxfield, and B. Dobson, (eds.), *Roman Frontier Studies 1989* (Exeter, 1991), 358–63.

COULSTON, J. C., 'Roman Archery Equipment', in M. C. Bishop, (ed.), *The Production and Distribution of Roman Military Equipment. Proceedings of the Second Roman Military Equipment Conference*, BAR 275 (Oxford, 1985), 220–346.

CREVELD, M. VAN, *Supplying War* (Cambridge, 1977).

—— *Command in War* (Harvard, 1985).

CRISAN, I. H., *Burebista and his Time* (Bucherest, 1978).

CUFF, P. J., 'Caesar the Soldier', *Greece and Rome*, 2: 4 (1957), 29–35.

CUNLIFFE, B., *Greeks, Romans and Barbarians: Spheres of Interaction* (London, 1988).

DAVIE, M. R., *The Evolution of War: A Study of its Role in Early Societies* (Yale, 1929).

DAVIES, R. W., *Service in the Roman Army* (Edinburgh, 1989).

DAVISON, D. P., *The Barracks of the Roman Army from the First to the Third Centuries AD*, BAR 472 (Oxford, 1989).

DEBEVOISE, N. C., *The Political History of Parthia* (Chicago, 1938).

DELBRÜCK, H., *History of the Art of War within the Framework of Political History* i. *Antiquity*, trans. W. J. Renfroe, (Westport, 1975).

DEVIJVER, H., *The Equestrian Officers of the Roman Army*, i–ii (Amsterdam, 1989 and 1992).

DIXON, K. R., and SOUTHERN, P., *The Roman Cavalry* (London, 1992).

DOBSON, B., 'The Centurion and Social Mobility during the Principate', in C. Nicolet, (ed.), *Recherches sur les structures sociales dans l'antiquité classique* (Paris, 1970), 99–116.

—— 'Legionary Centurion or Equestrian Officer? A Comparison of Pay and Prospects', *Ancient Society*, 3 (1972), 193–207.

—— 'The Significance of the Centurion and *Primipilaris* in the Roman Army and Administration', *ANRW* II. 1 (Berlin, 1974).

—— *Die Primipilares* (Cologue and Bonn, 1978).

DOMASZEWSKI, A. VON, *Die Rangordnung des römischen Heeres*, 2nd edn. ed. B. Dobbson (Bohlau and Cologue, 1967).

—— 'Die Fahnen im römischen Heere', *Aufsätze zur römischen Heeresgeschichte* (Darmstadt, 1972), 1–80.

DU PICQ, COL. ARDANT, *L'Étude sur le combat* (Paris, 1914).

EADIE, J. W., 'The Development of Roman Mailed Cavalry', *JRS* 57 (1967), 161–73.

ELTING, J. R., *Swords around a Throne* (London, 1988).

ELTON, G. R., *Political History: Principles and Practice* (London, 1970).

ELTON, H., 'Aspects of Defence in Roman Europe, AD 350–500', D.Phil. thesis (Oxford, 1990).

ENGELS, D. W., *Alexander the Great and the Logistics of the Macedonian Army* (Berkeley, 1978).

ESPÉRANDIEU, E., *Recueil général des bas-reliefs, statues et bustes de la Gaule romaine* (Paris, 1907–66).

—— *Recueil général des bas-reliefs, statues et bustes de la Germanie romaine* (Paris, 1931).

FEUGERE, M., *Les Armes des romains de la république à l'antiquité tardive* (Paris, 1993).

FINK, R. O., *Roman Military Records on Papyrus* (Cleveland, 1971).

FLORESCU, F. B., *Das Siegesdenkmal von Adamklissi: Troepeaum Traiani* (Bucharest: Bonn, 1965).

FRERE, S., and ST JOSEPH, J. K., 'The Roman Fortress at Longthorpe', *Britannia*, 5 (1974), 1–129.

FRERE, S., 'Hyginus and the First Cohort', *Britannia*, 11 (1980), 51–60.

—— *Britannia* (London, 1987).

—— and LEPPER, F., *Trajan's Column* (Gloucester, 1988).

FRYE, R. N., *The Heritage of Persia* (London, 1963).

—— *The History of Ancient Iran* (Munich, 1983).

FULLER, MAJ.-GEN. J. F. C., *The Generalship of Alexander the Great*, (London, 1958).

—— *Julius Caesar: Man, Soldier and Tyrant* (London, 1965).

GABBA, E., *Republican Rome: The Army and Allies* (Oxford, 1976).

GICHON, M., 'Cestius Gallus' Campaign in Judaea', *Palestine Exploration Quarterly*, 113 (1981), 39–62.

GILLIAM, J., *Roman Army Papers* (Amsterdam, 1986).

GLOVER, M., *Peninsula Preparation* (Cambridge, 1963).

GOLDSWORTHY, A. K., 'The *Othismos*, Myths and Heresies: The Nature of Hoplite Battle', *War in History*, 4.1 (1997), 1–26.

GREEN, M. J., *Dictionary of Celtic Myth and Legend* (London, 1992).

GREENE, K., *Archaeology of the Roman Economy* (London, 1986).

GRIFFITH, P., *Rally Once Again: Battle Tactics in the American Civil War* (Marlborough, 1987).

—— *Military Thought in the French Army, 1815–1851*, (Manchester, 1989).
—— *Forward into Battle: Fighting Tactics from Waterloo to the Near Future*, rev. edn. (Swindon, 1990).
GRIFFITHS, W. B., 'The Sling and its Place in the Roman Imperial Army', in C. van Driel-Murray (ed.), *Roman Military Equipment: The Sources of Evidence. Proceedings of the Fifth Roman Military Equipment Conference, BAR* 476 (Oxford, 1989), 255–79.
GROEMANN-VAN WAATERINGE, W., 'Food for Soldiers: Food for Thought', in J. C. Barrett and L. Macinnes (eds.), *Barbarians and Romans in North West Europe, BAR* 471 (Oxford, 1989, 96–107.
HANSEN, M. H., 'The Battle Exhortation in Ancient Historiography: Fact or Fiction?', *Historia*, 42. 2 (1993), 161–80.
HANSON, V. D., *The Western Way of War: Infantry Battle in Classical Greece* (New York, 1989).
—— *Hoplites: The Classical Greek Battle Experience* (New York, 1991).
HANSON, W. S., *Agricola and the Conquest of the North* (London, 1987).
HARMAND, J., *Une Campagne Césarienne: Alesia* (Paris, 1967).
—— *L'Armée et le soldat à Rome de 107 à 50 avant nôtre ère* (Paris, 1967).
HARRIS, W. V., *War and Imperialism in Republican Rome, 327–70 BC* (Oxford, 1986).
HASSALL, M., 'The Internal Planning of Roman Auxiliary Forts', in B. Hartley, and J. Wacher, (eds.), *Rome and her Northern Provinces* (Gloucester, 1983), 96–131.
HAWKES, C., 'The Roman Siege Works at Masada', *Antiquity*, 3 (1929), 195–213.
HEDEAGER, L., 'The Evolution of German Society, 1–400 AD', in R. Jones, J. Bloemers, S. Dyson, and M. Biddle, (eds.), *First Millenium Papers: Western Europe in the First Millenium AD, BAR* 401 (Oxford, 1988), 129–44.
HELGELAND, J., 'Roman Army Religion', *ANRW* II. 16. 2 (Berlin, 1978), 1470–505.
HIBBERT, C., *A Soldier of the Seventy-First* (London, 1975).
HOLDER, P. A., *Studies in the Auxilia of the Roman Army from Caesar to Trajan, BAR* 70 (Oxford, 1980).
—— *The Roman Army in Britain* (London, 1982).
HOLMES, R., *Firing Line* (London, 1986).
HOLMES, T. RICE, *Caesar's Conquest of Gaul* (Oxford, 1911).
HUGHES, BRIG.-GEN. B. P., *Firepower: Weapons Effectiveness on the Battlefield* (London, 1974).
HYLAND, A., *Equus: The Horse in the Roman World* (London, 1990).
—— *Training the Roman Cavalry* (Gloucester, 1993).
ILKJÆR, J., 'The Weapons Sacrifice from Ilerup Ådal, Denmark', in K. Randsbourg, *The Birth of Europe* (Rome, 1989), 54–61.
ISAAC, B., *The Limits of Empire: The Roman Army in the East* (Oxford, 1992).
JACKSON, K. H., *The Oldest Irish Tradition* (Cambridge, 1964).

JOHNSON, A., *Roman Forts of the 1st and 2nd Centuries AD in Britain and the German Provinces* (London, 1983).

JONES, A. H. M., *The Later Roman Empire: A Social and Administrative Survey* (Oxford, 1986).

JOSEPH, J. K. ST. and PITTS, L. F., *Inchtuthil: The Roman Legionary Fortress Excavations 1952–1965*, Britannia Monographs Series 6 (London, 1985).

JUNKELMANN, M., *Die Legionem des Augustus* (Mainz am Rhein, 1991).

—— *Die Reiter Roms*, i–ii (Mainz, 1990–2).

KEEGAN, J., *The Face of Battle* (London, 1976).

—— *The Mask of Command* (London, 1987).

——*A History of Warfare* (London, 1993).

KENNEDY, D. C., 'Parthian Regiments in the Roman Army', in J. Fitz, (ed.), *Limes. Akten des XI Internationalen Limeskongresses* (Budapest, 1977), 521–31.

KEPPIE, L., *The Making of the Roman Army* (London 1984).

KIMMIG, W., 'Ein Keltenschild aus Aegypten', *Germania*, 24 (1940), 106–111.

LABISCH, A., *Frumentum Commeatusque. Die Nahrungsmittelverson-gung der Heere Caesars* (Meisenheim am Glan, 1975).

LATHAM, J. D., and PATERSON, W. F., *Saracen Archery: A Mameluke Work, c. 1368* (London, 1970).

LAWRENCE, W., *The Autobiography of Sergeant William Lawrence: A Hero of the Peninsula and Waterloo Campaign*, ed. G. N. Banks (London, 1987).

LAZENBY, J., 'The Killing Zone', in V. D. Hanson (ed.), *Hoplites: The Classical Greek Battle Experience* (New York, 1991), 87–109.

LEACH, J., *Pompey the Great* (London, 1978).

LEANDER TOUATI, A. M., *The Great Trajanic Frieze* (Stockholm, 1987).

LE BOHEC, Y., *La Troisième Légion auguste* (Paris, 1989).

—— *L'Armée romaine sous le haut-empire* (Paris, 1990).

LIDDELL-HART, B., *A Greater than Napoleon—Scipio Africanus* (Edinburgh, 1930).

LINTOTT, A. W., *Violence in Republican Rome* (Oxford 1968).

LLOYD, A. B., *Battle in Antiquity* (London, 1996).

LUTTWAK, E. N., *The Grand Strategy of the Roman Empire* (Baltimore, 1976).

MACMULLEN, R., 'The Legion as Society', *Historia*, 33 (1984), 440–56.

MANN, J. C., *Legionary Recruitment and Veteran Settlement during the Principate* (London, 1983).

MARBOT, M., *The Memoirs of Baron Marbot* (London, 1988).

MARKLE, M., 'The Macedonian Sarissa Spear and Related Armour', *AJA* 81 (1981), 323–39.

MARSDEN, E. W., *Greek and Roman Artillery: Historical Development*, (Oxford, 1969).

MARSHALL, S. L. A., *Men against Fire* (New York, 1947).

—— *Infantry Operations and Weapons usage in Korea* (London, 1988).

MAXFIELD, V. A., *The Military Decorations of the Roman Army* (London, 1981).

—— 'Pre Flavian Forts and their Garrisons', *Britannia*, 17 (1986), 59–72.

—— 'Conquest and Aftermath', in M. Todd, (ed.), *Research on Roman Britain, 1960–1989* (London, 1989), 19–29.

McLEOD, W., 'The Range of the Ancient Bow', *Phoenix*, 19 (1965), 1–14.

MESSER, W. S., 'Mutiny in the Roman Army in the Republic', *Classical Philology*, 15 (1920), 158–75.

MILLAR, F., *The Roman Near East 31 BC–AD 337* (Cambridge, Mass., 1993).

MILNER, N. P., 'Vegetius and the Anonymous De Rebus Bellicis', D.Phil. thesis (Oxford, 1991).

—— ed. and trans., *Vegetius: Epitome of Military Science* (Liverpool, 1993).

MORAN, LORD, *The Anatomy of Courage* (London, 1966).

MORRIS, D. R., *The Washing of the Spears* (London, 1965).

NOCK, A. D., 'The Roman Army and the Religious Year', *Harvard Theological Review*, 45 (1952), 187–252.

NOLAN, L., *Cavalry: Its History and Tactics* (London, 1853).

NYLEN, E., 'Early Gladius Swords in Scandinavia', *Acta Archaeologica Copenhagen)* 34 (1963), 183.

OAKLEY, S. P., 'Single Combat and the Roman Army', *CQ* 35 (1985), 392–410.

OLIVER, J. H., 'A Roman Governor Visits Samothrace', *AJP* 87 (1966), 75–9.

PARKER, H. M. D., *The Roman Legions* (Oxford, 1971).

PEDDIE, J., *Invasion. The Roman Conquest of Britain* (London, 1987).

—— *The Roman War Machine* (Gloucester, 1994).

PETERSON, D., *The Roman Legions Recreated in Colour Photographs* (London, 1992).

PLEINER, R., and SCOTT, B. G., *The Celtic Sword* (Oxford, 1993).

PRITCHETT, W. KENDRICK, *The Greek State at War*, i–v (Berkeley, 1971–91).

RAEPSAET, G., 'La Faiblesse de l'attelage antique: la fin d'un mythe?', *L'Antiquité Classique*, 48 (1979), 171–6.

RANKOV, N. B., 'The Beneficiarii Consularis in the Western Provinces of the Roman Empire', D.Phil. thesis (Oxford, 1986).

—— 'M. Oclatinius Adventus in Britain', *Britannia*, 18 (1987), 243–9.

Regulations for Field Forces in South Africa 1879 (Pietermaritzberg, 1879).

RENEL, C., *Cultes militaires de Rome: les enseignes* (Paris, 1903).

RICHARDSON, F. M., *Fighting Spirit: A Study of Psychological Factors in War* (London, 1978).

RICHMOND, I. A., 'The Roman Army Medical Service', *The University of Durham Medical Gazette* (June, 1952).

—— *Roman and Native in North Britain* (Edinburgh, 1958).

—— 'The Roman Siege Works at Masada, Israel', *JRS* 52 (1962), 142–55.

—— *Trajan's Army on Trajan's Column* (London, 1982).

RIVET, A. F. L., *The Roman Villa in Britain* (London, 1969).

ROBINSON, H. RUSSELL, *The Armour of Imperial Rome* (London, 1975).

ROSENBERGER, V., *Bella et expeditiones. Die antike Terminologie der Kriege Roms* (Stuttgart, 1992).

ROSENSTEIN, N., *Imperatores Victi* (Berkeley, 1990).

ROSSI, L., *Trajan's Column and the Dacian Wars* (London, 1971).

ROSTOVTZEFF, M. I., BELLINGER, A. R., HOPKINS, C., and WELLES, C. B. (eds.), *The Excavations at Dura Europus: Preliminary Report of the Sixth Season of Work, 1932–1933* (New Haven, 1936).

ROYMANS, N., 'The North Belgic Tribes in the First Century BC: A Historical-Anthropological Perspective', in R. Burndt, and J. Slofstra, (eds.), *Roman and Native in the Low Countries: Spheres of Interaction, BAR* 184 (Oxford, 1983), 43–69.

—— *Tribal Societies in Northern Gaul* (Amsterdam, 1990).

SADDINGTON, D. B., *The Development of the Roman Auxiliary Forces from Caesar to Vespasian* (Harare, 1982).

SALLER, R. P., *Personal Patronage under the Early Empire* (Cambridge, 1982).

SCHALLMAYER, E. and others, *Der Römische Weihebezirk von Osterburken I. Corpus der griechischen und lateinischen Beneficiarier Inschriften des Romischen Reiches* (Wurttemberg, 1990).

SCHLEIEMACHER, M., *Römische Reitergrabsteine* (Bonn, 1984).

SELZER, W., *Römische Steindenkmaler. Mainz in römischer Zeit* (Mainz, 1988).

SMITH, F. W., 'The Fighting Unit: An Essay in Structural Military History', *L'Antiquite Classique*, 59 (1990), 149–65.

SMITH, R. E., *Service in the Post-Marian Roman Army* (Manchester, 1958).

SOUTHERN, P., 'The *Numeri* of the Roman Imperial Army', Britannia, 20 (1989), 81–140.

SPEIDEL, M. P., 'The Rise of the Ethnic Units in the Roman Army', *ANRW* II. 3 (Berlin, 1975), 202–31.

—— *Guards of the Roman Armies: The Singulares of the Provinces* (Bonn, 1978).

—— '*Exploratores*: Mobile Elite Units of Roman Germany', *Epigraphische Studien*, 13 (1983), 63–78.

—— *Roman Army Studies*, i–ii (Amsterdam, 1984–92).

—— 'The Soldiers Servants', *Ancient Society*, 20 (1989), 239–47.

—— 'The Names of Legionary *Centuriae*', *Arctos*, 24 (1990), 135–7.

—— *The Framework of an Imperial Legion*. The Fifth Annual Caerleon Lecture (Cardiff, 1992).

SPRUYTTE, J., *Early Harness Systems: Experimental Studies* (London, 1983).

STARR, C. G., *The Roman Imperial Navy 31 BC–AD 324* (New York, 1941).

STOCKTON, D., *Cicero* (Oxford, 1971).

STOUFFER, S. A., *The American Soldier*, i–ii (Princeton, 1949–65).

SYME, R., *Tacitus* (Oxford, 1958).

—— 'Tacfarinas, the Musulamii and Thurbarsicu', *Roman Papers*, i, ed. E. Badian (Oxford, 1979).

THOMPSON, E. A., *The Early Germans* (Oxford, 1965).

THORDEMAN, B., *Armour from the Battle of Wisby, 1361* (Stockholm, 1939).

TODD, M., *The Northern Barbarians* (Oxford, 1987).

TODD, M., *The Early Germans* (Oxford, 1992).

TROTTER, W., *The Instincts of the Herd in Peace and War* (London, 1947).

VAN DRIEL-MURRAY, C., 'A Fragmentary Shield Cover from Caerleon', in J. C. Coulston (ed.), *Military Equipment and the Identity of Roman Soldiers*, *BAR* 394 (Oxford, 1988), 51–66.

VERCHÈRE DE REFFYE, J. B., 'Les Armes d'Alise', *Revue Archéologique*, 2 (1864), 337–49.

WAR OFFICE VETERINARY DEPARTMENT, *Animal Management* (London, 1908).

WATSON, G. R., *The Roman Soldier* (London, 1969).

WEBSTER, G., *The Roman Imperial Army* (London, 1985).

—— *The Roman Invasion of Britain* (London, 1993).

—— *Rome against Caratacus* (London, 1993).

WELLER, J., *Wellington at Waterloo* (London, 1992).

—— *Wellington in the Peninsula* (London, 1992).

WELLESLEY, K., *The Long Year AD 69* (London, 1975).

WELLS, C. M., *The German Policy of Augustus* (Oxford, 1972).

WENHAM, S. J., 'Anatomical Interpretations of Anglo-Saxon Weapon's Injuries', in S. Chadwick Hawkes (ed.), *Weapons and Warfare in Anglo-Saxon England* (Oxford, 1989), 123–39.

WHEELER, E., 'The Roman Legion as Phalanx', *Chiron*, 9 (1979), 303–18.

WHEELER, R. E. M., *Maiden Castle, Dorset* (Oxford, 1943).

WHITEHOUSE, H., *Battle in Africa 1879–1914* (Camberley, 1987).

WINTER, D., *Death's Men* (London, 1978).

WOLSELEY, GEN. SIR GARNET, *The Soldier's Pocket Book for Field Service* (London, 1882).

WOOLF, G., 'Roman Peace', in J. Rich and G. Shipley (eds.), *War and Society in the Roman world* (London, 1993).

ZIEGLER, P., *Omdurman* (London, 1973).

ZIOLKOWSKI, A., 'Urbs Direpta, or How the Romans sacked cities', in J. Rich and G. Shipley, (eds.), *War and Society in the Roman World* (London, 1993).

INDEX